I0138018

# Tibet's Fate

# Tibet's Fate

Warren W. Smith Jr.

ROWMAN & LITTLEFIELD
*Lanham • Boulder • New York • London*

Published by Rowman & Littlefield
An imprint of The Rowman & Littlefield Publishing Group, Inc.
4501 Forbes Boulevard, Suite 200, Lanham, Maryland 20706
www.rowman.com

86-90 Paul Street, London EC2A 4NE



British Library Cataloguing in Publication Information Available

**Library of Congress Cataloging-in-Publication Data**

Names: Smith, Warren W., 1945- author.
Title: Tibet's fate / Warren W. Smith Jr..
Description: Lanham, Maryland : Rowman & Littlefield, 2023. | Includes bibliographical references and index.
Identifiers: LCCN 2022042118 (print) | LCCN 2022042119 (ebook) | ISBN 9781538173985 (cloth) | ISBN 9781538173992 (ebook)
Subjects: LCSH: Tibet Autonomous Region (China)—Relations—China. | China—Relations—China—Tibet Autonomous Region. | Tibet Autonomous Region (China)—History—Autonomy and independence movements. | Self determination, National—China—Tibet Autonomous Region.
Classification: LCC DS786 .S5576 2023 (print) | LCC DS786 (ebook) | DDC 327.51051/5—dc23/eng/20221026
LC record available at https://lccn.loc.gov/2022042118
LC ebook record available at https://lccn.loc.gov/2022042119

# Contents


Introduction . . . . . . . . . . . . . . . . . . . . . . . . . . 1
Chapter 1: Tibetan Testimonies . . . . . . . . . . . . . . . . . . 5
Chapter 2: Lhasa, 1982. . . . . . . . . . . . . . . . . . . . . . 119
Chapter 3: Tibet Studies . . . . . . . . . . . . . . . . . . . . 233
Chapter 4: Radio Free Asia . . . . . . . . . . . . . . . . . . . 291
Chapter 5: Tibet's Fate. . . . . . . . . . . . . . . . . . . . . 319
Afterword . . . . . . . . . . . . . . . . . . . . . . . . . . . 349
Notes. . . . . . . . . . . . . . . . . . . . . . . . . . . . . 365
Index . . . . . . . . . . . . . . . . . . . . . . . . . . . . . 369
About the Author . . . . . . . . . . . . . . . . . . . . . . . . 387

# Introduction

THE TITLE OF THIS BOOK, *TIBET'S FATE*, IS NOT MEANT TO IMPLY THAT the current fate of Tibet is an ultimate destiny, or the result of Tibet's karma, in the sense that it is fair or just or predetermined. It is not even meant to imply that Tibet's fate is already decided. It is only meant in the sense that if Tibet's fate is now determined, it has been determined not by the Tibetan people but by those of China. If it is to be determined by China, then Tibet's fate is indeed to be an integral part of China. However, if Tibet's fate were to be decided by the Tibetan people, if they were allowed their right to national self-determination, then it would definitely be different.

China's aggressive assimilationist policies in Xinjiang and Tibet make it obvious that the CCP has no tolerance for minority nationality autonomy, despite its own promises and laws. Its recent abrogation of the autonomy promised to Hong Kong further demonstrates that China under the CCP will pursue the traditional Chinese historical quest for an ever more centralized political authority. CCP promises of autonomy both to nationalities and to Hong Kong have been revealed to be in the duplicitous Marxist sense of promising autonomy when the ultimate goal is assimilation.

Those who still hope that China might eventually respect its own nationality autonomy laws, who include the Dalai Lama and the Tibetan Government in Exile, must rely on increasingly forlorn predictions that the CCP will collapse and a more democratic China will be created, or the even more unlikely hope that more Chinese will become Buddhist and thus more sympathetic to Tibet. However, the Tibetan Uprising of 2008 revealed that Chinese anti-Tibetan nationalism was a popular phenomenon and not just fostered by the government. Chinese Buddhists have expressed more interest in their own personal fate rather than any sympathy for Tibet or the exiled Dalai Lama.

This book is a memoir of what has happened in recent Tibetan history, as told by Tibetans themselves, as well as an analysis of the international Tibet support movement, as told by me. The most evocative accounts of Tibetans' experiences under Chinese rule and repression of Tibetan resistance are told by those who were of an age in the 1950s that made them aware of the situation or who were responsible for the Tibetan reaction as local leaders, lamas, or Tibetan government officials. They were mostly those who resisted, many of whom experienced Chinese repression and political indoctrination as prisoners in the many prisons and "reform through labor" camps that the Chinese set up after the 1959 revolt. Prisons and labor camps were an integral part of what were described as the "democratic reforms."

In the second part of the book, I relate something of my own experience of Tibetan history and international advocacy and activism in regard to Tibet. I realize it may seem somewhat immodest to include my own experience along with those of Tibetans, most of whom suffered and were damaged in ways that no non-Tibetan experienced or can even truly imagine. Nevertheless, having been deeply involved with the study of Tibetan history and politics for some forty years, or fifty years if I were to count living in Nepal during the 1970s, I too have a story to tell.

First, as a resident of Nepal in the entirety of the 1970s, I was deeply involved with Sherpas and Tibetans. I worked at the Hotel Everest View in the Khumbu region of Nepal, constructing a relief map of the Everest region that may still be observed in the hotel lobby. And I made a huge, 22-foot-long relief map for the coronation of King Birendra in 1975 under contract with the National Planning Commission of Nepal. As a contractor for the Nepal National Parks Department, UNDP-FAO, and the Nepal Department of Agriculture, I built a total of ten buildings in Rara National Park, Langtang National Park, and the town of Jumla in the Karnali district of Nepal over a period of four years. I worked with a crew of as many as thirty Sherpa masons and carpenters, all from the

Junbesi area. During this time, I, of course, became aware of the Tibetan political issue.

I became far more deeply involved in the Tibet issue after a five-month experience in Tibet in 1982, the subject of chapter 2. I then researched Tibetan history and politics in Dharamsala during three periods of the early 1980s totaling about eighteen months. I enrolled at the Fletcher School of Law and Diplomacy with the specific goal of writing a history of Tibet which, after ten years of research and writing, emerged in 1996 as *Tibetan Nation: A History of Tibetan Nationalism and Sino-Tibetan Relations.*

I worked for twenty-two years as the only non-Tibetan member of the Tibetan Service of Radio Free Asia, where I wrote more than a thousand programs on Chinese and Tibetan politics. During this time, I published *China's Tibet?: Autonomy or Assimilation* and *Tibet's Last Stand?: The Tibetan Uprising of 2008 and China's Response.*

I have been as deeply involved in the Tibetan political issue as any non-Tibetan can possibly have been. Some of my insights are the subject of the chapter titled Tibet's Fate, where I examine the sensitive question of the nature of the Tibetan political system and its role in the fate that has befallen Tibet. I conclude that the Tibetan political system of *Chosi Shungdrel*, or the unity of religion and politics, is implicated in the failure of Tibet to maintain its independence.

The only period when Tibet undeniably was independent, during the Tibetan Empire of the seventh to ninth centuries, was when it had a predominantly secular government. Tibetan Buddhism during the Empire and after is responsible for much of Tibet's uniqueness and attractiveness to outsiders, but Tibet could have had a flourishing religious establishment without it becoming the government. The religious establishment's dependency upon foreign political patrons was a fatal flaw that hampered Tibet's chances to remain independent. The stagnating effect of the Buddhist church's domination of politics meant that Tibet did not develop culturally or politically; it entirely missed the industrial revolution, and it was left unprepared to either refute China's claims to authority over Tibet or to resist China when it attempted to assert that authority. In every way except religious philosophy, Tibet was a relatively backward society, giving China the excuse that Tibet needed to be liberated from its own exploitative social and political system. This is not to say that Tibet under a more secular regime would have been able to maintain its independence against China's expansionist ambitions, only that its chances would have been greater.

Given all the criteria for independent statehood—territory, culture, language, religion, and government—Tibet surely should be an independent state. Tibetan territory, defined by altitude, was the very nearly exclusive habitation of people who identified themselves as Tibetans. Those people share a distinct culture, language, and religion. They had a central government that directly administered the territory of Central Tibet and indirectly that of Kham and Amdo. Had Tibetans been allowed to determine for themselves their political status—that is, if they had had the right to self-determination as specified in the most fundamental documents of international law—there is no doubt that they would have chosen independence. Whatever the flaws of the Tibetan social and political systems, Tibet should have had the right to determine its own fate, and could have done so, until deprived of that right by China.

# Chapter 1

# Tibetan Testimonies

After the initial surge of refugees from Tibet in 1959–1960, very few Tibetans were able to escape and there was therefore a dearth of information about the events during the 1960s and 1970s. The void was filled with a tremendous amount of Chinese propaganda about the "liberation of the serfs" after the revolt and the subsequent Democratic Reforms Campaign by which Tibetans supposedly became "masters of their own fate." The Chinese propagandized the establishment of the Tibet Autonomous Region in 1965 and the "democratic elections" by which Tibetans were supposed to have gained self-rule. Little was said about the chaos of the Cultural Revolution. Collectivization and communization were promoted as great successes without mention of the Great Leap Forward famine of 1959–1962 or the food shortages in Tibet in the late 1960s and early 1970s immediately after full communization was achieved. Nevertheless, Chinese propaganda dominated what little news there was about Tibet, leaving the impression outside China that Chinese rule in Tibet and its social and political reforms were a great success.

The contrary accounts of the few Tibetan refugees who managed to escape during that time were often dismissed as most likely exaggerated due to an assumed bias and their extreme contrast with the version of reality presented by the Chinese and their Tibetan spokespersons. By the mid-1970s the Tibetan Government in Exile had realized the need to publicize their own version of the reality inside Tibet to the outside world. They collected a series of interviews, twenty-seven of which were published by the Information and Publicity Office of His Holiness the

Dalai Lama in 1976 under the title *Tibet Under Chinese Communist Rule.* The publication of these very credible Tibetan refugee statements challenged the Chinese version of reality within Tibet and began the shift in international opinion away from the claims of Chinese propaganda and toward the facts as revealed by Tibetan eyewitnesses. As such, the publication of this collection of refugee accounts was an important event in the history of Tibetan exile politics and the international perception of the Tibet issue. I have included edited versions of three of the best of these accounts to which I have added some context and commentary.

A large group of testimonies, five in number, derive from my interviews in Dharamsala in 1989–1990. The remainder of the testimonies are from mostly far more recent publications by Tibetans of their accounts of the events they experienced in Tibet after the revolt and in the prisons and labor camps in which many of them spent long years, even decades, before escaping into exile, usually after the liberalization period began in Tibet in 1979–1980. Some of these publications are very obscure, having been published in Dharamsala in the 1970s. I have summarized four of the best of those accounts. The totality of these testimonies, I believe, gives a fairly comprehensive account of events in Tibet as told by Tibetans themselves. The accounts are ordered not by when they were collected but by the events and the periods they cover.

## DORJE TSERING[1]

Dorje Tsering describes himself as a middle-class farmer with nine members in his family. His family owned nine yak crossbreeds, six horses, 200 sheep and goats, and land on which he could grow 250 *khel* of grain (1 khel equals approximately 12.5 kg.).

The Chinese Army reached his homeland of Nangra and Hormuka in Amdo on the traditional frontier between China and Tibet on September 25, 1949. He says that all the Tibetans of the area resisted the Chinese Army's entry, telling them that Tibet was an independent and separate country. They had lived in their own country for thousands of years and had no need for reforms, least of all reforms brought by foreigners. The Chinese spokesperson retorted that the aim of the CCP was to control not only all of Tibet but to expand the communist revolution to the whole world; therefore, two small villages in eastern Tibet could not escape without any changes. Such exchanges went on for a while, with the Chinese steadily trying to impose their authority on the Tibetans.

The situation became increasingly unbearable, until December 1949 when all the people decided to fight against the Chinese. They chose as their leaders Pon Wangchen of Nangra and Pon Choeje of Hormuka. They had about 6,000 fighters and a considerable quantity of arms and ammunition. Their first battle with 5,000 Chinese PLA (People's Liberation Army) troops lasted for fifteen days. Twenty-five Tibetans and an estimated ninety Chinese were killed. The Chinese soon sent reinforcements from Rebkong, south of Nangra. The next battle lasted for a month and resulted in the deaths of 40 Tibetans and 150 Chinese. In mid-1950 another 2,000 Chinese arrived and the ensuing battle lasted for two months in which 90 Tibetans and about 200 Chinese were killed. By 1951 there were an estimated 30,000 Chinese troops in Nangra and in a battle lasting for three months, 150 Tibetans and 200 Chinese died. In Hormuka, in a battle in February 1951, 350 Tibetans and 500 Chinese were killed and the Chinese gained control of the area. The Chinese arrested fifteen Tibetans from the village and shot them. They took the body of one whom they thought was a leader and forced the local villagers to criticize the dead body for three days.

The deaths of so many local men caused many of the Tibetans, especially the women, to plead to the fighters to surrender to the Chinese in order to avoid further bloodshed. Some of the fighters then decided to abandon their defense of the local villages and to continue their fight from the surrounding mountains. During this time, the Chinese sent Tibetan collaborators as envoys to the resisters asking them to surrender, saying that they had no chance against superior numbers and promising that there would be no punishment for their resistance. However, the fighters refused to surrender since they could not accept the loss of their independence to outsiders. They thus vowed to fight until the end.

In three years, they fought five major and several minor battles with the Chinese. Due to their fierce resistance, the Chinese began to call the Tibetan area of Nangra and Hormuka "Little Taiwan." Dorje Tsering says that there were some former Kuomintang refugees hiding in the area and the Chinese Communists tended to attribute Tibetan resistance there to the intrigues of the KMT. In April 1952 the Chinese sent an official from Beijing who made a speech in which he said that the local Tibetans had resisted for three years and had killed many Chinese soldiers. Since they were a minority nationality, the PLA had made eighteen separate attempts to negotiate with them. Nevertheless, they had continued to resist and therefore, Chairman Mao had decided to send 32,000 additional troops to finally crush all resistance in the area. The promised PLA troops, in four divisions, were already in the vicinity and they attacked the very next day from all directions and soon surrounded the whole area.

Even against these hopeless odds some of the Tibetan fighters refused to surrender, since they could not accept the loss of their freedom and independence. However, they were soon separated into smaller and smaller groups and surrounded by Chinese troops. Many on both sides were killed. Finally, Dorje Tsering and a few others were surrounded on a high mountain for a month in freezing cold without food or firewood. The Chinese sent Lama Shabdung Karpo and Serti Rinpoche to convince the last eighty Tibetans to surrender. They were offered amnesty by the Chinese even though they had resisted for more than two years and had killed many Chinese soldiers. This at last persuaded them to surrender.

The Chinese allowed the last of the resistance fighters to return to their homes as they had promised. Pon Wangchen of Nangra was even taken to Beijing to meet Mao, who praised him for his brave resistance and then made him head of the Nangra village government. The Chinese did not persecute those Tibetans who had resisted nor did they implement any of their promised reforms for a few years. As Dorje Tsering says,

> *For one year, 1952–[19]53, people led a happy life and there was an opportunity for both the children and the old to play and laugh. Then came the Socialism and reforms [Democratic Reforms, which involved the persecution of those of the upper classes who were identified as exploiters as well as monks and lamas, all of whom were called parasites.] Henceforth, anybody who opposed the Chinese was arrested. Innocent people were accused of various crimes and put in*

*prison. Daily meetings took place where anybody and everybody was criticized for his previous behaviors. [Democratic Reforms involved "struggle" sessions, or thamzing in Tibetan, in which Tibetans were required to denounce those that the Chinese identified as exploiters or "enemies of the people."] . . . at least ten people were shot dead every day after these meetings.*

Chinese soldiers were posted around the village so no one could escape. Everybody was in danger of being arrested. Many people committed suicide during these times, including his brother and six others from Nangra. Many Tibetans had been killed in battle or died in prison and some had managed to escape to India. As he says, "Only a few of the blind, cripples, fools and children were left." Dorje Tsering knew that his past history of resistance made him a suspect in the eyes of the Chinese and that his arrest was probably imminent. He decided to escape to Lhasa, where he knew that the Chinese had so far not begun any of their reforms. He managed to escape and reached Lhasa in October 1954. He stayed in Lhasa until 1958 under the name of Rinzin, until he was informed that the Chinese were looking for him. He then left for India.

## Tsayul Tulku[2]

Tsayul Tulku was born in 1938 in Amchok, a mixed *rongpa* (farmer) and *drokpa* (nomad) area near the famous Labrang Tashikyil Monastery, then a part of the Tibetan region of Amdo, near the cultural frontier with China, now a part of Gansu Province. The Amchok Tibetans traced their history from the Tibetan Empire period of Trisong Detsen, who ruled during the second half of the eighth century. They were descended from soldiers who were sent from Central Tibet to protect the frontier against the Chinese. They were known as *Kamalok*, which means "not to return without orders," which, of course, never came. At five years of age, he was recognized as the reincarnation of Tsayul Rinpoche of Labrang Tashikyil Monastery. He stayed in his home until age 10 when he was taken to Labrang Tashikyil.

In early 1949 the Chinese PLA arrived in Labrang. At first, they were polite to the lamas and monks and promised to make no changes or reforms. They asked only for the cooperation of the monastery. However, there had already been some armed resistance in Amchok, in Choni to the south and in Nangra and Hormuka to the north. There was more resistance in 1956 due to Chinese soldiers and settlers taking local land. But only in 1958 was there open revolt when the Chinese began what they called democratic reforms, or the confiscation of private property of the well-off and harassment of traditional elites and lamas and monks, and socialist transformation, or collectivization.

The change in Chinese policy from one of no reforms to precipitous reforms was due to the Anti-Rightist and Anti-Local Nationalist Campaign, which had followed Mao's Hundred Flowers Campaign, during which he called for criticism of the CCP, with the slogan "Let a hundred flowers bloom, a hundred schools of thought contend," with confidence that the Communist Party's rule was widely accepted and could withstand what he anticipated would be minor criticisms. Instead, he was met with fundamental criticisms about the legitimacy of one-party rule and with objections to the Chinese right to rule over their territories from minority nationalities.

Tsayul Tulku says that even though none of Labrang's 3,000 monks participated in the revolt, and some of its lamas were even sent to nearby areas to try to convince Tibetans to not revolt, 2,000 of them were arrested and accused of sympathizing with or even instigating it. The people of Amchok revolted because they rejected the right of the Chinese to rule over what was traditionally Tibetan territory. A small monastery in Amchok was destroyed, the revolt there was put down brutally and some 600 people killed or imprisoned, many of the latter dying in prison. The Chinese rationale for focusing on monasteries and monks seems to be their belief that the religious establishment was a natural obstacle and opponent of Chinese control over Tibetan areas and reform of Tibetan society. Tsayul Tulku was personally accused of having instigated the revolt just because of his presumed sympathy with it. He and some twenty truckloads of lamas and monks, about thirty per truck, were taken to Lanzhou, then by train to Xinjiang and a prison at a place called Ansi. They were mostly lamas and tulkus like himself or monastery administrators.

There were four prison camps in the area that Tsayul was aware of: Yumen Xian, Mazong Xian, Zu Xian, and Ansi Xian. In his camp there was at first no food and even very little water available, the area being mostly desert. They had to subsist on only two cups of water per day. Eventually they got two *ti momo* (steamed buns) per day but only one if they were sick and unable to work. Informers were rewarded with an extra ti momo. The steamed buns were white, or made of wheat, only on special occasions. Usually they were red, made from *kaoliang* (sorghum), or green, made from *chaomi* (millet), or black, made from *mimei* (?). The buns were usually coarse and often contained grass and sand. There were approximately 1,000 Tibetans at the camp along with 2,000–3,000 Chinese prisoners. They were mostly employed in water conservation projects. The prisoners had to carry dirt in baskets until their shoulders were raw. After work, in the evening, there was indoctrination and mutual criticisms and thamzing. Tsayul was subjected to thamzing because he was accused of failure to convey Chinese instructions to Amchok Tibetans properly and was thus held responsible for the revolt.

Tsayul Tulku was assumed to be a reactionary because his father and six brothers had fought against the Chinese in Amchok. His father and four brothers were killed while the other two brothers were arrested and died in prison. Other Tibetans in the camp were also pressed to confess to having killed Chinese. He describes thamzing as a process of pushing, pulling hair, beating with a stick, breaking one's glasses, and withholding of food and water until one confessed. The subject was tormented by his fellow prisoners who themselves were subjected to the same ordeal. They were made to assume the "airplane" position (bent over at the waist with hands tied behind the back) and might be hung by the thumbs from the ceiling by a rope. The process could go on for several days until a confession, true or false, was obtained. Tsayul was asked during his thamzing if he liked the Chinese government. He said no, because his father and all his brothers had been killed. The Chinese said that they were all counterrevolutionaries and would have been imprisoned anyway.

Tsayul Tulku reveals that not only were he and his group of 600 lamas and monks of Labrang arrested and sent to labor camps but (he may have only learned this later) 2,000 of the 3,500 lamas and monks were arrested and sent to prisons or Reform Through Labor camps. The remaining monks were divided according to class. Many were sent to a labor camp near Labrang, the site of a remote *gompa* (monastery or temple), and put to work mining marble. They were there for three years and many did not survive. There was another prison at Lanzhou where there were Tibetans from all over Amdo. Some of the higher lamas from Labrang were also imprisoned at Lanzhou. Out of his group of 600 sent to Xinjiang, only 200 survived. Some of the survivors, including Tsayul, were eventually allowed to return to their villages (in late 1958) but not to their monastery. Only those of lower-class backgrounds were allowed to be monks. Tsayul says that the Chinese rationale for this repression of lamas and monks was because they were considered "rocks on the road to socialism" who must be removed even if they had to be killed.

In 1959, after the revolt in Lhasa, Tsayul was sent to a reeducation center near his home in Amchok. He was told that he was released from prison only because of the benevolence of the CCP. There were about 150 Tibetans at this center. Here he learned that the houses of all those Tibetans who had been arrested were sealed and all the possessions confiscated. All properties of monks had been confiscated. Monasteries had all of their large statues destroyed and all precious arts, jewels, and metals were taken by truck to China. Several of Labrang's large temples had been destroyed. Stones from destroyed monasteries were used to make houses for the Chinese.

At the reeducation center he had to study Mao's works, in Tibetan, about class struggle and the nature of religion. He asked to be allowed to study Chinese but was told that reactionaries and counterrevolutionaries had no such privilege. They were shown a film of the revolt in Lhasa and accused of collaborating with it even though they had been arrested a year earlier. They were also accused of contacts with imperialist countries via central Tibetans. The Chinese said that they came to Tibet to liberate the lower-class Tibetans, who supported the CCP. Only a handful of the upper class opposed socialism, they said, so they must be crushed. They also said that Tibetans and Chinese were the same race and were therefore of the same family. Lamas were enemies of the people. People all over the world were the same family (proletarian internationalism) and Marxism would eventually rule the world. Marx and Mao had the same philosophy; Mao had developed Marx's philosophy. India was a reactionary country, evidence for which was that it had given refuge to the Dalai Lama.

There were only two roads to be taken, the white and the black. The black road was that of reactionaries and would lead to repression. The white road was for those who supported unification of Tibet with China and who informed on others. This road led to more liberal treatment. Tsayul had to write his life story from childhood with emphasis upon how he had exploited others, particularly everything that had been given to him as a monk, including butter tea and tsampa. The others also had to write about their past histories with emphasis upon how they had exploited others. Failure to fully confess to exploitative activities consistent with what the Chinese imagined could subject one to thamzing by his fellows. At the same time, the Chinese justified everything they had confiscated from the Tibetan upper classes and the monasteries by saying that it was not for themselves but for all the people, of which the CCP was the legitimate representative. They also put all responsibility for the revolt in Tibet and the fate of people such as Tsayul on their past exploitation of the Tibetan people and their opposition to the liberation of Tibet by the CCP.

The fifty or so Tibetans at this reform and reeducation center were mostly upper-class monks and laymen who had committed no actual crimes except for their class or religious status. Because of their former status in local society, the Chinese hoped to reform their thinking so that they might influence others to support the new regime. Unlike prison, there was no fixed sentence. Release was contingent upon confessions, reform, and informing on others. Because Tsayul would not admit that the offerings he accepted from his devotees was a form of exploitation of them, and he would not inform on others and generally would not "reform" at all, he spent ten years in the reeducation center, from 1959 to 1969. He was given fifteen days of thamzing in 1968, two to four hours per day, for his failure to confess. During the Cultural Revolution he and other former lamas were paraded through Labrang with dunce hats and placards on which were written their offenses and were forced to shout "I am an enemy of the people!" This happened several times in 1966.

Tsayul was also taken around to local villages for thamzing. This was supposed to demonstrate to ordinary Tibetans how high lamas at places like Labrang Tashikyil had exploited them. He was told that the villagers themselves had demanded that he be brought there for thamzing. Some local Tibetans had been trained in how to conduct the thamzing sessions, but he says that they were actually sympathetic to him. They went to five villages by horseback, riding slowly in order to delay their arrival in each village. In the villages, the thamzing was relatively light, with few or no beatings. The villagers did not blame him for any supposed exploitation. Instead, they apologized to him saying that they had to follow the orders of the Chinese. Even his guards gave him tea and meat when the Chinese were not looking. When there were beatings, they were administered by the Chinese or nonlocal Tibetans working with them.

Indoctrination, thamzing, and torture for failure to reform were routine. Several of the former monks at the reeducation center committed suicide, one by jumping into the Ma Chu, one by cutting his own throat, and one by hanging himself. The prisoners were required to pledge their loyalty to a poster of Mao every morning and evening. During an anti-religion indoctrination session, they were told that it was ignorant to pray to invisible gods. One of them, Alak Kuncho Senge, said that the ritual they did to an image of Mao was the same because they had never seen him and didn't know if he really existed or not. He was given continuous thamzing for three years.

During lax periods Tsayul and the others at the center were allowed to go out for short times, but during political campaigns they could not even talk to their friends or relatives who came to see them or to deliver food for them. At the beginning of the Cultural Revolution, he had to rewrite his life history several times since he was accused of having failed to admit his exploitation adequately. Tsayul managed to survive by doing the bare minimum in regard to reform. However, when he was finally released, he was told that he had been given the opportunity to reform but had resisted; therefore, he was given a "black hat" as a reactionary and sent to do "released labor" at Nishi village nearby. He was there for the next ten years, from 1969 to 1979.

Tsayul says that of the three traditional Tibetan provinces of U-Tsang, Kham, and Amdo, there was as much resistance to the Chinese in Amdo as in Kham and U-Tsang, but it was lesser known because few Tibetans from Amdo had escaped into exile since it was far more difficult to escape from there. The commune system was introduced from 1958 with common kitchens and prohibitions on individual fires for cooking. There was one kitchen in small villages and two or more in larger ones. There was no crop failure during the next three years of the Great Leap Forward but Tibetans in Amdo suffered starvation because all their harvest was confiscated. People had to subsist on 25 grams of grain per day whereas formerly they had half a kilogram. People had to eat grass, bark, and leather. Bodies swelled before death and the young looked like the old, being unable to walk without a cane.

The Chinese had said that they came to liberate Tibet and help Tibetans and they would leave when Tibet was improved. After 1958 they stopped saying anything about leaving. They were not embarrassed by the failure of their policies and the starvation that resulted, saying that they had to pay back the Russians with grain and that Tibetans should be grateful for the assistance—like roads, manufactured products, and hospitals—they had received from the motherland.

After 1979 Tsayul remained at the reeducation center as a hired worker. In 1983 the name of the center was changed to a Political Consultative Committee and charged to implement the CCP's family planning policy. Tibetans could have two children except for those working in government offices who could have only one. There were fines for children in excess of the limits. Tsayul and the other former lamas were not allowed to say that sterilization or abortion were violations of Buddhist principles. Tsayul advised people to have as many children as possible and to pay the fines if they could. The medical staff was poorly trained and there were many accidents during medical procedures. One Tibetan doctor who opposed the family planning policy was sentenced to five to seven years in prison. In 1987 Tsayul was supposed to go to a conference in Chengdu but instead he took the opportunity to escape to India.

## Naktsang Nulo[3]

Naktsang Nulo was born in 1949 in the tiny nomadic town of Chugama, which consisted of only a few houses surrounding the Chugama Monastery, in Machu, now a part of Gansu Province. Although this area was close to the border with China, the local nomads had little contact with any Chinese, even in the early 1950s, except when they went to large monasteries such as Labrang Tashikyil. Although they were loyal to the lamas of Labrang, their ultimate loyalty was to the Dalai Lama in Lhasa, where the family went on pilgrimage in 1956. The Chugama nomads did not recognize any political authority of the Tibetan government in Lhasa, or any other government, but they strongly identified with central Tibet in a cultural and religious sense. They were one of the tribes known as Golok, which means those whose heads (*Go*) were turned against (*lok*) any outside authority.

Naktsang Nulo experienced both traditional Tibetan nomadic life as well as the Chinese imposition of Democratic Reforms and Socialist Transformation Campaigns at the beginning of the Great Leap Forward in 1958. Although he and his family revolted against the Chinese and were later imprisoned after being captured while trying to flee to Lhasa, he survived, was forgiven for his rebelliousness, presumably because he was still a child, and went on to have a career as a minor official in the local prison system in Chumarleb in Qinghai where he as a child was himself imprisoned. Much later in his life, in 2006, he wrote and privately published an account of his life, *My Tibetan Childhood*, which is one of the most important works of Tibetan literature of the post-1950 period of Tibetan history.

Naktsang Nulo reveals equally as much about the inequities of traditional Tibetan society as about the abuses under Chinese rule. While the author describes much about his early life as idyllic, he also reveals some of the inequities as well as the harshness of Tibetan life. His father was abused by a local monastic official for the minor offense of carrying a rifle near the Chugama Monastery. It is clear that the monk official had some sort of grudge against his father and was unrestrained in his ability to achieve his revenge.

The family's pilgrimage to Lhasa is one of the most memorable accounts of the book. On the way, although in a large group of more than 100 well-armed people, they were repeatedly attacked by bandits, all of whom were nomads like themselves from different local tribes. They also had encounters with large numbers of bears and wolves and one woman was actually eaten alive by wolves. In Lhasa they witnessed an aristocrat being carried on the shoulders of his servant. They visited all the major monasteries of Central Tibet. Upon their departure they managed to break one of their tribal members out of prison in Lhasa, in defiance of Lhasa's authority over any Goloks.

This part of Amdo remained mostly free of Chinese interference until 1958. In that year Amdo Tibetans were subjected to the Chinese Communists' political campaigns of Democratic Reforms and Socialist Transformation simultaneously, against which most of the local nomads revolted. Democratic reforms were supposed to be a cathartic experience for Tibetans during which the falsity of their religion would be exposed and they themselves would be inspired to destroy their own monasteries after they had realized that they had been kept in ignorance and exploited by the monks and lamas. The socialist transformation process was supposed to be gradual and voluntary, transitioning from mutual aid teams to collectives to communes as the local people themselves realized the economic advantages of each stage. However, in many parts of eastern Tibet outside the future Tibet Autonomous Region, communization was precipitous, coercive, and total. Naktsang Nulo's book contains what is perhaps the best account of these Chinese political campaigns as they were experienced by the local people.

Naktsang Nulo was only nine years old when the events he describes happened, but he was an eyewitness. The Chugama Monastery was just west of the Ma Chu (upper Yellow River) so the Chinese troops had to cross the river to reach it. There was only a ferry available for crossing, but the ferryman fled rather than ferrying the Chinese across. Local Tibetans had heard that Labrang Tashikyil had already been taken by the Chinese and that many lamas and monks had been arrested. However, the Chugama monks believed that the Chinese would have no reason to arrest any monks or destroy their monastery if they did not resist. The

Chinese soldiers had to link arms to cross the rushing river, during which six of them drowned.

The loss of their soldiers due to the ferryman's refusal to cooperate put the Chinese in a bad mood, which the monks attempted to counteract by greeting the soldiers in front of their monastery with *khatags*, the traditional greeting scarves. The soldiers returned the scarves in the traditional manner and were then welcomed into the monastery where they took up quarters in the monastery's chapels. The Chinese commander called a meeting of all the monks and local people for that evening in which he said that no one should be afraid, since Chinese and Tibetans were one family. He said that the troops would be there for only one week; however, during that time no one would be allowed near the monastery at night because the troops would be patrolling and would shoot anyone on sight. The next day the Chinese troops had abandoned any friendly pretenses and had adopted an angry and threatening demeanor toward the monks. Some of the monastic officials and high lamas were put under detention.

The Chinese commander called a meeting of all the monks. He was introduced by a subordinate officer who instructed the monks about the CCP's program called Democratic Reforms. The officer told the monks that the subject to be discussed was whether or not they needed the monastery anymore. They would be permitted to speak, but, as it turned out, only to agree with the proposal to eliminate the monastery. They were told that silence would be interpreted as opposition. Anyone who did not speak (in agreement) would be identified as a rebel. To make his point, the head monk disciplinarian was paraded in front of the monks in handcuffs to demonstrate the fate of any who resisted (even though this monk had not in fact resisted; his only crime was apparently his position within the monastic hierarchy).

Some monks immediately protested, saying that if they told the Chinese what they wanted to hear, then their monastery would be destroyed, whereas if they said nothing then they themselves would suffer. There was thus no way that the monks could say that they wanted to keep their monastery. Some monks who protested the Chinese methods were dragged out by Chinese soldiers, while the rest were asked if anyone else chose to speak out. Given no other choice, the monks finally had to accede to the Chinese demand that they agree that they didn't need their monastery anymore. The Chinese officer then interpreted this as a voluntary decision by the monks to not only abandon their monastery but to destroy it.

After this coerced agreement was reached, the Chinese commander spoke to all the monks, saying that because all the monks had agreed that they no longer needed their monastery then he had agreed to their request to close it. Then he told them that they should immediately destroy all the religious statues, scriptures, and any other religious objects. Most of the monks then stood up and declared that if the Chinese wanted to destroy the monastery, they would have to do it themselves. They tried to leave but were surrounded by the Chinese troops with guns aimed at them while others appeared on the roofs with machine guns. The Chinese officer fired two shots from his pistol and then told the monks that anyone who didn't want to destroy the statues should say so. The monks were now afraid to resist as they were surrounded by armed troops and anyone who had so far resisted had been carried away. The Chinese troops then made some of the monks start pulling down the main statues. Laymen who had gathered outside to observe what was happening also tried to protest but were threatened and driven away by the troops. Eventually the monks were made to pull down all the statues, scatter religious texts, and trample clay statues to dust. Because the destruction was done by the Tibetans themselves the Chinese were able to claim that it was voluntary.

Naktsang Nulo, who was watching from near the doorway, was amazed that even when the statues of wrathful deities were pulled down there were no immediate consequences for those who did so. He, like all Tibetans, had been taught to believe in the power of the wrathful deities to harm any who did not propitiate them as well as the protective powers of the more benevolent deities. He began to wonder if the deities had no power after all, which was precisely the cathartic effect the Chinese Communists hoped to produce by demonstrating to Tibetans the actual powerlessness of their deities.

The next day, all of the nomads, as well as villagers living on the east side of the Ma Chu, were forced to start moving to the west. Chaos ensued as people were made to leave possessions behind. The Chinese shot dogs who barked at them as the people were being led away. Naktsang Nulo was unclear about the purpose of this forced relocation, especially since he and his family fled the next day. However, during their flight they saw many other villagers that had been relocated and concentrated in larger groups. What he observed was the Chinese attempt to create communes by amalgamating various scattered tribes and villages, without regard to the sparse resources of the grasslands to which the locals had adapted with a dispersed settlement pattern for agriculture and a nomadic lifestyle for animal husbandry. The simultaneous Democratic Reforms and Socialist Transformation Campaigns inflicted on the Tibetans of this area of Amdo seem to reflect the Maoist belief that the most primitive minorities, among whom were included all Tibetans, but especially nomads, could go straight to communism, "skipping the stages of history," because they were at the stage of primitive communism, not corrupted by capitalism and bourgeois democracy.

Faced with this forced communization and news that the Chinese were asking about him as a possible opponent, Naktsang's father decided to flee toward Lhasa, where the Chinese Communists' reforms had not yet begun. They left in the middle of the night with his older brother and several monks from the monastery. On the way they passed the Kangsar Monastery, which was damaged and deserted. Monks' robes, remnants of religious implements, and pages of texts were strewn everywhere. The fate of the monks and the local people was a mystery. Farther on they came across the scene of a massacre of a nomad encampment of a hundred people or more. Men, women, children, horses, and yaks had all been slaughtered and left where they lay. Naktsang Nulo's father said that they appeared to have been pilgrims returning from Lhasa, who may have been mistaken by the Chinese for those fleeing toward Lhasa, who were now considered rebels and thus could be killed with impunity. They met two women survivors who confirmed that the group was returning from Lhasa; they said that the others had been killed by Inner Mongolian cavalry troops who were employed by the PLA to operate in the Tibetan grasslands.

Soon thereafter, while riding along a road at night, they themselves were fired upon by Chinese troops approaching in trucks. They came across valleys full of untended horses, yaks, and sheep, with no people anywhere to be found. They later found that the nomads had also been the victims of the Inner Mongolian cavalry, who had forced all the people into communes while leaving behind the animals upon which they were dependent for survival. They encountered another small group of survivors, mostly women and children and many wounded, from the clan Dzachuka that had opposed the Chinese entry into their nomadic area and had been wiped out as a result. As they proceeded to the west they came upon a clan of nomads, the Wujud, who had surrendered to the Chinese and had been disarmed by them and subjected to democratic reforms, including the arrest of leading figures who refused to cooperate as well as many lamas and monks. Because the Chinese now occupied the area, which lay upon the route to Lhasa, their further progress was blocked.

The presence of so many Chinese troops in the area led to a series of running battles. In each instance they were discovered by the Chinese and retreated to a defensible position, usually on top of the nearest mountain, from where they were able to kill many of the Chinese, while suffering no losses of their own. Finally, however, they found themselves in an indefensible position and confronted by more than a hundred Chinese. Here was the end of their road. Several of their party were killed and Naktsang's father was mortally wounded. Naktsang Nulo writes that he later came to know that the day his father died was the ninth of September 1958.

The remainder of the party surrendered and Naktsang was surprised to find that some of the soldiers were Tibetans of the clan that had been subdued by the Chinese and were now forced to collaborate with them. Some of these Tibetans even participated in the interrogation and torture of the prisoners. They later learned from some of the women of the tribe who took care of them that many of the more resistant men of the tribe had been arrested and taken away, forcing the rest to cooperate. They noticed that most of the remaining people of the tribe were women, children, and old men. The survivors of Naktsang's group, nine in number, were taken to a nearby camp where there were other Tibetan prisoners, some 100 men and 50 women. Most of the prisoners were from the Alak clan, which was part of the Wujud tribe, but which had resisted the Chinese. Most of them had been killed or arrested as a result. They said that the Wujud chief had taken money from the Chinese and surrendered his tribe but that some clans had resisted. The result had not been that different, since many of the men of the clans that had surrendered had still been arrested. They complained that they could have more successfully resisted the Chinese if their tribe had been united.

A few weeks later when the number of prisoners had reached about 300, they were all taken further west toward Chumarleb. They halted for a day at another nomad encampment along the way where six lamas among the prisoners were subjected to thamzing, or "struggle," by the locals, a ritual that would become well-known to all Tibetans. Naktsang, who had been led to believe that the highly respected lamas would be spared by the Chinese, was astonished to see them humiliated, stomped on, and finally beaten to death by the crowd and their bodies tossed over a cliff. The crowd shouted slogans about how they had been exploited by the lamas even though the lamas were from far away and unknown to them. Naktsang was unable to believe that Tibetans were capable of such acts of hatred, especially against revered lamas. It was explained to him by one of local women that the Chinese were the instigators and the Tibetans powerless to refuse to participate. While the Chinese remained on the edge of the crowd, allowing the Tibetans to be the actual perpetrators, and even rushed to subdue the beatings when it got too violent, they were the actual perpetrators. They were the ones who allowed the beatings to finally result in the deaths of the six lamas, all the while pretending to be restraining the Tibetans from expressing their resentments against their supposed exploiters.

They continued toward Chumarleb with ever more prisoners. Two of them tried to escape by killing two Chinese guards but were themselves killed by the other Chinese soldiers. An old man who was too weak to continue walking was left behind with two Chinese, who shot him when the others were out of sight. When they reached the town, late at night, the prisoners were all thrown through a trapdoor into an underground prison. Naktsang estimated that there were some 360 Tibetans, so crowded that there was no room to even lie down and so little air that it was hard to breathe. Some 1,000 Tibetans were captured and imprisoned at Chumarleb, where all but a small number perished due to starvation during the Great Leap Forward. Naktsang Nulo and his brother were some of the few who survived. Because they were young, they were allowed to live outside the prison and they subsisted due to their skill as hunters and trappers of small animals.

The following quote from the Chinese Communist propaganda publication, "Nationalities Unity," described the two campaigns considerably differently than did Naktsang Nulo:

> *On September 15 [1958], the entire Kannan Chou [Southern Kansu Tibetan Autonomous District] was completely communized. . . . The 46,000 Tibetan herdsmen, who only a short time ago basically lived in a feudalistic society, have now, on the basis of having secured victories in the suppression of counterrevolutionaries and carried out a social reform, flown over several ages in the short period of a fortnight, and, singing and dancing, have now reached heaven in one stride, taking them into People's Communes in which are carried the seeds of communism.*

> *In this violent class struggle, after a campaign of propaganda and education was deeply carried out and after contrasting the old and new societies, the class consciousness of the vast laboring herdsmen was rapidly promoted. After they perceived the reactionary essence of the feudalistic exploiting class, they were greatly surprised, and rose up with set teeth to accuse the exploiting class of their heinous crimes and they voluntarily bound the counterrevolutionary elements and bad elements and handed them over to the government, asking for them to be punished. After stripping off the religious cloak of the counterrevolutionary elements in religious circles, they exposed their fraud; and the masses say: "We shall never permit these man-eating wolves to do evil things while riding on the neck of the people waving religious*

*banners." At the debate meeting the masses were so excited that they shouted continuously: Long Live Chairman Mao! Long Live the communist Party! We Are Liberated!*

## Nyima Assam[4]

Nyima Assam was born in 1939 in the Markham area of western Kham. His father was the chieftain of one of the eighteen districts of Markham. He was schooled at home. He remembers the entry of the Chinese into Markham in 1950, after the invasion of Chamdo and Markham in October of that year.[5] He says that they were very sweet-talking at first. They called a meeting of the local leaders at which they said that Chinese and Tibetans were brothers. China, being the older brother, had the responsibility to help the younger brother. Tibet was very backward and undeveloped, they said, and its feudal system was oppressing the people. They promised to leave when Tibet was developed. They formed a Political Consultative Committee[6] in Markham in which his father and all other traditional leaders would continue in their positions with generous salaries paid by the Chinese. They also declared that no taxes had any longer to be paid to Lhasa and that all debts were forgiven. They promised that there would be no "democratic reforms" until the local people were ready for them—in other words, that they would be voluntary.

Markham had previously been administered by the Tibetan government in Lhasa, despite Chinese claims that it was what they called Sikang Province. Tibetans from the area contributed men for a local militia, with each large or every two small families contributing one man. This militia, along with some Tibetan Army units stationed in the area, resisted the Chinese invasion in October 1950. Nyima says that there was little Tibetan national consciousness in the area, more a local identity as Khampas, although the distinction between Tibet and China was clear, based upon conflicts with Chinese invaders in the past, including the recent past (1905–1912). Despite Chinese propaganda about familial relations between Chinese and Tibetans, the Chinese were considered as foreigners and their entry into Tibet in 1950 as an invasion.

Nyima Assam says that he thinks that Ngapo Ngawang Jigme was forced to sign the Seventeen Point Agreement, which was meaningless for that reason as well as because China forcibly invaded Tibet. He said that the Chinese would do whatever they wanted regardless of any Tibetan agreement or resistance. Also, the Seventeen Point Agreement had many seductive promises. He rejected the Chinese policy that the Dalai and Panchen Lamas were equal, saying that the Dalai Lama was the ruler of Tibet while the Panchen was only a lama. Among the PLA troops who entered the Markham area there were many propaganda troupes who gave dance and drama performances, showed movies (usually outside on the sides of large whitewashed Tibetan houses or monasteries), and distributed magazines. Their themes were that New China was powerful and its policies were modern and progressive, while Tibetan society was backward and its political system was exploitative and oppressive. They said that the CCP was supported by the progressive Soviet Union while the KMT was supported by the imperialistic Americans. Chinese propaganda contained both sweet promises for those who cooperated and threats for those who resisted.

In 1956 the Chinese called a meeting of local Tibetan leaders of Markham and Jomda at Gatok in Markham where they proposed that these two districts should agree to immediately implement democratic reforms. With the exception of a few Tibetan collaborators who approved, all others objected, based upon the promises of no reforms in the Seventeen Point Agreement until Tibetans were ready and specific promises that reforms would be voluntary. Tibetans of these two districts were quite aware that the Seventeen Point Agreement applied to their areas despite the Chinese having set up a separate "Chamdo Liberation Committee" there.[7] In fact, this proposal was made after the Chamdo Liberation Committee was abolished and the area "returned" to Tibet, or what was to become the TAR, when the Preparatory Committee for the Tibet Autonomous Region was created in 1956. They said that they would agree only if instructed to do so by the Tibetan government in Lhasa. The Chinese attempted to coerce Tibetans to agree by surrounding the meeting site with as many as 5,000 PLA troops, Nyima says, but Tibetans, who were also armed, managed to leave without making any agreement.

After this meeting, the Markham and Jomda Tibetans decided upon open armed resistance. Each chieftain was to provide five men and each of thirty-six monasteries would provide five men (presumably laymen attached to the monasteries). One of the lama leaders gave a speech in which he said that resistance was necessary since the Chinese intended to destroy Tibetan religion. The issue in their minds was not resistance to social reforms but defense of their country from Chinese control. Until that time the primary irritant for Tibetans had been Chinese road construction, which used Chinese PLA, KMT prisoners, and hired Tibetan labor. Tibetan road workers were paid in *dayan* (Chinese silver dollars) but Tibetan land had been taken for the road with no compensation. The resistance leaders managed to gather 6,000 men. They ambushed and killed 100 Chinese at Samba Droka and blocked the road to Yunnan. They had their personal weapons and made primitive cannon (*jindal*) out of bamboo. Otherwise, the Tibetans had only their swords and protective amulets. They fought several battles with the Chinese, who brought 40,000 reinforcements, Nyima says, from Chamdo and Batang.

In 1957 they ambushed a pack train of 400 animals carrying food supplies from Chamdo to Markham. The Chinese used Tibetan collaborators to get information about the resistance. Nyima says that it didn't matter whatever the Chinese said or what their current policy was, the ultimate goal of control over Tibet was always the same. The Chinese killed monks of Si Gompa as they were returning from saying prayers in a village. They bombed Lhora Gompa from the air as well as Sangchu village, to intimidate Tibetans, Nyima says. By 1958 Markham had become a center of Tibetan resistance as others had fled from east of the Dri Chu (Yangtze) and the Chinese forces were increased accordingly. By this time the Chinese were shooting at any Tibetans, all of whom they characterized as "reactionary bandits." They killed thirteen lamas at Nyemo Gompa. In a battle at Gande Gompa, 200 monks were killed as well as many Chinese and the gompa was shelled with mortars.

By 1959 the Tibetans still resisting the Chinese had to flee to the mountains due to overwhelming Chinese forces. The Chinese used aircraft to search for the Tibetans in the mountains. There were several groups of 10–30 men, some of whom lasted until April 1961. According to Nyima Assam it was only in early 1961 that any American assistance was received. There was one airdrop of arms, ammunition, and other supplies along with seven Tibetans trained by the CIA. However, by this time it was too late. The Chinese were aware of the arms drop and surrounded the area. Four of the CIA-trained Tibetans were killed; two took cyanide pills and died while one took the pill but survived. Nyima Assam says that his father, Nyima Pon (*Pon* means chieftain or headman), began with 500 men; 153 were killed and 300 were captured. Sixty of those who surrendered were eventually released because they confessed and promised to "reform." Forty-three held out until the end in the mountains, of whom thirty-eight were eventually killed.

Nyima was held along with an estimated 5,000 Tibetan prisoners at Vise Gompa in Markham Gatok. They were held there from 1961 to 1963. Four hundred prisoners were kept in leg chains while another two hundred were in handcuffs. The prisoners were individually interrogated with questions about how many Chinese each had killed, who were their leaders, who provided support, were there any connections with other countries, and did they know of any hidden weapons. They were asked why they had revolted and told that if they confessed, they could be forgiven, but if they refused, they would be shot. There were only two paths, the black and the white. The interrogators alternated sweet talk with threats; the interrogators themselves were changed every three days. He and his father were thought to have killed an important PLA officer and four others and to have wounded another two. They were told that they deserved execution but due to the CCP's liberal policy, they were each sentenced to life in prison and deprivation of political rights.[8]

They were gathered every three days for political lectures and movies, the themes of which were that Tibet had been liberated from foreign imperialism and its own backward feudal system. The three Tibetan ruling classes (aristocracy, government officials, and monks) had been exploiting all the others, but now the formerly exploited would be the rulers. Nobody should think that any help was coming from the American imperialists, Indian reactionaries, or the exiled Dalai Lama. Tibetans were now entirely under the control of China. They could either reform or be executed. They were shown movies about the backwardness of Tibet and the Chinese victories over the Americans in Korea and the Indians in 1962.

Nyima says that the Markham prison camp was only for interrogation. Once prisoners received their sentences, they were sent to more permanent prisons and labor camps. He says that sixteen received life sentences, fifty got 15–20 years, and thirty got 12–15 years. Nevertheless, he claims that fifteen prisoners were publicly executed there in 1961. While at Markham, the prisoners were subjected to thamzing in local villages. He and others were told that people in their home villages were demanding that they be subjected to criticism. The Chinese claimed that they were actually restraining the "enthusiasm of the masses" to criticize the prisoners because they were "aware of your crimes." In reality, he says, the Chinese coerced local villagers to demand that they produce the prisoners for thamzing and they instructed them in exactly what their crimes were. They promised rewards for those who demanded and actively participated in thamzing and threatened that those who didn't enthusiastically participate would be subject to thamzing themselves. During thamzing of prisoners, the Chinese cadres present would pretend to be controlling the "anger of the masses," while actually it was they who were inciting them. He says that some prisoners were beaten to death or injured during thamzings.

In 1963 he was sent to Tsa Pomda prison near Chamdo. There were some 5,000–6,000 prisoners there, 500 of whom were from Markham. Twenty to fifty prisoners were kept in each small cell. Two or three died every night. He claims that almost all prisoners at this camp, which was called an agricultural commune, died of overwork and starvation. He says that some 4,000 Tibetans died at this camp but the numbers never decreased because more prisoners were constantly being brought in. The diet was only a little tsampa (roasted barley flour) and some black tea. Paradoxically, those with the heaviest sentences were more likely to survive because they were kept in chains and did not have to work. Of the original 5,000 arrested in Markham, he thinks only 500 survived. In 1965 there was a public execution of seven Tibetans for refusing to confess and for "opposing the Communist Government."

There were several camps at Tsa Pomda. The first camp was for those with life sentences and was the strictest, although the prisoners did not have to work. There was an agricultural camp and a lumber camp from which timber was taken to China. There was also a "reform through labor" camp, to which "reactionaries" and "exploiters," which included lamas, aristocrats, and any others who resisted, were sent without any prison sentence. Still, they could spend far longer than the designated three years in this system, sometimes for as many as 15–20 years. This camp was engaged in vegetable growing, carpentry, tailoring, and building houses, offices, and barracks for the Chinese. Nyima was at this camp for six years. While there he heard that the Chinese had taken all the valuable statues from the large Chamdo Monastery in 1961 and that the rest had been destroyed at the beginning of the Cultural Revolution in 1966.

In 1969 Nyima and eighty other prisoners were sent to the prison labor complex at Po Tramo in Kongpo. He names the camps there as Dzongna, Chundo, Damchu, Nangdep, Talung, and Golingtang. These camps were engaged in forestry, agriculture, and construction. As at Chamdo, there was one camp here, Damchu, where the prisoners were all lifers. There were 220 prisoners in this camp who were kept chained and worked as tailors and carpenters. There were the usual political indoctrinations and thamzings, with executions of those who refused to reform. He says that there was a public execution in 1974 of thirteen prisoners who had refused to reform and therefore "chose to die, so we will kill them." One of them was a lama who had refused to give up his religion, while others had retained the "empty hope of help from the Americans, India, or the Dalai Lama."

Prisoners were subjected to thamzing for simply looking at the sky, which was interpreted to mean that they were hoping for more American airdrops, or for sitting quietly, which implied that they were secretly saying prayers. Some prisoners committed suicide by jumping into the river or into latrines, while others were executed for killing or injuring Chinese guards. Nyima says that of some 8,000 prisoners at these camps only 1,000 survived. In his unit 170 had died before he was transferred and of the 50 left there, only 3 survived. Most died of overwork and starvation.

In 1976 Nyima was sent to Drapchi, the largest prison in Lhasa. Other prisons in the Lhasa valley were Sangyip and Gurtsa, plus Yititu (First Labor Reform Camp) and Wutitu (Fifth Labor Reform Camp). There were about 7,000 prisoners in total. Gurtsa was for initial interrogations. Sangyip was where sentences were decided, after which prisoners were sent to Drapchi. Sangyip was also for old Tibetan government officials and aristocrats, "CIA Khampas," and "spies for the Dalai Lama" whose sentences were undecided.

There were six units at Drapchi, with 200–300 prisoners in each. One unit was a hospital for Chinese and cooperative Tibetan prisoners from all the prison and labor camps in the Lhasa area. Other prisoners were given no medical facilities at all. Sometimes all the prisoners in the Lhasa area were gathered at Drapchi for lectures and public executions. Nyima was there for four years during which time there were three public executions. There were also what were called "liberal and strict" meetings at which the policy of liberal treatment for confession and cooperation versus a strict policy for noncooperation was reiterated. At such meetings Tibetans were told that they should give up the "empty hope for independence of Tibet."

Nyima describes the visit of the Nepal King Birendra to Lhasa in 1978. He visited Drapchi, where the prisoners had bathed and cleaned the prison, and they had been given new clothes, shoes, bedding, and good food for the visit. Birendra came and looked around but asked no questions of prisoners, who were anyhow told not to talk to him. All of the clothes, shoes, and bedding were taken away after his visit. He was finally released from Drapchi Prison in March 1979 at the time that the liberalization policy was announced in Tibet and almost all political prisoners were released. However, he says that some of those directly involved in the 1959 revolt were not released even then.

He was still not free, he and eighty others being designated as released workers and required to labor at a small wage at a camp at Tsetang, in Lhoka, south of Lhasa. He was finally fully released two years later and told to return to his home in Markham. However, he said that he no longer had any relatives in Markham and was therefore allowed to go to Lhasa. He says that the Chinese remained suspicious of all former prisoners and it was therefore hard for any of them to make a living. After the demonstrations of 1987 he was told that he was suspected of being involved so he resolved to escape. He got a fake trade permit to go to the border with Nepal at Zangmu and crossed into Nepal by going through the forest around the border post.

## Tashi Palden[9]

Tashi Palden was born in Serdrag, Dragyab, Kham. In 1958 he was a monk in the Upper Tantric College at Ramoche in Lhasa. In October 1958 he began a three-year, meditational retreat (*tsam*) in the Tara Tsamkhang, which was on the top floor of the temple at the rear. He says that from there he could see everything that happened shortly thereafter during the uprising in March 1959.

He says that in March 1959 it was rumored that the Chushi Gangdruk resistance forces were approaching Lhasa and would soon drive the Chinese out of Tibet. In the city people were demonstrating everywhere, shouting slogans and carrying banners. All of the monks were being requested to hold special prayers for a swift and happy ending to the sufferings of the Tibetan people. He knew from his experience in Kham that in times like this the monks and monasteries became special targets of the Chinese wrath.

On the 17th of March, some Ramoche monks returned from the Norbulinka, where they had been holding special prayers, and reported that the Dalai Lama had already fled Lhasa. (He fled that night.) On the 19th, many gunshots were heard. Fifty Ramoche monks vowed to defend their monastery and armed themselves with whatever weapons they could find, including knives, axes, and even a few guns. They even made an unsuccessful attempt to raid the nearby Zimbook house, which was occupied by the Chinese, in order to steal more weapons. Some Tibetan policemen in a nearby house who were better armed also fired their weapons at the Zimbook house.

On the 21st, the Ramoche was damaged by Chinese artillery fire and then attacked by Chinese troops. A local beggar came around with a horse he had found to give to the monks. They later realized that the beggar was a spy for the Chinese to find out where the monks were gathered since immediately afterward the Chinese began shelling the inner courtyard where they were. Several monks were killed, the Ramoche was set on fire, and the remaining monks were forced to surrender or to flee. Tashi Palden and five others managed to escape in the night to the nearby Tsomoling Monastery.

The next day the Chinese made an announcement by loudspeaker that the Norbulinka, Potala, and Ramoche had all been captured and that the Tibetans holding out in the Jokhang should surrender so that it would not be damaged or destroyed. Since the fighting seemed to have died down, he and a few other monks went back to the Ramoche to help put out fires. They took khatags in hand with the intention to surrender to the Chinese. He saw that the streets were filled with bodies of dead and dying Tibetans. They and many other of the surviving Ramoche monks surrendered to the Chinese that day. They were told that they had killed an important Chinese general and many others during their attack on the Zimbook house, but he thought it more likely that it was the firing by the Tibetan police that had killed them.

The Ramoche monks were taken to the Zimbook house. They were guarded by 200 Chinese troops. An officer said to them: "You have seen the corpses all around Lhasa. You must remember that it need not have come to this if you Tibetans had not acted so foolishly. Now it is too late for you to repent. You will all end up like these corpses." They were given wheelbarrows and made to collect about forty dead bodies from the Ramoche courtyard.

The next day they and many others were marched to the Norbulinka where hundreds of Tibetans were detained. Along the way they saw many dead Tibetan bodies. They were told by a Chinese officer to look at the Potala, which now had Chinese flags flying from the top. The officer said, "your precious Potala now belongs to us." At the Norbulinka they collected and burned all the dead bodies, which took three days. The Tibetan detainees were sorted out according to their former roles and positions. The Chinese said that all government officials and high lamas would be released immediately, so they should identify themselves. However, this was just a trick since they were taken away and most were imprisoned.

Those who remained were lectured by a Chinese officer who told them that they should not have opposed them since they had come there to liberate them. They were taunted for thinking that the Chinese soldiers were just teenagers and that the Chushi Gangdruk could defeat them. Even the Tibetan women had been so confident as to demand that the Chinese should get out of Tibet. (This was an apparent reference to the women's march shortly before the revolt demanding that the Chinese leave Tibet.) They were told that they had as much chance of getting their independence as seeing the sun rise in the west. Then Tashi Palden was told that he along with many others would be sent to work on a hydroelectric project east of Lhasa named Nachen Trang.

Tashi Palden reports that there were 3,700 Tibetan prisoners in his group at Nachen Trang, guarded by 500 Chinese soldiers. His camp was all men but there was another camp of all women. The camp was along the banks of the Kyichu River and was fenced on the three open sides with barbed wire. The prisoners had no possessions except the clothes they had on when they were arrested. Their work was to dig out a channel adjacent to the river and to carry earth and stones to the dam construction site. At first the food was sufficient due to all the food supplies confiscated from the upper classes of Lhasa. However, food rations soon became little more than a handful of tsampa a day. They had to work all day and then attend propaganda meetings in the evening. They were questioned about their roles in the uprising and asked about who was responsible for it. Some learned to say that the reactionaries were responsible for the revolt, which was what they thought the Chinese wanted to hear, but most said that they were too confused and too busy trying to save their own lives to know what really had happened.

One day a former Gyume Monastery (Lower Tantric College in Lhasa) monk was brought before them to talk about how he had tried to join the Chushi Gangdruk in Lhoka but had been caught along the way. He was at first beaten but then decided to confess everything, including having killed some Chinese, after which he was congratulated and released due to his correct attitude in confessing. He was then sent to lecture to other Tibetans about the Chinese policy of leniency for confession as opposed to severity for opposition. The Gyume monk was obviously better off and especially better fed than the prisoners, so most of them decided to confess their attitudes toward the Chinese and anything they had done to oppose them. Tashi Palden had not done anything active during the revolt so he confessed to having prayed for the victory of the Chushi Gangdruk.

Another day some twenty-five prisoners, including former monks like Tashi Palden, some of the Dalai Lama's bodyguards, and former soldiers in the Tibetan Army, were selected by the Chinese and then taken to Lhasa. The monks were given good monks' robes to wear and the soldiers were given Tibetan Army uniforms. They were taken to the ruins of Kundeling Monastery (below the Potala in the direction of Norbulinka) where there was a Chinese film crew set up ready to film them. A Chinese officer addressed them:

> *We are gathered here to make an important documentary film about the uprising. You must display anger and other emotions exactly like you felt at the time of the uprising. Anybody who does not take the whole thing seriously and ruin the shooting by smiling or showing boredom will be severely dealt with afterwards.*

They were handed unloaded guns and made to enact mock battles ending with some pretending to be dead while others were shown emerging from the ruins of the monastery to surrender their weapons. One of the former soldiers burst into tears when he was handed a gun. He was arrested after the filming and taken away. They were instructed to never tell anyone that they had been involved in the propaganda film.

> *When you go back you must never tell anyone that have been participating in a film. If asked, you are to say that you were taken around Lhasa where you saw the Potala, Ramoche and other important buildings repaired and the people looking very happy.*

A few weeks later at Nachen Trang they were shown the same film that they were in, which the Chinese said proved that the revolt was caused by the reactionaries and that monks were involved in it. Everyone at Nachen Trang knew that the film was false propaganda, since they recognized the monks and soldiers who had participated in it, but this did not matter to the Chinese who showed the film all over China and Tibet and in their international propaganda. All the prisoners were made to sign a statement that they thought the reactionaries had started the uprising and that monks had participated in the fighting.

Prisoners were divided into companies of 100 and subdivided into groups of 25. Each group had a leader and an assistant leader chosen by the prisoners themselves. The group leaders were responsible for ensuring that everybody in the group worked strenuously without any rest. Each prisoner was required to carry at least 75 baskets of earth each day for distances up to a kilometer. In the evening each group leader had to report to a Chinese supervisor how many baskets were carried that day. The best performing groups were praised while the worst performing were punished with increased work or reduced food rations. Competition was thus set up between groups. Tashi Palden says that none of the workers at Nachen Trang ever walked; they were always running.

In their evening indoctrination sessions, the prisoners were required to declare who was responsible for the revolt. They learned to say that it was the reactionaries who were responsible but they were uncertain about who or what "reactionaries" were. Then they were told that they were not just prisoners but workers for the *Tang* (the CCP). They were told that they would have to bathe in the water of liberty and offer their hearts to the Tang. A celebration was held called "Offering Your Heart to the Tang." After that they were instructed about the need to oppose the social classes and institutions that the Chinese had defined as the exploiters of the Tibetan people: the feudal serf-owners, the Tibetan government, and the monasteries. They were told about democratic reforms, which meant liberation of the serfs and relief from all debts owed to any of the feudal exploiting classes. The Tibetan prisoners learned to say what they thought the Chinese wanted, mostly just to shorten the length of the evening meetings, but they understood little of the confusing Chinese terminology, mostly because what the Chinese believed about Tibetan society corresponded to their ideology but not to the reality.

The most confusing question the Chinese asked was, "What is oppression and deception?" The correct answer was, "the old society," because the old society was based upon deception and oppression. Then they were individually asked about whom they had oppressed and deceived or who had oppressed and deceived them. They usually made up answers about minor injustices or abuses they had inflicted or received. However, the former monks replied that they had neither inflicted nor received any deception or oppression since they did nothing but offer prayers for the betterment of others and were supported by society for doing so. However, the Chinese said that all these answers were insufficient since they all had agreed that Tibetan society was based upon deception and oppression; therefore, they must have inflicted or suffered from deception and oppression themselves.

The Tibetans were dumbfounded by this requirement to misconstrue their lives as well as the reality of Tibetan society in order to fit in with Chinese definitions. But the Chinese did not believe that anyone had never had anything to do with suffering, since they characterized Tibetan society as plagued by suffering. They were therefore required to reexamine their lives from an early age in order to realize how they had caused or had been the victims of the deception and oppression theoretically inherent in old Tibetan society. No one could avoid participation or maintain that there was no such oppression in the past or that they had no role in it. They thus learned to make elaborate, exaggerated, or false denunciations of the inequalities and evils in the old society and their roles as either perpetrators or victims just in order to satisfy the Chinese.

Some Tibetans from outside Nachen Trang, mostly former serfs, were brought in to provide examples of the inequalities and evils supposedly inherent in Tibetan society. These former serfs were practiced in their accounts of their sufferings and were taken around from place to place to convince all Tibetans about the evils of their own society. Many of the former serfs lived on their ability to tell their stories, often elaborated to emphasize their sufferings. They became semiprofessional complainers about the evils of the old society. They were very popular with the Chinese since they confirmed what they thought about old Tibet and justified the Chinese role in coming to Tibet to liberate the Tibetans from their own exploitative society. After the outside speakers left, the prisoners were required to make elaborate denunciations of the society that had allowed such outrages. They were also required to learn and to sing songs denouncing the old society and praising the new communist ideology. After some time, such meetings became so exhausting that they preferred hard labor. So, when the working hours were raised to twelve per day, nobody complained.

The Chinese soon introduced the process of mutual criticism, or thamzing:

> *Those who criticized others were praised and received special privileges. Those who did not were regarded with suspicion. Soon there developed a group of people who specialized in finding faults in others. After a while they were kept separately with the Chinese guards and they did not have to work. Their job was to watch others.*

Everyone was required to participate in the criticism in order to show their own enthusiasm for change. Failure to passionately participate could result in being the next victim of the thamzing process. Tibetans thus learned to make up false criticisms of others and to fake passionate energy for change. However, in reality, most Tibetans just went along with what they thought the Chinese wanted. The result of the Democratic Reforms Campaign was that Tibetans learned to speak falsely and to act falsely. What the Chinese thus achieved was to introduce the same sort of deception and oppression into Tibetan society that they imagined had been inherent all along, but that in fact they had brought to Tibetan society themselves.

One day it was announced that there was going to be a visit by foreigners. For days they were instructed on what kind of questions to expect from the visitors and what their answers should be. One Gyume monk confided in others that he intended to tell the whole truth to the visitors. He was betrayed by another Tibetan and subjected to thamzing after the visit. The day of the foreigners' visit an enormous amount of food was put before the prisoners for the foreigners to see. The visitors,

Russians they were told, did not ask any questions and just took photos. The prisoners were served four meals that day.

After that the work became harder and the food was worse. Some people committed suicide by jumping into the river. Loads were now carried in wheelbarrows, with one person pushing and another pulling with a rope. They had to run all the time and the wheelbarrows often overturned. Many prisoners were run over by wheelbarrows but the work continued without pause.

At the beginning of 1960, when the Nachen Trang hydroelectric project was almost finished, Tashi Palden and the other prisoners were told they would be sent either to farms in Kongpo or to mines at a place in the Changtang called Tsala Karpo. Most hoped to go to Kongpo, since farming in the relatively warm climate of Kongpo was considered preferable to mining in the cold and harsh conditions of the Changtang. However, they were told that more people were needed for the mines at Tsala Karpo; therefore, everyone between the ages of 20 and 50 would have to go there. They were also shown warm tents and clothes that were promised to be provided in Tsala Karpo.

Tsala Karpo was located in the northern Changtang near the lakes Nagtsang and Pongog. The name Tsala Karpo, or "white earth," usually refers to the common mineral borax, often found near salt lakes and used to make soap and other simple products. However, in this case the name apparently referred to the place where the mines were located since they were told that the mineral they were mining was more valuable by weight than gold. It was found in white, yellow, blue, and reddish lumps. (The valuable mineral mined at Tsala Karpo was probably chromium, used to harden steel especially for military uses.) The minerals mined there were taken by truck to Golmud and from there to Dunhuang and the railhead at Loyang in Xinjiang, the closest railhead to Tibet at the time.[10]

There was no food, fuel, or even water at Tsala Karpo. All had to be trucked in by the Chinese. There were no warm tents or clothing. Some wood for cooking could be found in the surrounding areas. Tashi Palden's group from Nachen Trang was about 500 prisoners. There were another 300 Tibetan prisoners from Nagchu and some 300 Chinese prisoners.

They were watched by 500 PLA troops. The regime of work all day and political meetings at night was continued.

Gradually the work at Tsala Karpo became more arduous and the food rations less. One day one of Tashi Palden's fellow prisoners approached him with a plan to escape, but he was afraid to trust him since the Chinese sometimes used provocateurs to test the loyalty of the prisoners. However, the prisoner did escape and Tashi Palden wished that he had gone with him. A few others also escaped, after which the Chinese resumed thamzings in order to find out who might have thoughts of escape. The Tibetans were even told that they could criticize the policies of the Chinese during the criticism sessions since this was part of democratic reforms. Tashi Palden took this promise seriously and criticized the Chinese for subjecting the Tibetan prisoners to such misery. He said that it was no mystery why some prisoners had escaped, because all the prisoners there were overworked, starved, and mentally tortured by all the Chinese political campaigns. The Chinese then tried to subject him to the usual thamzing process of beatings by his fellow prisoners but now, unlike at Nachen Trang, the Tibetans refused to participate in the process.

Despite his fellow prisoners' refusal to criticize or beat him, Tashi Palden knew that the Chinese would find some way to punish him. Therefore, he determined to escape. He was able to do so by pretending to be part of a group sent out to find firewood. He managed to escape and to reach Lhasa where he exchanged identity papers with and obtained a travel permit from his brother whose back had been broken at Nachen Trang. He went to Bathang and managed to get Rato Rinpoche and a few others to escape to India with him. They traveled by night and slept in the mountains by day and finally reached Bhutan in December 1960.

## Tashi Dorje[11]

Tashi Dorje was a nomad of the Hor Yetar nomadic area in northeastern Tibet. He was seventeen years old in 1959 and experienced the outcome of the revolt only in June when Chinese officials came to his area. The local Tibetans were told that the revolt had been put down by the PLA in a short time since it was supported only by the upper-class reactionaries and not by the common people. They were told that the reactionaries had tried to take the Dalai Lama to India but that he had been captured. Similarly, those Tibetans who had already escaped to India had been returned by the government of India because of India's respect for China. They should have no thoughts of fleeing because if they tried to escape, they would be captured and returned immediately. They were also instructed to surrender any weapons in their possession.

The local nomads replied that they would not surrender their weapons and that they would obey the rules of the Communist Chinese only if they did not conflict with their local traditions, culture, and religion. This reply made the Chinese very angry. They said that the Tibetans would have to obey each and every rule of the new government without any questions and that they would return shortly to collect the Tibetans' weapons. If they refused to surrender their weapons, they would suffer the same fate "as that of the reactionary Dalai Lama and his followers."

The local Tibetans had a meeting in which many spoke out against giving up their weapons. Tashi Dorje's uncle was one of those who spoke out:

> *As we all know, yesterday the Chinese officers claimed that they have captured Lhasa and His Holiness. But we must not be discouraged by what they say. It is their policy to make propaganda like that and we must not be influenced by it. As demonstrated by their actions in other parts of eastern Tibet, the Chinese see our religion as the main obstacle to their military advancement. I for one am not prepared to give in to their demands at all and further, I think that we must all jointly fight the Chinese for preserving freedom of religion, equal status and equality before the law.*

Some 600 of them vowed to continue resistance to the Chinese and left that same night for Damshung (northwest of Lhasa along the road to Nagchuka and Golmud in Qinghai) where they had heard that many resistance fighters were gathered. Only about 400 Tibetans, mostly women and children, were left behind, but they also vowed to continue resistance. Tashi Dorje and those who left for Damshung soon reached the Sokchu River, which they could not cross because the water was high. There was a bridge near the Sokchu Dan Monastery but it was guarded by the Chinese, who were busy dismantling the monastery. They were told that some thirty monks from the monastery had already left for India.

There they were joined by twenty-seven nomad families who fashioned a rope bridge by which they were able to cross the river one by one. They were told that Chinese troops were looking for them, so they traveled for eighteen days with no break. They reached a place called Tsam Lung where they stayed for three months. There were now some 900 in their group. They were told that there were as many as 20,000 Tibetans hiding in the area but, like their own group now that they had been joined by many nomad families, they were burdened by women and children as well as by many of their livestock and were thus not a very effective fighting force. They were nevertheless determined to fight whatever the outcome and only waited for an opportunity to attack. They stayed there until the winter.

In December they were joined by some monks from the nearby Patsang Monastery who told them that all religious activities at their monastery had been stopped by the Chinese, who were now using the main assembly hall for political meetings and thamzing of high lamas and former upper-class people. Almost all the formerly 500 monks had escaped or been arrested. The Chinese had taken away the monastery's valuable images in some fifty trucks. The rest of the sacred images and ritual implements, including religious texts, *thankas,* and *mani* carvings, were destroyed on the spot.

Many of the Tibetans at Damshung decided to join forces with others at Chakra Pembar to the east. They had gathered there because there were no Chinese there at the time and because the terrain was suitable for guerrilla warfare. (Here they were supplied with arms by several flights from the American CIA.) Until then none of them had thought to escape to India. All were determined to stay to fight for Tibetan independence. Then on February 9, 1960, his group was bombed by five Chinese jet airplanes. The bombing went on until noon and many were killed. Then the planes dropped leaflets calling on them to surrender. The leaflets reminded them that there was only one good path and one bad path. "The good path leads to the Great Motherland and the bad one leads to the reactionary Dalai. People should surrender and return to the Great Motherland. If they decide to follow the Dalai clique and go to America, we can easily destroy them by a handful of bombs." However, they were not discouraged because the leaflets revealed that the Dalai Lama had not been captured but had escaped.

The bombing continued for ten days; many were killed or captured and the group was reduced from 20,000 to only 12,000. His group was still determined not to surrender or to flee into exile so they left that place and headed back toward Amdo, being constantly attacked by the Chinese and losing more of their number. After twenty days, when they got to Sirhor in Amdo, there were only 280 of them left. However, they found that the whole area was under the control of the Chinese who were busy preaching the virtues of socialism to the people. There they again clashed with the Chinese. Several were captured, including his uncle and eleven others who were killed by being pushed from an airplane.

After the deaths of their twelve friends, the remaining 268 of them left Sirhor and went toward the lakes Tsaring Nor and Oring Nor. When they reached the lakes, their path was blocked by 1,000 Chinese troops. Although exhausted and poorly armed, they had no choice but to fight. Here they lost another 100 of their companions. Finally, the survivors decided that they had to try to reach India. Tashi Dorje and a few others traveled several months across the Changtang, subsisting on wild meat. They reached Ladakh in February1962, having fought against the Chinese for almost three years. His account reveals that most Tibetans in Amdo, especially the nomads, resisted Chinese rule but that only a small portion of them were able to escape to India.

## Rinzing Paljor[12]

Rinzing Paljor was born in Lhasa in 1930. He was trained by his father in traditional Tibetan thangka painting. He remembers hearing about the Chinese invasion of Tibet in 1950 on Radio Nepal. The PLA was reported to have entered Tibet from the east, from Sichuan through Kham, and from the north, through Qinghai. His understanding of the subsequent Seventeen Point Agreement was that Tibet would have to coordinate all government decisions with China. Tibetans consoled themselves with the provisions of the agreement that safeguarded Tibetan religion and did not change the position of the Dalai Lama or the customs and traditions of Tibet.

Given this understanding, citizens of Lhasa sent a letter to the Dalai Lama at Yatung on the border with India asking him to return to Lhasa.[13] However, they worried about the provisions of the agreement that required the Tibetan government to be incorporated within the Chinese administrative system and the Tibetan Army to be integrated within the PLA. They feared that the Chinese would change Tibet because they had no respect for religion. Also, the ideology of the Chinese Communists was to collectivize everything, the result of which was that everyone became equally poor rather than rich.

Rinzing was unimpressed with the condition of the first PLA troops who entered Lhasa, describing them as ragged and emaciated. He swears that the Chinese troops brought "herds" of dogs with them for food and collected stray dogs in Lhasa for the same purpose. The Chinese misinterpreted Tibetans clapping at their arrival as a welcome when it really was a Tibetan tradition to clap to expel demons. Tibetans were told by their government to be polite to the Chinese PLA troops. The Chinese immediately began to try to curry favor with the poor, whom they promised would become rich due to the policy of equalizing wealth. Tibetans' sentiments were expressed by a popular poem or ditty that went as follows:

> There is plenty of firewood to burn,
> No need for dog shit.
> No need to liberate Tibet,
> Already have the Dalai Lama.

The sentiment expressed by this ditty seems to be that the Chinese brought nothing to Tibet that Tibetans needed, thus questioning their motives for coming to Tibet at all. Many Lhasa Tibetans thought that the silver dayan that the Chinese were liberally dispensing to curry favor was "Siling money," Siling being the Tibetan pronunciation of Sining, the provincial capital of Qinghai; and that the image on it was of Ma Pufang, the Hui Muslim ruler of Qinghai before 1949, rather than Yuan Shikai. All the dayan that the Chinese distributed during the 1950s were confiscated in 1959, along with all Tibetan printed money. Paper renminbi was issued in exchange for dayan and Tibetan money, but only for those not involved in the revolt. Possession of Tibetan money became illegal after 1959. Much of the dayan ended up in Nepal and India where it was melted down for its silver content.

Rinzing's father, Sonam Rinchen, organized a Crafts Union in 1955 after the Dalai Lama returned from Beijing. It included not only artists but also all sorts of artisans like tailors, carpenters, masons, metal workers, shoemakers, and tanners. The purpose was to have an independent organization of Tibetan workers outside the control of the Chinese, who were also attempting to organize and propagandize workers. They collected dues that were used to support out-of-work members and also to gild the Jowo (Sakyamuni Buddha) statue in the Jokhang and to organize picnics. According to his father there had been trade unions in Lhasa since the time of the Fifth Dalai Lama (mid-seventeenth century). Artists like Rinzing and his father were actually Tibetan government employees. They were paid a small salary plus food and butter tea during their work. They painted thankas and frescoes for the Potala, Norbulinka, and Jokhang and for the monasteries of Drepung, Sera, and Ganden. Most were taught within their own families, but painters had to pass a government test. Eventually a painting school was established at the Potala.

The main activity of the union was to organize prayers for the Dalai Lama, including a ceremony at the Norbulinka, at which the Dalai Lama told them that the Chinese had come to help Tibetans and that they had a right to expel them if they were not really helping. This was similar to the version that the Chinese themselves were saying, that they had only come to help and would leave when Tibetans no longer needed them. During the 1959 revolt, the union members protected the Norbulinka and Jokhang and they also burned down the old KMT Chinese residence. Sonam Rinchen was arrested defending the Jokhang during the revolt and died in 1968 in Drapchi Prison. He was first detained at the

Taring house, then sent to Drapchi, Nachen Trang, and back to Drapchi. He was also subjected to public thamzing, the main accusations against him being that he had been the leader of the "illegal," or noncommunist, Crafts Union.

Rinzing was quite aware of the controversy over the Panchen Lama. He knew the history of the previous Panchen's flight to China in 1924 and the fact that his reincarnation was not recognized by Lhasa until the Seventeen Point Agreement, which characterized the status of the Dalai and Panchen Lamas as equal, which was not true, he said. The PLA escorted the Panchen Lama on his return to Tibet in 1951 and insisted that he should not have to prostrate to the Dalai Lama but instead should be accorded equal status, including thrones of equal height. The Dalai Lama did not have a problem with this, even though some of the people of Lhasa apparently did, being aware of the tradition that the seat of the Panchen was supposed to be equivalent only to a Regent. The Dalai Lama even came forward to greet the Panchen when he arrived. The young Panchen was not blamed for what was considered these bad manners because he was considered to be under the control of his own entourage and the Chinese.

Rinzing says that there were few changes in Lhasa before the revolt. The Chinese created many social organizations and tried to get the Tibetan aristocrats to join. There were no pressures to send children to China for education but very strong incentives to do so, especially for the aristocrats. The Chinese put great pressure on the Dalai Lama and the Tibetan government to stop the resistance in eastern Tibet, even though they themselves had put those areas outside the territory of the TAR and thus theoretically beyond the authority of Lhasa. Whenever the Dalai Lama gave a teaching, the Chinese insisted that the Panchen should give exactly the same teaching, whether he knew the scripture or not. Lhasa Tibetans protested the creation of the Preparatory Committee for the TAR in 1956 as a violation of the provision of the Seventeen Point Agreement that there would be no political changes. However, the Chinese said that if Tibetans did not want to participate, then the Chinese would run the committee themselves.

When the Dalai Lama went to India in 1956 for the 2,500th anniversary of the birth of the Buddha, about half the people of Lhasa thought he would stay there because of the deteriorating situation within Tibet. When he returned it was thought it was due to Zhou Enlai having gone to India to convince him to return with promises of no reforms in Tibet. The Chinese promised that there would be no reforms for six years with another six-year extension if Tibetans were not ready. They also promised to reduce their numbers in Tibet, but Tibetans had no way to know how many Chinese were coming or going. The Chinese retrenchment in 1957 led Tibetans to believe that the Tibetan government actually had the power to refuse reforms. Tibetans were happy with the no reform policy; particularly, a reduction in the numbers of Chinese in Tibet was welcomed since they were considered a burden.

The Chinese were fortifying their camps and positions in and around Lhasa before March 1959. By that time most people in Lhasa were supportive of the Chushi Gangdruk (Tibetan Resistance), despite their traditional prejudice against Khampas, and were hopeful that they could defeat the Chinese. Rinzing was among those who gathered at the Norbulinka to protect the Dalai Lama and prevent him from going to the drama performance at the Chinese military camp on the other side of the Kyi Chu. It was well known that he had been told to come without his usual entourage or guards and Tibetans were fearful that he would be kidnapped and taken to China.

Rinzing was a member of the *Mimang* (People's Assembly) organized at the Norbulinka. They met with the Kashag and demanded that Tibet should declare its independence, but the Kashag insisted upon diplomacy because the Chinese were clearly ready and even eager to put down any revolt with force. The Mimang sent messages to the Nepal, Bhutan, India, and Kashmir consulates declaring Tibetan independence. The Kashag advised against mass demonstrations and the organization of a militia, as did the Dalai Lama, but Tibetans felt that they had to take matters into their own hands.

Rinzing heard the first shots fired at the Norbulinka at four o'clock on the morning of March 20th. He claims that as many as 1,000 artillery rounds were fired at the Norbulinka and then at the Potala. By the

23rd, all of Lhasa was under the control of the Chinese and almost all Tibetan men were killed, had fled, or were in hiding. He was arrested and detained at Norbulinka with thousands of others, where he was kept for six months and interrogated daily. He was then transferred to Silingbu, the Chinese military headquarters where the highest government officials, lamas, and aristocrats were kept. His house was sealed but his wife and mother were allowed to live in the basement. They were taken out daily for labor and were struggled at night. He was imprisoned for five years but was not badly treated. He was labeled as a reactionary until 1977. He had to seek permission to go anywhere outside his home. He was not allowed to paint professionally but some of his old students got paints to him and he painted on Sundays. The Chinese found out and accused him of "fooling the people."

During the Cultural Revolution any house could be searched at any time by Red Guards, who were usually young Tibetans, looking for religious objects. If any were found, they were confiscated and the owners subjected to public struggle. The Tibetan Red Guards were usually students educated at the various minority nationality institutes in China; they were joined by locals recruited by means of coercion combined with promises of rewards for any religious objects they found. The Red Guards were also responsible for the ransacking of the Jokhang and the Ramoche, but only after the Chinese had removed all of the most valuable items. They cut open the Ramoche Jowo searching for jewels but found only black soot, which was actually burnt precious stones. The Chinese then criticized Tibetans for worshiping "bags of coal." The soot was thrown in the Kyi Chu but some was saved and used by Tibetans as medicine. Some was left and was given to the first Dharamsala delegation that came to Lhasa in the early 1980s.

I met Rinzing Paljor in Lhasa in 1982. He was the brother-in-law of Dolma Yudon Tenpa, a Tibetan American woman who befriended me in Lhasa and provided me with much information and most of the inspiration that led me into a career in Tibetan studies. Dolma was one of the first Tibetans to return from exile for a visit during the liberalization period that began in the early 1980s. Rinzing and his wife Sonam Cheodron were living in two small rooms in the old Phala mansion just east of the Barkhor. I spent many days there gathering information from the numerous Tibetans who came to visit Dolma and tell their stories.

Rinzing had been released from his house arrest in 1973 because the Chinese wanted to invite some foreign visitors to Lhasa, like the king of Nepal, and they did not want them to see the destruction caused by their own political campaigns. Rinzing was employed in the restoration of murals at the Jokhang at that time and, later, during the 1980s, at Drepung, Tashilhunpo, and Shalu. I worried about Rinzing and Sonam, but they, like so many older Tibetans, said that they had suffered so much already that they were no longer afraid. Fortunately, Rinzing Paljor and Sonam Cheodron were able to leave Tibet a few years later. They got a permit to visit India in 1985, where they remained, Rinzing becoming the Dalai Lama's private painter and head of a school for young artists in Dharamsala.

### Abu Chonga[14]

Abu Chonga was born in Shota Lhosum in 1935. Shota Lhosum means the three (*sum*) valleys or districts of Shopa Do, Ta Dzong, and Lho Dzong in the western part of Kham. He says that travel to Chamdo took seven days while to Lhasa it was twenty-five days. The area was mostly seminomadic with some purely nomadic areas. He remembers the arrival of the PLA in Shota Lhosum and that they were in a poor state, with not even very good weapons. They distributed dayan liberally and said that they had come only to help and would leave Tibet when certain unspecified reforms and benefits had been completed. They said that 95 percent of the Tibetans would benefit from their reforms, which implied that at least 5 percent, presumably the traditional rulers and landlords, would not. He reports that despite the Chinese promises, their arrival in Shota Lhosum was considered a bad omen.

At first there were no reforms and the local elites remained in their positions with lavish salaries from the Chinese. Only their office titles were changed to correspond to the Chinese system. The Chinese established hospitals and schools. There were no purges or public criticisms but there were mandatory public meetings to educate the locals about class exploitation. Some local children, particularly the poor,[15] were sent to China for free education. There were strong financial incentives for parents to send their children but no coercion.

Abu Chonga was aware that the Chushi Gangdruk resistance organization was formed in 1958 at a meeting in Lhasa under the guise of a golden throne-making and dedication ceremony for the Dalai Lama. He was not there but he assumes that many in the Tibetan government and in the monastic establishment were in collusion with the founding of the resistance organization or at least in sympathy. Active resistance began in Shota Lhosum around the same time, due to news of what the Chinese called democratic reforms having been implemented in Kham east of the Mekong, which was part of Sichuan Province, and Khampa refugees fleeing through the area on their way to Lhasa or staying there to organize resistance. He reports that Paksho Gompa gave 96 British rifles and 24 boxes of ammunition that they had hidden in the monastery walls to the Chushi Gangdruk.

The Chushi Gangdruk began organizing resistance in his area by requiring all men age 18 to 60 to enlist and inviting women to do so as well. They described the Chinese as like a bird with a sweet voice, but who talked like a parrot and whose real character was like an owl (a raptor or predator). Each district of Shota Lhosum was supposed to send 100 men to attack the Chinese at Po Tramo in Kongpo. However, the Chinese were well fortified at Po Tramo and the Tibetan attack failed with many being killed or wounded. The Chinese were able to call in reinforcements and surround the attacking Tibetans. The Chushi Gangdruk described this as their thirteenth battle with the Chinese. Shortly thereafter Abu Chonga heard through a radio that Lhasa had been lost.

After the revolt in Lhasa the Chushi Gangdruk withdrew from Shota Lhosum and told the locals to continue resistance on their own. But the locals were poorly equipped. There had been no CIA airdrops up to this time in this area. Some Tibetans from Chamdo and Derge joined the resistance in Shota Lhosum. The Chinese PLA, which had substantially neglected the area before March 1959, reentered in April. The local Tibetans lost several battles with the Chinese, with eighty killed in one battle and fifty each in two more. They had mostly only swords and axes and tried to capture weapons from the Chinese. Lho Dzong was lost and the Tibetan fighters had to withdraw to Shopa Do and Ta Dzong. In the sixth or seventh month (Tibetan calendar) came the first American airdrop of sixteen fighters and weapons at Pembar in Ta Dzong. They had radios and rifles, both Indian (8-shot) and American (5-shot), plus three mortars, grenades, and one 25-shot rifle (presumably a Bren gun, which had a 20-round magazine). The CIA-trained Tibetans radioed that there was an active resistance in the area and received another airdrop of additional weapons and ammunition.

The Tibetans tried to attack Lho Dzong, where the Chinese had fortified the local monastery. They fought eight battles but were unable to capture it, although they killed many Chinese. As at Po Tramo, the Chinese were able to call in reinforcements. The Chinese took the timbers from the gompa to make coffins for their troops, who filled a large cemetery. Abu Chonga believes that as many as 70,000 PLA were sent to the area from Chamdo. The large number of Chinese troops finally managed to surround the Tibetans on a mountain where they attacked from all sides. When there were only thirty Tibetans left, they accepted a Chinese offer to let them surrender. They were actually surprised that the Chinese kept their word and did not fire when they came down from the mountain. The PLA was disciplined, says Abu Chonga, unlike the Siling Tamak (Siling Cavalry), former troops of Ma Pufang, some of whom had joined the PLA. They were also good fighters, but were undisciplined, and would surely have killed the Tibetans even though they had surrendered as they had done in other instances.

This was in the first month of 1960. Abu Chonga was among a few Tibetans who were able to escape before the surrender. He and a few others continued to fight until the fourth month of 1960. They still held out hope for more assistance from abroad. During that time, they were approached by a Tibetan collaborator who had been appointed over their area by the Chinese. He was one of those upper-class Tibetans who hoped that by cooperation with the Chinese they could retain some of their wealth and privileges. He had already had some of his wealth confiscated by the Chushi Gangdruk commander, Gompo Tashi, because of his collaboration with the Chinese. Abu Chonga and his comrades offered to surrender but only to this Tibetan rather than to any Chinese.

He was lured up to their hiding place and then he and a companion were killed.

Abu Chonga says that there were 20,000 Chinese in Lho Dzong at that time. There were only seven left in his group who had still refused to surrender. They hoped to flee to India but were informed that all the routes were blocked by the Chinese. His group remained on the run until they were betrayed by what Abu Chonga calls a "low caste horse castrator" who had been cultivated by the Chinese. They were surrounded and attacked by the Chinese, the first of whom, carrying only a pistol and presumably an officer, Abu Chonga shot and killed. They were finally forced to surrender. The Chinese were surprised to find that there were only seven Tibetans in his group. One of the Tibetans had been wounded and six Chinese had been killed. The wounded Tibetan was thrown from a cliff by the Chinese.

They were interrogated by a three-star Chinese general who questioned why they were still fighting and who was supporting them. Some Chinese still seemed mystified why Tibetans would resist the "assistance" they had come to provide to Tibet. They were taken to Lho Dzong where there were another 2,000–3,000 Tibetan prisoners. Democratic reforms had already been implemented and all his family's property had been confiscated. He was kept in Lho Dzong until 1962. Some others were sentenced to long 15-year prison terms during that time, at Po Tramo and Chamdo, and many of them died in prison due to starvation because of food shortages during the Great Leap Forward (1959–1962). The prisoners at Lho Dzong were made to work cutting trees and sending logs down the river and plowing fields using eight men to pull a plow. They tried to hit stones while plowing so the plow would break and they could rest.

In Lho Dzong prison, relatives were allowed to bring food to prisoners. The prisoners were often taken out for thamzing in villages. The local Tibetans did not know how to do a thamzing, so the Chinese had to incite the poor to criticize the former exploiting classes. The poor were instructed with chalk boards about who were the exploiting classes. They were told that they had to either stand for socialism or for feudalism, there was no other way. Anyone who did not participate in thamzing must be for feudalism and must therefore be subjected to thamzing themselves. Anyone who was for socialism must subject others to thamzing until they confessed to their exploitation of others. They were told that everyone had something to hide about their past and that thamzing was meant to determine what that was. There were many suicides during thamzings.

Abu Chonga says that the real purpose of thamzing was so that the Chinese could find out who the upper class "exploiters" were and who were "reactionaries" and "counterrevolutionaries," that is, whoever resisted "reform" or opposed the Chinese in any way. Democratic reforms were conducted under the rubric of the "three antis and two liberations" policy. The three antis were opposition to the monasteries, the old regime, and feudal landlords, both monastic and aristocratic. The two liberations were freedom for the serfs and forgiveness of all debts. The property of all the upper classes was confiscated.

Religion was particularly attacked. Tibetans were told that monasteries and monks were the main exploiters; without the destruction of religion there could be no real liberation; only materialist ideology was real while all other ideologies were imaginary. Monasteries were looted of their relics by the Chinese and the most valuable articles were taken to China. Some less-valuable articles were distributed to the local people. Similarly, all the animals of the nomads were confiscated. The best animals were kept by the Chinese while the poorest were distributed to the Tibetans. The Chinese also collected most of the barley harvest. The best was taken as taxes while the worst was given to Tibetans. Tibetans were told that the socialist road was crooked but that the end was bright.

Abu Chonga says that by this time the reality of Chinese reforms had convinced even the lower classes, some of whom had believed the Chinese promises, that the Chinese had brought nothing good to Tibet. Taxes, thamzings, repression, and starvation had made them realize the reality. Poor nomads who had received more animals during democratic reforms ran afoul of Chinese quotas for milk and butter production. Tibetans traditionally tried to keep large herds since animals could starve during droughts or freeze during snowstorms. However, the Chinese insisted that production should increase every year without regard to weather. If the nomads had a good year with lots of milk, butter, and meat production, then the Chinese increased the quota for the next year and then took that amount regardless of the actual production that year. If the nomads were unable to meet the quotas, then they were subjected to thamzing. In contrast, rewards for good production were petty, including pens, small amounts of money, letters of recognition, and Mao's photos and his books.

In 1962 he was sentenced to death for the crime of being a reactionary but because he was a minority nationality, his sentenced was reduced to twenty years in prison, plus he was deprived of political rights for another five years. This was standard CCP practice, but deprivation of political rights had little meaning for most Tibetans. He was first sent to Chamdo Prison, where he was told that his crime was so large that the whole sky could not hold it and that he must reform his mentality through labor. He was then sent to the prison and labor camp complex at Po Tramo. His camp was named Dzongna and, along with Chundo and Damcho, was one of the three largest camps that held the prisoners with the longest sentences. Chundo was a former monastery that had been made into a prison. Other camps were Nangdap, Goshang, and Talung. His camp was actually in Bomi, about two hours by truck to Po Tramo.

Abu Chonga says that there were 7,000–9,000 prisoners altogether in the Po Tramo prison complex. They were chained by the legs at night and even in the early morning when they had to do exercises. One corner of the exercise yard was just for *tulkus* (lama reincarnations). Then they had to listen to readings from Mao. The labor was mostly clearing land and farming. This part of Kongpo is at a lower altitude than almost anywhere else in Tibet and therefore was suitable for farming, especially for wheat, which the Chinese preferred over the Tibetan barley. The prisoners were fed so poorly that they were dizzy and hungry after the work day.

After work they were gathered in the courtyard of the prison and given political indoctrination. Each prisoner was criticized for his performance that day and, if lacking, was told that they must be thinking of the old society. They were all told that they had been given the opportunity to reform for which they should be grateful. They were constantly told about how China had beaten the Americans in Korea and the Indians in 1962. The whole sky was conquered by China, they said; the old Tibetan way of thinking was useless and Tibetans should not hope for support from any imperialist and reactionary countries. They were thus harangued until the stars were shining in the sky.

In the winter months the prisoners were required to write self-criticisms and to examine their thoughts and actions before and since being imprisoned. They were rewarded for criticizing or informing on others and punished for not having a positive attitude for reform. Political education consisted of lectures on the power of China and its territory, of which Tibet was a part. At one time all the prisoners of the seven camps were gathered together and lectured by officials from Lhasa about the need to take the bright way, or reform, or the death way. To illustrate the point, fifteen prisoners who had refused to reform were paraded before them with their crimes written on placards around their necks and then executed in front of all the other prisoners. They were told that opposition to the communist government could only result in the same fate. Three more prisoners were executed for trying to escape, twenty-seven were executed in 1969, and sixty more in 1970 after the Nyemo revolt near Lhasa.

Before the Cultural Revolution, the prisoners could pray silently or finger their prayer beads, but during the Cultural Revolution even anyone making throat movements was suspected of reciting mantra and prisoners were sometimes shot just for that reason. Many lamas in prison committed suicide during that time. One prisoner who tried to escape had his severed head displayed to the others as an example. Abu Chonga believed that the campaign against the "Four Olds" during the Cultural Revolution (old thoughts, habits, traditions, and customs) was directly aimed at Tibetan tradition and culture. One Tibetan unit leader was killed by the prisoners for being too cooperative with the Chinese and for informing on others.

Abu Chonga and all other prisoners at Po Tramo were released in 1979, due to the liberalization policy, but they were required to remain at the same place as "released workers." After two years they were told they could return to their homes. In 1983 Abu Chonga got a permit to go on pilgrimage to Kang Rinpoche (Mt. Kailash) in far western Tibet from where he escaped to Nepal.

***Tsering Dorje Gashi*[16]**

*New Tibet*, by Tsering Dorje Gashi, is the story of a Tibetan who was educated at the Beijing National Minorities Institute from 1956 to 1961. He was one of many Tibetans educated at the various minority nationality institutes, most of whom were sent back to Tibet after the 1959 revolt. These Tibetans were supposed to become the cadres who would pursue Tibet's "democratic reforms" and "socialist transformation," and would eventually become the administrators of an "autonomous" Tibet. He worked for the *Tibet Daily* newspaper for eight months in 1962 before becoming disillusioned. He was then sent back to his home town of Phari where he engaged in manual labor until escaping to India in September 1966.

Having been educated by the Chinese Communists in their ideologies and ideals, he was able to contrast those ideals with the reality in Tibet under Chinese Communist rule. The author says that he was better able to understand China's policies in Tibet than most Tibetans because of his previous education and that he therefore felt an obligation to explain those policies to the best of his ability to Tibetans and to the outside world.

Tsering Dorje writes that his book is based upon his ten years of personal experience of China and its administration of Tibet, first in Beijing and then in Tibet. He particularly wanted to tell the story of Tibetans and other nationalities at the minority nationality institute who resisted Chinese indoctrination and protested against Chinese policies at great personal risk to themselves. Because of his experience, he felt a responsibility to reveal the facts of Tibetan resistance to the Chinese control of their country both in Beijing and in Tibet. He wanted Tibetans and the world to know that even many of the Tibetan youth educated and indoctrinated by the Chinese were not fooled by Chinese propaganda and they retained their Tibetan identity and will to resist. Some, of course, also became unwitting tools of the Chinese in their destruction of Tibetan culture and national identity. He writes that it is difficult for Tibetans or the outside world to penetrate Chinese propaganda, but that he is in the position to be able to do so because he was trained in that same propaganda.

Tsering Dorje was born in 1941 in Phari, a small high-altitude village in the Chumbi valley that extends south from Tibet between Sikkim and Bhutan and forms the primary trade route from Tibet to India. He went to school in Phari until age 13 when he transferred to a traditional medical school. His teacher was a renowned traditional doctor who was highly learned in medicine and astrology. He was at this school for only two years for reasons that he does not explain, perhaps due to his family's financial situation, and then returned to a small school in Phari. Perhaps it was due to this disappointment that he became interested in educational opportunities then being offered by the Chinese.

He became aware of the opportunity in 1956 when a Chinese official came to his Phari school to talk about scholarships to study in China. The Chinese were at that time offering to send Tibetans to school in China with all expenses paid by the Chinese government. Tibetan families were under a lot of political pressure to send their children to China for study and some were essentially coerced into doing so against their will.

Tsering Dorje was not at all coerced; in fact, he was eager to go and tried to persuade his family to allow him to go. He was enticed by the opportunity to see the world outside Tibet and to receive what he thought would be a modern education. He writes that he was young and longed for bigger and more exciting places, with lots of strange and new things to see. He finally persuaded his family that sending him to China for education was in his best interest. He was chosen along with six others from Phari. They joined another twenty youths from the Chumbi valley and were all given an elaborate send-off hosted by a local Chinese official.

The Chinese official told them that the Chinese Communist Party had great plans and great expectations for their futures, which were sure to be bright and secure. They would become pioneers in the socialist transformation of Tibet. They could also see the wonders and cities of China that they had previously only heard about. The students' parents were consoled by a promise that they would be sent back to Tibet after three years. The speech of the Chinese official upon their departure made it apparent that he expected that the simple Tibetans would be totally transformed by their experience and their education in China.

Tsering Dorje was chosen to go to the National Minorities Institute in Beijing in 1956 when he was fifteen years old. At that time many Tibetan youth were sent for education at the various minority nationality institutes in the Chinese interior. The largest ones for Tibetans were at Sining in Qinghai, Xiangang near Xian in Shanxi, which was started as a school for children of the Tibetan lower classes, and another at Chengdu in Sichuan for Tibetans from the parts of Kham that had been absorbed into that province. Only a few of the top students were chosen for the main minority nationality institute in Beijing. Tsering Dorje was not only a good student but he had consciously chosen the opportunity for himself. He was intelligent and self-aware, which contributed to his ability to withstand Chinese indoctrination and later to understand the fallacies of Chinese policies in Tibet.

Tsering Dorje and his group of 27 youths from the Chumbi valley traveled to Lhasa where they were joined by students from other parts of Central Tibet until their number reached about 300. There were both male and female students, although he does not say how many there were of each. They spent two months in Lhasa undergoing medical tests before leaving for Beijing via the northern route through Qinghai.

Upon their arrival at the minorities institute in Beijing, the students were greeted by the Tibetans already there, who had arrived in two previous groups in 1954 and 1955. The new students were served with hot water or weak tea and jokingly told that the clean water was better for them than the heavy milk and butter tea they were used to drinking in Tibet. He later came to realize that this was their way of carefully criticizing the scarcities in the diet at the institute.

There were approximately 1,000 Tibetan students at the institute, along with youths from almost all of the PRC's designated national minorities. The largest groups of students were from Tibet and Xinjiang. The Xinjiang group included Uighurs and Kazakhs. He says that the students from Tibet and Xinjiang were proud of their cultures and most resistant to cultural assimilation. Many of those from Xinjiang retained their national costumes and traditions better than any of the other minorities, including Tibetans.

> *The students from Sinkiang were intensely proud of their culture and their traditional costumes. Even after six years in the Institute the Sinkiang students did not discard their costumes to adorn the blue boiler suits of the Hans. This was a lesson to us, the Tibetans, I felt.*

He also mentions that there were large numbers of Mongols as well as some Han Chinese. The main subjects taught were Chinese language, mathematics, and politics. There were also sections of students from each nationality who specialized in dance and drama. Other subjects taught were history, science, geography, music, painting, and physical training.

In mid-1957 the atmosphere and conditions at the nationality institute began to change for the worse with the advent of the Anti-Rightist Campaign, which followed the Hundred Flowers Campaign introduced by Mao in early 1957. Based upon his conviction that the CCP and its policies were popular and well-accepted, Mao invited criticism of the Party in order to correct its presumably few mistakes. The slogan of the campaign was “Let a hundred flowers bloom, let a hundred schools of thought contend.” Mao introduced the campaign with a speech on the contradictions still existent within Chinese society, dividing them into nonantagonistic, or those among the people, and antagonistic, or those between the people and their enemies. Only a few contradictions were categorized as antagonistic, such as those with reactionaries, while most were defined as nonantagonistic, including relations between the national minorities and the majority Han Chinese.

Mao was subsequently surprised by an outpouring of fundamental criticisms of not only the CCP’s policies but of the legitimacy of its one-party rule. National minority CCP cadres, particularly Uighurs and Tibetans, took advantage of the opportunity to question the legitimacy of Chinese administration, if not Chinese rule, over their areas. Some minority party members, primarily Uighurs, called for administration of their areas by separate communist parties composed only of their own nationality.

So shocked was Mao at these criticisms that he characterized the Hundred Flowers that he himself had invoked as dangerous weeds that had to be cut down. He then instituted the Anti-Rightist Campaign to repress all who had dared to criticize the Party. Minority nationalities that had been critical were included; the official title of the campaign was the Anti-Rightist and Anti-Local Nationalist Campaign. Minority nationalism was defined as local nationalism, meaning a regional nationalism within China, which was meant to deny that there could be any sense of national identity among any of the current national minorities deriving from a history as a nation separate from the Chinese nation.

The attack on local nationalism, which had been expressed primarily by Uighurs and Tibetans, hardened the CCP policies toward those minorities and changed the atmosphere for them and all students at the National Minorities Institute. Tsering Dorje paraphrases the speech the teachers gave to introduce the new campaign:

> *The present campaign is a political movement to successfully implement throughout China the second five-year plan and to further consolidate the hold of socialism. Recently the rightists wearing the masks of the people, denying the party and Chairman Mao, blatantly made big plans for the restoration of capitalism. However, their efforts were turned to dust by the militant revolutionary power of the broad masses following the correct leadership of the party and Chairman Mao.*

He writes that at the institute the Anti-Rightist and Anti-Local Nationalist Campaign took the form of a rectification campaign that sought to expose and criticize students with rightist or local nationalist attitudes. This soon became an attempt by the more leftist students to criticize and purge anyone less leftist or less doctrinaire than themselves in their ostentatious support for Chairman Mao.

Each student was required to write a self-criticism and to criticize others. Students came under tremendous pressure to appear more leftist than others. Since many Tibetan students came from what the Chinese considered a feudal and backward society, they had difficulty proving that they were in fact revolutionary and progressive. One way to do that was to excessively criticize their own cultural background and to criticize other Tibetan students as more backward than themselves. Thus, the atmosphere at the nationalities institute degenerated into mutual criticism and distrust. Tibetans were indoctrinated into attitudes of contempt for their own supposedly backward societies that accorded with Chinese attitudes. Being removed from Tibetan cultural influences and surrounded by an atmosphere of leftist intolerance of rightist or local nationalist attitudes, some Tibetans succumbed to a similar intolerance of the supposedly backward nature of traditional Tibetan society and culture.

Leftist student organizations put up big character posters attacking students or teachers considered to have rightist attitudes. Students were forced into a competition to prove themselves more loyal to China than to their own nationalities. Those with strong national identities, like Uighurs and Tibetans, were no longer able to claim that it was possible to be loyal to both China and their own nationality. Among each nationality a few students were singled out by others of their own nationality as examples to be criticized. Traditional minority nationality song and dance performances were ended because they were characterized as backward and bourgeois. The culture and traditions of minorities were labeled as some of the poisonous weeds that needed to be rooted out in the Anti-Rightist and Anti-Local Nationalist Campaign.

Another part of the Anti-Local Nationalist Campaign was to purge students of what the Chinese Communists considered bourgeois and reactionary religious beliefs. Paradoxically, this was called a religious freedom campaign. The CCP was an atheist political party, but it claimed to allow freedom of religious belief. In fact, writes Tsering Dorje, religious practice was restricted and criticized. No one who retained any religious belief could be considered a progressive and a revolutionary nor could they ever become a member of the CCP. Students at the nationalities institute were challenged by teachers and their fellow students to examine their belief in spirits and gods and ghosts.

Tsering Dorje writes that before this anti-religious campaign began, the students held many different religious beliefs, including Buddhism and Bonism (pre-Buddhist Tibetan religion) among the Tibetans. "At the time a student could follow any religion of his choosing; no one questions him about it. As such there was no need to start a religious freedom campaign." Before the religious freedom campaign there was actual religious freedom, he says, but after the campaign there was none. Tibetans in particular were criticized for their strong Buddhist beliefs and Uighurs for their belief in Islam, and both came under intense pressure to abandon their religions in favor of the official atheism of the CCP.

The anti-religious campaign was conducted by the students themselves at meetings in their classrooms. Tsering Dorje writes that out of his study group of forty-six Tibetan students, there were three who had become or were trying to become Party members. The one who had already become a Party member led the first discussion on religion. He had obviously been instructed about what argument to take in regard to religious belief.

He said the time had come to debate the existence of gods and ghosts. He said that the debate was between backwardness and progressivism, between traditional and proletarian attitudes, between religious idealism and communist materialism. Those students who took a progressive attitude and abandoned their religious beliefs would be regarded as the best students, while those who lagged behind would be subjected to criticism by the more progressive. From this Tibetan CCP member Tsering Dorje first heard that the more backward students would be subjected to the Communist process called "struggle" by their more progressive fellow students and teachers. This is when he first heard the Tibetan word thamzing, which was to become so notorious in later political campaigns in Tibet.

The Tibetan CCP member explained that the Communist Party did not recognize nonmaterialist phenomena like spirits and gods and ghosts. He denounced religion as superstition promoted by the upper class to keep the common people in ignorance so that they could exploit them. The exploiting classes fooled the masses with lies and falsehoods, like the theory of karma which explained that their low status was the result of their own past lives and thus could not be altered by their own actions in this life. However, the Communist Party sought to liberate the common people from these beliefs and thus free them from their exploitation by the upper classes. Therefore, progressives should not have religious faith because religion was used to exploit the masses.

He said that Tibetans who wished to join the Communist Youth League should not have religious faith. Since this was the first step to becoming a Communist Party member and an essential requirement to advancement within the Chinese Communist political system, there was great pressure on the Tibetan students to renounce their religious beliefs. The Tibetan Party member said that anyone was free to have any religious belief, but the message that the students understood was that this freedom of religion was the freedom to be second-class citizens in the PRC and that those who had religious belief would be discriminated against and constantly propagandized and coerced to give up their beliefs.

Tsering Dorje describes the debate that followed this speech. Almost all of the Tibetan students were Buddhists and a few held to Bon beliefs. Only the Party member and two others who hoped to join the Party were atheists. They argued that religion provided nothing that anyone could eat or drink. On the contrary, Tibetans wasted tea and butter and tsampa on offerings to clay and metal images that represented their gods. However, some of the other Tibetan students argued that what the atheists criticized were only the superficial aspects of religion. The value of religion was that it helped people to bear their difficulties and sufferings in life and it taught moral lessons like how to eradicate hatred, envy, and anger from one's mind. No one forced anyone to make offerings to deities or to lamas and monks and no one thought that such offerings were essential in order to gain the benefits of religion. Study and devotion as well as good works were also important.

Another Tibetan student who aspired to CCP membership attacked the view that religious belief was socially benign. He denied that any monks or lamas ever attained enlightenment. Instead, he said, they spent all their time thinking of how to exploit the masses so that they could continue their privileged lifestyles. Many of the lamas and monks were those most affected by the sins of lust, jealousy, and hatred, he said. The masses of people should work for their own material livelihood and stop supporting the parasitic lamas and monks. This was countered by another student who said that he had never heard of any lamas and monks demanding that they be supported. Instead, support was freely and voluntarily given to them because they were devoted to achieving the highest spiritual aspirations of not only themselves but of Tibetan society as a whole.

The debate continued for a few days until another meeting was called, at which a former Tashilhunpo (Panchen Lama's monastery in Shigatse) monk argued forcefully in favor of religion. He said that there was no reason to blame religion for the erroneous actions of some monks and lamas. Any ideology, including Marxism, was likely to have those who would misuse it. He cited as an example the current Anti-Rightist Campaign in which some CCP cadres were criticized for their erroneous actions while the ideology itself was still considered to be true. The rightists, he said, were likely to be those who had only a superficial understanding of Marxism. Similarly, exploitative or erroneous lamas and monks were likely to have only a superficial understanding of Buddhism. Neither Marx nor Buddha should be blamed for the mistakes of their followers. This student argued, as did the Dalai Lama himself, that Marxism and Buddhism were compatible in their beliefs in some ways.

The argument was ultimately ended by an angry outburst by a Chinese cadre who was present. He denounced religion as poison and said that only the progressive atheist students should be listened to. After this, all further debate was prohibited and students were subjected to anti-religious propaganda, including big character posters on walls around the campus. The result of the religious freedom campaign was that animosity and conflict was created between those who retained their religious faith and those who abandoned it.

Tsering Dorje writes that the Chinese administrators and teachers promised open debate at the institute about religion and other subjects but shut down discussions when some students argued forcefully in favor of Tibetan culture and religion and against communist ideology. Tibetans thereafter continued their discussions, but only privately and in secret from the Chinese and their Tibetan converts. Soon an underground political opposition was formed that became known as the Ear Society. He says that the 100 or so members of the underground organization were the more nationalistic of the Tibetans and included some of the best students. The leader of the Ear Society was Nyetho Jigme of Gyantse.

There was another secret Tibetan group known as the Nose Society, which Tsering Dorje knew little about, indicating that they kept quiet about their activities even to other Tibetans. They were mostly students in the arts departments. Their leaders were not known to him until they were later exposed and subjected to public thamzing. He did not know the numbers of this group, given the secrecy involved, but assuming the two groups had similar numbers they could have represented as many as 15 to 20 percent of the 1,000 Tibetan students at the National Minorities Institute at that time. No doubt there were many more who were sympathizers.

Tsering Dorje writes that the Tibetan students who were members of the underground political organizations were those who cared the most for Tibet and its future and some who questioned why Tibet had fallen under the control of China. They were the students who were most interested in politics and they were the most politically conscious, but not in the way that the Chinese hoped. The more nationalistic Tibetan students reacted in a more negative way to Chinese political indoctrination and became more defensive of Tibetan culture and national identity precisely because of the Chinese attempt to denigrate Tibetan culture and to assimilate them to Chinese culture. They studied Tibetan history because of their interest in preserving that history. They rejected the Chinese narrative that Tibet had always been a part of China and had only a local history as a part of China, and no history or national identity as a state independent of China.

The main argument of the more nationalistic Tibetans was that Tibetans could benefit from Chinese assistance, but that ultimately Tibet must be ruled by Tibetans. Although this was consistent with what the Chinese also said about how they had come to Tibet to assist Tibetans and would leave as soon as that was done, they were intolerant of this argument when it came from the Tibetan students. The Tibetan students expressed their arguments by putting up wall posters at the institute in the middle of the night. Their posters were invariably torn down the next day by the Chinese administrators or students. Their posters carefully expressed gratitude for Chinese assistance but revealed some Tibetan skepticism about Chinese motives for helping Tibet. He lists some of the most prominent slogans:

> The development aid given by China to Tibet is welcome.
>
> The friendship between China and Tibet will last for thousands of years.
>
> The motorable roads in Tibet built by the Chinese assistance will boost trade between China and Tibet. This is welcome.
>
> All thanks to the Chinese, who without the Tibetans even asking for it, helped the Tibetans in the true spirit of proletarian internationalism.
>
> Since Tibet must be ruled by the Tibetans, we are doing our best to study under the guidance of the Chinese.
>
> For many centuries Tibet managed to stand on its own two feet. The fact that today scientifically advanced and technologically well-equipped China is helping Tibet is welcome.
>
> The main aim of our studies is to develop Tibet. Our desire is to implement in Tibet what we are learning in China.

The slogans were carefully worded but some were rather cynical in their expression of appreciation for Chinese assistance. Most implied that Tibet in the future should be ruled by Tibetans. Even though the Chinese had promised autonomy in which Tibet would be administered by Tibetans, the students' slogans implied more Tibetan political control than the Chinese apparently intended. Also, the use by the students of the terminology about Chinese relations with Tibet implied that Tibetans were claiming that Tibet had in the past and should have in the future an identity as a country separate from China.

Tsering Dorje writes that the Chinese administrators of the institute interpreted the Tibetan students' relatively moderate slogans as a devious plot to separate Tibet from China. They attempted to divide the nationalistic Tibetan students with promises of leniency for confessions of involvement with the posters or repression if one were found out without confession.

The students were thereafter subjected to continuous indoctrination meetings at which informers were present and the students were challenged on their beliefs. However, the attempts to intimidate the students did not stop them from putting up wall posters. The arguments on their posters evolved from merely claiming that Tibet was formerly independent and should be administered by Tibetans in the future, even if under Chinese sovereignty, into criticisms of current CCP policies. They had been lectured by their Chinese teachers about the benevolence of China in building roads to Tibet, but they replied with questions about whether the roads were for Tibetans or for enabling China to send military forces to Tibet. They were aware of Chinese repression of the revolt in eastern Tibet beginning in 1956 and escalating in 1958 due to the introduction of the Democratic Reforms Campaign, so they criticized the reforms and Chinese military repression in Tibet. And they began criticizing other Tibetan students at the institute who were informers for the Chinese.

One night one of the leaders of the underground group, Wangdu of Chamdo, was caught putting up wall posters. He was publicly arrested the next day in front of the other students and taken away. Nothing was heard about him for the next two years until finally it was learned that he had committed suicide in a prison labor camp. The school administrators held an exhibition of all the posters that had been put up by Tibetans as a warning to students of other nationalities not to engage in such activities. The students were told to inform on anyone who put up any such wall posters and that if they failed to do so, they themselves would be punished.

Even these attempts at intimidation did not stop some Tibetan students from speaking their minds in classes. Chinese teachers began confronting the more nationalistic students about their beliefs in order to identify those who needed to be repressed. One student, Yarphel from the Koko Nor area, was asked about his belief in regard to Tibet's former independence. He replied that whether Tibet was independent or not could be learned by studying Tibetan history. When confronted about whether or not he thought Tibet should be independent, he replied that every Tibetan would prefer that it be independent. Other Tibetan students also resisted Chinese attempts at indoctrination and intimidation. Several were subjected to thamzing and all were forced to undergo intensified indoctrination and warnings against local nationalism. A few were made examples of the danger of opposing the Chinese. Yarphel was taken away and never heard of again.

Struggle, or thamzing in Tibetan, was a political technique used by the Chinese Communists to identify opponents and repress them. At the National Minorities Institute, the students were assembled and told by the president that a few bad elements had organized underground nationalist student groups and were trying to divide the big family of the motherland:

> *At present our Institute is taking the road to progress. However, there are a few bad elements who are making every effort to divide the big family of the motherland. This evil wind is against the interests of the people of China. Consequently, some people must be subjected to thamzing to reform their minds. Every student must make every effort to avoid being influenced by the evil wind and must fully participate in the thamzing. Those who are neutral and fail to participate in the thamzing campaigns will themselves be subjected to thamzing. No one will be let off. The purpose of the thamzing campaign is to separate the students animated by local nationalism and those animated by the spirit of the great motherland.*

The local nationalists were accused of creating antagonism against the motherland and the Party. What this really meant was that the Party was accusing any minority student who harbored local nationalist views of being an enemy of the people. However, local nationalism was defined as practically any expression of respect for minority cultures and even any hopes that their cultures might be preserved under any sort of autonomous administration of the minority nationalities themselves as was in fact promised to them by the CCP.

The first Tibetan student to be subjected to thamzing was Amdo Gyakok, who had been exposed as one of the leaders of an underground nationalist student group. He was dragged before an assembly of about 1,000 students of all nationalities. They were worked up in advance by Chinese teachers and student activists into a frenzy of animosity toward Amdo Gyakok and his crime of local nationalism. Tsering Dorje writes that Gyakok appeared to have already been subjected to some physical abuse. The activists demanded that he confess his crimes. He admitted that he had been a leader of one of the nationalist student groups and that he was a local nationalist. However, he said that he was unsure whether or not his local nationalist views made him a reactionary. This was apparently his way of saying that his views of respecting Tibetan culture and expecting that the Party would honor its promise to allow local autonomy had previously been Party policy but were now denounced as being anti-Party and anti-China.

The Chinese and Tibetan activists demanded that Amdo Gyakok reveal the names of other members of the underground Tibetan student group. He named only Kesang Dekyi, who had already been exposed as one of the leaders. He refused to reveal any more names and was thus subjected to multiple thamzing sessions with shouts and intimidation and beatings over a period of almost a month. Tsering Dorje says that Gyakok appeared to be thoroughly intimidated and looked like a trapped animal. He submitted to the abuse without resistance and refused to defend himself. The Chinese teachers and activist students pretended to try to restrain the abuse heaped upon him by the students but in fact it was they who had instructed the students in how to conduct a struggle session and incited them to make it as violent and intimidating as possible. However, even though Amdo Gyakok appeared totally defeated, he still refused to name any more names or to repent his opinions. He was finally subjected to one final violently abusive thamzing session from which he had to be dragged out almost lifeless. This was the last time he was seen by any of the other students.

The thamzing of Amdo Gyakok was intended to intimidate the other Tibetan students, which it did, but they were also impressed by Amdo Gyakok's spirit of resistance. Tsering Dorje says that eventually some thirty Tibetan students were subjected to thamzing during the Anti-Local Nationalist Campaign. Many of them had been exposed as members of the nationalist student organizations. Despite this intimidating process, the Chinese had great difficulty in convincing Tibetans to denounce their own culture and religion and give up their belief that Tibet deserved an autonomous administration by Tibetans themselves.

Tsering Dorje writes that there were three different degrees of thamzing. The most severe was for those who had advocated local nationalism, while lesser degrees were for those who were thought to have been exposed to the poisonous weed of local nationalist thinking and those who were thought to be only somewhat sympathetic to such thinking. The most extreme form of thamzing was held before gatherings of as many as 1,000 students, while the lower degrees were held before two or three hundred people, presumably mostly of the same nationality, while the lowest degree was held in the classroom before only a few fellow students. Those subjected to the most severe form of thamzing were the students thought to have been the leaders of underground nationalistic organizations and those who had secretly put up wall posters advocating Tibetan independence or even just autonomy under Tibetan administration. Tsering Dorje says that about thirty Tibetan students were subjected to the most severe form of thamzing while 60 percent of the several hundred Tibetan students were subjected to lesser forms.

Tsering Dorje writes that the many nationalistic Tibetan students came from all parts of Tibet. They were generally some of the best students, but their education in Chinese propaganda had the opposite effect from what the Chinese intended. Their political consciousness was raised by the education they received in Marxist political doctrine, which made them more aware about how the Chinese failed to live up to the Marxist ideal in practice. In particular, they found the Chinese lacking in their promise to respect, promote, and preserve minority nationality cultures or to allow any real nationality autonomy in practice.

The Tibetan students mostly argued about the issue of whether Tibet was independent in the past or was a part of China. The Tibetans who had adopted the communist ideology argued that history proved that Tibet was always a part of China. However, their arguments were countered by other Tibetans, some of whom had more actual knowledge of Tibetan history. The Chinese position that Tibet became a part of China during the Tibetan Empire period due to two marriage alliances was easily refuted by others who asked why, then, didn't Tibet also become a part of Nepal, with which there was also a marriage alliance? They also pointed out that the history of that period was one of almost constant conflict between Tibet and China and that the treaty that finally ended that conflict clearly established that Tibet and China were separate countries with defined borders.

The Tibetan communist students had to constantly refer to the Chinese teachers to get arguments to refute the more nationalistic students. Their arguments gradually degenerated into threats. They declared that anyone who favored Tibetan independence was nothing but a running dog of the upper-class exploiters and their foreign imperialist supporters. That was countered by the question of whose running dogs were those who said that Tibet was an integral part of China?

The position of some of the more nationalistic Tibetan students was that Tibet was independent in the past and should again be independent in the future. However, others took the safer position that Tibet should at least have the high level of autonomy that the Chinese Communists had themselves promised in the Seventeen Point Agreement and in their nationality autonomy doctrines. Even this position was now precarious since the Anti-Local Nationalist Campaign was intended to restrict minority nationality autonomy because many nationalities, especially Uighurs and Tibetans, had proved insufficiently loyal to China.

In his analysis of the Anti-Local Nationalist Campaign, Tsering Dorje writes that the term local nationalism was nothing but a Chinese attempt to negatively label any pro-independence ideas or activities among any minority nationality peoples. Such ideas came to include even the right supposedly guaranteed to minorities by the PRC's system of national regional autonomy to determine their own cultural affairs. In regard to Tibet, many of the provisions of the Seventeen Point Agreement—that Tibet should enjoy cultural and political autonomy essentially equivalent to that it had enjoyed in the past—came to be denounced as local nationalism. Tibetans and other minority nationalities had been promised that China was only interested in helping them and would leave the actual administration of their areas up to the minority nationalities themselves.

However, they were now subjected to propaganda and pressure to politically integrate and culturally assimilate with China.

Tsering Dorje cites the address by the president of the National Minorities Institute to the whole student body in which the Anti-Local Nationalist Campaign was initiated. The president contrasted the policy of the CCP with that of Chinese regimes of the past that had exploited the minority nationalities. His speech reflected the typical Chinese view that minority nationality alienation from China was solely due to this mistreatment in the past. Since the policy of the CCP was for equal treatment of all nationalities, then all such alienation should automatically disappear. He, like many Chinese, had no conception of why any minorities would want to be culturally separate or politically independent of China. They imagined that the minorities were culturally backward and therefore could benefit from adapting the more advanced Chinese culture. And they imagined that the political independence of any nationalities, especially those on the frontiers like Tibetans, would only open them and China up to exploitation by foreign imperialists.

The Anti-Local Nationalist Campaign was a result of the realization by the CCP that the political integration and cultural assimilation of some minorities, particularly Uighurs and Tibetans, was not going to be as easy as previously anticipated. Their cultures and national identities were far stronger than the Chinese had imagined. The proponents of local nationalism were thereafter put into the Maoist category of antagonistic contradictions, or contradictions between the people and their enemies. Local nationalists were no longer just ideological opponents who could be debated but were now political enemies who must be repressed.

Tsering Dorje was still at the National Minorities Institute in Beijing in March 1959 when the revolt took place in Lhasa. He writes that he knew nothing of the revolt until the night of March 18th when the Tibetan students were awakened in the middle of the night and told to assemble for a meeting. They were then told that there had been a revolt in Lhasa. A Chinese instructor said that certain upper-class reactionaries in collusion with foreign imperialists had staged a revolt but that it had been put down quickly because it had no popular support. He claimed that the PLA had been very restrained and had only resorted to violence when they were attacked by the rebels. The rebels had been arrested or had fled to India.

The Chinese instructor said that the revolt would actually turn out to be a good thing since the defeat of the serf-owners would allow for democratic reforms to be implemented in Tibet:

> *Every student must clearly understand that the rebellion is neither a conflict between two races nor arising out of the fact that the person of the Dalai Lama was endangered. It is not a conflict between one country [and] another nor between Tibetans and the Hans. . . . This rebellion is but the last agonies of the dying reactionaries. The nature of the rebellion is basically class struggle. It is a struggle for the triumphant liberation of the Tibetan peasant serfs.*

The students were told that they all must write letters to their families advising them against joining or sympathizing with the rebels. They were instructed to hand their letters over to the school authorities in unsealed envelopes. Accordingly, the students each had to write a letter to their families once a week. However, none of them ever got a reply to their letters. Therefore, they knew little about what had actually happened in Tibet or even about the fate of their families.

A few months after the Lhasa revolt, the PLA military commander in Lhasa at the time of the revolt, Tan Kuan-san, came to Beijing. He had been the highest Chinese official in Lhasa in March and was thus not only knowledgeable about what happened but also responsible. Tan Kuan-san also visited the National Minorities Institute and addressed the Tibetan students. He said that the result of the revolt was that the Tibetan people could begin their own people's revolution and democratic reforms. He appealed to the students to be leaders in the socialist revolution going on in Tibet. Tsering Dorje quotes Tan as saying that the revolt had transformed a situation of repression by the old serf owners into a new era of liberation and prosperity for all Tibetans. It is clear that Tan assumed that the Tibetan students were all progressives, having been instructed in the communist ideology at the institute, and that none could possibly be reactionaries or have any sympathy for the reactionaries.

He reiterated the Chinese position that the revolt was about class and not nationality.

From the end of 1959 until the end of 1960, three batches of students, a total of about 500, were sent back to Tibet. Most of them were employed as interpreters for Chinese officials, but there were also some who were given work as teachers or accountants. However, Tsering Dorje remained in Beijing until the end of 1961. He was assigned to work in the institute's printing press. He said that after the revolt the remaining Tibetan students were given more practical education in subjects that might be useful in Tibet, like electricity, surveying, and agriculture, rather than the mostly ideological subjects taught before.

Tsering Dorje writes about the period of food shortages that began from the end of 1959. The students' grain ration was not enough to last the whole month even if one ate very little each day. When the grain rations ran out, they had to search for other foods like spinach and even leaves of trees. They were constantly lectured on the sacrifices that they must make to achieve socialism like the revolutionary heroes of the past had done. They were told stories about the sufferings of those who went on the Long March through eastern Tibet during the mid-1930s.

They were told, falsely, that thanks to the CCP, no one had died during the present famine. In fact, estimates of the number of Chinese who died of starvation during the Great Leap Forward of 1959–1962 range from 30 to 40 million people. They were also not told that the reason for the famine was the Great Leap Forward itself and not because of adverse weather as the CCP claimed.

By the end of 1961 people in Beijing were actually fighting over the leaves from trees. Almost everyone was on the edge of starvation, without any physical energy and possessed of thoughts of nothing but food. Even cloth was rationed and no one had more than one set of clothes, which were usually worn and patched. However, he found that Beijing was relatively well-off compared to other parts of China. When his group of twenty students was sent to Tibet in December 1961, they traveled by train first to Chengdu, Sichuan. They were issued new clothes and grain ration coupons for the journey. In Chengdu they saw people literally starving in the streets.

*The railway station at Chengdu was filled by starving people and when they saw new faces, they at once raised their thin, emaciated palms. I did not see anyone through feelings of human sympathy giving any food to these starving people, nor did we have anything to give. For in a socialist society everyone must act according to orders given from above. Such a society does not leave room for a person moved by human sympathy to come to another's help.*

During the two days they spent in Chengdu they were able to obtain steamed buns using their grain ration coupons but they had to guard them from starving people who would try to steal them. They saw posters of many people whose faces were crossed out in red, which meant that they had been executed. They were told that many people were executed for stealing food, especially those who had stolen from government grain stores. They saw two children dying of starvation on the street with no one offering to help them. They were told that the father of the children had been executed for stealing grain and that their mother had died of starvation shortly thereafter. And they were told that it was better for the children to die since there was no one to help them. This situation made Tsering Dorje and the other Tibetan students wonder what kind of world had been created by the Chinese Communists.

From Chengdu, Tsering Dorje and his group went by train to Liuyuan, on the unfinished railroad to Xinjiang, from where they went by bus to Dunhuang and then Golmud in the Tsaidam. When they crossed the Thongo La from Qinghai to Nagchuka, they experienced altitude sickness because they had spent so much time in China. Tsering Dorje thought that his weakened condition due to near starvation in China also contributed to his sensation of altitude sickness.

At Nagchuka he noticed that there were more Chinese, mostly well-armed PLA soldiers, than Tibetans. However, one of the PLA soldiers was a Tibetan, a former student at the National Minorities Institute. He had been involved in hunting down Tibetan "bandits" in the Changtang. He revealed that the atmosphere was still tense, almost three years after the revolt, and that there was a prison in Nagchuka with 600 prisoners and a labor camp at Tsala Karpo, which was notorious for its harsh conditions. He was also told about the large labor camps at Kongpo. He realized for the first time that some of his relatives or friends might have been involved in the revolt, which created doubts about how they would regard him or how he should relate to them. He would soon discover that such doubts and suspicions were a predominant characteristic of the lives of most Tibetans after the revolt.

Tsering Dorje was assigned to work at the *Tibet Daily* newspaper, located at the Teykhang house at Shol at the foot of the Potala. He worked there for the next eight months. He was happy to be back in Lhasa but he found that now the atmosphere was very different. There seemed to be more Chinese, mostly heavily armed soldiers, than Tibetans. Many of those who had participated in the revolt had been transported to far away labor camps, but even in Lhasa many Tibetans were in prison and most others seemed to be engaged in forced labor projects. He estimated that there were as many as 5,000 Tibetan prisoners in Lhasa and he heard of but did not see the Nachen Trang hydroelectric project just east of Lhasa where many Lhasa Tibetans were engaged in forced labor. Tibetans had been given a variety of labels that designated their class status or political status. They were coerced to engage in constant class warfare with other classes, which led to a pervasive atmosphere of fear and suspicion among everyone.

Tsering Dorje writes that the Chinese treated Tibetans as their serfs and Tibet as a conquered country, as indeed it was. He said that Tibetans had lost their freedom and had literally become the serfs of the Chinese, despite all their propaganda about how they had liberated the Tibetan serfs from the Tibetan masters.

> *Everywhere one looked in Lhasa, the most common sight was the Chinese. At the point of gun, the Chinese taskmasters took the Tibetans everywhere they liked, to the north, to the south and forced them to work hard. Those nationalists who had revolted against the tyrannical rule were transported to the worst places in Tibet, like Kongpo in the south and Tsala Karpo Lake in the Changtang, the "Siberia of Tibet." The others were kept in Lhasa as a free labor force. A rough estimate*

> *of prisoners in Lhasa when I was there could be 5,000. These prisoners were made to work like animals.*
>
> *To lose one's country means to become a serf to a foreign lord. Since 1959, the Tibetans have literally become the serfs of the Chinese overlords. Freedom, the essence of Tibet's distinct way of life, has been destroyed. While in China, I had always longed to be back in my own country. But when I actually got to Tibet, I saw that the Tibetans had been turned into serfs and servants of alien masters, and I got no happiness from being in my own land. Like other Tibetans, I too had to struggle to survive the whims and fancies of a foreign master.*

While in Lhasa he was able to hear a series of public sermons given by the Panchen Lama. Some two years after the revolt and after the famine that resulted from Mao's Great Leap Forward policy, more moderate CCP leaders, led by Liu Shao-chi, instituted some slightly more liberal policies in Tibet. One of these was that Tibetans should be allowed more cultural and religious freedom. These policies were conveyed directly from CCP leaders to the Panchen Lama, who announced them in Lhasa. However, Tsering Dorje said that the reality was that there was hardly any liberalization and that the Panchen Lama was deceived by the Chinese.

The Panchen Lama described CCP policy as intended to eventually allow Tibetans to administer their own autonomous region. However, they must first complete democratic reforms. He said that he had been promised that the Chinese would leave when Tibetans could finally stand on their own feet and were able to pursue economic development on their own. The central government would provide financial assistance, but Tibetans would run their own region. Tibetans would also be able to preserve their own culture and religion, but they themselves would be responsible for doing so. He said that the Chinese were in Tibet only to help Tibet emerge from its feudal and backward past into a more modern future. Once this was achieved, then there was no reason for any Chinese to remain in Tibet.

The Panchen Lama then repeated the Chinese claim that the Dalai Lama had been abducted from Lhasa and taken to India. Up until this point in his talk the Panchen Lama adhered strictly to Chinese policy. However, he then said that every Tibetan hoped that the Dalai Lama would be in good health, that he would live long, and that he would eventually return to Tibet. Even though he had said nothing that really deviated from Chinese policy, the Panchen Lama was later criticized by the Chinese for praising the Dalai Lama and expressing hope for his return. They interpreted this to mean that the Panchen hoped for a restoration of the old society.

In subsequent talks the Panchen Lama spoke about the need to preserve Tibetan culture. He said that Tibetan culture must be modernized but that there was no need for cultural destruction in the name of reforms. There had already been extensive destruction of monasteries during democratic reforms, but he had been promised by CCP leaders that this would cease under newly liberalized policies. He said that there would be religious freedom and that those lamas who remained would not have to betray their religious tradition by denouncing the Dalai Lama. Even though the highest CCP leaders had made these promises of cultural and religious freedom to the Panchen Lama, his favorable statements about the Dalai Lama angered Chinese cadres in Tibet, who considered the Dalai Lama a traitor. The Panchen's public talks in Lhasa made the Chinese begin to mistrust him. After this they began planning to label him as a reactionary and to remove him from his political position in Tibet.

In 1962 the Chinese announced that due to the previous three years of famine, some Tibetan cadres would be sent back to their home villages to help with agriculture. The Tibetan cadres were told that it was entirely voluntary whether they wanted to return to their villages, but Tsering Dorje says that this was not true, that the Tibetan cadres to be sent had already been selected. The Tibetans were coerced to volunteer to go back to their villages but even if they did not volunteer, they were sent anyway. Those Tibetans whose political loyalty was suspect were the first to be chosen to be sent back to their home villages.

Phari had changed tremendously in the seven years that he had been gone. Previously, Phari was not a wealthy place but it was moderately prosperous due to its location on the trade routes to India, Bhutan, and

Sikkim. Phari was the highest town in Tibet and probably in the whole world. Little agriculture was possible but local pastures were rich and therefore animal products were plentiful. In addition, almost anything could be obtained in the local markets because of the international trade that passed through. There were several local monasteries nearby and Tibetans enjoyed complete religious freedom.

When he returned to Phari in 1962, the first thing he noticed was the lack of the previous commercial and social activity. Trade with the neighboring countries had been cut off. He could only get food with a ration card issued by the CCP. Everyone was restricted in how much grain they could buy according to their work status. The best workers got the highest amount of grain while the worst, including the young, the old, and the disabled got barely sufficient for life. If their food rations ran out, there was no recourse; they could get no more food. The Chinese Communist system had turned a formerly prosperous area into one of poverty.

Much of Phari was deserted since many of the residents had fled to India or Bhutan. From 1959 to 1962 some 8,000 Tibetans fled Phari, mostly to Bhutan, leaving only about 1,700 people there. In addition, there were some 300 people from Phari in prisons in other parts of Tibet. Those who were left were put to work on public works and border defense projects. One project was called the Canal of Happiness, on which the people were made to work without any compensation. The only way to protest these hardships was to compose satiric songs that the Chinese could not understand.

Despite Phari being a high-altitude area where barley had never before been grown, the Chinese insisted that they could conquer heaven by making barley grow in Phari. However, Tsering Dorje writes that no matter how hard they made the local Tibetans work to grow barley, most of it was destroyed by frost before it could ripen.

Tsering Dorje was not in Tibet during the period of democratic reforms after the 1959 revolt; however, he asked many questions about it while he was in Phari. The predominant stories he was told involved the confiscation of the property of the upper class and the monasteries and the uncompensated work on public projects required of everyone. He says that of the 3,000 houses in Phari, the property of some 500 families was confiscated during democratic reforms. These families were usually accused of having taken part in or having supported the revolt, or even of having only sympathized with the revolt because of their upper-class status. The property of almost all the upper class, even those formerly cooperating with the Chinese under the United Front policy, was confiscated. Many of the upper class were arrested or fled into exile, which conveniently eliminated the nationalist opposition of this class to the imposition of direct Chinese rule over Tibet.

The residents of Phari reported that the confiscated properties included not only houses, livestock, and whole estates of the upper classes but all of their material possessions as well, including clothes, carpets, furniture, jewelry, works of art, and religious items. The monasteries also had all of their religious artworks and relics confiscated. The property of the upper classes was supposed to be redistributed among the lower classes, but the Phari people reported that they received only items that the Chinese had no use for. Valuable articles like jewelry, statues, thankas, other artworks, and religious items from both private homes and monasteries were confiscated and were presumed to have been taken to China.

> *The poor Tibetans did not even get a few crumbs of the edible things carted away to China. The material possessions and priceless works of art and piety painstakingly made and collected by the Tibetans generation after generation was emptied and taken away. The Tibetans were skinned dry and had nothing left for themselves but their miserable bodies. The outside world generally think that the "democratic reform" has benefitted the Tibetan people. But the only democracy in the reforms was the right of the Chinese masters to "liberate the Tibetan people of their wealth, works of art and priceless religious relics."*

Tibetans had to attend lengthy political meetings, usually at night after long work days. The main Chinese propaganda theme at these meetings was called "speaking bitterness." Tibetans were supposed to contrast the sufferings of the past during the feudal serf system with their happiness after liberation and democratic reforms. However, they described this as an exercise in falsity and deceit since for most of them the old society had been better than the new. The Tibetans described Chinese indoctrination as an attempt to create shadows where there were no objects. They said that Chinese indoctrination mentally killed them and emptied their minds, which were then filled with Chinese lies. At least in old Tibet they had more personal freedoms and usually a more adequate living standard than in new Tibet under the Chinese.

Phari Tibetans were mobilized by the Chinese for defense during the border war in late 1962 as well as in 1965 when there was another border dispute that the Chinese thought would result in war. Tsering Dorje describes the border war preparations in 1965. Local Tibetans were required to load into military trucks one evening when the Chinese expected war to soon break out. They were kept for three months on the border doing compulsory labor without any compensation except inadequate rations. Meanwhile, back in Phari, the horses that the Chinese had brought would not eat the locally grown but unripened barley, so they were fed on barley imported from other parts of Tibet. Tibetans meanwhile had no barley at all except what they could pick out of the horses' dung. Thus, there arose the expression that life was better for Chinese horses than for Tibetans.

Tsering Dorje also writes about Chinese attempts in 1963 to entice exiled Tibetans to return. This was during the relatively liberalized period after the disastrous failure of Mao's Great Leap Forward. Mao's role in the government was reduced for a period of about two years during which other leaders like Chou En-lai and Liu Shao-chi tried to implement slightly less radical leftist policies. In Tibet they hoped to reduce their international embarrassment in regard to Tibet by enticing exiled Tibetans, perhaps even including the Dalai Lama, to return.

The CCP tried to convince Tibetans to return by making promises of no punishment for participation in the revolt, return of confiscated properties, freedom of religion, and employment given according to past rank or experience. A propaganda campaign was mounted that portrayed Tibetans inside Tibet as living in freedom and happiness while Tibetans in India were suffering from poverty and sickness. Tibetans were coerced to persuade their relatives to return with these promises but also with the implied threats that their families inside Tibet would suffer if their relatives did not return. Tsering Dorje writes that the Chinese promises would be more convincing if they would implement for those Tibetans still in Tibet any of the promises that they offered to the exiles. Tibetans had none of the freedoms that the exiles were offered and of course the exiles knew this so few if any actually returned.

The failure of the Chinese attempt to entice Tibetans in exile to return was due to their misconceptions about the reality inside Tibet as well as in India. They tended to believe much of their own propaganda about how Tibetans were liberated from the abusive social and political system of the past and were now masters of their own fate. The reality for Tibetans was quite different. The Chinese also imagined that the exiles in India were suffering and could be enticed to return, but again the reality was quite different.

The period of relatively liberal policies did not last very long. Mao soon regained his political position and power and instituted the Great Proletarian Cultural Revolution, during which Tibetans enjoyed almost no freedoms, their culture was attacked, and more Tibetans were accused of disloyalty and repressed in a variety of ways.

In 1966 Tsering Dorje and his family escaped to Bhutan. In the last chapter of his book, he explains his reasons for fleeing his country, how he and many other Tibetans suffered under Chinese rule, and why they rejected China's justifications for its rule over Tibet. He writes that his experience at the Beijing National Minorities Institute had made him aware of the falsity of China's justifications for its rule over Tibet and its claim to have liberated Tibetans from their own misrule. He says that the Chinese had used what they called democratic reforms to identify and repress Tibetan opposition.

> *The deepest aspiration of every Tibetan is freedom from Chinese domination. The Chinese have tried to stifle this sign of "local nationalism" by killing hundreds of Tibetans at one time, as in the March 1959 Uprising. Power was grabbed from the hands of the Tibetans and they were not given even a dog's importance. They had to spend their whole lives obeying the orders of the Chinese masters. If any Tibetan*

> *exhibited the slightest signs of Tibetanness like worshiping or praying, showing respect for Tibetan culture, and undue respect for lamas, etc., he was at once condemned as "reactionary." He had to adorn a dunce hat, be ridiculed in public, locked in jail or sent to a labor camp.*

Tibetans were particularly discontent about how the Chinese had stolen much of the moveable property of Tibet while at the same time claiming to be selflessly helping Tibet with economic assistance. During democratic reforms they had confiscated most of the property of not only upper-class Tibetans but also of all traders and merchants. They had also confiscated all of the valuable metal and artworks from monasteries and private homes. Some of this—like thankas, printed religious texts, and clay statues—they burned or destroyed, often making Tibetans do the actual destruction. Woodblocks were used for firewood or to make furniture; *mani* stones were made into walkways or outhouses so that Tibetans would be forced to defile their own sacred objects. The most precious artworks and metal images and implements disappeared and were taken away to China.

> *Priceless works of art, literature and religious relics and works that were the model of Tibetan artistic perfection and achievement were taken out of the Potala and the various monasteries and temples and destroyed with a wanton disregard for artistic and cultural value. The sculptures were burnt, idols and religious articles made of clay were either thrown into rivers or destroyed on roads and people had to stamp on them. Idols and images made of gold, silver, brass and precious stones and metal were taken to China and eventually they found their way in the markets of Hong Kong, Shanghai and Tokyo where antique collectors from the West bought them for exorbitant prices. [Most Tibetan metal artworks were melted down without any regard for their cultural, artistic or monetary value.]*

The empty monasteries and temples were later destroyed during the Cultural Revolution; the Chinese again making Tibetans do the actual destruction. They tried to eradicate all aspects of Tibetan culture that distinguished Tibetans from Chinese. They had established communes mostly as an attempt to control all aspects of Tibetans' lives. By means of communization the Chinese even managed to steal from Tibetans their own food grown with their own hands.

Tsering Dorje writes that the Chinese created such oppression and exploitation of Tibetans that there was no difference between their so-called liberation and the serfdom that they condemned and used as justification for their rule. The only country guilty of aggression against Tibet was China. By 1966 the tensions on the border had decreased enough so that a few people from Phari were able to escape. Tsering Dorje waited until he was sure that those who had escaped had reached exile safely. Then, in September, he and his wife, child, mother, and brother took their own opportunity to escape to Bhutan.

## Tsering Wangchuk[17]

Tsering Wangchuk was born in Lhasa in 1951. In 1958 he entered a private Tibetan school in Lhasa. Both of his parents were from prominent families in Kham. His father was once a monk at Drepung in Lhasa; he came close to achieving the Geshe degree but "lost his celibacy" while on a tour to raise funds for his Geshe ceremony. He then became a businessman, using his family connections in Kham, China, and Lhasa to do trade in goods from China and India to Lhasa and lumber from Kongpo to Lhasa. He was a successful trader and businessman and the family had a large house in Lhasa. His father joined the Chushi Gangdruk resistance in 1958 in Lhoka and his mother was a member of the Tibetan Women's Association that protested against the Chinese occupation of Tibet.

His father escaped arrest in 1959 and spent the next three years hiding out in a cave near Drigung Monastery east of Lhasa. He was discovered in 1962 and sent to Sangyip Prison in Lhasa. Tsering and his mother were allowed to visit him with instructions to tell him to confess everything in exchange for leniency. Neither did so, however, his wife asking only why he hadn't escaped to India in 1959 when he was in Lhoka, close to the border. He was eventually taken to the Chinese military headquarters in Lhasa and released.

His father was given a position in the United Front, presumably due to his former high status. This was a time when there was a relative liberalization due to Mao having lost influence after the disastrous failure of the Great Leap Forward. The Chinese were trying to entice Tibetan exiles to return and thought he might have some influence. He also still had some influential Chinese contacts due to his past trade activities. However, their real purpose seems to have been to observe him and see who his contacts were. He knew this, however, and didn't associate with anyone he didn't want to get into trouble. He was eventually informed upon as someone who was still anti-Chinese and he was sentenced to fifteen years in prison at the beginning of the Cultural Revolution. He was in prison until 1979 when the Chinese again offered him a political position if he would cooperate by giving public speeches about how misguided he had been in the past. However, he refused and died in Drapchi Prison in Lhasa.

Tsering Wangchuk transferred to a Chinese school after the revolt, where he studied both Chinese and Tibetan. Other subjects were math, politics, songs (patriotic), and exercise. The teachers were all Chinese, none of whom spoke Tibetan. Tibetan teachers were there only as translators. All instruction except Tibetan language class was in Chinese. Tibetan was used only for reading the *Tibet Daily* newspaper and for writing letters. Tibetan students were taught mostly spoken Chinese; written Chinese was taught using Pinyin rather than characters, at least at first. Most children of the former upper class were not admitted to schools. Class status was important in the school, with the lower-class children getting everything free. However, he says that the children of the former upper class and their parents were actually now the poorest people in Tibet.

Tibetan students were taught about the evils of old Tibetan society and constantly told to contrast the old and new societies and to be happy in the new. They were subjected to lurid and exaggerated accounts of the old society by some "liberated serfs" who were paid by the Chinese to tell their stories at any and every venue. They were told to report any anti-government attitudes of their parents, who were allowed to practice religion themselves but not to teach it to their children. They saw films about the development of China and the backwardness of Tibet. They saw propaganda films about the progress made by socialist countries in contrast to the poverty and social turmoil of capitalist countries, where people were said to be demonstrating in favor of socialism. India was portrayed as very poor and Tibetan exiles there as having to eat grass to survive. This was during the Great Leap Forward, when many Chinese in the interior were actually eating grass and tree bark. They were young and tended to believe much of this Chinese propaganda.

After the 1962 border war, some Indian prisoners were paraded through Lhasa. Drama troops put on performances about the Indian defeat in the war. The Chinese said that the Indians were grateful to have lost the war since life was so bad for all but the very wealthy there. Indians were said to be hoping for liberation with the help of China, by means of the development of an Indian Communist Party, supported by China. The lack of the expected socialist revolution in India after 1962 was explained by India's alliance with the Soviet revisionists. The United States was denounced for its imperialism, especially in Asian countries like Vietnam, Laos, and Cambodia, where American soldiers were said to kill pregnant women and eat their fetuses. China was said to be the only honest country in the world.

Tsering Wangchuk was in Lhasa Middle School after 1963, the biggest school in Lhasa, which was directly administered by the government. After 1964, political indoctrination increased; the Panchen Lama and Buddhism were criticized. Tibetan language instruction decreased and Chinese increased, while traditional Tibetan culture was denigrated. In 1965 Chinese student activists, not yet called Red Guards, began to arrive in Lhasa. Some of them had already been to Xinjiang. They began the destruction of the already depopulated and looted monasteries. The Chinese students entered the, until then, undamaged Jokhang and destroyed some statues. They then went out the back and made Tibetan students carry the remains of the statues out the front as if they had done the destruction. This was propagandized as Tibetan students having spontaneously and voluntarily destroyed the remnants of the old society. The Tibetan students were also sent to the Ganden Monastery outside Lhasa and made to destroy some of the statues, mostly those made of clay, that had been left behind during the confiscation of all monastery valuables during democratic reforms.

Even before the Cultural Revolution, which began in 1966, Tibetans were required to cut their long hair, not wear any ornaments, and refrain from flying prayer flags or doing prostrations in front of monasteries or to deities. When the Cultural Revolution began, Chinese students who had been sent to Tibetan villages returned to Lhasa. Tibetans educated in China were also sent to Lhasa. The Destroy the Four Olds Campaign was announced and almost all remaining statues and frescoes in every remaining monastery were destroyed by the Chinese and Tibetan Red Guards. The Chinese made much propaganda about how the Tibetans themselves had destroyed the monasteries because they had realized that religion was the basis of oppression. Both Chinese and Tibetan Red Guards took the opportunity to steal any remaining valuables from the monasteries. At this time even the Tibetan Red Guards understood little about the meaning of the Cultural Revolution except the campaign against the "Four Olds."

Tsering Wangchuk says that the Tibetan monasteries were so rich in valuables such as statues and artworks that it took more than ten years, beginning after the 1959 revolt, to transport all the most valuable objects to China and to destroy the less valuable artifacts that remained. Even until 1976, he says, valuable articles that Tibetans had hidden were being discovered and taken to China or destroyed. Chinese in Tibet were allowed to keep things like statues and thankas for themselves while Tibetans were not. Tsering's family, like many of the upper-class families of Lhasa, had a shrine room in their home with some statues and thankas. They tried to hide these articles, which was a worry for him that they might be discovered. Other families threw valuables into the Kyi Chu rather than have them stolen by the Chinese. Some Tibetans gave their valuables to Nepali-Tibetan *Katsura* families, who were allowed to leave Tibet.

Tsering Wangchuk describes the very confusing period of the Cultural Revolution, especially in Tibet, when the Red Guards divided into two factions and began to openly battle with each other. In Tibet, there was a pro-TAR government faction, *Namdrel*, and an anti-government faction, *Gyenlok*. In China, there were the radical leftists and their less-radical opponents, associated with the later purged president Liu Shao-chi. Both factions of Red Guards claimed to be more radical and more loyal to Mao than the other, so it was difficult to see what their differences were. The less leftist faction was denounced as capitalist roaders, and the conflict portrayed as a struggle between two ideologies. Tsering Wangchuk says that it was obvious, even in Tibet where Chinese factional politics were little understood, that Mao was using the Cultural Revolution to destroy his opponents, particularly those who had finally curtailed his disastrous Great Leap Forward Campaign.

During the Cultural Revolution, young Red Guards were encouraged and allowed to travel, even being given free rail passes, in order to "exchange revolutionary experiences." Some of them went to Tibet for that reason and Tsering Wangchuk says that some Tibetan Red Guards went to China for the same reason. He says that most Tibetan Red Guards had little comprehension of the Chinese ideological factions and simply followed the lead of the Chinese. The Namdrel faction in Tibet was composed of Chinese and Tibetans who were more associated with the TAR government than those in the Gyenlok faction, who accused TAR officials of failure to implement Mao's more leftist policies. Tsering says that many Tibetans joined Gyenlok just for the opportunity to oppose the TAR officials and those associated with it.

Government officials and Tibetans in the official dance and drama troupes were in Namdrel while most Tibetan students, as well as some Chinese students, were in Gyenlok. At this time many Tibetans educated at the minority nationality institute near Xian were returned to Lhasa. They were mostly Namdrel, having been indoctrinated in the need to support the government. Gyenlok members took the opportunity to criticize major Chinese CCP cadres, like Wang Chimei, and Ngapo Ngawang Jigme, the foremost Tibetan collaborator who had signed the Seventeen Point Agreement, for being insufficiently leftist, while their real purpose was to make trouble for those Chinese who had abused Tibetans or Tibetans who had betrayed Tibet. Some of the Chinese officials were sent back to China where they were struggled and imprisoned. Tibetans criticized Ngapo for being a reactionary and for maintaining contact with the exiled Dalai Lama, although the Chinese were aware of his connection and wished to maintain it. Tibetan students claimed the right to struggle Ngapo, after which he was taken to Beijing. He suffered no further negative consequences, almost alone among all important Tibetan collaborators, perhaps because of his role in the Seventeen Point Agreement and the fact that, with the purge of the Panchen Lama, he was essentially the only important collaborator left.

The rivalry between the two Red Guard factions in Lhasa quickly degenerated into open street conflict, which evolved from sticks and stones to weapons. The Namdrel faction had greater access to weapons, which they were given in order to protect government officials but soon began to use against their rivals in street fighting. They also had the support of the Public Security Police and the PLA. However, the Namdrel was composed mostly of office workers while many of the Gyenlok were those that Tsering characterized as "toughs" and "miscreants" who were more adept at street fighting.

Conflict centered over control of the Lhasa Radio station and offices of the *Tibet Daily* newspaper. Factional fighting was also pursued through propaganda, mainly wall posters and loudspeakers, now mounted on every building, and controlled by Lhasa Radio and *Tibet Daily*. The PLA finally entered the loudspeaker battle against Gyenlok by using huge loudspeakers removed from the border with India. Tsering Wangchuk says that by this time Gyenlok was mostly Tibetan, with the exception of those Tibetans beholden to or indoctrinated by the Chinese, while Namdrel was mostly Chinese.

In January 1967 the CCP decreed that both factions of Red Guards should unite and in February the PLA took control in China and in Tibet. What this meant in Tibet was that Gyenlok should unite with Namdrel, or in other words, that Gyenlok should be eliminated. This resulted in the arrest and torture of some Gyenlok members. Others were gunned down by Namdrel members with automatic weapons. The Gyenlok faction held out at the Lhasa Radio station until overwhelmed by the government and PLA.

All of the confusion and conflict in Lhasa and all over China at this time reflected the competition between Mao and his opponents, or between the leftist and rightist factions in the CCP. The theme of the conflict was to "Bombard the Headquarters," or to remove opponents to Mao's radical leftism. Red Guard attacks on government officials were tolerated by the government and PLA, but they remained overall in charge. However, the decree in January 1967 that factional Red Guard fighting should cease had come from the more moderate faction of the CCP, while Mao still preferred that Red Guards should be allowed to purge his enemies. In February he prevailed and allowed the Red Guard fighting to revive, which in Lhasa meant that Gyenlok leaders were released and street fighting continued.

Before this time each side was armed mostly with primitive weapons, including some ancient Tibetan armor taken from monasteries. Tsering says that street battles thus resembled medieval warfare. After its revival, the Gyenlok faction began to prevail, due to its being the most radical and at that time supported by Mao. However, the PLA intervened to support the pro-government Namdrel by providing them with weapons. The fighting then became much bloodier, until finally in Lhasa and all over China Mao had to relent and allow the PLA to put a stop to the fighting. The Gyenlok held out at the Jokhang until it was stormed by the PLA, resulting in the deaths of 11 and 62 injured, mostly Tibetans, according to Tsering Wangchuk. He says that by this time some Tibetans took advantage of the confusion to attack Chinese and that the attacks on Tibetan culture resulted in a rise in Tibetan nationalist identity. There was a polarization between Tibetans and Chinese that overcame to some extent the Chinese attempt to cultivate Tibetan collaborators and to indoctrinate Tibetans against their own culture.

The most chaotic part of the Cultural Revolution ended with most of the same Party leaders in power and no result except a diminution of the Party's reputation among Chinese and a weariness among Tibetans about the irrationality and brutality of Chinese politics. The attacks on all aspects of Tibetan culture were a more damaging effect of the era for Tibetans, who responded as best they could with attempts to exploit the chaos for their own purposes and to protect their own beliefs and cultural traditions. Street fighting continued in Lhasa until 1968, Tsering says, even though the two Red Guard factions had been "reconciled." Because of the chaos of the Cultural Revolution, it was impossible to investigate past crimes. The Chinese administration limited itself to the investigation of "daylight killings," but all others were forgotten. There was no actual amnesty, however, so that all who had participated in fights or killings feared being found out.

Tsering Wangchuk was *xiafang*, or "sent down," to a rural village in 1969. In his case, however, the village was within the Lhasa valley, at its northern edge just south of Sera Monastery and near the Drapchi Prison.[18] He was "graduated" from the Lhasa Middle School even though that school had not held classes for the past three years. Among the aftereffects of the Cultural Revolution were millenarian rumors, such as that Tsongkhapa was still alive in his *chorten* at Ganden,[19] the Dalai Lama's face had been seen in the sun, implying that he would return to Tibet, and that Ling Gesar had been seen in or would return to Hor.[20] In Nyemo, a rural district west of Lhasa, a Buddhist nun had visions that led her to lead a revolt against the Chinese that took on such dimensions that Tibetans referred to it as the Second Tibetan Revolt.

What the Chinese referred to as the "counterrevolutionary Nyemo rebellion," had its origins in the arousal of Tibetan nationalism due to the Cultural Revolution as well as resistance against the collectivization of both agriculturalists and nomads that took place in the area in 1966. Tsering Wangchuk says that the sending of PLA propaganda teams to the area had also aroused resistance. This uprising was also called the 29 Districts Revolt, which indicates its wide spread. In contrast to the 1959 revolt, which at least for central Tibetans was mostly urban, in Lhasa, the Nyemo revolt took place in rural and nomadic areas. The primary target in each district was the district administrative center, manned by both Chinese and Tibetans, which had only recently been established in 1965 along with the inauguration of the Tibet Autonomous Region, by means of which Tibetans had theoretically achieved autonomy or "self-rule."

The Nyemo revolt expanded to areas from "west of Namtsho to Markham,"[21] according to Tsering Wangchuk. Many Chinese were killed. Tibetans did anything they could to harm the Chinese, including cutting telephone lines and destroying images of Mao. The PLA put down the revolt with great brutality; many troops were sent who were said to have shot indiscriminately at villagers and nomads. Tsering Wangchuk says that some Chinese leaders, including Hu Yaobang, said that it was a mistake to kill so many people like this. Even some PLA soldiers said that it was wrong to kill so many poor people. Some 100 were arrested in Nyemo and Nyemo Ani and 13 or 14 others were publicly executed in Lhasa. Tsering Wangchuk says that the execution, which all Lhasa Tibetans were required to attend, was obviously meant as intimidation. He also says that the Lhasa prisons, including Drapchi, were full after the revolt. Martial law was not officially declared but its equivalent was implemented.

Tsering Wangchuk went to Nyemo in 1976 as part of a "science research team," where he heard more stories about the revolt. Communes were supposed to be set up before the Cultural Revolution but because of local opposition they were not, so the PLA was used to set them up during the Cultural Revolution. Nyemo people said that democratic reforms after the 1959 revolt had created animosity; socialist transformation, meaning collectivization and communization, was the cause of the Nyemo revolt, while the chaos of the Cultural Revolution created the opportunity to revolt. Communization caused food shortages in villages and among nomads, mostly because the Chinese took most produce under the guise of a variety of taxes, while Tibetans were left with barely enough to survive. He quotes a nomad saying that they couldn't even have yogurt, a food previously in abundance, without permission from an official.

Tsering Wangchuk was in Lhasa in October 1979 for the arrival of the first Dharamsala delegation.[22] Chinese officials imagined that Tibetans were well-indoctrinated and would not have any sympathy for the "representatives of the serf-owners." However, Lhasa Tibetans gave them an emotional and ecstatic welcome, much to the surprise of the Chinese officials, who were thus discredited even in Beijing, which they had deceived with false reports of prosperity and ethnic harmony in Tibet. In May, 1980, Hu Yaobang was dispatched to Tibet where he announced immediate and comprehensive reforms, replacing Chinese officials, dissolving communes, and promising the removal of most Chinese cadres in Tibet and renewed respect for Tibetan autonomy. Hu promised to remove 85 percent of the Chinese cadres in Tibet and Tsering says that as many as 20,000–30,000 actually left.[23]

Many Chinese officials who left Tibet at this time took with them large quantities of valuables they had collected while in Tibet, particularly gold and artworks. Many had wooden furniture made before they left to take with them. Tibetans said that ordinary Chinese had been kings in Tibet but would be nothing when they returned to China. A Chinese saying was that each Chinese in Tibet could make enough to support sixteen of his relatives in China. The Chinese managed to monopolize much of the subsidies in goods that were provided to Tibet after 1979 as a part of the reform package and many were reluctant to leave. A Tibetan saying was that many Chinese goods came to Tibet only to "do a round" of the Jokhang Temple before they returned to China.[24] Many of the higher officials managed to stay in Tibet and others returned when the policy was reversed in 1983.

In 1983 Hu Yaobang's reform policy was reversed and it was decided that Tibet could not develop without Chinese "experts," who included many private entrepreneurs enticed by the subsidies provided to Tibet and newly allowed to travel due to the post–Cultural Revolution liberalization. Some Chinese officials who returned to Tibet after 1983 said that economic conditions were better in Tibet than in many places in China. Many Chinese came to Tibet without any permits but usually managed to stay using connections or sometimes having to go out to more remote villages and towns. Tibetans from outside Lhasa at the same time had a very difficult time getting permits to live there.

Tsering Wangchuk was by this time a reporter for *Tibet Daily*. He said that the purge of Hu Yaobang in 1985 was for being too liberal with Tibet, for which he was accused of "separatism."[25] However, Tsering says that Hu should have been given credit for lessening tensions between China and Tibet. Tensions were so high before the reforms announced by Hu that there could have been another revolt. Tsering Wangchuk left Tibet for India in the late 1980s. He says that not all Chinese were bad. Some even sympathized with Tibetans; some were opposed to their own government and thought that Tibet deserved independence. Some even said that he and other Tibetans should go to India where they could have a better life.

## Dhondub Choedon[26]

Dhondub Choedon was born in 1942 in the Nyethang district of the Lhoka region of Tibet. Her family was one of twenty families who had to do labor for the Dhargyal Ling Monastery in order to provide food for the monks. There were six members in their family. Three had to do what was called *wulag* service for the monastery, which meant doing seasonal farm labor or caring for animals or carrying grain or trade goods for the monastery. Two did not have to do wulag service, so they worked as hired hands for pay, and the sixth member of the family, her grandfather, did the household chores.

The family had their own plots of land that belonged to the monastery, on which they could grow their own grain and use it to pay off their wulag requirement if they had a surplus. She says that the labor requirement, which was like a tax or rent on the land belonging to the monastery, was not too difficult. The worst part of the system was that they were tied to the land that belonged not to them but to the monastery. One could just run away, of course, since there was no enforcement mechanism to prevent anyone leaving or any means to make them return. There were also legal means to escape the bondage to the monastery by becoming a monk or joining the Tibetan Army.

The author says that those who were bound to render wulag service to the monastery were said to be the descendants of former monks who had married and thus forsaken their vows. The monastery was some distance from the fields and pastures that it owned, so a monk representative was sent to oversee planting and harvesting of crops. Those doing this wulag service for the monastery were given their meals by the monastery when doing so. She says that she had never seen a monk abusing any of the villagers and that except for this supervision and work requirement, they were able to manage their own private lives.

Her home was a two-story house with a walled compound. The ground floor of the house was used for their animals, which included 4 yak, 27 sheep and goats, and 2 donkeys. They had land sufficient to plant four-and-one-half khel of seed and they harvested 70 khel of barley. Another 36 khel of barley was earned by the two members of the family who hired out their labor and the family earned another 22 khel by selling butter, blankets that they wove, and shoes that they made. The total income of the family was thus 128 khel of barley. Counting the food that was given by the monastery to those members of the family doing wulag service, they had about 42 khel of barley per year for each member of the family or 251 khel in total. They had plenty of milk, butter, and wool. They had no difficulty in earning their livelihood.

Dhondub Choedon says that they used to celebrate many festivals and enjoy themselves. Losar was a five-day festival, during which they enjoyed meat, *khabzes* (fried bread), and *chang* (barley beer). In the evenings they drank chang and danced. During another festival in the fifth month, *Saga Dawa*, which celebrated the birth of Sakyamuni Buddha, they were fed and entertained by the monastery for three days. They had freedom to visit relatives in other areas or to go on religious pilgrimages.

The Chinese came to her area in 1959. They declared that the wealth of the rich would be shared with the poor, like her family, so she and her family were initially happy. But they had never seen any Chinese before and wondered if they spoke the truth. They also wondered how many soldiers they would bring and what their real aims were in coming to Tibet. Above all, they hoped that they would not stay long.

She was only eighteen at the time and did not understand the political significance of the Chinese invasion. When the Chinese arrived in Nyethang, they occupied the Dhargyal Ling Monastery and made it their headquarters. Some monks were executed, some were imprisoned, some sent to labor camps, and the rest were secularized and sent home. The Chinese confiscated one nearby estate and redistributed the land. Her family got additional land sufficient to plant four-and-one-half khels of grain. They already had that same amount of land, which legally belonged to the monastery, but that they used as their own, so their land was doubled. However, the Chinese confiscated all of the wealth of the monastery and did not redistribute any of it. The valuable statues and metal implements were taken away in trucks and the Chinese used other items such as carpets in their offices.

Because she was young, she did whatever she was told to do. She was made a member of a song and dance troupe. In 1961 the Chinese started a school at the former Bentzang Monastery and she underwent political indoctrination there for three months. She was then made the political representative of her village in 1962. During the border war with India of that year, she was a brigade leader of Tibetans made to carry supplies for the Chinese.

She and her family were the supposed beneficiaries of what the Chinese called democratic reforms because they were of the former serf class. They could now grow 140 khel of barley on their land, which was more than the 128 khel they made before. However, they lost approximately 100 khel that had been what three of the members of the family had made while working for the monastery. The 140 khel they now had was thus less than what they had before. However, from this 140 khel, 7 khel were taken as *Chetral*, or Loving the Nation Tax. Another 35 khel were taken under what was called Surplus Grain Sales, which was supposed to be saved for years of low crop production but which was actually used to feed the Chinese cadres and the PLA. Her family was left with only 16 khel of barley per person whereas they used to have 42 khel.

Redistribution of the property of landowners and monasteries was also of little benefit to her family. The Chinese divided all that was confiscated from the former exploiting classes into what they called "wealth of production" and "wealth of livelihood" categories. Wealth of production included livestock and farming implements. Out of this category her family got one horse. Wealth of livelihood included clothes, houses, and household implements. Her family got some of the tools of a butcher, which were not of much use to them. Even the best of the horses, clothes, and household implements confiscated from private houses was kept by the Chinese for their own use. They justified this by saying that the wealth of the exploiters was confiscated for the benefit of the people, meaning all the Chinese people and not just Tibetans.

Dhondub Choedon was willing to work for the Chinese at first because of their promises to eliminate the inequalities in Tibetan society. However, she found that not only did the Chinese not eliminate the old inequality but they instituted a new regime of inequality of which they and their collaborators were the primary beneficiaries. Previously, her village had been poor but it was in a beautiful place and almost everyone was happy. There was a great deal of personal freedom, limited only by the requirement to labor on the lands belonging to the monastery. However, after what the Chinese called democratic reforms there was no happiness and no personal freedom.

Her village was at a relatively high altitude, filled with green meadows and surrounded in the distance by forests. There were no beggars; starvation was unheard of and they had few worries. The land was quite prosperous and peaceful. They had their own language, religion, culture, and traditions. In the old days people worked hard but were happy and often sang and danced. People were able to freely express their thoughts and move about freely. Even the serfs had many freedoms. The relationship between the serfs and their masters was usually friendly and the masters usually took responsibility to feed the serfs in time of shortage. They knew that Tibet was an independent country. The importance of this could only be fully appreciated once their freedom was lost and they lived under an alien rule, in which there was nothing they could call their own and no ancestral heritage that they were permitted to value.

In late 1965 her area was made into one of the first communes in Tibet. There were 120 families, consisting of 675 persons, including 18 former monks and 7 former Tibetan Army soldiers. Everything now theoretically belonged in common to the Tibetans, but the Chinese gave all the orders and made all the decisions. Overall production in the commune area increased, mostly because Tibetans were driven to work harder, but they did not have any more food, because the surplus was always taken by the Chinese.

> *The "great change" which the Chinese said would make us "the masters of our own house" resulted in the Chinese having power over everything that was in our land. The system of commune made the people's hearts beat faster with fear and anxiety because the people are kept under constant watch and their actions noted down. Anyone who opposed the commune authorities or disobeyed their rules is brought*

*before the "people's court" and denounced during thamzing or class struggle meeting.*

There was no more freedom of thought or opinion. "No one can oppose the commune because the Chinese constantly declare that opposing the commune is opposing Socialism, and that it is anti-people and that person is the enemy of the people." There was no more leisure time in which Tibetans could engage in activities like religion or enjoy their usual cultural festivals with singing and dancing.

The commune was run by Tibetan Communist Party members who took their instructions from higher level officials, who were almost all Chinese. Tibetan commune leaders were chosen by the Chinese. They were theoretically elected by all the members of the commune, but the Chinese arranged these so-called elections so that only their choices could be elected. Only those of the lowest of the six class divisions, the former serfs, were eligible for election. Each of the five production brigades of the Red Flag Commune were allowed to suggest candidates for leadership positions. All of the commune members were then divided into small groups to discuss the qualifications of each of the nominees. However, the Chinese authorities had already decided who they wanted to be elected, based mostly upon their loyalty to the Chinese administration. Each of the small group discussions was led by a higher official who directed the discussion so as to praise and to favor the candidate they wanted and to criticize and reject those they did not want. The discussions in the small groups would go on until it was obvious to anyone who the higher authorities wanted and then everyone would vote for the approved candidates. The Chinese could thus claim that Tibetans had achieved democracy and self-rule, when in fact all decisions were made by themselves.

The Chinese also appointed the leaders of other organizations like the Communist Youth League. There were about thirty-three of the youths in the commune chosen for this organization. They were supposed to lead other youths to support the revolution in Tibet and to appreciate the benefits of the socialist system. They were also supposed to criticize the Dalai Lama and the "three big serf-owners" and to praise the CCP for its liberation of Tibet from the old oppressive system. The youth leaders were also to lead the Destroy the Four Pests Campaign. The four pests to be destroyed were usually enumerated as sparrows, flies, mice, and rats, but Dhondub Choedon says that in the Red Flag Commune, the youths also had to kill all dogs, cats, and birds. This campaign was supposed to eliminate pests that ate food supplies, but it was also meant to teach the youth to be merciless, rather than compassionate as Tibetan Buddhism taught, and to commit the sin of killing that Buddhism prohibited.

The Tibetan youth leaders were told that they were the future leaders of Tibet because they were not corrupted by the old society like their parents. They were to be like a blank slate upon which the new culture could be written. They were taught that the CCP was more like true parents to them than their real parents. They were to inform upon their parents for any old thoughts like practicing religion, or for any criticisms of the Chinese or the CCP.

Other organizations in the Red Flag Commune included a Youth League of younger Tibetans, a Poor Farmers League, a People's Militia, a Women's Federation, and a Commune School. The People's Militia was made up of about 120 members, both men and women, who were supposed to support the PLA and to expose class enemies and spies. Class enemies were anyone who opposed the Chinese and their reforms of Tibetan society; spies were any who expressed any support or even reverence for the Dalai Lama. The militia was used during the 1962 border war with India to carry supplies for the Chinese PLA.

The Women's Federation was supposed to promote women's liberation from the conservatism of old Tibetan society. Mainly this meant that women were supposed to "support half the sky" by doing equal work with men. They were also supposed to be liberated from marriage customs of the past, which meant that they could choose their own marriage partners rather than having them chosen by their families. However, what this meant in practice was that they were to choose partners of a good class and political status. Good class status meant lower class, while good political status meant loyalty to the Party. Tibetan women were also encouraged to marry Chinese since they were the most loyal to the Party and had supposedly selflessly come to Tibet to help Tibetans.

The Commune School had one teacher and about seventy students. None of the formerly upper class, who were often well-educated, were allowed to be teachers. Teachers had to be of lower-class status and were therefore usually not well-educated and therefore unable to be good teachers. Only about 10 percent of the students were selected for any higher education outside the commune and this was based upon their class status rather than on merit.

Dhondub Choedon summarizes how the Chinese explained the communes to her as one of the designated leaders of the Red Flag Commune. She writes that although the Chinese promoted the commune as an exercise of Tibetan democracy and self-determination, the reality was that all power resided with the subdistrict Chairman of the Chinese Communist Party and the Party branch within the commune. No Tibetan could oppose the commune or any of the decisions of the Chinese officials without being accused of opposing socialism and being an "enemy of the people," the people being the supposed beneficiaries of socialism.

Despite total Chinese control over the commune in regard to all policies, when problems arose, the Chinese took no responsibility. Problems were supposed to be resolved by the Tibetan commune leaders. Dhondub Choedon complained about food shortages, but was told that it was wrong to take local problems to the higher authorities. She was told that the CCP authorities had bigger responsibilities, like promoting the liberation of the rest of the peoples of the world. Even though the local problems like food shortages were caused by the Party's policies, the solution to these problems was supposed to happen at the local level. Furthermore, this was supposed to be an example of local self-rule.

The Chinese explained that the progressive and revolutionary Tibetan people should favor the commune because of its administrative advantages. The commune allowed leaders to advise the people, to assign them work projects, to collect information about them, to lead them to reforms, to benefit the nation, to organize the people for collective labor projects, and to lead them to the socialist future. Dhondub Choedon says that all of these administrative advantages were actually about command and control, supervision, repression, and exploitation. The commune allowed the Chinese to control Tibetans, to tell them what to do, to supervise them, and to punish those who resisted or failed to perform. The commune allowed the Chinese to control all aspects of Tibetans' lives, to prevent their freedom of movement to other places, to expose opponents by means of criticism sessions, and to exploit the labor of the commune for their own use.

Dhondub Choedon writes that when the Chinese first came to Tibet, they divided the Tibetans into only two classes, the rich and the poor. "At first, they befriended the rich and the powerful to make them their agents. Then, after 1959, they befriended the beggars, criminals and the poor, who would have personal resentments against the establishment, to make them their tools." They divided Tibetans into further classes after 1959 in order to make their rule easier. These classes were the former serf-owners; the agents of serf-owners; rich farmers; poor farmers; and the former serfs. The serf-owners were the former aristocracy, high government officials, and monastic leaders. The agents of the serf-owners included lower-level monk officials, Tibetan Army officers, and lower-level government officials. There were differentiations within these two upper classes according to political status and wealth.

If a family had income above their expenses and if they had any hired labor, then they were classified as rich farmers. Farmers who had no excess income were classed as poor farmers. The two upper classes were to be opposed; the two middle classes were to be educated; and the lowest level farmers and the former serfs were to be relied upon. There were both political and economic criteria for class divisions. Anyone who had participated in the revolt or who opposed the Chinese in any way was included into the classes of those to be oppressed. In the beginning the Chinese thought that the majority of Tibetans could be relied upon, because they thought that they would naturally support socialist reforms that theoretically benefited themselves, while only a small percentage needed to be repressed, but the percentage to be repressed constantly rose as the Chinese discovered that more and more Tibetans opposed them.

In the Red Flag Commune, 41 people in nine families were classed as agents of serf-owners; 70 people in eleven families were classed as rich farmers; 364 people in seventy families were classed as poor farmers; and

200 people in fifty families were classed as serfs. Dhondub Choedon says that the Chinese classifications of the Tibetan social system did not correspond to the reality. The Chinese classification system intentionally misinterpreted Tibetan social relationships of the past in order to fit within Chinese Communist ideologies and their class system. Also, the Chinese had greater difficulty making their class divisions in the nomadic society—which, except for the tribal leaders, was very equalitarian—and in less socially stratified areas of Tibet like Kham and Amdo.

Traditionally, Tibetans used to barter grain for meat and butter from the nomads. However, the Chinese required the nomads to sell all their meat and butter to the Chinese state companies, which used these products to feed themselves and the PLA soldiers. Village Tibetans were not allowed to buy meat and butter from the nomads. The Chinese also paid reduced prices to the nomads; for instance, Dhondub Choedon says that the Chinese paid only 8 yuan for a large sheep, whereas in the Lhasa market a single leg of sheep sold for 15 yuan. The Chinese exercised strict control over what the nomads could do with their animals, requiring them to get permission to slaughter any animal. They also taxed the nomads just like they did the farmers.

Tibetans whose grain rations were insufficient were required to search for edible roots and herbs, but these were sometimes not sufficient. She cites the names and circumstances of several families in her commune whose food was insufficient and several people who died of starvation as a result. This was in the period around 1970 when Tibet again began to suffer food shortages due to the introduction of the commune system and the substitution of wheat for barley because the Chinese preferred wheat. Wheat did not grow as well as barley at high altitude.

The fallacies of the Chinese commune system were inherent in the attempt to control every aspect of people's lives and their production. The inefficiencies came from this strict control system, but the control was also necessary for the Chinese so that they could exploit the Tibetans for their own needs. Given the inequalities and inefficiencies in the Chinese commune system, plus the obvious fact that the Chinese were exploiting Tibetans for their own food supplies and were living far better than the Tibetans, even the former serfs began to realize that the old system had been better than the new. The Chinese tried to tell Tibetans that they had risen up and become the rulers of their own land and the masters of their own lives. However, the fact obvious to all Tibetans was that Tibet was now owned and controlled by China and every aspect of their own lives was controlled by the Chinese. No matter how much they produced, which increased due to their being forced to work at a frenzied pace, they still received the same subsistence rations while the rest was taken away to feed the Chinese.

Dhondub Choedon's production brigade of twenty-nine households and 121 people in the Red Flag Commune was able to produce 3,900 khel of grain. After the Chinese took their taxes, only 1,783 khel was left, which was barely sufficient for the Tibetans to survive. Nearby nomads also had their animal production strictly controlled. They were allowed to keep only the minimum amount of meat, milk, and butter for their own use while all the rest was taken by the Chinese for their own use and for export to the Chinese interior. Nomads were not even allowed to keep their own wool. They used to make cloth for their tents and bedding and clothes by weaving their own wool with their own looms. Now, however, all wool was taken by the Chinese and used in weaving factories that they had built in places like Nyingtri in Kongpo. They made mostly blankets which were exported to China. Only the lowest quality of woolen cloth was made available to Tibetans. Tibetans either wore their old woolen *chubas* that were now patched and worn out or they wore Chinese cotton clothes.

Even the wild animals in Tibet no longer had any freedom. In the past, big herds of wild animals had roamed freely. However, since the PLA had come to Tibet, they had slaughtered the animals from their jeeps to feed themselves. Wild animal meat had also been exported in large quantities to China. The Chinese had created many small industries in Tibet using local materials, which they proclaimed as the result of their assistance in the economic development of Tibet, but they served mostly the interests of the Chinese military and bureaucrats in Tibet or were meant for export to China.

Dhondub Choedon also complained about the restrictions on Tibetan cultural festivals. The Tibetan youth had already forgotten about these traditional festivals because their parents could not even talk about them without being accused of trying to reestablish the old society. The Chinese had even confiscated household utensils of brass and copper. They paid a small price for the household utensils they confiscated, but Tibetans had to pay inflated prices for Chinese-made aluminum pots to replace them. For instance, the Chinese paid 12 yuan for a large copper pot, but an aluminum pot one-fourth its size cost 25 yuan. Some Tibetans simply could not afford to replace the household utensils confiscated by the Chinese.

The Tibetan social structure was disrupted because no one could trust anyone else due to Chinese cultivation of informants, including one's own children. The Chinese policy on religion proclaimed that anyone was free to practice religion and also free to not practice religion. However, in reality, the Chinese did everything to destroy the Tibetan Buddhist religion. They knew that Tibetan Buddhism was incompatible with Chinese communism in ideology and thus something that they had to destroy in order to get Tibetans to believe in communism. They claimed that Buddhism was superstition and thus backward and incompatible with modern science, but what was really the most intolerable aspect of Tibetan Buddhism to them was that it was such an important component of Tibetan national identity. The Chinese were intent upon transforming Tibetan national identity into Chinese identity and therefore they had to eradicate Tibetan belief in Buddhism. The Chinese also characterized monks as parasites who must be made to work to earn a living and improve Tibet's economy.

Dhondub Choedon says that in her Nyethang district alone there were previously thirty-seven monasteries with some 2,700 monks and nuns. Now, in all of Lhoka, of which Nyethang was only one district, there were only thirty monks. Even these thirty monks were not really monks but had been made to marry and now worked as farmers, herders, or construction workers. They were kept only to pretend that there was religious freedom. They were made to perform religious ceremonies on religious holidays at the Tramdub Dolma Lhakhang, which was the only one of the previous thirty-seven monasteries that was not destroyed or transformed into military barracks or office buildings. Even the Yumbu

Lhakhang, built by the first Tibetan king, Nyatri Tsanpo, was destroyed by the Chinese in 1968 even though it was not a real monastery.

Dhondub Choedon lists each of the thirty-seven monasteries that were destroyed and the number of monks and nuns in each. She says that all scriptures were burnt, clay statues were destroyed, and all idols of gold and with precious gems were taken away to China. All statues of brass and copper and all religious implements and even kitchen utensils like the large brass pots used to make tea for the monks were also taken away to China. The destruction of monasteries was done to teach Tibetans that their gods were powerless and their religion useless, but it was also done with utter contempt for the feelings of the Tibetan people.

The Chinese were constantly proclaiming that Tibetans had achieved self-rule and democracy. However, she says, democracy means the right to choose one's own culture and beliefs. Tibetans had believed in Buddhism for more than a thousand years. Was it believable, she asks, that they would have voluntarily destroyed their own religious monuments and persecuted their own monks and given up their own religion? She says that this is not believable despite the Chinese claim that Tibetans did all this voluntarily. She says that this involuntary destruction of Tibetan monasteries and abandonment of ancient traditions and culture is evidence that all of this was done under Chinese coercion and is proof that Tibetans enjoyed no democracy or freedom of religion.

She also asks if it is credible that Tibetans would have willingly abandoned all other aspects of their cherished traditional culture in favor of Chinese culture. Would they have voluntarily given up all their traditions in favor of everything Chinese? The Chinese had proclaimed all Tibetan traditions and culture backward and reactionary, and Chinese socialist traditions and culture as modern and progressive, but was it credible that this was true or that all Tibetans were convinced of this voluntarily and without coercion and had adopted all aspects of Chinese culture democratically? Was it possible that Tibetans had democratically decided that their political system of government by the Dalai Lama was as feudal and reactionary as the Chinese said and that they had voluntarily decided to abandon their own government in favor of government by the Chinese?

Dhondub Choedon writes that when the Chinese wanted to be pleasant, they would say that now that Tibetans had been liberated, they were the owners of the nation, meaning not only Tibet but all of China. They were represented by the Chinese Communist Party, which was the provider of peace and prosperity wherever it went. However, when the Chinese wanted to be more coercive, they would proclaim that the Chinese Communist Party had created a dictatorship of the proletariat, which no one was allowed to disobey. Tibetans were supposed to be a part of the proletariat since they were workers, like all Chinese workers. However, the majority of the proletariat being Chinese, its leaders were also Chinese and all of its institutions that enforced the dictatorship, like the Communist Party, the PLA, the police, and the judicial system were also Chinese. Even in Tibet, all these institutions were dominated by Chinese and not Tibetans. What the dictatorship of the proletariat in Tibet meant was the dictatorship of the Chinese.

Dhondub Choedon writes that the Chinese considered the cultivation and training of Tibetan cadres as essential to their administration of Tibet. However, at the time that she was writing, the Chinese had failed to create very many loyal Tibetan cadres. They had sent thousands of young Tibetans to minority nationality schools in China, but those who had been to the Chinese schools were not the ones that the Chinese trusted most and they did not place them in the most prominent and responsible positions. Instead, the most trusted Tibetan cadres were those of the lowest classes, most of whom still remained uneducated. There were several former serfs that the Chinese had elevated to symbolic positions based almost solely upon their loyalty and willingness to repeat all of their propaganda. They were sometimes very clever and scheming in order to promote themselves, but they could only repeat Chinese propaganda without being able to understand it or to analyze it.

Those Tibetans who had been sent to the minority nationality schools, on the other hand, did not often rise to the most responsible positions. The reason was not that they were not smart enough or talented or educated. In fact, the problem was that they were too educated. Many of those sent to the Chinese schools to learn the Chinese Communists' Marxist doctrine had become educated enough to question that doctrine. Their study of the Marxist anti-imperialist doctrine often led them to identify the Chinese conquest of Tibet as imperialist and its control there as colonialist. The more these Tibetans were educated, the more they learned to think and analyze the situation for themselves.

Even many of those of the former lowest classes, whom the Chinese thought should be most loyal to their doctrine, were able to see through the pretensions of that doctrine as applied to Tibet. They did not agree that the inequalities of the former Tibetan social system were sufficient justification for the Chinese occupation and control of Tibet. If the Chinese were so concerned with the welfare of Tibetans, then why did they not leave after the social system had been changed as they had previously promised to do? Tibetans who were not of the former lowest classes knew that their families had suffered during what the Chinese called democratic reforms and their property had been confiscated. Tibetans of all social classes were aware of the brutal Chinese repression of any and all Tibetan resistance and that many thousands of Tibetans had been killed, imprisoned, or had been forced into exile. They also learned of the continual Chinese Communists' intolerance of any opposition among the Chinese people as well as among Tibetans. They could see that the Chinese claims of having brought freedom and democracy to Tibet were false.

Dhondub Choedon writes that the Chinese perpetuated their rule by dividing Tibetans and setting them against each other. They did this by means of class divisions, political indoctrination, speaking bitterness campaigns (about the old society) and mutual criticisms, and thamzing. Political education was given to all lower-level cadres, of whom she was one. They were taught natural science, atheism, social evolution according to Marxism, class consciousness, national consciousness, and socialist consciousness. Natural science was meant to counter what the Chinese characterized as the superstitious and unscientific beliefs of Tibetan Buddhism; social evolution was about the natural and inevitable progress from primitive societies like the Tibetan to the ultimate highest social system of socialism or communism; class consciousness meant that class identity always took priority over ethnic or national identity; national consciousness meant that Tibetans should identify as Chinese or as

Chinese of the Tibetan nationality; and socialist consciousness meant that Tibetans should strive to create the socialist society and to support the unique role of the Chinese Communist Party and the correctness of its policies.

Tibetan cadres were indoctrinated with a negative portrayal of old Tibetan society in order to disguise the foreign imperialist nature of the Chinese conquest of Tibet:

> *The Chinese make us retail the evils of the old society without the least regard for the truth. They collect some instruments of punishment, bones of dead men and bits and ends about the old social practices and make the people recount their sufferings before these exhibits. They make effigies dressed in aristocrats' and poor beggars' clothes and make us describe, with details, about the old society—its backwardness, darkness, oppression, etc.—and declare that all these were true. The most elegant and convincing speakers would then be praised for speaking the "truth" and made to do it again before public meetings. They declare that the root of all these "sufferings and evils" of the "three big serf-owners" is the "Dalai rebel traitorous clique." The meeting will not stop until the whole audience denounces the Dalai Lama and later, the Panchen Lama. If anyone does not join, the Chinese will declare that he is infected with "blind faith and empty hope," and saying that he must be "relieved of his mental burden," he will be subjected to thamzing in that meeting and made to confess and denounce his own "wrong thinking." During these meetings everyone had to cry and say, "The gods, lamas, religion and monasteries are the tools of exploitation, the three serf-owners made the Tibetans poor; the Chinese Communist Party liberated us and gave us food, clothes, houses and land; the Chinese Communist Party is more kind that our own parents; may the Chinese Communist Party last for ten thousand years; may Chairman Mao live for ten thousand years!"*
>
> *This would strike any outside observer as absurd; you cannot make a people love and hate by demanding it. The purpose of all these charades is obvious; innumerable repetition of similar stories mixed with*

*half-truths make falsehood convincing; the humiliation and denunciation destroy the self-respect of the old folks; and, most importantly, it seeks to make the struggle for the independence of Tibet synonymous with "restoration of hell on earth." The Chinese are also guilty of wiping the history of Tibet from the minds of Tibetan youths and filling their minds with falsehood—they have given official sanctity to the creation of lies.*

However, Dhondub Choedon says that the Chinese were unable to eradicate all Tibetan culture and all Tibetan pride in their own history. This, she says, was typical of all conquerors who try to eradicate another culture. They may be somewhat successful because they have a monopoly on coercion and the use of force, but they cannot completely change everyone's minds. The Chinese claimed to have given so much to Tibetans, but she says,

*The Chinese say that they have given this and that to the Tibetans. But who are they to give us anything? The land is ours and the wealth therein is our property. They belong to us, not the Chinese. By what right do the Chinese live on our land and control our property?*

In her last chapter Dhondub Choedon returns to the theme of the Cultural Revolution, which began in the Red Flag Commune at the end of 1966. Two Chinese and six Tibetan officials came to the commune and selected thirty young Tibetans from the former serf class who were then declared to be Red Guards. The Red Guards were only youths but were empowered to do anything they wanted, and therefore often became tyrannical in their actions. They patrolled the commune and denounced all Tibetan habits. All Tibetan signs and symbols written on house walls were eradicated and replaced by photos of Mao. All colorful house decorations were painted over in dull colors. Tibetans were not allowed to exchange khatags. Tibetan songs and dances were banned and replaced with revolutionary Chinese songs and dances that everyone was required to learn. They had to replace their Tibetan dress and hairstyles with Chinese dress and hairstyles. The Chinese tried to make Tibetans learn

Chinese and they even tried to alter the Tibetan language by incorporating Chinese words and phrases. This was called the Chinese-Tibetan Friendship Language.

The Red Guards pulled down prayer flags and destroyed shrines, *chortens*, and *mani* walls. They also destroyed any remaining monasteries and all their murals. They confiscated any remaining personal religious items like statues or thankas. They burned any religious scriptures they could find. The Red Guards accused anyone attempting to keep religious items or any old traditional items of trying to resurrect the past and described them as the enemy within. Prayer beads were confiscated. Even those caught burning incense were charged with attempted arson and paraded with dunce caps. Old people praying silently were denounced for being superstitious.

The Red Guards went from house to house and forced everyone to buy portraits of Mao and they painted his sayings all over the walls. Everyone was required to carry Mao's Little Red Book with them at all times and had to recite quotations from Mao on demand. Anyone failing to correctly recite Mao's sayings was subjected to criticism or thamzing.

Dhondub Choedon says that the Cultural Revolution was a time when the Chinese tried to destroy Tibetan culture and replace it with Chinese culture, causing great cultural anguish for Tibetans. She denounces the Chinese attempt to destroy Tibetan identity as essentially a cultural genocide. The violence and destructiveness of the Cultural Revolution lasted only a few years, but the anti-Tibetan policies lasted a full ten years, from 1966 to 1976. She says that the Cultural Revolution was typical of the style of rule of the Chinese Communists who meant to transform society by means of violent political campaigns.

Dhondub Choedon writes that for many years she did what the Chinese ordered, even participating in the destruction of monasteries and religious monuments. She says that it would not have done much good to have done otherwise since they had all the power and they repressed all who opposed them. She acknowledges that Tibet was in need of some reforms in its social and political system and even that the religious system was in need of reform. She believed that Communism was not all bad, at least in theory. However, her experience finally led her to understand that everything the Chinese said was nothing but lies and she felt that she had no choice but to attempt to escape into exile. She has many unhappy memories of what happened in Tibet and what she participated in but she believes that the oppression and the suffering in Tibet cannot continue forever and that, one day, Tibet will be free again.

She fled Tibet even though she was among those so-called liberated serfs who were favored by the Chinese. Her husband, whom she had married in 1962, was also a former serf and had been made a local cadre. They had two children, born in 1962 and 1969. However, Chinese policy was that spouses were often separated because they were assigned to different areas. They first thought to escape in 1967 because of the disparity between what the Chinese had promised and the reality in Tibet. They realized that freedom and happiness were impossible without the independence of Tibet. Her husband soon fell into trouble because he said something about how Lenin's thoughts were superior to those of Mao. This was such an offense that she was encouraged to divorce her husband with the threat of thamzing if she refused. For this reason, in 1973 they decided to escape even though they would have to leave their children behind.

## Rinbur Tulku[27]

Rinbur Tulku was born in 1932 in Markham, western Kham. He was recognized as the reincarnation of Rinbur Tulku of the Rinbur Monastery in Markham. At age 14 he was sent to the Sera Monastery in Lhasa for studies. In 1950 he was back in Markham when the Chinese arrived. Like most Tibetans, he recalls that the Chinese said that they would protect religion and that they had come to Tibet only to help it develop and would leave when that was accomplished. However, he says that most Tibetans did not believe the Chinese promises. They distributed dayan very liberally, both for hired labor and to pay the salaries of local officials. Tibetans were only interested in the silver content of the dayan and did not accept them as a new currency. The Chinese were very polite at first but this did not change the Tibetan impression that they were bad people.

Rinbur says that the Chinese tried to convince Markham Tibetans to demand democratic reforms as early as 1955. However, Tibetans knew that Markham was part of the territory covered by the terms of the Seventeen Point Agreement that stipulated that reforms would not be implemented until Tibetans were ready. He says that the Chinese strategy was to gradually increase their control. The Democratic Reforms Campaign could not be implemented in Markham until 1960, after the revolt in Lhasa.

Rinbur returned to Lhasa in 1955 because of Chinese anti-religious propaganda in Markham. The Dalai Lama asked him to be the vice chairman of the Tibet branch of the Chinese Buddhist Association in Tibet in 1956, a request that he could not refuse. He was still uncomfortable doing so but Trijang Rinpoche, the Dalai Lama's tutor, who was the chairman, also urged him to accept. He was aware that the associations that the Chinese were setting up, all under the auspices of the Preparatory Committee for the TAR, were an attempt to co-opt Tibetans in the demise of their own institutions and that their promises to protect and preserve religion were insincere. He argued with the Chinese many times about their suppression of lamas and monasteries in Amdo and Kham, including his own area of western Kham. By late 1957 or early 1958, they were so dissatisfied with his obstructionism that they had him replaced, after which he returned to his studies at Sera.

He was arrested immediately after the March 1959 revolt and kept at the Silingbu Chinese military headquarters along with many of the higher-level Tibetan aristocrats, government officials, and lamas. He was interrogated about his role in the revolt. He was not involved but some of his relatives had been members of the Chushi Gangdruk resistance. They, however, had all escaped or been killed so there was no one to contradict his story that he had no involvement. He was subjected to the usual Chinese tactic of trying to elicit confessions by promising leniency for cooperation, but he replied only that he trusted the CCP to investigate him fairly and honestly. His Tibetan interpreter told him that if he stuck to his story the Chinese couldn't prove anything. This proved to be true and he was released after only a few months, unlike many others at

Silingbu who were sent to harsh prison camps in Xinjiang from which only a few returned and only in 1979.

He rejoined the Tibet Buddhist Association in 1961 but again was so resistant that he was removed in 1963. As a high lama he was persecuted during the Cultural Revolution, being subjected to thamzing a total of thirty-five times and labeled as a reactionary. In his autobiography, Rinbur Tulku described his experience of the beginning of the Cultural Revolution in Lhasa and the looting and destruction of cultural relics.[20]

Rinbur Tulku's account reveals the typical process of the looting and desecration of Tibet's temples, monasteries, and household shrines. Even at the beginning of the supposedly chaotic Cultural Revolution, the process was deliberately organized and controlled by the Chinese authorities. Before the "revolutionary masses" were allowed to vent their animosity against the exploitative Buddhist religion and the religious establishment, all shrines were emptied of their valuable contents by Chinese officials and soldiers. All implements made of precious metals and all ornamentations of precious jewels were removed before any more random destruction was allowed. In Lhasa it appears that all such valuables were stored at the Cultural Relics Bureau and then eventually trucked to China. Rinbur's account also reveals the coercion that the Tibetans came under from Chinese cadres to participate in the destruction of their own cultural relics.

Contrary to the version of events, often promoted by the Chinese themselves, that the process of destruction of Tibet's monasteries began with the Lhasa Jokhang and was confined to the period of the Cultural Revolution, the sacking of the Jokhang actually came near the end of a process that had begun during the Democratic Reforms Campaign that had begun in the summer of 1959 in the TAR and earlier in Tibetan areas outside the TAR. By the beginning of the Cultural Revolution, only the Potala, the Jokhang, and a few of the most important of Tibet's temples and monasteries had escaped the process of looting, desecration, and physical destruction. Such was the volume of religious art in Tibet that the process of looting and destruction of Tibet's cultural and artistic heritage took almost ten years, beginning during the Democratic

Reforms Campaign and continuing during the Cultural Revolution until only some ten major monasteries were left standing.

Rinbur was rehabilitated again in 1979 and restored to his position of vice chairman of the Tibet Buddhist Association in 1980. In 1982 he led a team of Tibetans to try to recover Tibetan artworks still in China.[29] In particular, they hoped to recover the upper half of the Sakyamuni Buddha statue brought to Tibet by the Nepalese princess, known as the Ramoche Jowo because it had been kept in the Ramoche temple in Lhasa. The Ramoche had been badly damaged during the revolt and the statue was cut in half and its contents removed at the beginning of the Cultural Revolution. The lower half had been found in Tibet but the upper was thought to have been taken to China.

They went to Chengdu in Sichuan, where they found no one willing to respond to their requests, so they went on to Beijing. In Beijing they were told that some Tibetan artifacts had been recovered from a foundry, the Precious Metal Smelting Foundry, in 1973, during a brief period of slightly liberalized policies. In a warehouse they found 26 tons of "statues and offering vessels," as well as "nearly a thousand burnished copper statues with gold tracery." One of the large statues they recognized as the upper half of the Sakyamuni Buddha. This statue, along with the 26 tons of statues and religious objects from this site and 6 tons from another, 13,537 statues in various states of damage in all, were recovered and returned to Tibet. Almost all statues made of gold or silver had disappeared.

Although many statues were recovered, many more statues and religious implements of brass or copper had been melted. Rinbur Tulku was told by one of the Chinese workers in Beijing, who had recovered the statues from a foundry in 1973, that they had found some 50 tons of damaged Tibetan artifacts and had managed to salvage 26 tons of "serviceable items and pieces." This was the remnant of some 600 tons of Tibetan statues and vessels of "gilt copper, bronze, burnished copper and brass" that the foundry had acquired and, after removing all gold gilding, had "melted down load by load and used in the production of goods for the state or public consumption." Later, they heard that the foundry had acquired another 30 tons of Tibetan artifacts, from which they were able to salvage 6 tons. This Chinese worker told Rinbur that Tibetan artifacts were taken from Tibet to Liuyuan (in northwestern Gansu, near Dunhuang, on the railroad from Gansu to Xinjiang, the closest railhead to Tibet at that time) and then on to foundries in Taiyuan (Shanxi), Beijing, Shanghai, and Tianjin. He estimated that other foundries melted comparable amounts as the one near Beijing.

Upon their return to Chengdu, Rinbur was able to recover another 5 tons of artifacts from a foundry in Sichuan, mostly so damaged that nothing could be salvaged. Another 1 ton from Taiyuan (Shanxi) was salvaged and 2 tons from another foundry at Man Shan in Sichuan. Most Tibetan artifacts left in Sichuan had already been smelted.

While Rinbur had gone to Sichuan and Beijing, another Tibetan team had gone to Qinghai, where artifacts from central Tibet were also reportedly taken. The leader of that group, Gatar Tulku, found several warehouses at Huang Yuan, just west of Sining, some still full of statues and some showing signs of having held great quantities of metal objects. One warehouse was empty except that the floor was still covered with Tibetan coins. This team also returned several tons of statues to Tibet. Gatar Tulku relates that he had in his possession a list of all the warehouses in China that had stored Tibetan artifacts, the total tonnage they received, and the foundries to which the articles had been sent for melting. He regrets that he was required to return the list to Chinese officials and was unable to retain a copy. He also met in Chengdu with Rinbur and together they went to a nunnery where they found some one hundred baskets, each containing dozens of small and valuable Tibetan statues carefully packed and ready for shipment to some undisclosed location. They were unable to recover these statues because they had been "bought" by the current owner and had already been sold to a buyer.[30]

What this information reveals is that the confiscation of Tibetan art and metal works was systematic and was organized by the Chinese government. Art and metal works from central Tibet were taken to warehouses at Liuyuan in Gansu and Huang Yuan in Qinghai. Presumably, artifacts from Amdo were also taken to Huang Yuan and perhaps other locations. Artifacts from the areas of Kham that were part of Sichuan were taken to Chengdu or some other location in Sichuan. From each of the primary warehouses, the artifacts were sold to foundries that melted them down for their metal content. These foundries were state-owned enterprises and the metal was designated by the government for other purposes. Given that Rinbur Tulku recovered some 13,537 statues and religious articles in various conditions, or 32 tons out of the 630 tons acquired by the foundry near Beijing, and that several other foundries were rumored to have smelted comparable amounts, the magnitude of the Chinese looting of Tibet's wealth can be imagined. One can see from these figures that the total number of statues and religious articles taken from Tibetan monasteries was many hundreds of thousands. This, of course, does not include any of the most precious statues of gold and silver, most of which simply disappeared, or the thousands of priceless thankas, some of which later appeared on the international art market but most of which were reportedly burned at each site where they were confiscated, along with religious texts and the woodblocks used to print texts (although woodblocks were sometimes used for firewood or other purposes in wood-scarce Tibet). The recovered Jowo statue was restored at the Jokhang in Lhasa and replaced in the Ramoche in a ceremony in 1985. Rinbur and his team redistributed the other recovered statues and religious vessels and implements to the undestroyed monasteries of Tibet "in accordance with their actual situation." The large monasteries of Drepung, Sera, Sakya, and Tashilhunpo that had preserved some of their treasures intact did not receive any of the recovered statues. Rinbur writes that they were distributed to the most important monasteries of each sect and in each area, presumably as these monasteries were being restored:

*The destruction of Tibet's monasteries is often mistakenly attributed to the later Cultural Revolution and excused as an aberration in the history of the CCP or as having been suffered not only by Tibetans but by all the Chinese people. However, the repression of the Tibetan upper class and the looting and destruction of Tibetan monasteries was not an aberration, but rather a planned and systematically executed transfer of power and redistribution of wealth, not from the former upper class to the liberated serfs, but from the Tibetan people to the Chinese. The destruction of Tibetan cultural monuments and*

> *artifacts was an immediate aspect of Chinese policies that began as soon as China gained complete political control over Tibet. The Chinese state used the confiscated wealth for its own purposes in the name of "all the people." The destruction of the Tibetan state, the purge of its ruling class and the destruction of the most visible aspects of Tibetan culture and national identity was pursued not for the benefit of the Tibetan people but to secure Chinese control by destroying the culture and the national identity of Tibet.*

Rinbur says that the liberalization policy that the Chinese instituted in Tibet after 1979 was intended to create conditions just good enough to entice the Dalai Lama back from exile and finally resolve the problem of the "unity of nationalities." The Dalai Lama's absence was a big problem for China, he says. Many older Tibetans wanted him to return because they wished for his presence and blessings, but others, mostly the younger Tibetans, did not think it wise for him to return because they did not trust any Chinese promises to allow any autonomy or religious freedom in Tibet. They feared that the Dalai Lama would be exploited as a powerless figurehead while the Chinese retained full control over all aspects of Tibetans' lives. Rinbur said that many Tibetan cadres were very nationalistic at that time but most did not think it wise for the Dalai Lama to return. Even a Chinese "head of the TAR" told him to tell the Dalai Lama not to return.

In early 1985 Rinbur was in Beijing for a conference on Buddhism. This was at the height of the liberalization period when he says it "was possible to talk" with the Chinese about Tibet. Most thought that the Tibet problem had essentially been resolved, with the exception of the absence of the Dalai Lama. At that time, he requested permission to visit India. Travel was relatively liberal at that time, with Tibetans from exile visiting Tibet and many Tibetans allowed to visit India. The Chinese hoped that Tibetans from exile would be impressed with newly improved conditions in Tibet and could be persuaded to return with promises of return of confiscated property and provision of jobs and stipends. Tibetans who were given permits to visit their relatives in India and Nepal were instructed to convince their relatives to return to Tibet. Salaries for

Tibetan officials were generous at that time with high sounding titles but little responsibility.

Rinbur was given a permit to visit India. He says that the Chinese thought he would return. He visited with the Panchen Lama in Beijing who sent his regards to the Dalai Lama with him. He says that the Panchen Lama also thought that he would return and that he and the Chinese may have hoped that he could persuade the Dalai Lama to return. He planned everything for his staff at the Buddhist Association as if he planned to return within a year but he says that he had no intention to return. He left Tibet in late 1985 and went to Dharamsala where he remained.

# Chapter 2

# Lhasa, 1982

In February 1982 I participated in a Chinese-language study program at Inner Mongolia University, organized by the US-China Education Foundation. My interest was not so much to study Chinese but to learn something about an autonomous region in the People's Republic of China, the Inner Mongolian region having been the first, established in 1947, even before the establishment of the PRC in 1949. A more far-fetched hope was that I might somehow get to Tibet, which had been closed to almost all foreigners since 1950 but where a liberalization of Chinese policy under Deng Xiaoping had already seen the dissolution of communes and Chinese promises to finally allow some semblance of actual Tibetan cultural and religious, if not political, autonomy. My interest in Tibet derived from a ten-year residence in Nepal, where I worked with Sherpas and became acquainted with the Tibetan political issue.

My group of fifteen students at Nei Mongu Daxue (Inner Mongolia University) turned out to be mostly undercover Christian missionaries, from whom an opportunity to extricate myself came when I encountered an American English teacher passing through Huhohaote, the capital of Inner Mongolia, who had just received an individual travel permit to Lhasa. I immediately went to the Public Security Police in Huhohaote to avail myself of an individual travel permit, to replace the group permit I was then on, only to be told that they had given permits to Lhasa for two weeks only on a trial basis and had stopped just the day before! China gave permits to Lhasa for only a few weeks in only three small cities, one of which was Huhohaote. I got a travel permit for other places but was very disappointed to not get one to Lhasa.

However, upon return to the university guest house, a young Inner Mongolian student housekeeper with whom I had been friendly offered to forge a Lhasa permit for me. She looked at the permit, which listed a few cities, like Urumchi in Xinjiang, that I had requested. There was no full stop after the last place name. She said that she had the same kind of ink and she thought she could copy the writing style. She made a few trials on another piece of paper, which looked exactly like the writing on the permit! So, I gave her the go-ahead and she wrote in the characters for Lhasa. It looked exactly the same as all the other names! Armed with my new forged permit, I was ready to go.

I went first to Urumchi with the hope to get to Kashgar and from there into western Tibet, which would truly have been a first. However, Kashgar was off-limits to foreigners so I had to backtrack along the railroad to Liuyuan and take a bus from there to Dunhuang, the site of the famous Silk Road Buddhist caves. From there I hitchhiked on a truck to Golmud, at that time a small town on the Tibetan Plateau in what is now Qinghai Province. From Dunhuang the road heads south toward the edge of the Tibetan Plateau and enters at the plateau's lowest point, the *Tsaidam* Basin, which means salt marsh in Tibetan. The Tsaidam is a high-altitude marsh marked by tufts of grass that are practically the only vegetation. Here and there Mongol yurts were visible in the distance.

At Golmud I was asleep in a dirt floor hotel room when, at about 3:00 a.m., my door opened without the courtesy of a knock, the light went on, and I found my bed surrounded by six Chinese Public Security Police in immaculate white uniforms. Speaking in Chinese, which I suddenly realized that I could understand more than previously thought, they demanded to see my travel permit. I managed to produce my passport and my Chinese travel permit, which fortunately included Lhasa, which was the only possible destination from Golmud. Still, they wanted to know how I got there. I told them that I had come overland, by hitchhiking from Dunhuang, about a hundred miles almost directly north of Golmud. That route was illegal, they said, only the route from Sining to Golmud being open to foreigners. The road from Sining, to the east, the capital of Qinghai, meets up with the one from Dunhuang just north of Golmud. The police conferred and decided that the way I had come was illegal, but now, having reached Golmud, I was legal again.

They said I could go to Lhasa, since I had a permit, but only by plane, since the road was under construction. They instructed me to buy an airplane ticket to Lhasa the next day. And then they left, almost as abruptly as they had come. Their middle-of-the-night surprise visit had obviously been meant to impress and intimidate. In the morning I bought a plane ticket to Lhasa.

They were paving the road to Lhasa that summer, which was why I was not allowed to go by road. Some of the few foreigners who made it to Lhasa that summer did travel over that road and reported that trucks had to detour off the road in places where paving was being done. Trucks often got mired in mud, making an ordeal for those who reached Lhasa this way. The flight by contrast gave an exciting view of the northern plateau.

I was the only foreigner, with the exception of three Hong Kong Chinese students, on the plane from Golmud to Lhasa. The scenery was magnificent as expected, but mostly featureless plateau terrain punctuated by the occasional snow peak. There was no visible evidence of human habitation with the exception of occasional sightings of the road from Golmud to Lhasa. We must have flown past the magnificent Nyenchenthangla mountain range just northwest of Lhasa, the abode of the protector spirit of Central Tibet, but I was insufficiently attuned to its significance at that time to identify it from the other peaks. The famous Nam Tso, or lake of heaven, was also visible off to the west of our flight path. The plane landed well south of Lhasa in the valley of the Tsangpo River, 50 kilometers from Lhasa, the nearest sufficiently flat spot for an airport. There was a bus available that took about three hours to traverse the one-lane dirt and gravel road to Lhasa. I had read many travelers' accounts of traversing this very road on their way from India or Nepal.

As the bus approached Lhasa, my eyes strained for the first sight of the Potala, as had those of thousands of pilgrims and travelers before me. The sight was as exhilarating as expected, but as we arrived at our stop, I was disappointed to see that the magnificent Potala was now surrounded by a dingy Chinese city of ugly concrete buildings, much like every other Chinese city I had seen. The Potala still rose majestically above the city, but it now appeared like the last surviving relic of Tibetan civilization left unconsumed by the typical Chinese urban ugliness.

As I arrived, I had in mind the history of Tibet's isolation, both before and after 1950, and my fortune at being in China just when Tibet was opened to a few individual tourists on an experimental basis. Tibet had been closed to all but a few communist sympathizers since the last British Government of India representative, Hugh Richardson, left in 1947, when India achieved independence. The last foreigners to leave Tibet before the Chinese took over were the two Austrian mountaineers, Heinrich Harrer and Peter Aufschnaiter, who had escaped from British internment in India and spent the war years in Tibet. Harrer wrote the famous book *Seven Years in Tibet*, since made into a movie, about his experiences with the young Dalai Lama. Aufschnaiter hung on even longer than Harrer, until the Chinese had entered Tibet in 1950, and wrote his own book, *Eight Years in Tibet*.

Another Brit, Robert Ford, who was employed by the Tibetan government as a radio operator in Chamdo, was arrested by the Chinese when they invaded in October 1950 and was subjected to five years of "thought reform" in a Chinese prison. He wrote a book, *Captured in Tibet*, later republished under the wonderful title *Wind Between the Worlds*, about his experiences. The title captures the extreme dissonance between the free-spirited and relaxed Tibetan lifestyle that Ford experienced before his arrest compared to the Chinese Communists' attempt to control his existence in both body and mind. Ford wrote that there was no escape from the Communists' thought reform either in resistance or the pretense of conformity. The first requirement was admission of guilt, which for Ford was to admit that he was a British spy. He feared pretending to go along because the Communists' thought reform methods were so coercive and sophisticated that he thought he might lose his mind. He never did admit to being a spy and was finally released after he confessed to the lesser charge of "entering China illegally," meaning that he was in Tibet with the permission of the Tibetan but not the Chinese government.

Since then, the Chinese had allowed in only a few foreign communists who were sympathetic to their attempts to transform Tibet. Those who were allowed closely supervised trips to Lhasa obliged their hosts by writing books that repeated the propaganda they were told about how China had liberated the Tibetan serfs, who were now singing and dancing in the streets. From 1950 to 1980, there had been no reports from objective observers about what was happening in Tibet. The few accounts from Tibetan refugees tended to be dismissed as biased or exaggerated. Like many of my friends in Nepal, I had long hoped that Tibet would open to the outside world. But, unlike my friends, I had guessed that it would be the front door from China that would open, not the backdoor from Nepal, and I was fortunate to be in China just at the right time when the Chinese decided to give out the first experimental individual travel permits to Lhasa.

I was directed from the bus stop near the foot of the Potala to #2 Guest House, which was nearby and was the only place in Lhasa at that time where individual foreign travelers could stay. I didn't actually have to ask for directions; someone nearby simply waved me toward where it was known that foreigners could stay. There was a much fancier place for tourist groups, far outside the city in the direction of Drepung Monastery. Group tourism had been allowed for perhaps a year before individual permits began to be given, but there were few groups so far. There were no tourist groups in Lhasa when I arrived and only a few individuals. When I got to the Guest House, I was able to count them all. There were precisely six foreigners in Lhasa that day, July 4, 1982. The Guest House was mainly for Chinese cadres working in Tibet, so they had little idea what to do with foreign tourists. We were thrown together, four to a room, without regard to gender, nationality, previous association, or anything else.

My new roommates, an American couple who had been working as English teachers in China, informed me that the Panchen Lama was giving blessings at the Jokhang that very day and urged me to go there and get one, as they had. They didn't know that there was anything unusual about the Panchen Lama giving blessings, only that all of Lhasa seemed to be there and that there was an air of excitement among the

Tibetans. I was very surprised to hear that the Panchen Lama was there. I knew that his very existence had been a mystery since the early 1960s, when he was arrested for his criticisms of Chinese policies in Tibet. Most Tibetans had regarded him as a collaborator during the 1950s, but he had redeemed himself in 1962 by refusing to denounce the Dalai Lama and by his criticisms of Chinese policies in Tibet in the form of a lengthy petition to Mao and Zhou Enlai. His subsequent fourteen years of imprisonment and house arrest had further enhanced his credibility. This was his first visit to Lhasa in almost twenty years, hence the Tibetan excitement. He had arrived in Lhasa that very day, or perhaps the day before, but he had begun giving blessings only that day.

I went directly to the Jokhang. The street that the Guest House was on, named People's Road, led directly there. As I approached, I saw a long line of Tibetans stretched out the door of the Jokhang and winding around the Barkhor, the street that is the circumambulation route around the Jokhang Temple. As I was about to go to the end of the line, several Tibetans waved to me to get into the line close to the front. I was a foreigner, so I was allowed this privilege. It may also have had something to do with the Tibetan habit of cultivating foreigners in the hope that they will become supporters of their cause. It worked on me.

As the line entered the second courtyard, where the Panchen Lama was seated on his throne, he looked up to see the tall foreigner. As I got near him, I could see his attendants preparing a special blessing cord for me. The usual blessing, with which I was familiar from Nepal, was a thin red cord suitable for wearing around the neck. Tibetans and Sherpas and even many foreigners were used to wearing one or more of such blessing cords they had obtained from different lamas until the cords disintegrated. I received my touch on the head from the Panchen Lama and was presented with a broad red ribbon by one of his subordinates. This was meant as a special blessing for me, but it was not suitable for wearing. I tried to make it known that I preferred the ordinary cord that everyone else was getting. After some confusion and misunderstanding, I managed to get one of those, too, without, I hope, making too much of a scene. It was special enough to me that I wore it for years until it fell apart. I considered this a pretty auspicious first day in Lhasa.

The Panchen Lama stayed in Lhasa for a few days before going to his monastery of Tashilhunpo in Shigatse. He made a speech at Sera Monastery at the northern edge of the Lhasa Valley in which he described some of his suffering in prison. According to Tibetans who were there, he said that he still suffered from partial paralysis on one side of his body, having been forced to lie on one side facing the cell door so that he could be observed, a common regimen at the Qinghe Prison for high-level prisoners near Beijing. This only increased his stature among Tibetans, who until then were still somewhat ambivalent about him. They sympathized with him, knowing that he had shared their suffering after he had stood up to the Chinese leaders on their behalf. His return to Tibet was a major event, but as one Tibetan said, his return was only a "small joy" compared to a return of the Dalai Lama, which is what most Tibetans really wanted.

Lhasa was just beginning to emerge from the Cultural Revolution and to experience the reforms initiated by Deng Xiaoping. In Chinese cities this meant the reemergence of individual capitalism, but in Tibet it meant the revival of Tibetan culture. Tibetans were relieved, at least partially, not only from the chaos and destruction of the Cultural Revolution but from the economic and political restrictions of collectivization. The Cultural Revolution ended with the death of Mao and the arrest of the Gang of Four in 1976, but it took until late 1978 before Deng was able to establish his predominance over other Party leaders and to initiate true reforms. In 1979 the few surviving Tibetan government leaders who had been arrested in 1959 were finally released from prison. The Panchen Lama was rehabilitated, communes in Tibet were dissolved, and Hu Yaobang made his famous visit to Tibet in 1980 in which he said that the Chinese role in Tibet looked like colonialism, if only in the economic sense, and declared that the numbers of Chinese in Tibet would be reduced by 85 percent. Tibetans were still talking about the 85 percent number in 1982, and I actually saw Chinese regularly leaving by bus from the compound behind #2 Guest House. The implication of Hu's policy changes for Tibet was that Tibetans would finally be allowed to enjoy some of the autonomy they had long been promised. The removal of Chinese cadres at the local level allowed Tibetans to begin reconstruction of their monasteries and religious monuments like *chortens*, or Buddhist stupas.

After thirty years of the Chinese occupation, Lhasa appeared to be about half Tibetan, half Chinese. There was a predominantly Tibetan section around the Jokhang and the Ramoche Temples, now beginning to take on the character of a ghetto. The new additions to the city were mostly to the west and the north. The area between the Jokhang and Potala was built up with government offices, the Guest House, a department store, and a *Xinhua* (New China News Agency) propaganda bookstore. The area to the south of the Potala was occupied by the PLA military headquarters and Chinese government offices. The one-floor department store was adjacent to the Guest House. Some items in the store, particularly packaged food items, were actually for sale, while others, mostly locally made handicrafts, were for display only. I was able to buy tinned ground coffee from Shanghai and canned peaches, from where I don't know. There was also canned tuna, convenient for trips outside Lhasa. To the west of the Potala was mostly new Chinese housing, with the exception of the Norbulinka, formerly the Dalai Lama's summer palace, now a "People's Park." Old photos of Lhasa show almost nothing between the old city and the Potala except the *Yutok Samba*, or Turquoise Bridge, which could still be found now hidden among other buildings. Now the whole area was filled with ugly, drab, and undistinguished buildings.

There was not a single private hotel and only one restaurant to be found in the area between the Jokhang and Potala. The only Tibetan establishment that could be called a restaurant was near the Jokhang. It had *thukpa*, or noodle soup, and *momos*, meat-filled dumplings, but it was dirty and filled with beggars. The Guest House had meals of cabbage soup and steamed buns (*baozi* in Chinese, *ti momo* in Tibetan). At the rear of the Guest House there was a small VIP annex where Chinese officials stayed and a solar bath house where anyone could buy a ticket for a hot shower. The two Tibetan exile delegations that had so far visited Tibet had stayed there and it was the scene of demonstrations by Tibetans during both the first delegation visit in 1979 and the second in 1980.

The delegations were sent from Dharamsala, India, home of the Tibetan government in exile, after Deng Xiaoping invited the Dalai Lama's brother, Gyalo Thondup, to send representatives to see how things had changed in Tibet. Deng presumably thought that conditions were so improved that the exiles would be sufficiently impressed to give up their exile and return to China. Chinese officials in Tibet had typically lied to Beijing about how loyal Tibetans were, or perhaps they deceived themselves with their own propaganda. They were shocked to find that Tibetans still revered the Dalai Lama and had not given up their desire for independence. The demonstrations in 1979 led to the arrest of some Tibetans who had shouted slogans for Tibetan independence; more demonstrations in 1980 led to the termination of the second delegation visit.

Most Tibetans still looked poverty-stricken, with dirty and patched clothes. Lhasa was traditionally a city of beggars, of course, Tibetans being famous for their generosity due to the good karma to be gained by giving to the poor. Lhasa was still full of beggars, this being something the Chinese had done little to change. Both Chinese and Tibetans wore the shapeless Chinese proletarian shirts and trousers in green and blue. Some village or poor Tibetans wore the traditional chuba but usually in a very patched and torn state. Lhasa was still extraordinarily colorful, despite Chinese attempts to "proletarianize" Tibetans and their city. They had made Tibetans abandon their colorful costumes and the prayer flags, door curtains, and door and window awnings of their houses. The colorful interior decorations were painted over. It was as if the Chinese wanted to remove all that was colorful, joyous, or unique about Tibet and Tibetans and replace it with the drab uniformity and sterility of Chinese proletarianism.

Even the Chinese had been unable to change some unique Tibetan characteristics, however, like the extraordinary Tibetan climate, which made Tibet so unlike not only China but any other country. Lhasa lies at 12,000 feet (approximately 3,700 meters) and is surrounded by peaks that reach 18,000 feet (almost 5,500 meters). The dry air and the high altitude created a stimulating sense of otherworldliness that even the Chinese could not deflate. The air was of a sparkling clarity that stimulated the senses and the night sky was magnificent with innumerable stars. The dramatic changes and extremes in the weather only added to the sensual excitement of the Tibetan atmosphere. The climate is dry but remnants of the Indian monsoon reach the plateau in the summer, producing dramatic thunderstorms, hailstorms, and rainbows.

Everything about Lhasa was less colorful and certainly less Tibetan than it had been before, but the Potala still loomed in all its majesty over the city and proclaimed its uniquely Tibetan character. The Potala is indisputably the finest example of Tibetan architecture and one of the architectural wonders of the world. The Chinese had tried to claim the Potala as an example of the skill of the "Chinese people," an unsubtle way of saying that Tibetans are Chinese, but the distinctive way its soaring architecture fits into the Tibetan landscape proclaims it entirely Tibetan. The Potala seems to grow out of the rock of the Marpori hill upon which it is built, its golden temple roofs giving it the appearance of soaring toward the vast Tibetan sky. The Potala dominates the landscape of Lhasa and provides a thrilling sight from any angle and any distance.

The 300-foot high (100 meter) Marpori (Red Hill) upon which the Potala stands was first used as a fortress palace by Srongtsan Gampo in the seventh century. Some of the original palace still exists in the lower level of the Potala. The structure as it now appears was built by the Fifth Dalai Lama in the mid-seventeenth century. The White Palace, built by the Fifth Dalai Lama, was meant for his residence and for Tibetan government offices and functions. The large assembly hall in the White Palace was used for governmental functions like meetings with foreign dignitaries and enthronements of Dalai Lamas. The Red Palace was built mostly after the Fifth Dalai Lama's death by his regent, Sangey Gyatso, who concealed the death of the Dalai Lama for twelve years in order to finish the palace. The Red Palace was built to house the reliquary chorten of the Fifth Dalai Lama and to house the Dalai Lama's personal Namgyal Monastery. The Red Palace assembly hall was used for religious functions as in any monastery. Additions were made to house the reliquary chortens of subsequent Dalai Lamas, each of which is indicated by a golden temple roof directly above it. The most substantial addition was made for the very large chorten of the Thirteenth Dalai Lama when he died in 1933.

The walls of the Potala are massive at the base and taper toward the top, another distinctive characteristic of both Tibetan monastic and domestic architecture. This gives a receding effect that makes the Potala seem even more lofty. The effect is accentuated on the Potala and most Tibetan buildings by the exterior window trim, a painted black border that is wider at the bottom than the top and adds to the receding effect. The broad white front of the building was used to display huge thankas during religious festivals. At the top of the Potala there is a frieze of darker maroon that distinguishes all Tibetan monasteries. The band is composed of branches of the tamarisk bush cut in short lengths and placed with the ends outward. These bands can be a few feet in height to several feet as on the Potala. The irregular ends of the sticks painted a dark maroon give an effect of depth almost like velvet.

The Potala was open a few days every week. I went at the first opportunity. You had to buy a ticket, but then you could explore all day long if you wished. You entered by ascending the long stairway that goes up first to the left and then to the right as one faces the Potala. The entrance continues up a long, sloping corridor through the building on the right side and then turns left and emerges in the large courtyard in which the religious *Cham* dances used to be held. A group of Tibetan women there were tamping down the earthen surface of the courtyard and singing as they did so. From this courtyard one enters the central part of the Potala via a series of stairways that lead to the top of the building. On the top floor are the Dalai Lama's empty quarters and the rooftop from where he used to observe his subjects through a telescope. On the western side of the rooftop one can see the Chinese-style pagoda structures.

From the roof one wends down through different floors and innumerable shrine and relic rooms, always clockwise in the circumambulation fashion, until you reach the lowest levels of the Potala dating from the empire period of the seventh century. In the oldest cave-like chamber are statues of Srongtsan Gampo, who unified Tibet, and his queens Bhrikuti from Nepal and Wencheng from China. Bhrikuti is placed to the left of Srongtsan Gampo and Wencheng is to the left of Bhrikuti, one place removed, because Bhrikuti preceded her as queen. Despite their claim that Wencheng began the "inevitable unification" of Tibet and China, the Chinese have not removed Bhrikuti or altered her place in this oldest shrine of the Potala. Also on the lowest level are the large chortens of the previous Dalai Lamas, those of the "Great Fifth" and the "Great Thirteenth" Dalai Lamas extending up many stories through the building almost to the roof.

Despite its massive size, the Potala, like all Tibetan monasteries, is ingeniously built to allow light to reach the interior all the way down to the lower levels. The Potala is thus not a mass of dark chambers, as it might seem from its outside appearance, but a surprisingly light and livable space with interior illumination and delightful sun-filled atriums at the center of each main structure. Both the White and Red Palaces are rectangular structures of many stories, the lower levels being filled with massive assembly halls of two interior stories each into which light penetrates by means of skylights. Above the assembly halls of each palace are multistoried atriums built like small interior temples, each level diminishing in size like a pyramid. The upper-level atriums do not reach the height of the surrounding walls; thus, they are protected from the wind but still receive plentiful sunlight. They are now glassed but originally must have been protected by wooden shutters. These central atriums are like sunrooms that were probably reserved for high lamas and the Dalai Lama himself. There is sufficient space around this central structure to allow light to reach into the interior of the building and at least partially illuminate shrines on all levels.

Since there were no tourists in Lhasa, foreign or Chinese, the Potala was filled exclusively with Tibetan pilgrims. There were also none of the cameras and listening devices that the Chinese would later install. Each relic room had caretakers who were usually willing to let you sit with them in one of the windows that look out over Lhasa. I returned to the Potala many times and spent many hours with these caretakers or just sitting on the roof near the pagodas and observing the city of Lhasa below. It was on my first visit, however, that the most memorable event occurred. I sat down with two Tibetans on the stairway entrance from the first courtyard. I attempted to ask a simple question in Tibetan about conditions in Lhasa. My question was innocuous but the reply was profound. "*Rangzen mindu*," said one of them. "No freedom." Then they left, perhaps in fear of the possible consequences of what they had said. This was my introduction to the reality of life for Tibetans.

Beneath the Potala is the area known as Shol, site of several Tibetan government buildings, the most prominent of which is the Parkhang Chenmo, or Great Printing House, built in 1926 by the Thirteenth Dalai Lama to replace the old printing house. The new printing house, where religious texts were printed from woodblocks, is a massive structure whose size is not apparent because it is overshadowed by the Potala. The printing house has the largest interior hall in Lhasa, larger even that the assembly halls of the Potala. The interior hall, meant to create space for woodblock printing, is three stories high, supported by eighty wooden pillars. Another building to the rear once housed a standing Maitreya (Buddha of the Future) statue in an interior space four stories high, lit by a skylight. Other Tibetan government buildings at Shol are the original printing house, Shol Parkhang; a government office building, Shol Lekhung; a Tibetan Army building, Magshikhang; and a paper money printing house, Ngu Barkhang.[1]

Other buildings in the Shol area include stables for horses, one-story houses, and the famous Potala Prison, incongruously named Shol Dekyiling, or "Happiness Place," a name not meant to intentionally taunt prisoners, as it may seem, but the original name of the residential house that was later converted into use as a prison. The house is small with an interior courtyard around which are the few cells. The interior is dark because the courtyard is small and does not allow much light, but the cells are not underground, like a dungeon, as is sometimes thought. Chinese propaganda makes much of the supposedly infamous Shol Prison, where Tibetans were supposed to have been starved and stung by scorpions. One Tibetan acquaintance, Tseten Wangchuk, later told me about the Chinese making a propaganda film about the Shol Prison in which they wanted to show a scorpion on a prisoner. But the scorpion wouldn't stay still, so it had to be tied with a string onto an actor's body in order to show how Tibetans were tortured!

Tseten Wangchuk also claimed to have been the model for one of the life-size clay sculptures in the "Wrath of the Serfs" exhibition that used to occupy the Museum of the Tibetan Revolution at the southeastern corner of the Shol area, just outside the wall. One of the sculptures depicted a small boy trying to resist an evil lama who wants to use him as a ritual sacrifice for the construction of a temple, a practice not current in Tibet in the twentieth century, if ever, but a popular theme of Chinese propaganda about old feudal Tibet. The exhibition was supposed to show how Tibetans had suffered as serfs before being liberated by the Chinese. The museum, built in 1965 for the inauguration of the Tibet Autonomous Region, was still there in 1982, but had been closed when the liberalization began, perhaps on the orders of Hu Yaobang, who might have thought this sort of propaganda insulting to Tibetans and unsuitable for foreign tourists. Later, even the building was removed and the location of the sculptures, which are rumored to have been preserved, is a mystery.

In front of the Potala, on the south side of Dekyi Shar Lam, is a stone pillar commemorating the Tibetan capture of the Tang dynasty capital of Changan, now Xian, in 763. Some of the text on the pillar is damaged, by Chinese, according to Tibetans, during the period in 1910–1912 when China invaded in response to the British invasion of 1904 and the Dalai Lama sought exile in India. The damaged text supposedly lists the Chinese cities captured by the Tibetans.

Behind the Potala is the lovely Lukhang, or Naga Temple, on a small island in a pond created when clay was dug out to make mortar for the building of the Potala. The Lukhang was built by the Sixth Dalai Lama around 1695 to fulfill the promise made to the *nagas*, or serpent spirits, to build a temple for them if they would allow the digging of the earth there for the construction of the Potala. The temple is reached by a stone bridge. The small pond was a popular boating place for the Lhasa aristocracy. The three-story temple interior is decorated with unique wall paintings depicting tantric subjects.

The Potala is Lhasa's most prominent and most famous structure, but the Jokhang is its most sacred. When the Potala attained its present magnificent form in the late seventeenth century, the Jokhang had already been the center of the Tibetan spiritual universe for a thousand years. The

Jokhang is the destination for Buddhist pilgrims from all over Tibet and beyond and the first site they visit in Lhasa. A Tibetan saying, no doubt apocryphal, is that pilgrims, upon reaching Lhasa, do not even have a cup of tea before visiting the Jokhang. The Jokhang, or Tsuklhakhang (Central Cathedral), is the center of the old Tibetan part of Lhasa.

In 1982 the Jokhang was still approached via a narrow street, allowing it a pleasant seclusion. The approaching street was lined with old buildings on the northern side and the street itself was filled with merchants, beggars, and pilgrims, giving it a decidedly medieval atmosphere. I remember a street dentist with a foot-powered drill among the sights of this street. (Many years later I learned that the US Army used foot-powered dentist drills for field use in World War II. Given that Tibet was full of US Army surplus articles after the war and even to recent times, the drill I saw may have been made in the USA!) In 1985 the Chinese demolished the buildings in front of the Jokhang to create a plaza. The Jokhang is not an imposing building from the outside; the effect of the plaza was thus to diminish its appearance. The special character of the Jokhang is due to its contents, the sacredness of which was accentuated by its seclusion, now reduced by its exposure.

In front of the Jokhang was a small stone enclosure within which was a stone stele on which is carved the treaty of 823 between the Tibetan Empire and Tang dynasty China that ended an almost two-century period of warfare between Tibet and China. Tibet was mostly the victor in these wars, establishing control over the Tibetan Plateau and making incursions beyond, including into the Tarim Basin of what is now Xinjiang, controlling the area of Dunhuang, and briefly capturing the Tang capital at Changan, now Xian. The stele acknowledges Tibetan successes by declaring the mutual recognition by both Tibet and China of their separate territories and establishing the border between them. Tibetans emphasize the lines of the treaty that say that Tibet and China are separate countries, each of whose borders shall not be violated, and that Tibetans should be happy in the land of Tibet and Chinese in the land of China. The Chinese emphasize the line that says that China and Tibet have a relationship like uncle and nephew, meaning that Tibet should be subordinate to China.

Within the stone enclosure was a dead tree propped up by a pole that was supposed to be the willow tree planted by Wencheng in the seventh century. The tree was now little more than a stick, Tibetans saying that it died shortly after the Chinese invaded Tibet. The stone enclosure was preserved when the plaza was built in 1985, as was the treaty stele, but the dead tree was replaced with a living one.

I went every evening to the Jokhang to observe the Tibetans prostrating in front of the temple and to participate in the daily *kora*, or circumambulation of the Jokhang around the Barkhor. Barkhor means "middle kora." The inner kora, *nangkor*, is inside the Jokhang, while the outer kora, *lingkor*, is a 5-mile (7.5 km.) route circling the old city, the Potala and Chakpori (leaving out the Norbulinka). The Barkhor is a broad promenade with shops on both sides and lined with street vendors. The Jokhang and the Barkhor were the place to be in the evening. Many Tibetans did their daily prostrations and circumambulations after work. Since Lhasa was on Beijing time, it didn't get dark until almost midnight. All of China is on one time zone, the rulers in Beijing apparently being uncomfortable with nonconformity even in regard to time, or perhaps this reflects their insecurity about control over all of their empire. Tibetans had to go to work in the morning in darkness and the sun didn't set until midnight, which must have been a daily reminder of China's paranoid insistence upon control over all aspects of Tibetans' lives.

The Barkhor is the center of life for most Lhasa Tibetans. Every morning and evening, thousands of the devout would do their kora around the Barkhor, allowed since 1980, often making several circuits. Many Lhasa residents were there every day and there were also Tibetans from all over the plateau, many in the traditional colorful costumes representative of each of their areas. Tibetans from outside Lhasa, and particularly those from eastern Tibetan areas outside the Tibet Autonomous Region (TAR), had until recently been prohibited from traveling to Lhasa. Since the liberalization began in 1980, Tibetans from all over the plateau had been flocking to Lhasa to do the religious pilgrimages they had been unable to do for years. Conspicuous among them were the nomads in their traditional sheepskin chubas and the nomad women with their long, braided hair, the braids supposed to be 108 in number.

Often attached to the end of the braids was a horizontal ribbon of corals and turquoises. Several pretty nomad girls with ruddy cheeks were so adorned and were the shy subjects of my photography attempts. A joke among the foreigners in Lhasa that summer was that Tibetans around the Barkhor were so colorful and attractive that one could set up an automatic camera to take photos at random intervals and still come up with fantastic photographs.

Everything was for sale around the Barkhor. One could find traditional Tibetan products as well as articles from Nepal, China, and almost anywhere in the world. There were contemporary articles from all over the world as well as artifacts like old Tibetan coins and paper money. In front of the Jokhang, khatags, or silk scarves, were available as offerings for the deities inside. I remember finding Nescafé instant coffee from Nepal and meeting some of the half-Tibetan, half-Newari traders from Nepal known as Katsara, with whom I could speak in Nepali. I also recall that PLA soldiers in small groups intentionally went around the Barkhor circuit the wrong way. I couldn't resist bumping into one or more of them. I also saw an old Chinese woman with bound feet toddling around the Barkhor, just like the Tibetans. Occasionally, particularly tall Tibetan men, usually Khampas from Eastern Tibet, approached me, standing shoulder to shoulder, and drawing a hand quickly along my shoulder to mark their height. Those few who matched my 6 feet 3 inches were considerably proud of themselves.

The area in front of the Jokhang was always full of Tibetans doing prostrations. Many had a goal of several thousand prostrations, so they would lay leather pads or rugs on the smooth flat stones and be there all day. The stones were rubbed smooth by hundreds of years of such use. This area had been blocked off by an iron fence until only the year before. Films made of the first delegation visit to the Jokhang in August 1979 show the delegation members within the fence and hundreds of Tibetans outside pushing and shoving and clamoring to get in to meet them. One of the delegation members was Lobsang Samten, the Dalai Lama's younger brother, whom the Tibetans were most desperate to greet. Finally, they managed to break through the gate in the iron fence and then mob the delegation members, lifting them on their shoulders, sobbing uncontrollably, and tearing away pieces of their clothes and even their hair in their frenzy.

This was one of the first events that so surprised the Chinese, who had warned Tibetans not to spit on or throw rocks at the "representatives of the serf-owners," whom the Chinese had attempted to teach them to hate by years of propaganda. The iron fence, which had prevented Tibetans either entering the Jokhang or doing prostrations in front of it from the time of the Cultural Revolution, was a visible symbol of the Chinese Communist policy on religion. They made every attempt to eradicate religion and were actually surprised that their propaganda and prohibitions had not convinced Tibetans, many of whom went to the Jokhang to make offerings and do prostrations as soon as they were allowed. The remnants of the iron fence could still be seen embedded in the paving stones.

Every day there were dozens of people doing prostrations before the Jokhang and every day, when it was open, there were thousands of pilgrims visiting. One could sit outside and watch the prostrators and those doing kora, or one could sit inside, in a spot in front of the Jowo, the Buddha image that is Tibet's holiest religious icon and the goal of every pilgrim, and watch the colorful Tibetans as they made their offerings. The Jowo is the statue of Buddha brought to Tibet in the seventh century by Wencheng, the Chinese bride of the Tibetan king, Srongtsan Gampo. The statue is of Indian origin, having been presented by the king of Magadha to Wencheng's father, Tang Taizong. But the Jokhang was built by the king's bride from Nepal, Bhrikuti, who preceded Wencheng by almost ten years. Bhrikuti also brought a Buddha image that was originally installed in the Jokhang. Wencheng built the second most sacred shrine, the Ramoche, sometimes called the Ramoche Tsuklhakhang, and her Buddha statue was originally there. The Ramoche is also known as Gyatak, or "Chinese temple," further confirming its association with Wencheng.

The site of the Jokhang was supposed to have been suggested to Bhrikuti by Wencheng for geomantic reasons. Since the site was a small lake or marshland, inhabited by serpent spirits or nagas (*Lu* in Tibetan), Bhrikuti supposedly suspected that Wencheng was jealous of her attempt to build the first Buddhist temple. Bhrikuti consulted Srongtsan Gampo, who consulted his tutelary deity, who confirmed the choice of site. Bhrikuti and Srongtsan Gampo went to the lake, whereupon a stupa magically arose from the water. This story is almost identical to that of the self-arisen (*svayambhu*) stupa that arose in the Naga Lake of Nepal and became the first Buddhist temple of Nepal. It seems that part of the mythology of Nepal was transferred through the Nepalese princess Bhrikuti to the mythology of the founding of the Jokhang in Lhasa.[2]

The lake was then filled in with timbers in a grid pattern, as illustrated in paintings in the Potala and Norbulinka, and the Jokhang temple was built in the Nepalese style by Nepalese artisans. Its original name was Trulnang Tsuklhakhang, meaning self-arisen temple, a Tibetan version of the Svayambhu stupa in Kathmandu. At the time that the Jokhang was built, Bhrikuti's brother, Narendradeva, was in exile in Lhasa, along with his followers and many Newari artisans, who worked on the construction and decoration of the Jokhang. Narendradeva returned to Nepal to become king in 641, just as the Jokhang was being finished.

Wencheng is supposed to have arrived in Lhasa only in 641, so the legend of her choice of the site for the Jokhang, which must have been started several years earlier, may reflect the rivalry that developed between the elder queen, Bhrikuti, and the younger rival, Wencheng. Wencheng also brought with her experts in architecture, agriculture, medicine, and other subjects, igniting a competition for cultural influence in Lhasa. China now claims that the arrival of Wencheng in Lhasa inaugurated Tibetan cultural development and began the "inevitable merging of nationalities" leading to Tibet's present incorporation in China's "big family of the Motherland."

The orientation of the Jokhang and Ramoche confirm their original associations with the two princesses. Almost every other temple and monastery in Tibet faces to the south, to collect the warmth of the sun, with architectural innovations to allow the sun to enter into the inner sanctuaries. But the Jokhang faces to the west, directly toward Nepal, or toward the route to Nepal, and the Ramoche faces east, toward China. The site layout of the Jokhang is said to be based upon the Indian Buddhist Vihara style while the architectural style is that of the Newari Buddhists of Nepal. The Ramoche is said to have a ground-level plan based upon the Indian Vihara style while the second-floor architecture is Tibetan and the third floor and roof is the Chinese temple style. The Ramoche is taller than the Jokhang because of its prominent Chinese temple-style roof and, at a time when the two were the tallest buildings in Lhasa, their relative heights may have reflected the rivalry between the two queens and, perhaps, between Nepal and China for influence in Tibet.

At some time in Tibetan history the Buddha images in each of the temples were switched for reasons that remain mysterious even to Tibetan historians. The Chinese Jowo (Jowo Sakyamuni) thus ended up in the Jokhang and the Nepalese Jowo (Jowo Aksobhyavajra) was in the Ramoche. Why the Nepalese Jowo was moved to the Ramoche and the Chinese Jowo to the Jokhang is the subject of several unconvincing legends. The most persistent story is that the Chinese Jowo was removed to the Jokhang—some say by Wencheng, who is supposed to have lived until about 680—and was concealed there due to the rumor of an approaching Tang Chinese Army. Why Wencheng would be unable to defend the statue against a Tang army is unexplained. The Tang army, according to one version of the story, entered Lhasa briefly and carried off the Nepalese Jowo but got only a short distance away before abandoning the statue, which was then installed in the Ramoche for some mysterious and unexplained reason. Some Tibetan historians say that the Tang army story is a fabrication.

The Chinese Jowo remained concealed in the Jokhang until it was removed from its hiding place and installed as the central image in the Jokhang by a later Chinese princess, Jincheng, who arrived in Lhasa in 710 as bride for the Tibetan king Megasthom. There are other versions of the story, none of which offer an adequate explanation for the switching of the images. The switch may reflect the legacy of the rivalry for influence in Tibet. The Jokhang had already become the center of Lhasa and the primary site of religious pilgrimage and devotion, while the Ramoche was decidedly secondary. Jincheng may have decided to correct this situation by placing Wencheng's Jowo at the center of the Jokhang and thus at the center of devotion. It may be that she was also responsible for the removal of the Nepalese Jowo to the Ramoche, an event intentionally obscured by the legends.

After the 1959 revolt, the Jokhang Jowo was preserved, but the Ramoche Jowo, or at least its top half, disappeared. It was only found in China, returned, reunited with the bottom half that was found in Lhasa, and replaced in the Ramoche in 1985. The Jowo brought from China became Tibet's most holy image and thus Wencheng is credited, especially in Chinese sources, with having been instrumental in bringing Buddhism to Tibet. But her image achieved its sacred status only because it was moved to Bhrikuti's Jokhang, Tibet's first and most sacred Buddhist temple. Bhrikuti and Nepalese Buddhist influences were thus probably more significant than those of China in introducing Buddhism to Tibet.

The Jokhang that was built in the seventh century was a square, Vihara-style temple built to house the Jowo. Later additions included an inner kora, the nangkor, decorated with 108 paintings depicting scenes from the life of the Buddha, a courtyard at the entrance to the temple, and then subsidiary buildings that eventually housed the Jokhang's monks as well as several Tibetan government offices. The temple reaches as high as four stories at some places and is decorated with Chinese-style gilded roofs, as are many of the temples and monasteries of Lhasa. One enters the Jokhang past prostrating pilgrims and through the massive front gate into the main courtyard. From the courtyard one enters the original temple, which is lighted only by butter lamps and has an appropriate atmosphere of darkness, ancient sanctity, and medieval mysteriousness.

There are numerous statues and shrines in the Jokhang to which pilgrims offer money and butter for the constantly burning lamps, but the Jowo is by far the most important. The statue was almost obscured behind the thousands of khatags that pilgrims throw upon it. I was told that every night the Chinese took all the money offerings and they even took the butter to be used in a government bakery. Chinese rarely if ever entered the Jokhang, making it one of the last of the totally Tibetan places in Lhasa. But one day as I was sitting before the Jowo, making my observations of Tibetan pilgrims, a young PLA soldier came strutting through the pilgrims, going the wrong way of course. Perhaps, like those of his comrades who went the wrong way around the Barkhor, he thought he was educating the Tibetans about the futility of their religion. But it may have just been confrontational and intended to intimidate, to show the Tibetans who their master was. As he approached, I stood up and blocked his way, motioning with one hand for him to turn around and go back the same way he came. His previously arrogant demeanor collapsed into shock at being confronted by this previously unobserved and very tall foreigner and he meekly turned around and went back. He was the only Chinese and certainly the only PLA soldier I ever saw in the Jokhang.

Beyond the Jokhang and the Barkhor is the old Tibetan city of narrow alleys and old manor houses. The streets, too narrow for vehicles, give the old city a medieval character and uniqueness that contrasts with what has been built around it in modern times. Directly behind the Jokhang is the Meru Nyingpa Temple (which means Old Meru), so named to distinguish it from the larger Meru Monastery nearby with which it was affiliated. Meru Nyingpa is supposed to date from the seventh century and is said to have been the place where Thonmi Sambhota, who was sent by Srongtsan Gampo to India to acquire a script for the Tibetan language, finished his creation of the alphabetic Tibetan script. The Tibetan choice of an alphabetic script of Indian origin, instead of the more archaic Chinese-style script based on pictographic characters, demonstrates the Tibetan orientation toward India and Nepal rather than China, despite later Chinese claims to the contrary. Meru Nyingpa was later the Lhasa seat of the Nechung oracle. It, like the adjacent Jokhang, suffered damage from Red Guard vandalism during the Cultural Revolution and was used as a granary and stable.

The old city is a fascinating maze that took many days to explore. There seemed to be an endless number of narrow alleys that invited exploration. I admired the magnificent granite stone construction of the old manor houses that were often to be found inside plain, nondescript gateways. Monastic buildings and old government buildings also were constructed of granite, each course of large stones divided by a layer of small stone chips that is characteristic of Tibetan building techniques. The old manor houses are now divided up into small apartments and assigned to a variety of Tibetan families. I later became familiar with one such manor house, that of the aristocratic family of Phala, just off the southeast corner of the Barkhor.

Another fine example of Tibetan stone architecture is the old Lhasa municipal building and jail, the Nangtsesha, on the north side of the Barkhor. The Nangtsesha jail was the Lhasa city jail, while that at Shol was the state jail. The Lhasa city jail had only eight small cells; nevertheless, the Chinese later turned it and the Shol prison into museums of the evils of the old Tibetan society, despite the fact that they themselves had imprisoned tens of thousands of Tibetans and created a vast complex of prisons and labor camps, as well as smaller prisons in every village and town. I also discovered the old Nepalese embassy, a magnificent building of fine stone work in a secluded courtyard to the south of the Barkhor. To the east of the Barkhor there is a small mosque for the Ladakhi Tibetan Muslims. The mosque had an outdoor teahouse under a grove of trees where one could have Arab-style mint tea.

To the north of the Barkhor there is a section of the old city surrounding the Ramoche Temple, divided from the Barkhor area by a straight road that begins in front of the Potala, named Dekyi Shar Lam by Tibetans and Beijing Street by the Chinese. This street was once a narrow, crooked lane but was straightened and widened by the Chinese with the result that the old city is now more than ever divided into two sections around the Jokhang and Ramoche, respectively. There was previously a long mani wall here and the entrance to Ramoche Lam was much wider, as is visible from pre-1950 maps. The mani wall, along with a chorten and an incense burner, were in front of the Jebumgang Lhakhang on the entrance to the Ramoche Lam, the whole area being something of an inner-city plaza which must have been one of the more pleasant spots of Lhasa. Now there is only a narrow entrance to the Ramoche Lam and the most holy building at the site, the Jebumgang Lhakhang, is in ruins.

The Jebumgang Temple was at this time surrounded by more recent shoddy constructions, including a public toilet, and was impossible to reach. The site was once a chorten containing 100,000 (*bum*) clay mold images of Je Tsongkhapa, the founder of the Gelugpa sect of which the Dalai Lamas were the heads. The chorten collapsed into a heap (*gang*) at the end of the nineteenth century and a temple, or lhakhang, was built to house the clay images. The Jebumgang Lhakhang was a small, square, three-story temple with a prominent gilded roof that once stood out in the Lhasa skyline. There were four smaller roof turrets on each of the building's corners. The Jebumgang Lhakhang was once one of the finest examples of Tibetan sacred architecture and decoration and one of the most sacred pilgrimage sites. It was damaged and closed after 1959 and until recently was used as a grain storage warehouse.

The Ramoche Tsuklhakhang still showed the damage it had suffered during the 1959 revolt, when it was partially burned, and during the Cultural Revolution. The roof area was particularly damaged, but the interior was intact except that all religious statues and implements had been removed and the wall paintings were damaged. In the place where the Jowo formerly was there was now a huge portrait of Mao, the Ramoche having been used until recently as a site for neighborhood committee meetings and public indoctrination. Mao's presence in the second most holy temple in Lhasa appeared to signify the Chinese attempt to substitute his image for that of the Buddha in Tibetans' minds and as the object of their reverence. In the fifteenth century, Ramoche became the Upper Tantric College, or *Gyuto*, with as many as 500 monks from Drepung, Sera, and Ganden studying there. The temple was extensively restored by the Fifth Dalai Lama in the mid-seventeenth century. Ramoche was restored in 1985 and the Jowo image, since recovered from a warehouse in China where images were stored before being melted down, was returned in a procession from the Jokhang where the image was restored to the Ramoche.

The Potala, Jokhang, and Ramoche are Lhasa's most famous historical sites, and they, along with Drepung and Sera and the more distant Ganden, are the most famous temples and monasteries of the Lhasa area. Drepung and Sera were the home of as many as 10,000 monks and, if Ganden is added, then there were as many as 20,000 monks in the Lhasa area, who would fill the city for religious events. Less well-known is that there were several very large monasteries within the city, all of which were now destroyed or damaged, and none of which had any remaining religious functions. Despite their very large size, these monasteries were somewhat difficult to find since they now had different functions and were surrounded by more recent structures. They could be located by their dark maroon friezes. Old photos of Lhasa show these monasteries as prominent landmarks. Their size indicates that their monk populations could have totaled several thousand, revealing that Lhasa was not just a secular city—with some temples and holy sites but with most of the monk population outside the city—but that it was inhabited by thousands of monks.

From the roof of the Jokhang, one could see to the north several very large buildings whose maroon friezes revealed them to have been temples or monasteries. All were on the north side of the Dekyi Shar Lam, two to the west of Ramoche Lam and two to the east. Having spotted these large monastic structures from the Jokhang, one could then go and find them on the ground. They turned out to be, from west to east, or from left to right as viewed from the Jokhang: Shide, Tsemoling, Gyume, and Meru Monasteries. Each was once a large monastic college (*dratsang*), second only in size to the great monastic universities, Drepung, Sera, and Ganden, each of which were composed of several dratsangs. Meru and Gyume were now obscured by other buildings, while Shide was in an advanced state of destruction and Tsemoling was being used for secular housing.

Of these four great monasteries, Shide Dratsang had suffered the most damage. One had to do some exploration to find it as it was surrounded by other housing, some of which was converted from the former monks' dormitories. What was left of Shide was now a scene of dramatic ruins. On what remained of interior walls were paintings defaced during the frenzy of the Cultural Revolution and slogans scribbled by Red Guards. Other monasteries in or near Lhasa had suffered similar damage, but Shide was the only one where it appeared that little or no attempt had been made to clean up the ruins. It thus gave an impression of only recently having been raided by Red Guards. Shide was closed and looted by the Chinese authorities after 1959, and nearly completely destroyed during the Cultural Revolution. Shide is still a magnificent ruin—its massive size perhaps preventing its total destruction, the remains revealing that it was once a truly impressive example of Tibetan monastic architecture. Even its ruins are of a massive size, with enough of its original four stories still intact to create an image of its former size and imposing presence.

Shide was founded by the Tibetan king Ralpacan in the early ninth century as one of the lhakhangs meant to surround and protect the Jokhang. It was originally very small, meant to house (*de*) only four (*shi*) monks. In the fourteenth century it became associated with Reting Monastery and was the residence of the Reting Rinpoche when he was in Lhasa. Shide became a large monastic complex in the typical style, with its entrance from the south into a courtyard surrounded on three sides with monks' cells, and its main temple, or lhakhang, at the northern end. Shide's main lhakhang, parts of which are still standing, is four stories in height and was formerly one of the most prominent buildings in Lhasa. Its courtyard is very large, some 150 feet (about 50 meters) across by 200 feet in length (approximately 60 meters), with two stories of monks' cells of varying size on three sides, with an inner veranda on the upper floor, perhaps 100 such cells in total, indicating that Shide could have housed several hundred or even a thousand monks. Its eventual large size was due to its association with the Reting Rinpoches, some of whom were regents during the minority of Dalai Lamas.

Tsemoling Dratsang is just to the northeast of Shide. It suffered less destruction and was converted to housing. Tsemoling is built in the same style as Shide, with a southern entrance to a very large courtyard surrounded by two stories of monks' cells. The only difference is that Tsemoling has two lhakhangs at its northern end. It is not as old as Shide, having been built in the eighteenth and nineteenth centuries. It was associated with Drepung's Loseling college. Like almost all of Lhasa's and Tibet's monasteries, it was closed and then looted after the 1959 revolt. Almost all its religious artifacts are gone and all its decorations are damaged or eradicated but the building itself survived, with the exception of a third story on the main lhakhang that is now missing. Tsemoling was almost as large and prominent as Shide, its temple roof being three rather than four stories and therefore somewhat less prominent on the Lhasa skyline. Like Shide, its size indicates that it could have housed hundreds of monks. Both Shide and Tsemoling were of fine architectural style and construction and were reportedly very finely decorated. Before 1950 both Shide and Tsemoling were isolated from other buildings. The nearest building was Ramoche. The area was dotted with streams and parks (*linka*) and each monastery had a lovely small summer house of fine architecture and construction in the open area to the north. Each of the summer houses is still existent but is so surrounded by other constructions as to be almost impossible to find.

On the eastern end of Dekyi Shar Lam are the equally large monasteries, Gyume and Meru. Meru is also known as Meru Sarpa, "New Meru," to distinguish it from Meru Nyingpa, "Old Meru." Both Gyume and Meru are magnificent examples of Tibetan architecture. Like Tsemoling, each suffered looting and damage to decorations like wall paintings but little structural damage. Both now serve secular purposes, Gyume being used as grain storage and housing and Meru housing the Lhasa dance and drama troupe and their costumes and equipment. Neither monastery, despite its size, is obvious from the street. Gyume is behind a long apartment building that now fronts on the street. Meru's long three-story row of monks' cells on its southern entrance formerly occupied some 250 feet (nearly 80 meters) of street frontage on Dekyi Shar Lam but are now obscured by small shops. Meru is much the larger of the two, being comparable in size and layout to Shide and Tsemoling, with a large courtyard bordered on three sides by rows of monks' cells. Gyume was supposed to be limited to 555 monks chosen from Drepung, Sera, and Ganden. A comparison in size to the other three monasteries indicates that each of the three larger monasteries could have housed a thousand monks or more.

Gyume Dratsang suffered the least structural damage of the four great monasteries along Dekyi Shar Lam. Gyume's four stories remain intact while Tsemoling's third story and Meru's fourth story have both been removed. Gyume thus might serve as a model for the restoration of both Meru and Tsemoling as well as Shide. Gyume was founded in the fifteenth century as the Lower Tantric College at the same time that Ramoche became the Upper Tantric College. The "upper" and "lower" designations refer to the physical site of each monastery rather than to their relative levels of Buddhist studies. Both tantric colleges were known for their scholarship, arcane rituals, and discipline. To find Gyume one has to go through the residential building in front. Once inside, Gyume is revealed as one of the most impressive of Lhasa's monastic buildings, even though all Buddhist artifacts and decorations are gone and the building is now divided into residential housing. Gyume does not have the traditional plan of a southern courtyard flanked by monks' cells. Gyume has an adjacent courtyard just to the west of the lhakhang. The Gyume monks were housed in a long two-story building on its west side that was demolished when the Dekyi Shar Lam was widened.

Gyume has a large (55 by 75 feet, or 17 by 23 meters) main assembly hall of forty-eight pillars with a two story central skylight section supported by four pillars. In the rear is a three-story inner altar room with eight pillars and a skylight on the third-floor level. The altar along the north wall once had three 15-foot tall (4.6-meter) clay statues of Je Tsongkapa and his two disciples. The inner sanctum is not open but it can be viewed through the skylight. The clay images are just piles of rubble and the walls show the usual signs of Red Guard defacement. The architectural effect of the skylight to the inner sanctum, which allowed sunlight to penetrate to the main images on the lower level, is very impressive, as is the skylight that illuminates the main assembly hall. Gyume is a fine architectural construction on all levels, from its innovative use of light to its fine stone and woodwork. When Gyume's Buddhist statues, wall paintings, thankas, and decorative woodwork were extant, it must have been an impressive sight indeed.

Meru Dratsang dates from the early ninth century and, like Shide, is supposed to have been founded by the Tibetan king Ralpacan. It may have been destroyed and rebuilt in the tenth century. It is said to have been the most important monastery in Lhasa before the Gelugpa era that began in the fifteenth century. Meru, like Shide and Tsemoling, has a large inner courtyard (120 by 150 feet, or nearly 40 by 50 meters) which is entered by an impressive gateway from the street. The courtyard was used for public indoctrination and struggle sessions, or thamzings, after 1959. The courtyard is lined with three stories of monks' cells on all sides and a double row of cells on the west side. It is now filled with a new building owned by the Lhasa Religious Affairs Department, which houses woodblocks for printing religious texts that survived the Cultural Revolution. Meru is the largest monastery of Lhasa in size and second only to the Jokhang as Lhasa's largest temple and monastic complex. The architectural layout is similar to Gyume, with a large 48-pillar assembly hall with a central skylight and a rear sanctum that is two stories in inner height, compared to Gyume's three stories. A fourth floor above the sanctum has been removed. As at Gyume, one can see into the damaged inner sanctum through a skylight. Meru is larger than Gyume but not quite so impressive in architecture, mostly because of the innovative placement of skylights at Gyume and its three-story inner sanctum.

Sera and Drepung Monasteries can be reached by bicycle rented at the Guest House. Sera Monastery sits at the northern edge of the Lhasa Valley about three miles from the center of the city. It is the smallest of the three great Gelugpa monasteries of Lhasa, having, according to tradition, 3,300 monks. Drepung supposedly had 7,700, while Ganden, which is about 25 miles east of Lhasa, was supposed to have had 5,500 monks. However, these were symbolic numbers indicating the traditional importance of each institution. While the numbers for Sera and Drepung were approximately accurate for most periods, Ganden may have had as many as 10,000 monks.

Sera was founded in 1419 by one of the disciples of Tsongkhapa. Its small size gives it a very pleasant atmosphere, like a well-situated small college in another country. At one time, Sera had three dratsangs or colleges: Sera Me for novices, Sera Je for monks from Kham, and Ngapa, the tantric college. It had thirty *kangtsens* or dormitories for monks from different areas of Tibet and beyond. There were paths between the great halls and small groves of trees where one could imagine monks congregating in the past. There were only a few monks remaining in 1982, so Sera, like most of the few surviving monasteries in Tibet, was like an empty museum, which was exactly what the Chinese intended. Sera had suffered little damage except that all of its lamas and monks were gone and all its religious and scholarly activities were no more. Its lhakhangs, or great monastic meeting halls, were all intact and statues, thankas, and decorations were all in place. The long rows of cushions that were formerly the seats of thousands of monks were now filled by only a few dozen. One could browse cabinets of precious metal statues as if visiting a museum.

Drepung was founded in 1416 by another disciple of Tsongkhapa. It suffered more damage than Sera, some of which is still visible. Drepung is situated at the northwestern edge of the Lhasa Valley about three or four miles from the city center. It appears as a small city of white buildings, hence the name Drepung, meaning "rice heap." In the early sixteenth century, a Drepung abbot built the Ganden Podrang, which became the name of the Tibetan government when this abbot was posthumously named as the second Dalai Lama. The Fifth Dalai Lama moved his residence and the government to the Potala in the late seventeenth century but retained the name Ganden Podrang. Drepung had four dratsangs and innumerable kangtsens. It was particularly known for its kangtsens for monks from Amdo and Kham as well as Mongolia, China, and Buddhist areas of Russia, like Buryatia, Tuva, and Kalmykia. Drepung's dratsangs were Loseling, which specialized in logic and had twenty-one kangtsens; Gomang, which had sixteen kangtsens made up of monks from Amdo, Kham, and Mongolia; Deyang for the study of medicine; and Ngapa, the tantric college.

Drepung has six large lhakhangs, one for each of its dratsangs, one for the Ganden Podrang, and one huge assembly hall, the Tsomchen. The Tsomchen is a massive building with a large courtyard and seventeen granite steps that give it an air of grandeur. The assembly hall is 150 feet (46 meters) wide by 100 feet (30 meters) deep and is supported by 183 wooden pillars. The central portion of the ceiling is raised to make an atrium and skylight. Most of the huge lhakhangs are intact, if empty, but one that had been destroyed still had propaganda slogans scratched on its walls. Below Drepung is Nechung, the monastery of the state oracle. The oracle was consulted in all the most important political decisions of the Tibetan government and was rumored to be subjected to bribery attempts by interested parties.

The Norbulinka summer palace is also reachable by bicycle or even by walking, being only about a mile directly west of the Potala. It was from here that the Dalai Lama fled in 1959. The Chinese opened it to the public and renamed it "People's Park." The Norbulinka is a large open area of trees and small palaces previously occupied by the Dalai Lama and his government during the summer months. The Norbulinka was first created by the Seventh Dalai Lama in the early eighteenth century, but most of its current buildings date from the time of the Thirteenth and the early years of the Fourteenth Dalai Lamas. It was somewhat damaged in 1959, but the Dalai Lama's residence and those of some previous Dalai Lamas are still intact. The Dalai Lama's palace has wall paintings depicting Tibetan history as well as the events of his time as Dalai Lama, including his meetings with British representatives of the Government of India. In one old structure on the grounds of the Norbulinka I discovered the remains of the Dalai Lama's old automobile, a small yellow Baby Austin, which had been carried in pieces over the mountains from India.

Ganden was founded in 1409 by Tsongkhapa himself as the main seat of his Gelugpa sect. Unlike all other Tibetan monasteries, the abbot of Ganden, or Ganden Tripa, was chosen not by heredity or incarnation but by scholastic merit from among the lamas of the Gelugpa monasteries of Lhasa. Ganden is about 30 miles (45 km.) east of Lhasa, too far to reach by bicycle. I was fortunate to meet a French geologist who was staying at the VIP guest house who invited me to share his jeep on a trip there. He was accompanied by a high-level official from Beijing and a driver. The gravel road to Ganden heads east for twenty miles or so on the main road to Sichuan, then turns off to the south on a narrow dirt track. The monastery is not visible until the road curves around toward the west and Ganden appears high above within a bowl-shaped mountain facing to the south. The track ascends to the monastery, or its remains, along a series of switchbacks. As you approach, the magnitude of the monastery and its destruction takes the breath away. Even the Chinese official seemed awestruck.

Ganden was at that time almost completely unrestored and appeared like a bombed city. Unlike some other monasteries, Ganden had been too big to completely eradicate. Most of the large structural timbers had been removed and some of the stone, but most of the stone walls of the buildings remained in a partially deconstructed state. Ganden is very remote and there are no large villages nearby, so it had not been possible to remove most of the stone. The Chinese were said to have resorted to explosives to destroy many of the largest buildings. Restoration work was being done on one or two of the largest buildings, but most of the huge complex was still in ruins. The restoration work was being done privately, by Tibetans themselves with no government assistance, although the government would later claim credit for the restoration.

We spent several hours there in constant awe at the magnitude of the destruction. As we prepared to leave, even the Chinese official seemed visibly moved; perhaps this sort of destruction was not what he had been told about Tibet. As we left, he said to the French geologist that he was moved not only by the magnitude of the destruction but by the Tibetan determination to rebuild this monument to their religion. Then he turned and said to his Chinese driver, "*Women keyi xia Xizang*," which I interpreted to mean, "We [Chinese] should leave [go down from] Tibet," or "It would be alright [*keyi*] if we left Tibet." The French geologist also shared my opinion that this was what he meant. If my interpretation is correct, then this would be the most extraordinary statement I heard from any Chinese about Tibet. He was apparently so shaken by the contradiction between what he had seen in the ruins of Ganden and what he had been taught about China's civilizing role in Tibet that he thought that China perhaps should leave the Tibetans to themselves, much as the treaty carved onto the stone stele had said they should.

In Lhasa I continued my routine of exploring the neighborhoods in the old Tibetan quarter, circling the Barkhor with pilgrims in the evening and sitting in front of the Jokhang. One evening as I was standing among the usual crowd of Tibetans in front of the Jokhang, I was approached by a Tibetan woman who asked, in English, where I was from. When I said "America," she said that she too was an American. Her name was Dolma Yudon Tenpa. Although dressed in the traditional Tibetan woman's chuba and *pangden,* she appeared almost as from another planet compared to the local Tibetans. Her chuba, the long gown traditionally worn by Tibetans, both men and women, was clean and new. Local Tibetans who still wore the traditional dress were shabby in comparison, their chubas usually being dirty, worn, and patched. Dolma's chuba was made in India, nothing comparable even being made in Tibet anymore. Her pangden, the apron worn by married women made of thin horizontal striped wool, was also new and finely made. Even though traditionally dressed, she stood out in the Tibetan crowd nearly as much as I did. Meeting Dolma was a momentous event for me, since she was to change the direction of my life.

I soon learned that Dolma lived in Pennsylvania with her husband and two children. She and her husband had been among the first group of Tibetans from exile in India to come to the United States, in the early 1960s, as workers for the Great Northern Paper Company in Maine. The company hired some thirty Tibetan men as lumberjacks and some of them brought wives. The company tried to exploit the Tibetans with low pay and by keeping them isolated in forests, but the Tibetans soon learned that they had political rights. They contacted their Maine congressman, who managed to get them out of their contracts with the paper company.

Dolma had an interesting history. She was a young girl in the 1950s, when other Tibetan youth were recruited by the Chinese to go to schools in the Chinese interior, but she refused to go. She was known for her independent nature even as a young girl. She told me that she was well-known to Tibetan soldiers and policemen, who sometimes harassed young girls, because she carried a small pearl-handled pistol in her chuba. As an aristocrat and as someone who was known to be opposed to the Chinese, she had to flee Tibet in early 1959 after being informed that she was in danger. She said that she regretted having to surrender her pistol at the Indian border.

Dolma was one of the first Tibetans from exile to visit Tibet since the liberalization began in 1980. Even at that first meeting in front of the Jokhang, I noticed that many Tibetans approached her, recognizing that she was from exile. They had questions about their relatives in exile, or messages to send to them, or they wanted to tell their stories of suffering since 1959. Dolma invited me to walk with her around the Barkhor and then to where she was staying with her sister and brother-in-law in a room in the old Phala mansion, the former residence of the Dalai Lama's chief minister who arranged for his escape in 1959. They had one large room in the old mansion, now the residence of many families and considerably run down since no one had any personal responsibility or interest in its maintenance. Their room was one of the best, however, being a large, glass-enclosed sunroom.

One of the first things I noticed at the old Phala mansion was the absence of the large brass and copper cooking pots and utensils, which are prominently displayed in every Sherpa house I had visited in Nepal and, I assumed, were also once common in Tibet. I was told that no one had such decorative kitchen utensils anymore, not even monasteries that used to have huge copper or brass cauldrons for making tea for thousands of monks. All metal utensils, as well as all metal statues and religious implements in monasteries, had been confiscated after the revolt, trucked to China, and melted down. This was a part of what China described as "democratic reforms." Tibetans were told that the wealth of their former upper classes and exploitative religious classes were to be redistributed to "the people," meaning not just the Tibetan people but the Chinese people. I also noticed that the former colorful woodwork of the Phala mansion had been painted over in proletarian blue or green; this, I was told, was done during the Cultural Revolution.

Dolma's sister, Sonam Choedron, was a few years older than Dolma but looked very much older. Dolma said that this was because of what she, like many Tibetans, had suffered since 1959. Her first husband was a government official who was arrested after the revolt and died in a Chinese prison camp. Because of her upper-class status, Sonam was subjected to "reform through labor" and forced to work on a hydroelectric project at Nachen Trang east of Lhasa. Many of the upper classes, monks, and those arrested for minor participation in the revolt were forced to work at Nachen Trang.

In the months that I was to spend at the Phala house listening to Tibetans tell their stories to Dolma, I heard the name Nachen Trang many times. Tibetans there were forced to work long hours at a frenzied pace, after which they were subjected to political indoctrination and struggle sessions of designated "reactionaries" until late every evening. Many Tibetans died at Nachen Trang or suffered injuries there from the dangerous conditions. Sonam, like many of those who worked there, was released when the project was finished, but she was labeled with a "hat" signifying her status as politically unreliable, in what was essentially a communist caste system. This meant that she could not be employed and had difficulty even obtaining sufficient food. This was during the time of famine produced by Mao's disastrous Great Leap Forward of 1959–62.

Sonam Choedron told of being forced, during the Cultural Revolution, to produce every day a quota of the dead bodies of one of the "four pests": flies, mice, rats, and sparrows. This was of course anathema to the Buddhist Tibetans and, of course, one of the reasons for imposing it upon them so that they might be "reformed" of their superstitions. Many Tibetans spoke of this requirement to kill sentient beings as one of the most repugnant of the Chinese political campaigns. This campaign did not have its desired effect. Tibetans are famous for their reverence for all living beings, even going to the extremes of rescuing worms disturbed by plowing and fishing flies unharmed out of cups of tea. This latter practice I observed with regularity at Dolma's. A group of people would be sitting quietly having tea when a fly would buzz into someone's cup. There was then a collective panic until the poor fly was rescued, lifted carefully to a windowsill or some other safe place, and even fanned to dry out its wings.

Dolma's sister had been "rehabilitated" during the 1970s, but life for Tibetans, even in Lhasa, was still hard and food shortages continued. There was a minor famine in the early 1970s due to the introduction of the commune system, which resulted in less rather than more agricultural production in Tibet as well as everywhere it was tried, despite the predictions of the communists. Sonam's face bore the tale of all that she had suffered, even though she had fared better than many others. Dolma told me to examine other Tibetans for evidence of similar effects, especially children born during the past twenty years. Soon I was able to recognize the effects on not only people who were not as old as they appeared but on a whole generation of stunted Tibetan youth.

Despite this record of famine and repression, Tibetans had been told that they were not only liberated from their suffering due to the feudal serf system but that they now enjoyed freedom and prosperity unequaled by most of the world, particularly those Tibetans who had fled to India, who were said to have all become beggars. Even those Tibetans who had made it to countries like the United States were said to be worse off than those upon whom had been bestowed the benefits of Chinese socialism.

Dolma told of visiting another sister in a rural area east of Lhasa. Upon leaving, Dolma was given a sack of potatoes by a villager, who said that they had been told that Tibetans in America were so poor that they did not even have potatoes to eat!

Sonam's husband, Rinzing Paljor, was an accomplished artist. He was a member of a guild of painters, artists, and artisans during the 1950s. He told of his guild trying to organize resistance during the 1959 revolt. Rinzing had been arrested after the revolt and remained in prison until 1972. His first wife was subjected to "reform through labor" and died at Nachen Trang. Rinzing was released during a period of relatively moderate policies under the leadership of Zhou Enlai and Deng Xiaoping. Because the Chinese knew that the destruction of almost all of Tibet's monasteries and cultural monuments would not make China look too good to the outside world if and when China might open up, they decided to restore some of the more famous temples and monasteries, like the Jokhang, Potala, and Norbulinka.

Since Rinzing was one of the best and one of the only remaining traditional painters, he had to be released from prison. Deng was soon purged by Mao and the Gang of Four, and restorations in Tibet were stopped, but Rinzing was not returned to prison. Instead, he married Dolma's sister, Sonam, and when the real liberalization began, once again due to the ascendancy of Deng Xiaoping, Rinzing was again in high demand for his painting skills. He had resumed work at the Jokhang and at Drepung, where I was shown the huge multistory standing Maitreya statue that he had been in charge of restoring, and later at the famous monasteries of Shalu near Gyantse and Tashilhunpo, the Panchen Lama's monastery at Shigatse.

I began going to visit Dolma almost every day. I started spending hours there every day, at Dolma's encouragement. I was worried that my visits might cause political problems for Sonam and Rinzing, but Dolma assured me that they weren't worried about it. They, like many older Tibetans, felt that they had suffered so much that they had a certain sort of immunity. Not that they were immune to repression, but just that they didn't care enough anymore to still be fearful about everything they did. I admired their courage born of suffering and Dolma's fearlessness, but I still wasn't sure. Dolma hadn't had the same experiences with the Chinese political system as her relatives. The situation was not too repressive at that time but everyone knew that it could change without warning. Sure enough, the Public Security Police, or *Gong An Ju*, soon visited the house, with questions about Dolma and me. Probably someone at the Phala house had informed, either because to do so was their responsibility or due to political fears left over from the past. The Gong An Ju, who were Tibetans, weren't too aggressive or demanding. They were just playing their role, in the Chinese style, of reminding everyone to be fearful of authority. They did not tell Dolma or her relatives that they could not allow me to visit.

My association with Dolma and her family gave me a unique perspective on my own experience in Tibet. Before, I had been little more than a tourist, more informed than others perhaps, due to my prior familiarity with the Tibet issue, but limited in what I could learn. Now I had an association with a Tibetan who was well-known and absolutely trusted and to whom many were anxious to tell of their experiences. I accompanied Dolma and her family on numerous excursions to many of the places I had already visited, like the Jokhang, Potala, Norbulinka, Sera, Drepung, and Ganden, but now my experiences were greatly expanded. I was told by Dolma not only the identity of every deity but the history of each monastery. We were also greeted by lamas and monks everywhere we went and Dolma would make generous donations.

I was also learning much more during my visits to her sister's home. There were always other Tibetan visitors there, relatives, friends from childhood, or those who wanted to send letters with Dolma to their relatives in exile. Nobody trusted the post, assuming that anything from Tibet to India or any other country would be opened and read by the police. I would sit quietly and listen, understanding little until the visitors left and Dolma explained to me what they had said. Some visitors seemed a bit nervous at my presence, but none stopped talking. Their stories had been bottled up so long that now they poured forth without restraint. It was always about their sufferings and the repressions of the Chinese. The themes were similar and consistent, creating a valid narrative simply because all the stories were consistent in their facts and details. Dolma could tell that I was more than a little interested in what was being related in these sessions and that I was moved by the evidence of Tibetans' sufferings under Chinese rule. Soon, Dolma proposed a bargain. She would interpret for me everything that was being said by all her visitors. In exchange I had to promise to write a book about the history of Tibet under the Chinese. I promised, and Dolma delivered for the next four months.

Not everyone who came to visit Dolma had suffered under the Chinese or had come to unload their grievances. There were a few of her contemporaries from the 1950s who had accepted the offer of schooling in China and had prospered as officials in the Chinese administration of Tibet ever since. I began to understand some of the dilemmas faced by Tibetans at the time. The Dalai Lama and the Tibetan government had accepted the Seventeen Point Agreement and its stipulation that Tibet was a part of China. The Dalai Lama and Tibetan government officials all had to cooperate with the Chinese. In the early 1950s, before the Chinese had begun to closely control Tibet or Tibetans' lives, there was even an enthusiasm, promoted by the Dalai Lama, for the Chinese model of progress, and optimism that Tibet could modernize under China's so-far benevolent rule while retaining what was best of Tibetan culture and religion. Children of the era were often very attracted by the offer of all-expense schooling in China. The alternative was to remain uneducated and to be identified as less than enthusiastic about the Chinese presence in Tibet and possibly an opponent. The Chinese Communist system had many ways of cultivating supporters and collaborators and ways of identifying and repressing opponents. The choice of whether to go to school in China was just one of the ways in which one was forced to choose between cooperation with the Chinese or resistance. Some of Dolma's childhood friends chose to accept the offer of schooling. They often prospered thereafter and never suffered, as did many others. Dolma chose to refuse the offer and, not too much later, had to flee into exile.

Another Tibetan whom I met had tried to straddle the choices. I met Tashi Tsering soon after I arrived in Lhasa when he came to the Guest House. He was looking for foreigners with whom to practice his English and to help him with an English-Tibetan-Chinese dictionary. Tashi had been in India in the 1950s, having been one of the Tibetan government officials sent with the Dalai Lama's gold that was removed from Tibet when the PLA invaded Chamdo in October 1950. Most of the gold had been lost in poor investments in India, but Tashi was still there in 1959. He secured a position with the Sakya Lama, who was invited to the University of Washington in the United States. The first Tibetan studies program at an American university evolved around the Sakya Lama, his family, and a few Tibetans like Tashi Tsering.

Tashi could have stayed in Washington and had a safe and secure career. But he was an idealist. He decided that Chinese rule over Tibet was an undeniable and irreversible fact and that a real Tibetan patriot should return to help his people. Thinking that his return would be welcomed by the Chinese, because his sincerity was proven by having given up a secure position in the United States, Tashi returned to China, via Cuba, in 1964. He was sent to teach at the Tibetan nationality school at Xianyang near Xian. In 1966 he went to Lhasa where he became a victim of the Cultural Revolution's need for scapegoats. His role in India in the 1950s was considered suspicious, while his residence in the United States made him a likely American spy. He was imprisoned in Xian until 1973 and only allowed to return to Lhasa in 1981.

I helped Tashi with one or two letters in his dictionary, checking his spelling and definitions, and suggesting other words to include. His dictionary was finally published and I got an acknowledgment in the foreword. Tashi later became somewhat famous for his school projects. He cultivated many foreign friends and solicited donations for the building of schools in Tibet. Tashi was fairly outspoken, claiming that all the mistakes of the past in Chinese politics were now being corrected and that there was now freedom of speech. Nevertheless, he was uncritical of the Chinese regime or its history in Tibet, having not experienced the worst of it himself and having made his choice to support it by returning to China. He was also the subject of a laudatory book by the American Tibetologist, Melvyn Goldstein, who had known him at the University of Washington.

Tashi seemed something of a tragic figure to me, if not to his biographer, because of his naïve decision to return and the price he paid for it. His decision illustrated a famous saying about the difference between Tibetans and Chinese, that Tibetans are condemned by their hopefulness and the Chinese by their suspiciousness. He revealed his undying naivety by asking me to send him a toaster from the United States. He had become accustomed to an American-style breakfast while there and now he wanted to make toast. At that time, he was living with his wife in one room near the Jokhang, not the larger quarters he later got even closer to the Jokhang where his wife opened a chang shop. His apartment at that time had a single 25-watt light bulb suspended from the ceiling. There was no other electrical outlet anywhere in the room. Still, Tashi imagined that he could somehow plug in a toaster, where I don't know, that required at least a thousand watts!

My meetings at the Phala house continued and I often went with Dolma and her family on excursions to various places around Lhasa. Dolma's relatives were sometimes able to get a vehicle so that travel to more distant sites was possible. She and her family also had places of interest that I would never have known about. One of those was Pabongka, in the northern corner of the Lhasa Valley to the east of Sera, an ancient seventh-century site that predates even the Jokhang. Srongtsan Gampo was said to have lived here, and it was where Thonmi Sambhota spent three years, after returning from India, compiling the Tibetan alphabet and written language (presumably before moving to Meru Nyingpa). Three stories of the once nine-story temple remained, built upon a massive rock that was said to represent a turtle, symbolic of the cosmos. To make a pilgrimage to Pabongka was supposed to be particularly auspicious.

We also went to cave shrines at the base of the Chakpori hill to the southwest of the Potala and to Ganden. I began going places with Dolma alone, usually by foot, like to tea and momo shops in the Barkhor area. She invited me to go with her to the military parade on the first of August, the anniversary of the PLA. We lined the street along with hundreds of Chinese and Tibetans. Many of the Tibetans were just curious, but some who had obviously opted for collaboration with the Chinese regime were conspicuous in their enthusiasm. I was told by one of the Public Security Police that photographs were not allowed, even though there was no military equipment on display in the parade, only marching troops. I believe there was a display of some military equipment, like armored vehicles, at another area restricted to VIPs. One other foreigner who tried to take photographs, having not been warned or who decided to ignore the warnings, had his camera angrily snatched from his hands by a Chinese policeman and the film removed and exposed. The parade was of several companies of PLA troops, plus one company of precision marchers who did some impressive maneuvers with their weapons. The crowd was suitably impressed, this seemingly being the purpose.

Dolma also invited me to go with her to the Serthang ("Golden Thanka") festival at Ganden. The Serthang festival involved the unveiling of a huge appliqué scroll Buddha image, traditionally held every full moon in August. The Ganden Serthang had been banned since the 1959 revolt. This would be the first time it was celebrated since then.

In July 1980 Tibetans had taken advantage of the presence of the second delegation from Dharamsala in Lhasa to accompany them to Ganden to observe both the destruction and reconstruction of what was once one of Tibet's largest and most important monasteries. Film of the delegation at Ganden shows them being mobbed by tearful Tibetans expressing both their grief and their hopes that the visit of Tibetans from exile representing the Dalai Lama meant that the situation was about to change for the better.

This seems to have been another event that the Chinese did not anticipate, perhaps still believing their own propaganda. Thousands of Tibetans managed to get to Ganden in trucks belonging to various work units whose drivers were Tibetan. The Chinese were able to retaliate only after the fact by confiscating the licenses of some of the truck drivers. This was the first time since the 1959 revolt that Tibetans had been able to organize such a spontaneous event. Because the Chinese had not anticipated it, they did not have their usual collaborators, spies, and informants in attendance, so Tibetans had a rare experience of freedom from Chinese control. Ganden was the first monastery founded by Tsongkhapa in the thirteenth century. His reform movement became the Gelugpa sect of Tibetan Buddhism and eventually the government of Tibet under the Dalai Lamas. Because of Ganden's role in the political history of Tibet, plus the presence of the Dharamsala delegation and the welcome they received there, the event took on nationalistic overtones.

The second delegation received an equally enthusiastic reception at the Guest House on their return to Lhasa, which was observed by a group of foreign journalists who were coincidentally in Lhasa and staying at the same guest house. This led to the expulsion of the journalists, the termination of the second delegation visit, and the cancellation of further visits. After the second delegation visit, the Chinese attempted to intimidate workers at Ganden and stop donations by Tibetans. The Chinese suspected Dharamsala's involvement in the reconstruction because of Ganden's political significance. Nevertheless, work there continued. In 1981 Tibetans tried to celebrate the Ganden Serthang, but all traffic was stopped at the bridge over the Kyichu. By the summer of 1982 the burial chorten of Tsongkhapa had been reconstructed as well as three of the largest lhakhangs, including the one from which the Serthang was traditionally hung. Tibetans were determined to once again try to celebrate the Serthang.

As we climbed into the back of a truck early one morning at the full moon in August 1982, we were uncertain whether we would be allowed to go to Ganden or if all trucks would be stopped at the bridge over the Kyichu, like the year before. The decision to allow Tibetans to go to Ganden for the Serthang in 1982 was no doubt the subject of political struggles between liberals and hardliners within the Chinese administration of Tibet. This was only two years after the visit of Hu Yaobang to Tibet and his decree that Tibetans should be allowed some cultural autonomy. However, Chinese and Tibetan cadres had to worry about the political implications of the reconstruction of Ganden. They were aware of the inseparability of religion and politics in Tibet. Some cadres were probably confident in their Marxist ideology that decreed that religion and nationalism were relics of the past. Others, however, had to fear that the revival of religion was certain to lead to the revival of Tibetan national identity and thus inevitably to Tibetan nationalism and separatism, as indeed it did.

Our truck as well as many others reached Ganden that day, whether due to a decision to allow it to happen or the lack of sufficient resolve to prevent it, I don't know. There were tens of thousands of Tibetans there, no Chinese that I observed, and only one or two other foreigners besides myself. There was an atmosphere of relief and celebration, no doubt much like in 1980, due to the sense of revival of Tibetan Buddhism and the escape, temporarily at least, from stifling Chinese control and supervision. I had no personal experience of Chinese control or repression myself, except what I had heard from Tibetans, but I could share the sense of relief to be in an entirely Tibetan atmosphere. Certainly, Tibetans are naturally more relaxed and free-spirited than the Chinese, especially those in Tibet who represented a colonialist administration.

Before the hanging of the Serthang, I visited the three lhakhangs so-far restored and Dolma instructed me about where to leave donations that would do the most good. The Ganden monks and workers certainly collected enough that day to keep the reconstruction going. The authorities tried to halt the reconstruction only a year later by arresting many of the workers there and restricting the number of monks. They didn't succeed in halting it but the work went on more slowly thereafter.

The Serthang is an enormous appliqué thanka with gold trim, perhaps 40 feet across and 60 feet long. It was carried by some twenty monks to the top of the tallest reconstructed building and then slowly unfurled from top to bottom. Later, many of the pilgrims did a kora of the monastery along a mile-long path that goes around the north side of the mountain behind the monastery. Along the path were several holy spots where miraculous events were supposed to have taken place. I also got a spectacular view of the monastery from a peak to the south that is perhaps a thousand feet above the level of the monastery and where most of the famous photos of Ganden are taken. After the ceremonies and rituals were performed, we all piled back into our trucks and drove back to Lhasa. There seemed to be a real sense among the Tibetans that this Ganden Serthang signified a religious and cultural revival. Given the inescapable association of religion and politics in Tibet, it also had political implications that were inspiring to Tibetans but ominous to the Chinese and perhaps to some of their most loyal Tibetan cadres.

After the Ganden Serthang, I went on an excursion to Gyantse and Shigatse. The first stage of the journey, from Lhasa to Gyantse, was by bus. The road from Lhasa goes to the southwest along the course of the Kyichu River. At the point where the Kyichu joins the Tsangpo, the road crosses the river and ascends upward toward the Khamba La (*la* meaning pass) at 15,580 feet (4,750 meters). The Tsangpo flows east from Shigatse but a gorge intervenes, along which travel, at least by motor vehicle, was difficult. So, the main roads to Shigatse went through Gyantse or through Yangbachen, north of Lhasa and then south to Shigatse. The Khamba La is about 3,500 feet above the Tsangpo and, once there, one sees Yamdrok Yumtso Lake about 1,000 feet below the pass to the south. The lake is of a serpentine shape and, like all lakes in Tibet, a brilliant turquoise color. This is where the Chinese later built a hydroelectric plant that generates power by taking water from the lake and dropping it down in a long penstock to the Tsangpo. Excess power from other sources was supposed to be used during the night to pump water back up into the lake. This would theoretically leave the lake undisturbed, but that seemed unlikely. They also eventually built a road along the Tsangpo to Shigatse.

After descending from the Khamba La, the road winds along the western shore of the lake, passing the Nangkartse Monastery, at about 14,750 feet (4,500 meters), home of Dorje Phagmo, Tibet's only female tulku, or reincarnated lama (who became a rather notorious Chinese collaborator), and then ascends toward the Karo La at 16,700 feet (5,090 meters). On the far side of this pass is where the Tibetans made their last stand against the British invasion of 1904. After the fall of Gyantse, the Tibetans constructed a stone wall about halfway up toward the Karo La leading to Lhasa. Like all the Tibetans' defensive measures, this also proved ineffective, the British simply outflanking the wall by scrambling up the scree slopes on both sides. Along this road, as well as on others in the area, one could still see propaganda slogans on nearby hillsides made with arrangements of white stones. They were the usual "Defend the Motherland," "Support the Communist Party" type of slogans, but I was told that Tibetans sometimes rearranged the stones to express anti-Chinese sentiments. All the roads in Tibet were gravel, with huge amounts of dust that made a dust mask necessary. They were also subject to "washboarding," the phenomenon of dirt roads being eroded by traffic in narrow horizontal ridges just far enough apart to cause a bone-rattling vibration.

Gyantse is a small town in a large fertile valley dominated by a fortress on a steep crag. The Gyantse fortress was the only real obstacle to the British invasion. Gyantse was basically only two streets, the road that leads through the town from east to west and a short spur to the monastery to the north, along which was the old business district. Gyantse illustrates the typical Tibetan settlement pattern, with a small town and other scattered houses and farms in the larger valley, all protected by a fortress to which the inhabitants could retreat in case of attack during the many periods of unsettled political authority in Tibet. The large fertile valley eventually supported the growth of a large monastery. Unlike Lhasa, Gyantse still had much of its Tibetan character. There was less destruction than in other places and very few new "improvements" to spoil the traditional Tibetan character.

The first Gyantse fortress was supposed to have been built by the last Yarlung dynasty king in the ninth century. The fortress was later expanded and the temple added in the fourteenth century. It was now in ruins, having been damaged both during the British invasion in 1904 and during the Cultural Revolution. Halfway up the hill to the fortress was a temple with very old wall paintings that were apparently the target of the later destruction. The fortress was inaccessible, the Chinese having not yet constructed their "Resisting Imperialism" museum there. Now they claim that the Tibetans were bravely defending China, rather than just Tibet, against the British invasion.

Behind the fortress is the Pelkor Chode Monastery, which dates from the early fifteenth century. The monastery is enclosed in an earthen wall, within which are the original Pelkor Chode lhakhang, the famous Gyantse Kumbum, and a bare stone multistory wall on which the monastery's large thanka would be displayed in Gyantse's version of the Serthang festival. Formerly, within the wall were several dratsangs or monastic colleges of various sects, including Sakyapa, Shalupa, and Gelugpa, in a dozen or so buildings, all now destroyed. Both the Pelkor Chode and the Kumbum were apparently too famous to be destroyed during the Cultural Revolution. As was the case with all such monuments that survived, credit was given to Zhou Enlai, who was said to have designated certain cultural monuments in Tibet and China to be spared. Zhou probably just ordered that all Tibetan monuments that had been designated as important cultural heritage sites by a Chinese survey in the early 1950s should be preserved from destruction. The Panchen Lama's monastery of Tashilhunpo in Shigatse and Sakya to the west were also among those that were saved from most of the official looting that took place after the revolt and the frenzy of destruction of the Cultural Revolution.

The Gyantse Pelkor Chode combines Newari- and Tibetan-style decorations and wall murals, most of which were still intact. The assembly hall is large, supported by forty-eight pillars. Inside one sees the large rolled-up thanka, also dating from the fifteenth century, that was displayed once each year until 1959 (Gyantse had not yet revived the ceremony). The Gyantse Kumbum is a large chorten, or Buddhist stupa, of several levels and many shrines entered from walkways that circle on the outside. The lower four floors are supposed to have a total of sixty-eight chapels; the fifth level has four chapels while the sixth and seventh have one chapel of four rooms each. The eighth level has one small chapel. Most of the chapels and their artifacts and paintings were reportedly preserved but only a few of the shrines were open so I couldn't see much about the state of the chorten or its images.

The Tibetan chorten is a Buddhist reliquary but it also has a pre-Buddhist symbolism as a connector between earth and sky. The pre-Buddhist Tibetan religion shares with shamanism the symbolism of human descent from the gods and attempts to reascend through the rituals of the shamans. Mountains, like Kang Rinpoche, and chortens are supposed to be symbolic connectors between heaven and earth. The first Tibetan king was supposed to have descended from the sky, via a sky cord, to a holy mountain in central Tibet.

There was a small hostel on the main road where one could stay, but at that time there were no provisions made for foreign tourists. There was one tiny momo shop whose most memorable feature was a loudspeaker hanging from the wall blasting Chinese music and propaganda. There were still a few such loudspeakers in Lhasa but they were not as numerous as in smaller sites like Gyantse, where every shop seemed to have one.

They were once a ubiquitous presence all over Tibet, blaring their martial music and exhortations to Tibetans to increase production and love the Motherland. This was one of the most intrusive, irritating, and offensive aspects of the Chinese occupation of Tibet, altering the peaceful and relatively quiet atmosphere of every city, town, and even private house in Tibet from the 1960s to the early 1980s.

Gyantse is only a short way from Shigatse. I took a truck headed for Shigatse that was loaded with Tibetans and a few Chinese PLA soldiers. Along the way we passed Shalu, an ancient fourteenth century monastery famous for its combination of Tibetan architecture, a Chinese-style turquoise tile roof, and its Newari paintings. The first temple at Shalu dates from the tenth century and is supposed to be the first temple constructed during the second diffusion of Buddhism in Tibet after its decline in the ninth century when the Yarlung dynasty ended. It had not yet been restored and was not open. Dolma's brother-in-law, Rinzing Paljor, was later employed on the restoration of paintings there. The road from Gyantse is level, following the Nyang River. At one point we stopped and some got out for a pee. One of the PLA soldiers looked around for a place to put his AK-47, so I offered to hold it for him. I wanted to see what it felt like. There was no clip in it, so it was not loaded, but it still surprised me that he readily handed it over.

Shigatse is on the Tsangpo River at 12,800 feet (3,900 meters). In Shigatse I met up with some other foreigners, one of whom was a female Dutch teacher who spoke good Chinese. We went to the local state store to try to buy coffee and beer. The store had a large pyramidal display of Shanghai ground coffee tins. When we asked the Chinese shop girl if we could buy coffee, we got the not entirely unexpected reply, "*meiyou* coffee," meaning "no coffee," even though she was perfectly framed by the pyramid of coffee tins behind her. Pointing out the pyramid of coffee did no good. She still insisted, with the unashamed mendacity common in China, that there was no coffee. So, the Dutch teacher said in her good Chinese that she wanted to see the manager, who came and was persuaded to sell us at least one tin of coffee.

Instructed to part with one tin, the shopkeeper still spent a few minutes searching behind the pyramid and elsewhere for a stray tin so she wouldn't have to disturb the perfect pyramid. Finally, reluctantly, she had to pull out one tin, the pyramid fortunately remaining undisturbed. Having already called the manager once, we thought the salesgirl would not resist when we asked for two bottles of beer, a large number of which were also prominently displayed. But her reply was the same, "*meiyou pijou*," or "no beer." However, knowing that her lies would not be accepted this time, she gave up two bottles of beer after only a small protest. We considered our purchase of one tin of coffee and two warm beers a major victory over the Chinese Communist system and went back to the guest house to celebrate.

Another time while walking through the small streets of Shigatse I came upon a *Xinhua* bookshop being emptied of all its contents. Mao's Little Red Book, propaganda posters, and all other items were being unceremoniously swept into a pile on the street. During the Cultural Revolution these were sacred items and one could be denounced, struggled, sentenced to labor camp, or even executed for any sign of disrespect to them. Times had changed, however, and now all such propaganda was apparently considered less than worthless, at least in Tibet. I found a book of Mao's quotations in Tibetan with an introduction by Lin Biao, Mao's now disgraced heir apparent who had tried to mount a coup in the late 1960s and had to flee to the Soviet Union. His plane crashed, or was shot down, and he was not spoken of again. The little red books with his introduction were all confiscated, except those that were forgotten in Tibet. I also found some propaganda posters with themes such as Tibetan women being trained by PLA soldiers to defend the Motherland. The sight of the *Xinhua* bookshop being emptied of Chinese propaganda seemed to be a sign that times had really changed in China and Tibet.

The small town of Shigatse is dominated not by Tashilhunpo Monastery but by the ruins of the huge fifteenth century Shigatse fortress built on a hill to the northeast of the city. In size and architectural style, the fortress is comparable to the Potala and is said to have been the model for it. It had been deconstructed, on orders of the Chinese, in 1961, for its stone, which was used for other construction. It was finally restored in 2007. Tashilhunpo is the head monastery of the Panchen Lama, who was on good terms with the Chinese until 1964 and therefore his monastery suffered relatively little damage. The monastery was founded in the fifteenth century by a disciple of Tsongkhapa who posthumously became the First Dalai Lama. There are several large well-preserved lhakhangs, particularly one with a standing statue of Maitreya, the Buddha of the Future, several stories high. Rinzing Paljor was later employed on restoration of statues and paintings here, too. Tashilhunpo once had four colleges, or dratsangs, only one of which still existed. When the Panchen Lama was purged in 1964, even Tashilhunpo suffered some damage and most of its monks were secularized. There were hundreds of Tibetans visiting the shrines of the monastery and making a circumambulation of the whole walled monastic complex, activities prohibited before the liberalization period.

From Shigatse I went by truck to the large monastery of Sakya. Just west of Shigatse the road passes the site of the famous monastery of Narthang, one of only three sites in Tibet where the complete Buddhist canon, the Kangyur and Tengyur, were printed from woodblocks. Narthang was completely destroyed and its woodblocks were all burned or turned into utilitarian items like furniture. The road to Sakya turns south from the main road to Nepal and western Tibet. Sakya Monastery is at an isolated site on a broad plain at about 14,000 feet (roughly 4,270 meters). On the north side of the small river that bisects the town is the oldest part of the monastic complex, dating from the eleventh century. There were said to have been 108 temples and shrines there, but 108 is the Tibetan auspicious number so anything reasonably close to that number is usually said to be 108. This part of Sakya was almost completely destroyed and had not been restored.

On the south side of the river is the huge Lhakhang Chenmo, enclosed in a massive earthen wall. The Sakya Lhakhang Chenmo was preserved almost intact because of its historical relationship with the Mongol Yuan dynasty of China (1272–1368). The main lhakhang, built in the thirteenth century, is supported with huge timbers, said to be cedars, far exceeding in size any trees now existent in this part of Tibet. Presumably they were cut at some distant site, perhaps to the south closer to the Himalaya, where there were forests of large trees when Tibet was less dry than today. The lhakhang is lined with the 108 volumes of the

Buddhist canon, the Kangyur, and the even more numerous volumes of scholarly commentaries, known as the Tengyur, and displays of relics of the Sakya rule over Tibet. Especially prominent are gifts from the Mongol Yuan dynasty emperors, communications between the Sakya and the Mongol emperors, and any other artifacts that demonstrate Tibet's connection to China or tend to substantiate China's claim to authority over Tibet. Sakya Monastery is also the repository of ancient Indian Sanskrit manuscripts, Tibetan manuscripts, and printed texts to the number of 20,000 volumes. There are also some 3,000 thankas, 20,000 metal statues, and 2,000 pieces of porcelain from the Yuan and Ming dynasty periods.

It was the Sakya hierarchs, Sakya Pandita and then Phagspa, who made the arrangement with the Mongols that saved Tibet from Mongol invasion. The Sakyapas inaugurated the so-called Patron-Priest relationship with the Mongols in which Tibetan lamas provided spiritual legitimacy to the Mongol Khans and the Mongols provided political patronage to the Sakyapas and Tibet. The Sakyapas were elevated to become the rulers of Tibet by this relationship, their monasteries were enriched by gifts from the Mongols, and Tibet was unified under their leadership. The downside of this arrangement was that the Tibetan relationship with the Mongol rulers of China was later used by Chinese dynasties, including the Chinese Communists, to claim Chinese sovereignty over Tibet. China now claims that Tibet became a part of China in 1270, when the Yuan dynasty was established, ignoring the fact that the Sakya relationship with the Mongols dates to 1247, before the Mongols under Kubilai Khan had conquered China, thus bolstering the Tibetan claim that their relationship was with the Mongol Empire, not with China, which, like Tibet, was only a part of that empire.

From Sakya I hitched back to the main road from Shigatse to Nepal and went a bit west to the small town of Lhatse (13,290 feet, 4,050 meters) where the road divides south toward Nepal and west toward Xinjiang. Its original route to Xinjiang was up the course of the Tsangpo to the holy mountain of Kailash and from there north to the border with Xinjiang. Now the road went west only a short way to Dzongba and from there straight north to the almost uninhabited northern plain, or Changtang. It then went west across the Changtang to Rutok and Gartok in the

Tibetan area of Ngari, which the Chinese call Ali, being unable to pronounce the "*ng*" or the "*r*" sounds. From Gartok another road went south to Kailash. Ngari is the historical site of the Zhang Zhung kingdom that was conquered by central Tibet in the seventh century, thus increasing the territory as well as the human resources of central Tibet and leading to the conquest of the whole plateau.

The road to Kailash, or Kang Rinpoche, the "precious mountain" in Tibetan, was now far longer than when it had gone directly along the Tsangpo. The route was diverted in the early 1960s to avoid the guerrilla raids by the Tibetan Resistance forces from the Mustang region of Nepal. The resistance had been relocated to Mustang by the CIA after the failure of the revolt in Tibet in 1959. The main road was not restored to the Tsangpo route (until recently) even after the threat from resistance raids ended because the Changtang route, although longer and much higher, needed less maintenance. The road was little more than a dirt track across the dry and relatively flat Changtang Plateau. The more southern route along the Tsangpo is subject to more rainfall and has more marshy areas along the river.

I wanted to try to get out to Kailash, having not yet given up that goal. When I was living in Nepal, I had read dozens of books about the sacredness of the mountain and the two nearby lakes and the constant unsuccessful efforts of foreign explorers to reach it. The mountain is not the highest in Tibet (21,840 feet, 6,657 meters) nor are the two sacred lakes at its foot, Mansarovar and Rakshas Tal (15,920 feet, 4,852 meters) the largest or highest. But Kailash stands almost alone in a stark terrain, like the connector between heaven and earth of both Indian and Tibetan mythology. The lakes are the source of the Karnali, which becomes the Ganges, and the Tsangpo. The area north of Kailash is the source of the Sutlej and the Indus, making the Kailash area the source of all the major rivers of the subcontinent.

I waited for two days on the roadside in Lhatse, but only a very few trucks passed by going that way. One Tibetan driver told me that the trip took a week and one had to bring along food and water or else starve. He offered to take me, but only if I got permission from his work unit in Lhasa. This gave me the excuse to give up and return to Lhasa, intending to get permission from the work unit whose address he had given me, but of course I never did, ending my quest to be the first foreigner to reach the holy mountain in modern times.

Back in Shigatse I encountered a group of about twenty Tibetans from Nepal, with whom I could speak Nepali. They had rented a truck and were going to Lhasa and offered to take me along. One woman said that she hoped to get the blessing of the Panchen Lama, who she had heard had been in Lhasa. I had to tell her that he had indeed been in Lhasa, and in Shigatse too, but by now had gone back to Beijing. She looked so disappointed that I gave her the ribbon I had been given by the Panchen as a blessing cord. She was very grateful and now I was in the good graces of the whole group for the trip to Lhasa. We went not the way I had come, through Gyantse, but east from Shigatse along the Tsangpo for a few miles and then across the river and north toward the Nyenchenthangla mountain range. We were all in the open back of the truck. The road crosses the 5,300-meter Suge La south of the main peak and descends to the hot springs at Yangbachen and from there connects to the main road from Golmud to Lhasa.

Since Nyenchenthangla is the holy mountain of central Tibet, I thought this was something of a compensation for having failed to reach Kailash. As we crossed the pass there was a most wonderful view of the mountain, one of the most beautiful sights I saw in Tibet. From the road to the east, from where one most usually sees Nyenchenthangla, it is a broad massif of several peaks running from southwest to northeast. But from the pass at the southwestern end of the range, it appears as one magnificent, perfectly shaped, pyramidal peak of 24,000 feet (7,315 meters). This sight was one of the most memorable visual experiences of my whole time in Tibet.

August was probably the high point for foreign visitors to Lhasa that summer. Still, there were never more than fifteen or twenty foreigners at the Guest House at any time. We occupied three or four rooms together on the third floor. Altogether that year perhaps as many as 150–200 foreigners availed themselves of an individual travel permit to Lhasa and reached there. Most were foreign teachers in China. There were some others, like myself, but the window for visas was opened and shut so quickly that you almost had to already be in China to hear about it. None of my friends from Nepal, many who had waited for years for Tibet to open, managed to get there. I wish they had—it was an extraordinary experience, but it would have been even more so if more knowledgeable people had been there. As it was, I was the only one there that summer who had any previous interest in Tibet. There were also a few groups of tourists in Lhasa. One would see them at the Jokhang. They were there for only a few days, so they hardly counted among those of us who shared the Tibet experience that summer. There were a few backpacker types who tended to be more interesting than the teachers. One was a young German named Jurgen Dahm who stayed for several months and with whom I shared some adventures.

Every evening Jurgen and I would go to the Jokhang after having dinner at the Guest House, which was about the only place to eat. Not that it was any good. The fare was usually watery cabbage soup that may or may not have ever seen a piece of pork, and steamed buns, or *baozi*. Baozi are quite good when still warm and a bit damp from the steamer, but they soon become hard as rocks. The Guest House was generous in its supply of baozi, so Jurgen and I would load up with as many as we could smuggle out of the dining room and give them to the Tibetan beggars at the Jokhang.

Food was still scarce in Tibet, due to the aftereffects of one of the most recent of China's many disastrous policies imposed upon the Tibetans. In the 1970s, the Chinese decided that Tibetans should grow more wheat, which Chinese preferred, and less barley, which is the Tibetan staple. Barley is so important in the Tibetan diet that Tibetans identify themselves as "tsampa eaters." Barley is better suited to cold and high altitude than wheat, which even the Chinese had to admit after several failed wheat harvests. Rationing of wheat and wheat products was still in effect in 1982. To eat outside government canteens or to buy baked products one had to have *liang pao*, or grain ration coupons.

Early one morning in July, Jurgen and I got up early to ride our bicycles out to the "sky burial" site near Sera. This was a popular excursion for all the foreigners since everybody had heard of this Tibetan funeral custom. One had to reach the site early or it might all be over. Those who had preceded us had sometimes been allowed to respectfully observe from a distance, or been chased away by those who cut up the bodies, or found that nobody had died the day or night before. Several had observed that Chinese were invariably chased away and never allowed to observe the Tibetans at the site, exercising a rare power over the Chinese to deny them their prurient interest in watching what they regarded as primitive and barbaric Tibetan death rituals.

The "sky burial" site was a large rock just beyond and to the east of Sera. To get there one has to pass by Drapchi Prison, Tibet's main prison for political prisoners. Like most Chinese constructions in Lhasa, it is a group of nondescript concrete buildings within a surrounding wall that is unrecognizable as a prison unless one knows what it is. Also nearby are the newer and smaller Sangyip, Sitru, and Yitritu Prisons. The sky burial site is near the execution grounds where some Tibetans were supposedly executed after the 1959 revolt and where Nyemo Ani, the nun who led a revolt in 1969 during the Cultural Revolution, was publicly executed in 1970.

We were lucky, I suppose, that three Tibetans had died the day or night before. There were three bodies laid out naked on the rock and two Tibetan *rogyapas*, or corpse cutters, preparing to dismember them. Two of the deceased were elderly men, but the third was a fairly young woman. No family members had come to the site. Since we were the only foreigners there and we were properly respectful, we were allowed to observe but were told that we couldn't take photos.

As the rogyapas began cutting up the three bodies, the process seemed as awful and barbaric as most imagine. They began by cutting off the large fleshy parts of the bodies into small strips, much as the Chinese used to do in their notorious "slicing process," a method of public execution using the cruelest and most humiliating means possible. Then the internal organs were also cut into small pieces. Next the bones were separated, crushed, and mixed with tsampa. Finally, the skull and brain were similarly crushed and mixed with tsampa. Once the bodies were dismembered, and became just pieces of meat, some of the awfulness of the process dissipated. As the human forms were transformed it just seemed like a butcher shop on the rock.

The process took about half an hour; all the while one could not help but notice the ultimate beneficiaries of the ritual approaching ever closer. Hundreds of large Griffon and Lammergeier vultures had gathered on the adjacent ridge that separated the site from Sera Monastery. As the process proceeded, they hopped from rock to rock, gradually descending the mountain until they surrounded the site at a close distance. The rogyapas had to throw occasional bits of the bodies to the nearest vultures to keep them at bay. When the bodies were all dismembered, the cutters hurried to finish before being overwhelmed by the now very large number of vultures.

As they finished, the two rogyapas jumped down from the rock. This was the sign the vultures were waiting for and they swarmed over the rock. Within what seemed like less than a minute, the vultures had consumed all of the meat and crushed bones and internal organs of the three bodies. Then they all flew away. And just like that it was finished. Now it seemed anything but barbaric. There was even a certain elegance to it; the bodies had simply vanished into the sky and were gone. The rock was once again bare and there was nothing but a memory of the dead bodies that were there only an hour before. Now the whole process seemed clean and efficient and as civilized as any other way of dealing with death and the disposal of human bodies. It even seemed an almost enlightened way of disposing of the dead. Once finished with their task, and I suppose as a reward for our respectfulness, the rogyapas invited us to share their Tibetan tea, which we did. No Tibetans would have done that, since the rogyapas are the only actual caste in Tibetan society with whom others will not intermarry or share food.

Among the interesting people I met in Lhasa that summer was a young Indian woman, Ami Bhatt, who had been studying Chinese in Beijing for the past two years. She intended to work for the Indian political establishment as a China expert. She spoke excellent Chinese and was a helpful companion on several excursions, including one to the Gong An Ju when I needed a visa extension. She chatted up the Chinese officer there and told him that I, too, was a student at a Chinese university. I knew little Chinese in comparison to Ami but I had retained the ability to write the characters for my university, Nei Mongu Daxue, and *Wo Lun*, my name in Chinese. I got my visa extension, there apparently being no limit to how long individual foreigners could stay in Tibet that year. The Chinese officer was later to be helpful when I ran afoul of the law.

Among Ami's friends in Beijing was a Tibetan woman who was the daughter of an important Tibetan collaborator, Phuntsok Wangyal, usually known as Bapa Phuntsok Wangyal or Phunwang. Bapa means a person "pa" from Ba, or Bathang, and Phunwang is a typical contraction of Tibetan names using the first syllable of each name. Phuntsok Wangyal was one of the first Tibetan communists and is credited, or blamed, for leading the Chinese into Lhasa in 1951. Bathang is a town in southern Kham, just outside the current Tibet Autonomous Region, where some Chinese and a few Western Christian missionaries had settled before 1950, mostly because it lies at a relatively low altitude in the gorge carved out by the Yangtze River as it flows south through Kham. Both the Chinese and the missionaries were the source of new ideas that influenced some Bathang Tibetans. Phuntsok Wangyal studied Marxism and Marxist nationalities policies and decided that they provided a solution for Tibetan autonomy in relation to China as well as Kham's autonomy in relation to both Tibet and China.

Phuntsok Wangyal, like Tashi Tsering, is the subject of a study by the Tibetologist Melvyn Goldstein, who lauds him as a visionary nationalist who sought a political solution for Tibet in the promises of Marxist nationality policies. Unfortunately, Phuntsok Wangyal had only the books about nationality policies and no experience of their actual application in any communist country. If he had, he would have known that Marxist promises of nationality autonomy were a cynical subterfuge to gain nationalities' acquiescence to absorption within a communist state, after which they were subjected to relentless coercion to assimilate.

Phuntsok Wangyal, like most Tibetan nationalists, even if they were communists, was purged after the 1959 revolt, when Chinese policies became intolerant of autonomy, and he spent twenty years in a Chinese prison. One of the "crimes" of which he was charged was that he continued to adhere to Marxist nationality theories, including carrying a copy of Lenin's treatise on nationality policy. Even his prison experience did not dull his enthusiasm for Marxism; after his release he wrote a huge, three-volume treatise on Marxist dialectics, by means of which almost anything can be proven, which he demonstrated by another volume using dialectics to "prove" that there should be water on the moon! The water on the moon thesis was just a theory he used to demonstrate the efficacy of the dialectical method, but he was proved correct when water was actually discovered on the moon!

Phuntsok Wangyal's daughter, Ami's friend, visited Lhasa for the first time that summer. At that time, she was using her Chinese name, Ping Ni. She was known to have been the girlfriend of the Chinese democracy activist, Wei Jinsheng, who was then in prison, and to have influenced his thinking. She was still loyal to her father's legacy and was as yet unaware that the propaganda she had been subjected to about Tibet was less than the reality. Her experience in Tibet was a shock to her. I saw her several times with Ami and the transformation she underwent was dramatic. She appeared to be trying to avoid rejecting her father's legacy while at the same time being confronted with undeniable evidence that the reality of Tibet was far from what she had been taught. I arranged for her to meet Dolma and the resulting encounter was of two Tibetans with experiences as radically opposite as imaginable. Ping Ni was unable to deny that Dolma's version of Tibetan reality was confirmed by everything she saw and everyone she met in Lhasa, while her version was refuted by all actual evidence. She stayed in Lhasa only perhaps a month, but her transformation was obvious. The next time I saw her, some ten years later in Washington, DC, she bristled when I greeted her as Ping Ni. Now she went by her Tibetan name, Phuntsok Dekyi, and didn't even want to be reminded of her Chinese name.

While in Lhasa I made some attempts to learn Tibetan. As part of my learning exercise, I attempted to translate signs posted in various places around the city. The Tibetan alphabet is fairly easy to learn, after which one is able to read Tibetan even without knowing the meaning of all the words. There was one sign in particular I wanted to translate, since it was posted on the front whitewashed wall of the Jokhang and thus, I imagined, had some significance. At the foot of this wall, as well as at the foot of many buildings in Lhasa, were white chalk stripes along the bottom with stripes every few feet running about five feet out into the street. I had also wondered about these chalk stripes but didn't imagine that they had anything to do with the written notice. As I stood at the right side of the Jokhang laboriously trying to translate the notice, I attracted the attention of several Tibetans, some of whom seemed to find my endeavor extremely humorous. Once I had translated the sign I understood. The sign said, "Please do not urinate on the wall." The white chalk stripes, I later found out, meant the same thing.

Walking the streets of Lhasa, one was likely to see almost anything. One day I saw a Tibetan man approaching who appeared to be holding something in his arms. As he neared, I saw that it was a small animal and as he got closer, I saw to my surprise that it was a snow leopard cub. He was a nomad who had found the cub, perhaps after killing the mother, and was now taking it to the Norbulinka Zoo. I was aware from living in Nepal that human sightings of snow leopards, or at least sightings by Western wildlife biologists, were very rare.

The Chinese had not yet created the plaza in front of the Jokhang but they had one in front of the Potala. They would later also destroy much of the Shol area below the Potala and build a horrendous mountain-shaped monument to their liberation of Tibet, but at this time there was only a water park and a MiG jet parked in the Potala plaza. One day as I was standing near the MiG, I was asked by three Chinese who appeared to be local officials if I liked "their" Potala. Their possessiveness set me off, so I replied, in Chinese, "*Bu shir nida Potala*," or "It's not your Potala." Then I quickly hurried off, now fearful, like Tibetans, of the consequences of whatever I said. Nearby, along the road to the east of the plaza, there was still a line of aging anti-American posters, encouraging Tibetans to defeat the imperialists.

Besides Dolma Yudon, the only other notable Tibetan from exile I met in Lhasa was Sharpa Tulku. He was an American citizen and had known Dolma in Dharamsala. He was one of the *tulkus* who had given up their Buddhist robes for marriage to Western women. He and Dolma had been involved together in the United States in Tibetans' second experience (after the Great Northern Paper Company) with the American political system. When these first Tibetans became eligible for US citizenship, they refused to have China written as place of birth on their passports. They lobbied to have a city rather than state of birth entered into passports for those political exiles who did not recognize the sovereignty of conquerors over their countries. They were successful and got Lhasa, or some other Tibetan place name, on their passports rather than China. The new regulation applied to others, like exiles from the Baltic countries, Latvia, Lithuania, and Estonia, who did not want to recognize the sovereignty of the Soviet Union over their countries. The first Tibetan-American political organization, the US Tibet Committee, grew out of their political organizing.

Sharpa Tulku was a bit more careful about his activities in Lhasa than was Dolma. He was of the aristocratic Rampa family, some of whom were current government officials. He told the story of his family receiving many letters from the outside world in the 1950s addressed to Lobsang Rampa. The letters were written by readers of the popular Lobsang Rampa series of books in English that purported to be the writings of a real Tibetan but were actually the fantasies of an English plumber. Such was the universal ignorance about Tibet at that time that almost anything could pass for the truth. The famous Madame Blavatsky had not long before created an entire philosophical-religious system and an organization to promote it, the Theosophical Society, out of wholly fictional contacts with some "Mahatmas" in Tibet. The Tibetan Post Office did not know what to do with the letters to the fictional Lobsang Rampa, so they delivered them to the Rampa family in Lhasa!

Sharpa Tulku was very careful while in Lhasa, but he did invite Jurgen and me to attend a wedding at his family's house. The invitation may have been prompted by Dolma, who was also invited but who was ill at the time and did not attend herself. If he was nervous about inviting foreigners to the wedding, he had good reason, since the event was attended by several high-level Tibetan cadres. The ceremony was very traditional; my main memory is of being served by several chang girls who would immediately refill your cup after every sip. Chang girls were usually chosen for their attractiveness and were encouraged to flirt with guests. Foreign guests were no exception and in fact it seemed that we were tested to see how much we could drink.

It was apparent that Sharpa Tulku's family was somewhat nervous about our presence since they had no doubt survived to that time by being very careful about their politics. The presence of Sharpa Tulku himself was also likely somewhat sensitive since he was an American and, given the paranoia of Chinese political culture, was probably suspected of being a spy. At the least, he was someone who had obviously expressed less than enthusiastic support for the Chinese regime in Tibet simply by his act of fleeing into exile. Now, during the liberalization period, exiles were being invited back in the hopes that they would see the correctness of the new policy and would stay; nevertheless, both Chinese and Tibetan cadres didn't really know what to do with them or how safe it was to associate with or even be seen with them.

Dolma, Sharpa Tulku, and all other Tibetan visitors from exile had to go to meetings with an official Reception Committee that had been set up to convince returnees to stay by means of promises of return of property, appointment to political positions with good salaries, and other enticements. Most returnees, however, had no intention of staying. They only wanted to visit their relatives, whose conditions were usually bad enough to convince them that they were far better off in their countries of exile, no matter what those conditions were or what they were promised if they were to return.

The Chinese were substantially ignorant about conditions in the outside world and tended to believe their own propaganda that Tibetans in exile were little more than beggars. They assumed that their newest "correct policy" would alleviate all discontent left over from the past and therefore any Tibetan exile, the Dalai Lama included, could be enticed to return, thus ending the Tibetan political issue. Despite Chinese and Tibetan cadres' expectations that returnees would be impressed with the situation in Tibet due to the new liberalized policies, returned exiles tended to be appalled with the evidence of destruction and suffering they observed. The Chinese may have thought that everything was fine in Tibet now, but few of the exiles' relatives agreed and few encouraged their relatives to stay. The main complaint, of which the Chinese were unaware due to their own assumptions that Tibetans were now completely reconciled to Chinese rule, was what I was told on the steps of the Potala: "Rangzen mindu."

Because of the atmosphere of fear that they themselves instill, colonialist or repressive regimes typically do not know what their subjects really think. Tibetans had learned to repeat the slogans they had been taught while concealing their true beliefs. The Chinese assumed that Tibetans had long ago given up their own "reactionary local nationalism" and were now loyal to the Chinese regime. The only remaining issue, they thought, was to improve economic conditions and allow the minimal cultural autonomy that had long been promised, after which the Tibet issue would finally be "resolved." Little did they know that a liberalization of the former repressive regime would result in a revival of Tibetan culture and thus a revival of the political issue.

In September I set off on a trip to eastern Tibet, or Kham. Kham is one of the most beautiful regions of Tibet due to its deep valleys and lush forests. The Tibetan Plateau is comparable to the American west in climate and geography. The plateau is roughly equal in area to the American mountain states from the Sierra Nevada to the Rockies, but at twice the altitude. Kham is something like the Colorado of Tibet. The western parts of Tibet are dry and almost desert, like Nevada and Utah. The Tibetan Changtang is somewhat like the terrain of Nevada, with mountain ranges interspersed with dry flat basins. Montana and Wyoming are very much like the rich grasslands of the eastern Changtang in Amdo.

To travel to Kham and return to Lhasa would require leaving the Tibet Autonomous Region (TAR) and reentering, but I knew that travel permits were checked only at Kangding, in Sichuan. Kangding (Tibetan *Dartsendo*) was on the traditional border between China and Tibet and it was also the geographical border between the lowlands of China and the highlands of the Tibetan Plateau. West of Kangding, at the first Tibetan town of Gatar, the road divides into the southern route through Lithang and Bathang and the northern route through Derge and Chamdo. The two routes rejoin about halfway to Lhasa at Bomi, so it was possible to go east from Lhasa on the southern route to just short of Kangding and then back along the northern route to Lhasa without encountering the Kangding checkpoint. The few travelers who had come to Lhasa that way had not reported being checked at the border between Sichuan and the TAR. So, this was my plan. I left some gear at the Guest House in Lhasa on the assumption that I would be back. I walked out to the far side of the bridge over the Kyichu with only a small backpack. I had to wait for only about an hour before I was picked up by a truck with a Tibetan driver.

My first ride was only for one day as far as Giamda. The road goes past the turnoff to Ganden and then climbs up to the Mi La (16,400 feet, about 5,000 meters) before descending into the small town of Giamda, at 10,500 feet (3,200 meters). This town, about 275 kilometers from Lhasa by road, was the western extent of what the Chinese had claimed as Sikang Province, based upon the Chinese invasion of eastern Tibet in 1905 in response to the British invasion of 1904. When the PLA invaded Chamdo in 1950, the PRC claimed that this was not an invasion of "Tibet" at all, based upon the preexisting claim that this area was already a Chinese province, never mind that this was also the result of military invasion. Therefore, since Tibet's subsequent capitulation was achieved by "negotiation," even if coerced by the threat of further invasion, Tibet was "peacefully liberated." From 1950 to the present, Chinese propaganda has never deviated in referring to the invasion of Tibet as a "peaceful liberation."

Giamda was my first experience staying in one of the small guest houses set up for cadres and travelers, mostly Chinese but also Tibetans, at every town along the major roads in Tibet. They were usually very simple, offering meals of cabbage and rice and communal sleeping arrangements. One needed only a *danwei*, or work unit affiliation, to stay there, which I had as a former student at Nei Mongu Daxue. I was able to sign in using characters for my Chinese name and the university. This affiliation proved very useful for the entire journey through Kham, since local officials could shift responsibility for travelers onto their danwei. It was assumed that my university must in some way be responsible for me, so locals didn't have to worry about who I was or what I was doing there. One downside of many of the guest houses was that they kept the lights on all night. At one place I waited until everyone else was asleep and then searched for the light switch, but found that there was none!

The lights, often just a single bulb hanging from the ceiling, remained on day and night!

I was on the gravel road early the next morning and soon secured a ride in a truck owned by a Tibetan who was going all the way to Dartsendo. This, like almost all the trucks in Tibet, was one of the old green Liberation Army models. The driver already had two passengers in the cab and at least another dozen in the open back sitting on wooden boxes or arranged in any way they could. I found a spot on a crate near the rear from which I had the most wonderful view of the magnificent Tibetan scenery as we drove along. From Giamda the road goes about 150 kilometers to the east into the Kongpo area, one of the most richly forested areas of Tibet. Nyingtri, the main town in Kongpo, was the center of a complex of forced labor camps where Tibetans arrested after the revolt were put to work cutting down the forest. The Kongpo area was still heavily forested, at least near the road. It was something of a conifers' paradise; I saw pines and firs and spruces with yearly growth rates of three feet or more. We arrived in Nyingtri at night after about two days on the road.

One disadvantage of this means of travel was that I had no control over the schedule. I couldn't stay in Nyingtri for a few days and enjoy the scenery. My Tibetan driver was going all the way through on this road and I was not about to give up this ride and look for another. After two days on the road, I became more familiar with the driver, who said he was the owner of the truck and that he did private business between Lhasa and Chengdu, in Sichuan. Now he insisted that I, as a foreign visitor, should not have to ride in the back but should assume a coveted seat in the cab. However, I preferred my spectacular seat in the rear, there being little threat of rain, which was the only disadvantage of being in the back of the truck. However, the driver insisted and implied that it would be something of an insult to his hospitality if I didn't sit in the front. So, I agreed and lost my open platform in the rear for a cramped seat in the cab of the truck. The Liberation Army truck has a hold-bar in the passenger side that hit me right in the knees, making the higher status seat in the front a big decrease in comfort.

We proceeded through Kongpo and the equally forested area of Bomi which lies at the relatively low level of about 9,000 feet (2,743 meters). From Kongpo one can see the beautiful Namche Barwa peak (25,400 feet, 7,742 meters) to the south. From here the Tsangpo turns south through the jungles of Pemako and descends to the plains of India and Bangladesh as the Brahmaputra. The Pemako area was once so impenetrable that it was a mystery whether or not the Tsangpo and Brahmaputra were the same river. One goal of the British Indian spies who were sent into Tibet in the nineteenth century was to determine if they were the same. The road through Kham was completed in 1954 along with the other main road to Tibet from the north through Golmud. China was in a hurry to complete both roads in order to consolidate its physical control over Tibet. When both roads were completed, China began its political transformation of Tibet, knowing that it could support its cadres in Tibet and bring in troops in case of revolt.

The road (northern route) through Kham is said to be 2,255 kilometers long and at an average altitude of 12,000 feet. The northern route through Derge was finished first and the southern route through Lithang and Bathang later. It is a truly impressive achievement, testimony to the intensity of the Chinese desire to control Tibet. At one time, the horse was the dominant military machine, allowing grassland cultures like Turks, Mongols, Manchu, and even the seminomadic Tibetans to dominate the sedentary agricultural areas of China. In the machine age, roads and railroads allowed sedentary China to dominate the surrounding grassland cultures. Completion of the roads into Tibet gave China the logistical control over Tibetans and the Tibetan Plateau that it had long claimed but had never been able to actually realize.

The northern route from Qinghai via Golmud to Lhasa is also more than 2,000 kilometers long and is at an even higher average altitude, but is easier than either of the two routes through Kham because it traverses the relatively level heights of the plateau that are not yet dissected by rivers as the plateau is in the east as it slopes down toward China and Southeast Asia. The northern route is subject to snowstorms and crosses many small streams and marshy areas, but it was the preferred route when travel was by horse and yak and it was the easiest route for the first primitive dirt and gravel roads into Tibet. The northern route was the first to be paved, in 1985. This was also the route of a petrol (gasoline) and kerosene (also used as jet aviation fuel) pipeline built in the 1970s, and the railroad, finally completed in 2006 after decades spent trying to solve the problem of permafrost.

The road to the east through Kham has to cross a series of mountain ranges and the deep gorges of the Salween, Mekong, and Yangtze Rivers. The difference in altitude between mountain pass and river gorge can be as much as 10,000 feet. The traditional name for Kham, adopted for the Tibetan Resistance, is Chushi Gangdruk, or "Four Rivers and Six Ranges," all of which run from north to south, while the road has to traverse from east to west. The road typically climbs up each range by a series of switchbacks, then descends into the next valley in the same way. The sloppy construction of roadbeds and shifting alignments betrayed the haste in which it was built. One could see where whole sections were abandoned for better routes as the road was reconstructed over the years. Sometimes, areas of landslide had to be bypassed, while other times it appeared simply that one route had been abandoned in favor of another. The road was hastily constructed but well-maintained. At 20-kilometer intervals there were road stations manned by Chinese workers, often one or more families, who no doubt thought they were suffering the worst sort of exile in Tibet. There was little traffic on the road except for the occasional military convoy of 50 to 100 trucks identical to ours loaded with petrol and rice or wheat.

From Kongpo and Bomi the road goes to the north a bit where it joins with the road coming down from Chamdo. The southern route then crosses the Salween and Mekong and reaches Markham, the last town in the TAR. From Markham it crosses the Yangtze to Bathang. The three rivers, each separated by a high mountain range, are only 150 kilometers apart, straight line distance, at that point. The plateau slopes downward from northwest to southeast, so all the rivers cut gorges through the southeast corner as they rush down from the plateau. Bathang is at a relatively low altitude in a rare flat spot alongside the river, with fields of wheat and apple trees. We stayed at both Markham and Bathang, making four or five days on the road at this point. From Bathang the road ascends via an endless series of switchbacks to a 15,340-foot (4,675-meter) pass and then descends slightly to a broad plateau of rich grasslands in the Lithang area where we saw nomad encampments. The driver had some business with one of these groups of nomads so we stopped there for several hours.

There were about fifty yak-hair tents in the encampment and one white canvas tent in which about twenty monks from Lithang Monastery were performing a ritual. The nomad tents are supported from the outside by yak-hair ropes, each of which is propped up by a vertical post about halfway between the stake where the rope is anchored and the tent, making the interior free of supports. The yak hair for the tent is woven by the flat-weave method on backstrap looms. The backstrap loom has a simple strap that goes around the back that allows a length of woolen threads to be anchored in the ground by stakes at one end and tightened at the weaver's end simply by leaning slightly backwards. All nomad weaving is done in this way since a real loom would be too heavy to transport. The tent interiors are large and spacious, with only a few possessions like a bellows for the fire, a butter churn, and a few low tables. Nomads sleep on yak-hair blankets that are woven just like the tents. Another type of blanket is woven from the soft underwool of the yak and can be used as a softer blanket or as a water-repellent coverall to be worn outside. In the corners of the tent are stacked yak dung for the fire and butter sewn into yak-hair bags. The women all had silver ornaments woven into their braided hair.

Each tent was protected by fierce mastiffs and one did not enter until the dogs had been quieted by the tent owner. I spent my time being entertained by the nomads with immeasurable quantities of butter tea, which, fortunately, I had already come to love while living in Nepal. It is made with tea, butter, salt, and a little soda and is the perfect drink for cold and high altitude. It is not, contrary to the accounts of many old travelers to Tibet, made with rancid butter. Yak butter has a strong smell, but rancid means spoiled and nomads have no reason to use spoiled butter. They may store butter for trade or sale, but the butter they use for their own tea is the freshest imaginable. Even butter stored in yak-hair bags doesn't become rancid in the cold and arid climate of Tibet.

I watched butter being churned from milk as I sat having tea. The tea is boiled on the fire and then poured into a cylindrical wooden tea churn, called a *domo*, along with butter and salt. It is churned with a wooden piston and then poured into a kettle and placed back on the fire. Also, it's not yak butter. This is a huge joke among Tibetans since the yak is the male animal. Butter is made from the milk of the *dri*, the female yak. If you tell a Tibetan you had yak butter tea, they will think this is the funniest thing they have ever heard and will say things like "Well, if it was yak butter, it must be very rare," meaning that it must have been made from the semen of the yak. Another favorite joke, this time at the expense of nomads, is to compare some difficult act to a nomad trying to have a bowel movement, since the nomadic diet is almost all protein from meat and milk and butter with little or no grains or vegetables.

After leaving the nomad encampment, we reached the town of Lithang the same day. Lithang is in a broad valley and is the largest town in southern Kham. Lithang is regarded as the center of the Tibetan revolt that began in the spring of 1956 as the Chinese began their "democratic reforms." What China's reforms actually meant was the overturning of Tibetan society, replacing the authority of traditional chieftains and lamas with lower-class collaborators who were actually puppets of the Chinese. Traditional leaders were subjected to public accusation and humiliation by lower-class activists in what was a primary technique of the Chinese Communists to eliminate the former ruling class and promote social catharsis, leading to "people's democracy." Lamas were particularly singled out for humiliation, typically accused of being charlatans who exploited the superstition of the people, and subjected to torture while being challenged to summon divine assistance to relieve them of their ordeal. These public sessions were particularly traumatic for Tibetans who were forced to abuse their respected leaders and revered lamas, who were sometimes tortured to death on the spot or, more often, sentenced to prison or reform through labor.

Tibet inside the TAR was at that time exempted from any such reforms out of lingering respect for the terms of the 1951 Seventeen Point Agreement, which specified that reforms would be undertaken only voluntarily by the Tibetans themselves. However, the Chinese defined only the TAR as the "Tibet" to which the agreement applied. One half the territory of Tibet and more than half the population was excluded from the provisions of the agreement. Those Tibetan areas outside the TAR were designated as autonomous districts of the provinces of Sichuan, Qinghai, Kansu, and Yunnan. The Chinese imposed their democratic reforms on the Tibetans of eastern Tibet so arbitrarily and so harshly that the result was widespread and open. The revolt that began in Kham in 1956 and Amdo in 1958 was repressed by the PLA with such brutality that thousands of Khampas and Amdowas fled to Lhasa and Central Tibet, leading to the revolt there in March 1959.

Lithang Monastery had been one of the first centers of the revolt in Kham. Thousands of local Tibetans sought refuge in the monastery, which was then bombed by the Chinese air force, killing many and hardening the resolve of Khampas to resist the Chinese. The monastery was almost completely destroyed, but it had been partially rebuilt. As we approached Lithang, I saw two Khampas on horseback, one of whom had an AK-47 slung across his back. In Nepal some Tibetans claimed that the Khampas of Lithang were still resisting Chinese control. The issuance of automatic rifles to nomads, for predator control, seemed conclusive evidence to me that there was no more revolt in Lithang. We arrived early, so I was able to tour the monastery, but it was all new so not very interesting. The Lithang Valley is at about 10,000 feet altitude and is one of the most beautiful places in all of Tibet.

From Lithang my truck proceeded the next day all the way to Dartsendo, but I got out at the junction with the northern road to Derge. I got another ride in short order, again in a Tibetan-driven truck. The small town of Gatar at the road junction is the first purely Tibetan town one encounters when coming from China. It is very picturesque, with many very substantial and well-constructed two-story stone houses. Gatar Gompa is further up the northern road and is the site of the temporary exile of the Seventh Dalai Lama and the birthplace of the Tenth.

The road runs along the river in which one could see logs being floated down to China. Alongside the river there were also large tree nurseries, which indicated that deforestation was accompanied by attempts at reforestation. In my travel through the most densely forested area of eastern Tibet, I had seen some areas of clear-cutting but also dense undisturbed forests even in accessible areas along the road. The Chinese admitted that they had cut more than half of the forest in this area but they had also made some efforts at reforestation, including aerial seeding and the nurseries I had seen. Reforestation was not able to keep up with deforestation, however, and eventually, in 2005, the Chinese government had to ban logging in the area after devastating floods downstream in China. Everywhere in Kham I saw small hydroelectric power plants, often of the diversion type in which a small overflow dam is built in a stream off which a canal channels water until it gains sufficient height above the stream to drop through a penstock to a small turbine. The same sort of mini-hydro projects were being promoted in Nepal at the time, but Tibet was farther ahead.

The next town to the north of Gatar is Dawu, where my ride ended and I was able to visit the local monastery. One of the lhakhangs of Dawu Gompa was restored while another still showed evidence of the destruction of the Cultural Revolution. Murals in the unrestored lhakhang showed evidence of hacking at the faces of deities while all the clay statues were reduced to rubble. I stayed in Dawu for two days and sat in on a ritual at the monastery, which the monks seemed to appreciate. Another short ride took me through the town of Luhou, or Zhaggo in Tibetan, a town that, like Dawu, seemed already more Chinese than Tibetan, all the way to Kanze (11,750 feet, 3,581 meters).

Kanze seemed to be still very Tibetan in character. As in most towns in Tibet at that time, the local monastery was being reconstructed. Kanze was still subjected to constant screeching blasts from loudspeakers exhorting Tibetans to follow the Party line and be loyal to the Chinese Motherland. Here I saw a different building style that made use of the abundant forest resources in the area. Instead of the stone or rammed-earth style used in less-forested areas, houses were built using a half-log technique. Logs were sawn lengthwise, presumably in a saw mill or perhaps using pit saws like my Sherpa carpenters did in Nepal, so that the outer wall looked like the typical log cabin while the inner wall was the flat-sawn side of each log. This style of house was as attractive as log cabins are everywhere.

From Kanze I got a ride over the beautiful Cho La (15,090 feet, 4,600 meter) to the famous monastery town of Derge. Derge is a small village centered around the monastery in a deep and narrow forested valley (10,800 feet, 3,292 meters) with a small river running through it from the Cho La in the east to the Jinsa Jiang (Yangtze) only a short distance to the west. Derge Monastery is one of only three or four places in Tibet where the full Tibetan Buddhist canon, the Kangyur and Tengyur were traditionally printed. Derge monastery printed with metal printing blocks rather than the usual wood. Only Derge's printing blocks had been saved, and printing of the Kangyur, Tengyur, and other texts had resumed.

In Derge I stayed in a tiny guesthouse meant for cadres. One of my fellow guests was a Tibetan from Lhasa who was there to collect texts printed by the monastery. I noticed him because his door was open and I could see that his small room was filled with hundreds of texts. His name was Tubten Khétsun and he was associated with the Tibetan Academy of Social Science that had sent him to Derge to collect one copy of every text for which there were extant printing blocks, some metal, most wooden. Such was the state of destruction of Tibetan Buddhist texts and printing blocks that Derge was the only place where many still existed. Khétsun had been there several months already, which explained his room full of books. I stayed several days in Derge during which I went to the monastery with Khétsun. At the monastery, we saw texts being printed as fast as one monk could ink a block and another could press locally made paper to it. It seemed that the traditional goal of quality had been replaced by the Chinese Communist ideology of increased production without regard to quality, which produced a lot of almost unreadable texts. The monastery's printing press was now organized as a *danwei*, or a state enterprise, so there was no escape from the goal of rapid production. This was a big problem for Khétsun who needed perfect copies to take back to Lhasa.

One evening, Khétsun asked if I wanted to go to a movie. It was outdoors, shown on the side of the largest whitewashed building available. We had to take stools to sit on and it was raining, so we took raincoats. The rain didn't stop many of the Derge Tibetans, for whom a movie was a rare entertainment. It hardly mattered what the movie was either; this one, like most, was a revolutionary drama about the victory of the Communists. A few hundred Tibetans and I sat through the movie in the rain despite having absolutely no interest in the subject. Movies shown on the side of houses had been part of China's propaganda campaign from the early 1950s. Along with PLA dance and drama troupes, outdoor movies were a favorite means to reach the Tibetans with China's revolutionary message.

I met Tubten Khétsun again, fifteen years later, in Washington, DC, at a Losar (Tibetan New Year) party. He had escaped from Tibet a few years after we met. He had spent a few years in India and then he was able to join his brother in the United States; his brother happened to be one of my colleagues at Radio Free Asia. Tubten Khétsun had written the story of his arrest after the revolt in 1959, his imprisonment for two years, and an account of Lhasa after the revolt and during the Cultural Revolution. His book had been published in India in Tibetan and attracted the attention of several people, including the Dalai Lama, who remarked favorably on it. An English scholar living in Kathmandu, Matthew Akester, translated it into English without even knowing the author. I became aware of the translation and I knew Khétsun, so I was able to make the connection between Matthew and Khétsun. The book was eventually published by Columbia University Press with the title *Memories of Life in Lhasa Under Chinese Rule*.

To my knowledge fewer than ten foreigners had come through Derge that year, and maybe a few the year before, so a foreign face was still a sight to see. I remember being stared at almost as if I was some sort of a strange-looking yak rather than a human being. The local Tibetans would look at me in wonder and then be shocked when I made some human gesture like smiling or speaking. Another thing I noticed in Derge as well as in all other Tibetan towns I visited was that there was always a state store that, if it sold nothing else, was well-stocked with cheap liquor.

By now I had only a few days left on my visa and needed to get back to Lhasa. I went out to the road early one morning to flag a ride to Chamdo to the west. As I was waiting there, I saw a Tibetan leading two young yak to a spot nearby. As the man tied each yak's legs together,

I cringed as I realized what was about to happen. Unable to move, each yak was easily toppled over and then suffocated with a cloth placed over its mouth. This is considered the most humane way of killing a yak, which many Tibetans consider a symbol of their country and thus are particularly reluctant to slaughter. The two yaks were then butchered as I watched and the meat sold to people who came out to what must have been the usual place for this business.

After a few hours standing by the side of the sparsely traveled gravel road, I still did not have a ride. However, a Chinese driver came along who was going the opposite way, back toward the east and then north to Jyekundo in Qinghai. He offered to take me along. Jyekundo was the most important town in the eastern grasslands (12,000 feet, nearly 3,700 meters) and almost surely had not been visited by any foreigner since the 1940s, if then. Going to Jyekundo was almost irresistible, but it would mean that my visa would expire before I could get back to the TAR, much less to Lhasa.

The road went through the richest grasslands of Tibet and the legendary kingdom of Ling, site of the famous epic poem "Gesar of Ling." The poem is entirely oral, having never been written until recently. It has many versions and is one of the longest epic poems in the world. Traditional performers of the epic would memorize as much of the poem as possible and make their living by public recitals. Now it is available in written and published forms, the Chinese having promoted Gesar research and publishing because this was a rare part of Tibetan secular culture that did not have the political implications of Buddhist scholarship. Gesar's brother married a Chinese woman, so the epic was also favored because it demonstrated the "natural and inevitable merging of nationalities." The name Gesar is said by some scholars to derive from the Roman Emperor "Caesar." The main square of Jyekundo is now decorated with a huge statue of Gesar on horseback.

I had to decide quickly, and I did and was soon on my way to Jyekundo with the Chinese driver. We had to cross back over the Cho La between Derge and Kanze and then turn north at a tiny town called Maniganggo. From the turnoff, the road was little more than a dirt track across the grasslands. The narrow valleys of the Kanze and Derge area broadened out and there was no longer any forest, only grass. The terrain is beautiful in the extreme with rounded snow peaks arising out of rolling high-altitude plains. The grasslands were rich and the yak and horses were fat and sleek. This is the best area of the plateau for animal husbandry. There were large numbers of yak and many horses, the latter a luxury animal since it was only used for transport and sport and was now not even used that much for transport. The richness of the grass was indicated by the fact that even luxury animals could be supported here. Farther to the west the plateau is far more arid and the grass more sparse. In the western part of the plateau, the predominant animals are goats and sheep, which can nibble the shorter grass and reach terrain inaccessible to yak and horses. There were no goats or sheep to be seen in these lush grasslands.

We stopped at a few places along the way. There were several small monasteries in the area, all destroyed and none so-far reconstructed. I saw many destroyed mani walls and places where mani stones had been used as paving. I used a photo of broken mani stones from here for the front cover of my history of Tibet, *Tibetan Nation*. At one place where I was taking photos of mani stones used for paving, I attracted a group of young Tibetan boys. My respect for the broken stones seemed to impress them. It reminded me of how foreigners' interest in the temples and stone sculptures of the Kathmandu Valley had influenced the attitudes of many people in Nepal about the value and need for preservation of their own cultural monuments. In Tibet, it had a political component, since an outsider's respect for what the Chinese had coerced the Tibetans themselves to destroy contradicted China's attempt to pressure Tibetans to devalue and disrespect their own culture.

As we approached the town of Serxu, the last place before the border of Qinghai Province and Jyekundo, the Chinese driver went slower and slower, finally traveling at only about five miles an hour. I knew what he was thinking. I had revealed to him that I had no travel permit to Jyekundo, so he was getting worried. I didn't want to get him in trouble, so when he suggested that he take me to the Gong An Ju in Serxu, I readily agreed. He seemed immensely relieved, especially when he dropped me at Serxu and he was allowed to go on his way. I was told that

I would have to go back the way I had come. It was too late to return that same day, and there was no traffic on the road.

I was told that I should stay in the local guest house and not go out, but that was no problem because almost everyone in the town came to see me. I was besieged by a crowd of Tibetans, young and old, all of whom just wanted a sight of a foreigner. I was rescued by some local Tibetan officials, who invited me to dinner at the only small canteen in town. They were all very friendly and interested in what had brought me to this remote part of Tibet. They seemed very flattered that anyone would want to visit their town. The next day they provided me with transportation back down the road to Maniganggo. So I didn't reach my goal of Jyekundo, but I saw the finest grasslands of Tibet, so rich that they had produced a kingdom of epic legend.

At Maniganggo, which was little more than the junction of two dirt roads, I waited beside the road headed back to Derge. My visa had expired at this point. To hitchhike in Tibet, one does not stick out a thumb like in some countries. Instead, you "wave down" approaching vehicles by a repeated downward wave of the hand, palm down. Soon, three Liberation Army trucks came along from the direction of Kanze and the first truck driver stopped to look me over. Asked where I was going, I said Derge and was offered a ride. The driver was a friendly and talkative young Chinese from Chengdu who drove this route regularly. My Chinese wasn't good enough for complex conversations, but I suppose I satisfied his need for companionship on this lonely road. I was surely the only foreigner he had ever seen, at least on this road. No doubt, his two fellow drivers wondered about the stranger their compatriot had picked up. He, like all the Chinese drivers I observed, carried a glass jar in which he made "tea" by repeatedly pouring hot water over a few tea leaves that were rarely replaced. The resulting brew had almost no color. Tibetans mocked this Chinese habit by calling hot water "Chinese tea." The weak and colorless Chinese tea could not be more different from the Tibetan salt and butter tea that was usually as thick as soup.

We went back over the Cho La again, for my third time, and reached Derge near dusk. By that time, I knew that the three trucks were going to Chamdo, so when we reached Derge I asked if they would take me all the way to their destination. They didn't stop at all in Derge; we drove along the river to the west as it got dark. A short distance from Derge, we stopped at a road maintenance station where the three drivers had friends and where, it seemed, they usually stopped for meals. We had dinner with a Chinese family that manned the road station and who seemed even lonelier than the drivers. Road stations were apparently not where drivers could stay overnight, so we continued driving after dinner. Around midnight we reached the Yangtze River and the border between Sichuan and the TAR.

On the far side of the river was a border post where the driver stopped and turned on the cab light, presumably so the border guard could see his passenger. I didn't want to be seen, however, so I reached up and turned it off. The driver looked at me in some surprise but didn't turn it back on. I was afraid of being turned back because my visa had expired. I supposed the driver figured he couldn't be blamed if the border guard failed to see me in the cab. And I didn't feel that I was really jeopardizing the driver, not like the one who took me north toward Jyekundo, because I did have a permit for Lhasa, even if it was expired. Maybe they would have sent me to Lhasa to get it renewed, but I didn't want to find out. The driver didn't seem too concerned and didn't ask why I had turned off the light, but he knew that I had done it for a reason, a reason that he didn't want to know.

We stopped at a guest house in Jomda shortly after crossing the border. The next day we crossed the pass (15,060 feet, 4,581 meters) between the Yangtze and Mekong Rivers and descended toward Chamdo in the rain. The descent was so steep and so slippery that the drivers had to put snow chains on their tires to deal with the mud. We finally arrived at Chamdo and my Chinese driver friend deposited me at the local guest house. Chamdo is built at the junction of two of the main tributaries of the Mekong (Dza Chu and Dzi Chu join to become the Ngom Chu). At that time, there were two bridges over the branches of the river that were of the old traditional Tibetan cantilever style. Both streams were perhaps 200 feet wide, so square timber structures were built near each bank, close enough that one log length reached the shore. The distance between the two square structures was greater than even the longest log's length, so the cantilever method was used. One row of logs is stretched out at an angle from the lower level of the square structure and then another row on top of that until there were four or five layers, each one protruding further out until it was possible to bridge the chasm with a set of the longest logs. This was the traditional style of bridge building in Tibet for bridges that could carry heavy loads. Smaller footbridges were built with iron chains from an early time, the inventor of this method, Changchung Gyalpo, also being the founder of Tibetan opera. It is said that he used opera performances to raise funds for his bridges.

Chamdo is the largest town in Kham and was the headquarters of the Governor of Kham and the Tibetan Army in Kham when the Chinese invaded in 1950. Since the Chinese claimed that the area was already part of the Chinese province of Sikang, they separated it from the rest of Tibet under what they called the "Chamdo Liberation Committee." They also created a separate area in Tsang (Shigatse) under the Panchen Lama, thus dividing central Tibet into three parts, not to mention the half of Tibetan territory and two-thirds of its population placed outside of what was to become the TAR. The Chamdo region was returned to the TAR in 1956. The Chamdo Monastery was the largest in Kham; it was looted like almost all monasteries in Tibet but the main monastic buildings were not destroyed. One of the largest lhakhangs had been restored in 1982. There were perhaps a hundred monks who were performing a ritual that I sat in on for most of three days. The monks seemed impressed and I hope encouraged by my respect and interest.

In Chamdo I met a young Tibetan who was in the Chinese Navy, a seemingly unlikely role for a Tibetan for geographical as well as political reasons. He was one of those Tibetans who had benefited by accepting rather than resisting China's authority over Tibet. He was disdainful of my interest in the Tibetan political issue, a lack of interest in that issue being a prerequisite for his own relative success. Chinese policy toward Tibetans was one of great incentives for cooperation and harsh disincentives for resistance. The Chinese political system did not allow any middle ground. Tibetans either had to escape into exile or they had to somehow adapt to the Chinese regime. The struggle sessions of the post-1959 period were meant to ferret out all opponents, even if only passive. One had to exhibit enthusiasm for the regime, even if false, and to inform upon and denounce others who exhibited less enthusiasm. Those who could not bring themselves to act out this play or who could not disguise their dissatisfaction were quickly identified and suffered the consequences. They were sometimes sentenced to "reform through labor" but that also meant learning to play along with the indoctrination and learn the slogans required to demonstrate loyalty. Many Tibetans were too simple and honest to perform this false act and they usually were the most easily identified and repressed and were the objects of the worst treatment in prisons and labor camps.

I stayed in Chamdo for three days because I had heard about a bus that had come from Lhasa with some government officials that would be returning empty. I managed to get a place on the bus for a fee, the only time I had to pay for transportation on this trip. The bus, a relatively modern model, departed Chamdo about half full, proceeding to the south along the Mekong River. We had gone only a few miles when we passed three Khampas standing beside the road. They tried to flag us down but the Chinese driver did not stop. No sooner had we passed them when the large rear window of the bus disintegrated with a loud crash. The bus skidded to a stop. It was obvious that one of the Khampas had thrown a rock through the bus window. The three Khampas, who appeared to be somewhat drunk, denied their obvious guilt even though the rock was lying there on the road near where they were still impassively standing. One of the passengers was a Tibetan policeman who had a pistol that he displayed to the Khampas while demanding that they pay for the broken bus window.

This scene was another stark juxtaposition between those Tibetans who had accepted the regime and those who still resisted it. The Khampas were drunk and surly and had probably thrown the rock out of a general frustration at their marginal status that allowed the Chinese driver of the bus to pass them by as if they didn't exist. The driver and the Tibetan policeman demanded that the Khampas pay for the window, which they said would be about 160 yuan, although interestingly both the Khampas and the policeman referred to the currency not in yuan but in rupees, which I suppose showed Indian or Nepalese influence in the

Tibetan economy over that of China. Finally, they managed to coerce out of the three Khampas all the money they had, which amounted to about six yuan. Given what the Khampas had to pay, one would have to say that they had won in this confrontation with the bus and with the Chinese authority. Once we resumed driving, the movement of the bus created a vacuum that sucked the road dust into the bus through the open rear window. Everyone had to move toward the front of the bus; for the rest of the journey to Lhasa we had to wear face masks and ended each day covered in dust. If the three Khampas could have seen our suffering, they would have been even happier with what they got for their six yuan.

The return to Lhasa was uneventful, perhaps because the dusty bus was much less exciting than the back of the truck in which I had come the other way. I had been a month on the road and had seen a lot of Kham. I had seen and learned a lot. It was like everything about Tibet; nothing was pure black or white. There was a great deal of deforestation, but there were also attempts at reforestation. Not all Chinese thought Tibetans were barbarians and not all Tibetans hated the Chinese. Some Chinese were friendly toward Tibetans and some Tibetans reciprocated. But I also saw that Chinese and Tibetans were generally separate communities. The Chinese I saw in Kham kept to themselves. Many seemed to regard Tibetans as backward, if not barbarian, and Tibetans confirmed their backwardness by refusing to participate in Chinese-style modernization. Tibetans often had surly attitudes toward Chinese. Chinese often treated Tibetans rudely, especially if they didn't speak Chinese.

The greatest barrier between Chinese and Tibetans was one of attitude. Tibetans regarded the Chinese as colonists and the Chinese knew it. Many Tibetans adopted attitudes of noncooperation and were therefore denied whatever benefits there were to be gained by cooperation. They reveled in their opposition to everything Chinese and thus perpetuated their own backwardness. They tended to reject modernity because it came with the Chinese. They reminded me of the American Indians who were mired in poverty because of their refusal to accept and participate in the culture that had overwhelmed and destroyed their own cultures. Some Tibetans, like those who threw the rock at the bus, seemed headed down that road. Like the American Indians, they sometimes sought refuge in alcoholism, which the Chinese government appeared willing to oblige. Tibetans' only chance was to compete with the Chinese but many seemed to have withdrawn into the defeat and depression typical of conquered peoples.

When I got back to Lhasa, it was October. My visa had expired a week before. I went to the Gong An Ju where I saw the Chinese official who had extended my last visa. I was told that I had violated China's laws and I was in big trouble. I would have to write a self-criticism! This was the Party's remedy for all minor offenses among its own officials and the Chinese population. Self-criticisms were meant to enforce conformity and to publicly humiliate those who failed to conform. It was a serious sentence for Chinese, since everyone had a personal record that was kept with the security police. Minor offenses could be taken into account on all sorts of issues, from jobs to housing to education for one's children, and they could influence punishments for more serious offenses if one already had a record of transgressions. Chinese who were forced to write self-criticisms therefore debased themselves to the greatest extent possible and pledged strict conformity and undying loyalty in the future. Self-criticisms were taken very seriously, both by the offender and the authorities. No one was immune from self-criticisms. Even Party leaders sometimes had to make self-criticisms, if only to get themselves back on the right side of Mao and the Party hierarchy.

The CCP tended to treat foreigners in China the same way as Chinese, at least in regard to enforcing conformity. Those foreigners who had come to work in China were considered to be sympathetic to the Communist regime and, until recently, many had been members of communist parties in their own countries. They were thought to be susceptible to communist-style discipline, and many were because they were intent upon proving their loyalty to the ideology. However, in the recent era of liberalization, many more foreigners had come to China who had no interest in or loyalty to communism or to the CCP. Some came as teachers just for the adventure of working in the still-isolated and mysterious China. Some, like my colleagues in Inner Mongolia, hoped to convert the Chinese to their (religious) ideology. Some were just backpackers or adventurers who took advantage of China's opening. For those of us who were hardly pilgrims of the Marxist faith, self-criticisms were a joke. I had already heard stories of those who had made minor transgressions and were solemnly told that they would have to write a self-criticism. Often, they used this as an opportunity to feign remorse and abject submissiveness while subtly mocking what they regarded as the ridiculous Chinese system.

I was already so angry at that system and at the Chinese for what they had done to Tibet that I was afraid that I would not be able to contain my opinions if I began criticizing myself for what had been nothing less than a great adventure for me. I had seen too much, and had been told too much by Dolma and her friends, to be able to restrain myself once I started writing a criticism of myself that I feared would turn into a criticism of everything that was wrong with the Chinese political system and their repressive and destructive role in Tibet. Informed of an option to pay a fine of 600 yuan, about $80, instead, I jumped at it, much to the surprise of the police official. The fine was high enough that no one, not even foreigners, had ever taken that option, at least in Lhasa. Writing a phony self-criticism was so easy that no one had even considered paying the fine. I had a little bit of money at the time so this was the best option for me. Once I paid the fine, I got another extension on my visa. There were hardly any foreigners left in Lhasa by now, mostly because the period when one could get a visa had been so brief and so long ago. Once in Lhasa, there seemed to be no limit on how long one could stay, but I was just about the last one left.

For the rest of October and November, I spent most of my time with Dolma and her family. Everyone seemed to know that Dolma would be leaving soon, so an even greater number of people visited in order to send letters with her to relatives in exile. Dolma also began to attract more attention from the authorities because of the salon she was conducting at her sister's apartment, because she was often seen in public with me, and because she was now well-known to the Reception Committee as someone who totally rejected their enticements to return and their propaganda about how wonderful life was now in Tibet and how it could only get better under the Party's leadership. She later told me that she thought that she started being followed at this time and that the Phala house was under observation. Dolma remained fearless, however, as did her sister and brother-in-law who, like so many older Tibetans, said that they had suffered so much already that they were no longer afraid. The last two months that Dolma and I were in Lhasa were when I learned the most about Tibetans' experiences since the early 1950s. The information I gathered at these informal salons formed the basis of my understanding of Tibetan history since 1950, but some of the following observations also derive from my subsequent studies.

Many of Dolma's informants were of the former upper class, of aristocratic status, or associated with that class as managers or retainers. All Tibetans who resisted the Chinese occupation of their country suffered adverse fates, but those of the former upper class tended to have lost the most because they had the most to lose. The lower classes were promised the wealth of the rich, in an overturning of society, but they were deceived when the Chinese became the owners of Tibet's wealth. Those of the upper classes had the opportunity to cooperate with the United Front, but very few survived the purges of those later identified as Tibetan "local nationalists." Many of the upper class were arrested and sent to prisons after the revolt, unless they managed to escape into exile, and even then, they lost their property and their country. Those of the lower classes usually suffered according to their role in the revolt, but the upper class suffered just because of their class status.

Marxist ideology was particularly efficacious in justifying the Chinese "liberation" of Tibet. Marx's class-based analysis of history decreed that the working class was destined to overthrow the exploitative capitalist class. In both Russia and China, revolutionary activists considered themselves authorized by Marxist theory not only to act on behalf of a nonexistent proletariat among their own nationality but also to act on behalf of an equally nonexistent proletariat of other nationalities in order to incorporate them within a larger socialist state. Thus, the Russian communists created the Union of Soviet Socialist Republics by incorporating many non-Russian nationalities and the Chinese communists created the People's Republic of China by incorporating Inner Mongolia, Xinjiang, and Tibet. Both Russian and Chinese communists thus perpetuated the conquests of the Russian and Chinese empires, respectively, while denying that they were imperialists. Instead, they claimed that they were actually liberating those nations.

The Chinese Communists thus declared themselves more legitimate judges of Tibetans' interests than the Tibetans themselves. The Chinese Communist Party (CCP) claimed to have liberated Tibetans from their own feudal misrule and to have achieved class self-determination for the Tibetan "serfs," while denying national self-determination to Tibet. This was justified by the theory that Tibetans would "naturally and voluntarily" opt for union with the more advanced socialist Chinese state rather than cling to their own barbarian backwardness. The Chinese Communists believed in the efficacy of their nationalities policies, an important aspect of which was respectful treatment of Tibetans and their customs until firm Chinese control could be established, after which the intended "reforms" of Tibetan society would begin.

According to Marxist ideology, the achievement of socialism would eliminate the exploitation of one class by another as well as the exploitation of one nation by another. With the elimination of class exploitation, the right of nationalities for national self-determination would disappear because the need would disappear. In Marxist ideology the self in self-determination was a class rather than a nation. Since Tibetans' genuine interests, as defined by the Chinese, were for union with China, then any separatist sentiments or actions had to be a reactionary response of the exploitative upper class or inspired by foreign imperialism.

Marxist ideology was compatible with the Chinese Communists' cultural chauvinism toward what they thought were the barbarian Tibetans, who should be grateful for the gift of Chinese socialist culture and who, most Chinese believed, were already Chinese and therefore had little reason to resist the actual imposition of Chinese administration. China's real motive for annexing Tibet was openly revealed by Mao, who offered to Tibetans what he imagined to be a mutually beneficial bargain. Since Tibet lacked population, he said, which China had in plenty, and China lacked natural resources, which Tibet had in abundance, then China should provide people to help develop Tibet while Tibet would provide its resources to help develop China. Mao was apparently unable to see any reason why Tibetans would oppose this "bargain," even though it meant giving up their country and their freedom.

To put their nationalities policies into action, the Chinese Communists had to gain actual control over Tibet. This was accomplished by the October 1950 invasion of eastern Tibet and the subsequent "Seventeen Point Agreement for the Peaceful Liberation of Tibet." The preamble of that agreement stated that Tibet would "return to the Motherland," which implied that it had been part of China all along but had been temporarily estranged due to the intrigues of foreign imperialism. There was therefore no question of any Chinese "invasion" of Tibet. The Seventeen Point Agreement essentially co-opted the Tibetan upper class, the class that would normally be the most resistant to the loss of its own rule, because the Dalai Lama's government had recognized Chinese sovereignty over Tibet. All Tibetans, but especially Tibetan government officials, were therefore required to cooperate with the Chinese.

The CCP's initial policy in Tibet was to cooperate with the Tibetan upper class, despite the eventual goal that the lower class would become the "rulers" of Tibet while the upper class was to be disposed of its privilege, its power, and its property. The Tibetan upper class was not unaware of the fate that Chinese policy decreed for their class. However, they were effectively co-opted as individuals by the hope that their personal cooperation would prove their loyalty to the new regime and make them essential in the functioning and legitimizing of the Chinese regime in Tibet. This strategy saved a few of the upper class from persecution, but only a very few of the most loyal and most essential. The Tibetan lower classes, designated as "serfs" because Tibet was, according to Marxist theory, at the feudal stage of history, were to become the beneficiaries of Tibetan "self-rule" under the PRC's system of National Regional Autonomy (later changed to Regional Ethnic Autonomy, to demote national identity to ethnic identity). In fact, those of the lower classes who were elevated to positions of nominal authority were little more than puppets of the Chinese, who exercised all real authority.

While Tibetan government officials automatically became collaborators with the Chinese regime, due to the terms of the Seventeen Point Agreement, their families and many others of the upper and middle class often had to make difficult choices. The Chinese offered significant incentives for cooperation, such as education in the interior for children and leadership roles in the myriad social organizations they created. Disincentives for noncooperation were unspoken but were as ominous as the incentives were attractive. As the Chinese gained ever more control over Tibetan social and political life, their collaborators benefited, while those who were less cooperative were increasingly isolated, deprived of economic and political benefits, and identified as opponents of the new regime, which could only have negative consequences. As Dolma and her friends and relatives experienced in Lhasa in the 1950s, one had to accept offers of education and membership in social organizations or be identified as actual or potential opponents.

The dilemmas faced by all Tibetans in the 1950s were described by many whose stories I heard. Tibetans' nationalist and patriotic sentiments were undercut by the fact that the Dalai Lama had accepted Chinese sovereignty over Tibet and thus cooperation with the Chinese was obligatory. For Tibetans to be loyal to their country and their national identity, they had to be disloyal to the Dalai Lama. Disloyalty to the Dalai Lama was almost unthinkable; Tibetans' sense of religious identity and devotion was at this stage in their history far more developed than was their sense of national identity.

As Marx predicted, nationalist identity and resistance is usually aroused by outside threats, or as he said, by colonialism. Tibetan identity was more local, until outside threats, such as the British invasion of 1904, the Chinese response in 1905, and the Chinese invasion of 1950 caused them to unify in response to the foreign threat. While Tibetans were forced to develop a more modern sense of nationalism in response to the Chinese invasion and occupation, the Tibetan government was engaged in a contradictory attempt to preserve a semblance of their traditional relationship with China, based upon the religious ideology of "Patron-Priest," an archaic system from an era that time had already passed.

The "Patron-Priest" relationship only worked when the patrons were Buddhist, which the Chinese Communists decidedly were not. The CCP promised to preserve Tibet's religious system and the status and role of the Dalai Lama and his government, but only until such time that the "Tibetans themselves decided for reform." By cultivating lower-class collaborators, the Chinese had a large percentage of Tibetans for whom they claimed to speak and who they said were in favor of reforms. Many indeed were in favor, since they were promised an overturning of society in which the rich would become poor and the poor would be rich. Other Tibetans who were in official positions or were members of Chinese social organizations were coerced to favor such reforms at least outwardly. Tibetans were placed in a dilemma in which they were forced to favor the abandonment of their own government and their own culture in favor of Chinese political control and an unknown "Chinese socialist culture."

Tibetans in the 1950s were put in an untenable position, both individually and collectively, by China's invasion and occupation of their country. Their government's acceptance, under duress, of the Seventeen Point Agreement forced them to collaborate with their invaders in the demise of their nation, while the CCP's United Front policy forced them to participate in the destruction of their own culture. The Chinese offered to assist in the modernization of Tibet while at the same time promising to preserve Tibetan cultural and political autonomy. If one could believe the Chinese promises, and ignore the contradiction between those promises and their ultimate plans for Tibet, then one might cooperate with them while still considering oneself a patriot to Tibetan national identity and culture.

Some Tibetans were willing participants. There were many Tibetans who were frustrated with the archaic nature of the Tibetan political system or who were opposed to the domination of that system by the Buddhist church. There were those, not only of the lower classes, who had been abused by aristocrats or landlords and were all in favor of change. There were some progressive intellectuals, like Bapa Phuntsok Wangyal, who believed the ideology of Communist nationality policies and were ignorant of the reality. The result of these circumstances in which Tibetans found themselves was to cause divisions in the society. Such divisions were a stated goal of CCP class warfare policies, which were intended to instigate turmoil and conflict in society, leading to "socialist transformation."

Despite their open intention to exploit the natural resources of Tibet, the Chinese denied that they were colonialists. Even Mao, in explicating his bargain for Tibetans—which was essentially colonialist in that it implied development of Tibet by Chinese for the benefit of China—did not admit that the Chinese role in Tibet was colonialist. Many Chinese in the first PLA units to enter eastern Tibet repeated the slogan that they were there to assist Tibetans to develop, and that they would leave once Tibet was developed, even if Tibetans begged them to stay! Many Chinese cadres who were sent to Tibet imagined that they were there to elevate the backward natives; they often had benevolent, if patronizing, attitudes toward Tibetans. Only when they realized that they were regarded as colonialists did they begin to act like colonialists. This is the nature of all colonialisms, which start with the rationalization that the natives are incapable of ruling themselves and rapidly degenerate into the arrogant defensiveness typical of all colonialist regimes.

Tibetans told stories of increased tensions in Lhasa leading up to the March 1959 revolt. Tensions had increased since 1956, when the Chinese began implementing their deceptively titled "democratic reforms" in areas of eastern Tibet outside the TAR. These reforms were democratic in the sense that they overturned society, based upon the Marxist theory that those on the top were guilty of exploiting those on the bottom, who therefore deserved to be on top.

That same year, 1956, the Dalai Lama was invited to visit India for the 2,500th anniversary of the enlightenment of Buddha, and the Chinese reluctantly had to allow him to go. China had only recently, in 1954, concluded a treaty with India by which India had recognized Chinese sovereignty over Tibet. "Panchshila," the Indian name for the treaty, means "five principles of peaceful coexistence," one of which was noninterference in the affairs of other countries. China later made this principle the cornerstone of its foreign policy. China meant to distinguish itself from the foreign imperialists in declaring that it would not interfere in the affairs of other countries, but its original purpose was to prevent any Indian challenge to China's interference in Tibet. China's invasion and occupation of Tibet was now past history and China now posed as the champion of the principle of noninterference. Since China's relations with India were good, the Chinese could hardly refuse Prime Minister Nehru's personal request that the Dalai Lama visit for such an important Buddhist anniversary. They insisted, however, that their collaborator, the Panchen Lama, should also be invited and that he should be treated as of equal status to the Dalai Lama.

While in India, the Dalai Lama spoke to Indian Prime Minister Nehru about seeking asylum, which prompted a quick visit by Zhou Enlai to New Delhi and promises that China would not implement any reforms in "Tibet" until the Tibetans wanted them and that the numbers of Chinese in the TAR would be greatly reduced. These promises were included by Mao in his "Hundred Flowers" liberalization policy, and they enticed the Dalai Lama to return to Lhasa. However, the Chinese still did not see the need to stop their reforms in eastern Tibet outside the TAR, with the result that revolt continued there and spread to central Tibet as refugees fled there. Tensions increased in central Tibet during 1958, when refugees arrived in Lhasa and the resistance forces relocated to southern Tibet.

A few of the Lhasa aristocrats had the foresight to leave for India as early as 1951, usually relocating in Darjeeling and Kalimpong. Others held out until the end, many hoping for the best, often until it was too late to escape. In the chaos of the revolt, some managed to escape but many more were captured. Dolma was one of the few who opted to escape in early 1959. She went to Shigatse in February and after a few weeks there escaped to India. She had to hide in a wagon under a pile of wool and at the border was able to cross only with the assistance of a Chinese businessman who befriended her.

Dolma told me many years later that she knew some Chinese officials in Lhasa as well as some anti-communist Chinese who had small shops in the area near the Yutok Samba. She remembers returning from Ganden one day, where she had witnessed the Dalai Lama's final *geshe* exams, to find that those Chinese had all disappeared, apparently having been rounded up by the government. This was one of the events that convinced her to leave Tibet. She says that she was better informed than most Tibetans, partly because of her friendships with some Chinese. She describes many Tibetans as refusing to recognize the reality that the situation was about to deteriorate rapidly. They tended to believe that as long as the Dalai Lama was in Lhasa, everything would be all right. However, Lhasa was full of refugees from Kham and Amdo and everyone knew what had happened there.

Dolma also had other sources of information. Her fiancé was one of those young Tibetans who had accepted the offer of schooling in China. He had first been sent for schooling to India in the early 1950s but then was pressured to go to the National Minorities Institute in Beijing. Despite his indoctrination there, he remained a Tibetan patriot and rejected communist ideology. He warned Dolma that the Chinese would eventually institute their reforms in the TAR as they had in eastern Tibet. He and Dolma planned to escape to India together. However, Dolma, as is the Tibetan custom, consulted an oracle at Sera Monastery who told her that she must leave immediately. She knew that the situation would ultimately result in a revolt, but the oracle indicated, accurately as it turned out, that the revolt was more imminent than anyone imagined. Because of the oracle's advice she was able to escape. Most Lhasa Tibetans were not so lucky. Most remained in Lhasa and were either killed in the revolt or arrested afterward. Dolma's fiancé was in Beijing at the time so was unable to escape with her. He was one of those who visited her in 1982.

Most of those who came to visit Dolma in 1982 had chosen various levels of noncooperation with the Chinese in the 1950s. There were a few exceptions, like her fiancé who had avoided trouble after 1959 and had a seemingly successful career as a minor official. But he didn't seem any happier or satisfied with the choices he had made than those who had resisted and had suffered as a consequence. At least the latter could claim some dignity in their lives and consistency in their beliefs. Many, if not most, of those who had collaborated had eventually run afoul of Chinese suspicion and the system of mutual denunciations and constant scrutiny and testing of the loyalty of Tibetan cadres. Even the Panchen Lama, whose role as the highest remaining religious leader was apparently essential to the legitimization of Chinese rule, was purged and imprisoned for his criticisms of the excesses of the post-revolt period. His purge and that of any Tibetan who revealed "local nationalist" sentiments was because the Chinese could not admit any fault in their policies in Tibet lest all their justifications for Chinese rule should come into question.

Most of the stories I heard were not about active resistance in 1959. Those who had participated in the resistance had been killed, or they had fled into exile, or they had been arrested and imprisoned where most had died from overwork and starvation. Many Tibetans told stories of the Tibetan government officials who had been arrested after the revolt, whether for participation or not, and were sent off to prison in Xinjiang (or Gansu, near the border with Xinjiang). Everyone knew this story since many were the relatives of those officials, almost none of whom survived. Out of some 170 Tibetan government officials who were sent to this prison, only some seven survived until their release in the late 1970s. Most of the family members who told their stories had themselves been sentenced to "reform through labor," simply for the crime of their class status, and had labored at Chinese construction projects, usually at the hydroelectric project at Nachen Trang.

Dolma's sister as well as many of those who came to visit had labored on the hydroelectric project a few miles to the east of Lhasa on the Kyichu River. Some had been arrested for participating in the revolt or as Tibetan government officials or employees, and many were monks, but many seem to have been guilty of nothing more than the "crime" of being of the upper class. There were different sections of workers at Nachen Trang according to their crimes. These work units were forced to compete with each other, which contributed to a frenzied work pace and a large number of injuries and deaths at what was already a dangerous site because of landslides and rockfalls. Each worker was required to earn a set number of work points per day; failure to do so meant having one's sentence extended, rations reduced, or being subjected to struggle by one's comrades. Dolma's sister remembers having to run with a wheelbarrow nonstop all day under the urging of Chinese supervisors.

My friend Tubten Khétsun had also been at Nachen Trang. He wrote in his book that he and his group of prisoners were sent there in November 1959. They were greeted by a lecture from a PLA officer who told them that old Tibet was a dark, barbaric, and cruel feudal society, the upper strata of which had not voluntarily accepted reforms, so the heroic

PLA had put down their revolt so that the reconstruction of Tibet could begin. The benevolent and correct policy of the Party was that he and other exploiters of the people should be given the opportunity to become new people through labor reform. They were subjected to the same sort of lectures every evening and had to learn to repeat such slogans themselves.

Khétsun estimated that there were as many as 10,000 Tibetan laborers at the site. On the way to work, they had to sing revolutionary songs such as "Socialism is Great, Socialism is Good!" They were forced to work thirteen hours per day, after which there were two hours of meetings, lectures, and struggle sessions for those who failed to meet their work quotas or who failed to show the proper revolutionary spirit. His group of prisoners had to carry jagged rocks all day and suffered sores on their hands and backs. He said that there were many accidents in which Tibetans were killed, as well as numerous suicides of those who could not stand the hardship. He felt that the Chinese plan was to break the spirit of the Tibetan people under the guise of reform through labor.

The workers at Nachen Trang were allowed visits from their families in Lhasa, who were allowed to bring them food packages, and who told them that the houses of anyone whose relatives had been arrested had been seized and all their possessions confiscated. Permission from the Party was needed not only to visit relatives at Nachen Trang but to go anywhere, even between neighborhoods in Lhasa. Many Tibetans said that after the revolt, the Chinese revealed their true attitudes toward Tibetans and their real intentions in Tibet. Before the revolt, the Chinese had been at least outwardly polite and respectful toward Tibetans. Chinese policy was to seduce Tibetans with favors and good treatment, especially for collaborators, in order to convince them to give up their own culture and political system in favor of "reforms" leading to Chinese socialism. However, after the revolt, they were in full control and no longer had any reason to conceal their real intentions or to treat Tibetans with any respect. In fact, they now tended to regard most Tibetans as traitors since they had also revealed their true sentiments by revolting.

Some, especially lower-class "activists," continued to benefit from their association with the Chinese, but most Tibetans felt that they had been dispossessed of their country, their property, their freedom, and their lives by their invaders, who arrogantly claimed the right to lecture them about their exploitation of "the people" and their crimes against the "Motherland." Tibetans were forced to denounce their own friends, relatives, respected leaders, revered lamas, and Tibetan patriots as exploiters, traitors, and "enemies of the people." This was when they began to understand that the Chinese intended to possess Tibet and Tibetans not only physically but mentally as well. In order to justify their invasion and occupation of Tibet, Tibetans had to be made to believe that they had been "liberated" from their own misrule and that Tibet had "always" been a part of China.

Many Tibetans spoke of their relatives who had been imprisoned or forced to labor at reform through labor camps. Some camps were notorious for starvation conditions, overwork, and deaths. Particularly mentioned was Tsala Karpo, a camp in the Changtang, west of Namtsho. One Tibetan who survived this camp told of being so starved and weak from overwork that it was an effort even to lift his head, which he had never before realized was so heavy. In Lhasa many Tibetans were imprisoned at Drapchi, Lhasa's first large prison, where there were both prison and "reform through labor" sections. Tubten Khétsun, who was there in 1960, says there were several hundred prisoners at Drapchi. Another notorious camp was in Kongpo at Nyingtri. This was actually a series of camps all engaged in logging. There was a camp at Chamdo where many Tibetans starved to death and another, a lead mine east of Dartsendo, where thousands of both Chinese and Tibetans were worked and starved to death.

The year of the Tibetan revolt and the next two years were the three years of famine that resulted from Mao's disastrous Great Leap Forward policy. Mao tried to collectivize Chinese agriculture all at once in order to use the "surplus" thus produced to industrialize, as Stalin had done in the Soviet Union. Both produced disastrous famines. Mao possibly did not even know the Chinese peasants were starving, since he received false reports from provincial officials about the glorious success of his policies. The Chinese Communist political system inculcated mendacity since cadres wanted to curry favor by claiming success and no one was willing to incur the wrath of those above by admitting failure. An estimated 30 to 40 million Chinese starved to death while Mao and the CCP leaders imagined that the Great Leap was achieving fantastic increases in production. They also imagined that their policies in Tibet were equally successful and popular, since that was what they were being told by Chinese cadres in Tibet.

The Panchen Lama was purged in 1964 for respectfully informing the Chinese leadership of how they had failed to win the Tibetans' loyalty due to the irrational repression, starvation, and other such failures in their policies in Tibet. The Panchen Lama reported that large numbers of Tibetans had starved to death, especially in the Amdo area. In his petition he said that 5 percent of the population there had been imprisoned and of those, about half had died. However, in 1987 he said in a speech that the real number was more like 10 to 15 percent, half of whom had died. He had not dared to report the real number in his report in 1962. The number of Tibetans who died due to the revolt and imprisonment and starvation thereafter is the subject of much controversy. The Tibetan Government in Exile has estimated that 1.2 million Tibetans died. China has ridiculed this number, saying that there were only 1.2 million people in "Tibet" at that time; therefore, if 1.2 million had died there would have been none left. However, "Tibet" in the Chinese definition is only the TAR, or what would become the TAR, leaving out another 1.5 million Tibetans outside that area. Dharamsala's number may be somewhat exaggerated, the real figure probably being more like half of their claim, but no objective observer can deny that some hundreds of thousands of Tibetans died.

After the revolt, all Tibetans were subjected to the Chinese Communists' techniques intended to expose opponents and impose ideological conformity. One word I often heard repeated by Tibetans was "thamzing," the Tibetan translation of the Chinese for "struggle," which was supposed to have a cathartic effect upon Chinese society by empowering the exploited to overthrow their exploiters and thus become their own masters. Such struggle sessions were characterized not only by verbal accusations but by spitting, hair-pulling, and beating, sometimes even beating to death, all encouraged by Party cadres. In Tibet, lamas were subjected to accusations of exploitation not only as landowners but for deceiving the people with superstitions. Tibetans were encouraged by the

Chinese or Tibetan cadres to torture lamas, who were then taunted to prove the power of their religion by summoning divine assistance. Their inability to do so was supposed to have a cathartic effect upon Tibetans by demonstrating to them the falsity of their religion. However, what most impressed Tibetans was the brutality of the Chinese and their political system.

Thamzing was part of what the Chinese Communists called "democratic reforms," the main tenets of which were class struggle and redistribution of property. Tibetans were divided into different class statuses in order to facilitate the process of class struggle. In Tibetan society, there was the obvious class distinction between the Tibetan aristocracy and all the rest. But there were no obvious class distinctions in society below the aristocracy. Arbitrary distinctions were therefore made, such as whether or not one had employed others for labor or whether a nomad had many yaks or few. The poorest were considered the most virtuous because they were the victims of class exploitation. However, every other category was defined as having exploited others to some extent. These divisions were necessary so that the transformation of society by means of class conflict could take place.

Thamzing also provided an opportunity to pursue personal grudges or to prove one's revolutionary credentials. Everyone had to prove themselves by criticizing others. No one was exempt. Failure to participate was regarded as evidence of a reactionary attitude. Everyone had to confess to any exploitative activities in the past, even if it were only to have engaged in private commerce or to have hired labor. Tibetans had to prove their loyalty to the new regime by denouncing the old society. This was important to the Chinese, since an exaggeration of the supposed evils of the old society was necessary for them to justify their overthrow of the old government and imposition of their own rule. Tibetans had to compete with one another to denounce the old society as barbaric, cruel, and feudal, and in doing so they had to denigrate their own culture. The result was to create a society where everyone informed on everyone else and no one could trust anyone else, even members of one's own family. Even children were encouraged to inform on their parents if they were observed muttering a prayer, fingering prayer beads, or turning a prayer wheel.

What the Chinese produced by their supposedly transformative methods was a society that they could control. Thamzing facilitated their investigation of the real loyalties and opinions of Tibetans. Those most honest and unable or unwilling to conceal their real opinions were the most easily identified and repressed. Honesty thus became a liability and Tibetans were taught to conceal their true beliefs. No one could speak truthfully to another. All had to learn to repeat Chinese lies and propaganda that they knew to be false. What "democratic reforms" actually achieved for the Chinese in Tibet was the identification and repression of all Tibetans who could not conceal their opposition to Chinese control.

Democratic reforms included a redistribution of wealth from the rich to the poor. Many Tibetans, such as Rinzing Paljor, said that the Chinese came to Tibet as beggars. The first PLA troops who reached Lhasa were poor and bedraggled and decidedly unimpressive. Many Tibetans of the Lhasa aristocracy were indeed wealthy in comparison, not only to the PLA soldiers but to many CCP cadres who had joined the Party precisely because of their poor and lower-class status. The Chinese Communists' attitude toward the Tibetan aristocracy and the religious establishment was that all their wealth had been gained by unjust exploitation.

Many Lhasa mansions had shrine rooms with precious statues and valuable thankas. Shortly after the revolt, the houses of Lhasa Tibetans who had participated in the revolt in any way, or had escaped, or any of those whose family members were government servants, were sealed and their contents confiscated. Then all Lhasans were ordered to bring all their jewels and artworks of value to collection points to be confiscated. Many told of throwing valuables into the Kyichu rather than surrendering them to the Chinese. The poorest Tibetans received some of the property confiscated from the rich, but Tibetans in Lhasa maintained that the Chinese took the best of everything, particularly the finest furniture, rugs, and jewelry. One popular item in Chinese cadres' houses at the time were Buddhist statues used as table lamps. A hole was drilled through the top of the head of the statue and an electric lamp inserted.

The attitude of the Chinese was that Tibet was part of China; therefore, the Tibetan aristocracy and monasteries were exploiters of not just the Tibetan people but of all the Chinese people, of whom the cadres were the representatives and thus the proper recipients of Tibetans' confiscated wealth. Private commerce was also prohibited and merchants had their property confiscated. Handicraft workers and artisans were no longer allowed to pursue their trades, which led to shortages of many needed items. Shortages of all but the most basic items distributed by the state immediately resulted, which contributed to the subsequent famine.

Monasteries had great wealth in gold- and jewel-encrusted statues. The Chinese maintained that the wealth of the monasteries was the result of the exploitation of the Chinese people; therefore, this wealth should be confiscated for the benefit of China. With this justification, the collected cultural and material wealth of the Tibetan people and the Tibetan nation was stolen by the Chinese under the guise of redistribution of wealth. Monasteries that had supported or participated in the revolt or whose monks had fled or had been arrested were closed and sealed after the revolt. Most monasteries were closed and their monks dispersed during democratic reforms since they lost their financial means of existence when their lands were redistributed. Monks and nuns were sometimes lined up and forced to pair off as spouses. Chinese trucks soon arrived at each of the closed monasteries and carted away all portable items, such as all statues of metal and all other metal articles and artworks.

Every monastery in Tibet, with the exception of about ten of the largest that had been designated as cultural monuments, received such a visit over the two years after the revolt. Such was the material wealth of Tibet's monasteries that it took many years to loot them all. The trucks went north from Lhasa and central Tibet to Golmud and from there to Dunhuang and the railroad at Liuyuan, which was then the closest railroad to Lhasa (and was the route I had taken into Tibet). From Kham and Amdo, the loot was trucked to points in Kansu and Sichuan. Several sites in China melted the Tibetan statues and other religious implements into metal that was then used to make proletarian tools "for the benefit of the Chinese people." Thankas were destroyed; some were sold on the international art market through Hong Kong, as were some of the most valuable statues.

The result of China's "democratic reforms" in Tibet was that the Tibetan nation was disenfranchised, decapitated, and dispossessed. The

Tibetan upper class was compromised, exiled, or repressed. The upper class was the cultural and political leadership of the nation, whose elimination removed any actual and potential competition for political influence in Tibet. The persecution of lamas and monks and the closing and looting of the monasteries was a destruction of the most important material and spiritual characteristics of Tibetan culture, upon which Tibetan national identity was built. All this was done under the guise of "liberation of the serfs" and "democratic reforms." Tibetans complained that they were not even allowed to mourn the deaths of their relatives, the persecution of their lamas, the loss of their freedom, and the demise of their religion and culture. Instead, they were required to denounce their own culture and mouth the Chinese slogans about how they had been liberated and were now, for the first time in their history, the "masters of their own fate."

Most of the stories Dolma's friends told were of the revolt and its aftermath. China's repression of all its opponents was something that anyone could understand. The Chinese need to control Tibetans' minds was less comprehensible. Still, Tibetans, at least those who had supported the revolt, knew that they had lost their country and their freedom. Some younger and lower-class Tibetans, who had been indoctrinated by the Chinese, no doubt believed the Chinese propaganda line that the Tibetan serfs had really been liberated and that China had only benevolent intentions in regard to Tibet. With the exception of those Tibetans who were the activist vanguards of the Chinese, all others had their lives upended and experienced repression and hardship previously unknown in their personal lives or in Tibet's history. They could little comprehend many Chinese ideological themes except to learn to repeat slogans during meetings.

The Cultural Revolution in Tibet was even more incomprehensible to most Tibetans. It was characterized by repression of all aspects of Tibetan culture and factional fighting between groups of youths, both Chinese and Tibetan, whose primary difference was in how fervently they claimed to be followers of Chairman Mao. These two themes combined to eradicate the remnants of Tibetan cultural distinctiveness, artifacts, and monuments and to abrogate all semblance of the autonomy promised by the establishment of the TAR in 1965, shortly before the Cultural Revolution began. Mao launched the Cultural Revolution to continue his socialization of China and he let loose the Red Guards to defeat his opponents in the Party who had opposed his radical policies and who had rescued China from the results of the Great Leap Forward. To further the transformation of Chinese society, Mao demanded the eradication of the "four olds." The cultures and traditions of minorities in the PRC, especially the Tibetans, epitomized the "four olds" and thus were a particular target.

The Cultural Revolution was initiated in Tibet in the summer of 1966 by Chinese students sent from Beijing and Tibetan students from the minority nationality institutes in Beijing and Xianyang near Xian. These "Red Guards" began by instigating Tibetan students in Lhasa to attack the Jokhang and destroy its artifacts, which were denounced as reactionary remnants of the old society. The Jokhang was one of the few temples or monasteries in Tibet that had not already been emptied during democratic reforms. Official supervision of the activities of the Red Guards was indicated by the fact that some of the most precious items were removed from the Jokhang before the Red Guards were allowed to enter. Some Tibetans were willing participants in the destruction of their own cultural heritage, having been indoctrinated by the Chinese; others were coerced to participate in the destruction by threats of persecution as reactionaries if they did not.

The ransacking of the Jokhang initiated the destruction of all the remaining monasteries in Tibet. Most were already empty, but now they were defaced and dismantled by local Tibetans instigated by Chinese and Tibetan activists. With the exception of some ten major monasteries, all of the thousands of temples and monasteries and religious monuments in Tibet were physically eradicated, in some cases down to the last stone. Mani walls—previously one of the most distinctive characteristics of the Tibetan landscape, constructed with stones carved with the Buddhist mantra, *Om Mani Padme Hum*, and images of lamas and deities—were dismantled and the stones used for walkways or public toilets for the express purpose of forcing Tibetans to defile their religion. Chortens that once dotted the landscape were similarly eradicated. The very face of the Tibetan cultural and spiritual environment was altered. Tibetan households were required to eliminate all their decorations. Prayer flags were removed and the colorful furniture and wooden interior decorations were painted over in dull proletarian green or blue. The only decorations now allowed in Lhasa were portraits of Chairman Mao and posters with his slogans.

Those few upper-class Tibetans who had survived to this time were dragged out by Red Guards, paraded around the Barkhor in their finery, and subjected to public thamzing on the streets of Lhasa. Any valuable articles they still possessed were confiscated. Tubten Khétsun says that many Tibetans, especially those who had been labeled "class enemies," had to sell whatever valuable items they still possessed at this time in order to survive. They had no food and no fuel to cook what they had, while the Chinese seemed to have plenty of everything. The electricity from the Nachen Trang project went mostly to Chinese offices and neighborhoods of Lhasa while the Tibetan area had little at all.

Lhasa was chaotic due to fighting between two Red Guard factions, each of which was supported by a different faction among the Chinese cadres in Lhasa. Each faction competed with the other to prove itself more revolutionary and more loyal to Mao than the other by being more intolerant of Tibetan cultural distinctions and destructive of Tibetan cultural monuments. The chaos of the Red Guard fighting eventually led to a rural revolt in the Nyemo area west of Lhasa that took on nationalist implications and was repressed by the Chinese with public executions of its leaders in Lhasa. In 1970, an organization of Tibetan youth opposed to the Chinese was similarly repressed with public executions. Tubten Khétsun wrote that the peaceful, religious, and prosperous character of Lhasa was now one of drab destruction, chaos, violence, hunger, and fear.

Khétsun also said that in 1970, the Chinese authorities required every Tibetan household to buy and install its own loudspeaker. Loudspeakers in public places were already one of the most offensive intrusions on Tibetan life, but now they were to be inside all houses and thus even more inescapable. He says that what was broadcast was propaganda about how great were the achievements of the Communist Party, how great and prosperous and powerful China was, how the imperialists and reactionaries had been defeated, and class struggle would be relentlessly pursued, all without a single word of real news. Tibetans of the favored lower classes could escape the screeching propaganda by cutting the wires of the loudspeakers and claiming they had malfunctioned. However, those of the despised "class enemies" did not dare do so and even had to make sure the loudspeakers worked lest they be accused of lack of enthusiasm for the Party's policies.

Collectivization was pursued during the Cultural Revolution and after. Rural Tibetans were organized into collectives, which were then amalgamated into communes in which individual liberty was restricted to the greatest extent at any time in the history of Tibet under Chinese rule. Communization allowed the Chinese to control Tibetans individually as well as collectively and to gain access to their agricultural production. Harvests were confiscated and Tibetans received a set ration that was often insufficient, because officials overestimated harvests in order to promote themselves in a competition like that which had produced the famine of the Great Leap Forward. The chaos of collectivization led to another food shortage in the early 1970s. Another grain shortage in the late 1970s was the result of a Chinese attempt to grow wheat instead of barley in high-altitude fields. The effects of this misguided program were still evident in 1982 in the grain coupons necessary for the purchase of any grain or its products.

One policy in which the Chinese were successful, or apparently so, was in coercing ideological conformity among Tibetans. After the revolt, the Chinese had coercive powers sufficient to enforce ideological conformity, at least outwardly, among all Tibetans or to repress any who resisted. Some Tibetans, mostly the young of the lower classes who had been indoctrinated in minority nationality institutes, may have been true believers in the Communists' ideology. They accepted that Tibet was backward and needed a revolution; their elevation to positions of ostensible authority made them loyal to the Chinese and led them to believe Chinese promises about the economic and social development of Tibet. If any harbored doubts about Chinese intentions or were troubled by the harsh treatment of other Tibetans, their best option was even greater ideological conformity in order to avoid that fate themselves.

All Tibetans had to learn to repeat Chinese slogans with believable sincerity and to outdo each other in denunciations of the "old society" before "liberation." They were subjected to relentless propaganda in a variety of forms and mediums in order to inculcate that ideology. Schoolchildren were taken to the exhibit of life-like clay sculptures, "The Wrath of the Serfs," in Lhasa and taught to believe that old Tibet was a backward, cruel, feudal "hell on earth." A common theme of neighborhood and communal meetings was to compare the suffering of the past to the happiness and prosperity of the present. Despite the fact that most Tibetans, particularly the old, knew very well that the past was far better than the present, they became adept at performing in the Chinese ritual of denouncing their own culture and society and praising the Chinese Communist Party and the joyous new life it had provided.

Thus, it was a shock to the Chinese in Tibet and no doubt to some of the more ardent Tibetan activists as well when the liberalization period began in 1980 and Tibetans welcomed the exile delegations from Dharamsala as their potential liberators from the very real "hell on earth" of Chinese rule. Hu Yaobang's liberalized policies in Tibet were based upon the assumption that Tibetan nationalism was dead and Tibetans were as loyal and grateful to the CCP as they said they were. Therefore, he underestimated the political danger in allowing Tibetans to exercise some of the cultural autonomy they had long been promised.

Beyond what I learned from Dolma and her informants, I also made my own observations and gathered my own impressions about Lhasa and Tibet, particularly in regard to what the city and the country were like before the Chinese came and what had happened since. My initial impressions upon entering Lhasa still held: that the old Lhasa was in the process of being surrounded and overwhelmed by the new city, characterized by ugly, Chinese-style buildings. Not only had the new rulers of Tibet disregarded the historic character of Lhasa but they had intentionally destroyed much of it. As for what was once Lhasa's charm, deriving from parks and open spaces along with attractive monasteries, temples, and manor houses, almost all was now eradicated. One had only to explore the formerly great monasteries of Shide, Tsemoling, Gyume, and Meru to get an image of what had been destroyed.

Old photos of Lhasa, taken by British visitors in the first half of the twentieth century, show the Lhasa Valley as a mostly open area, except for the Potala and the Shol settlement beneath it and the old city around the Jokhang. The population of Lhasa at that time was estimated at about 50,000 to 60,000. The Shol area beneath the Potala is thought to have been the first area of settlement in Lhasa. The Shol settlement was protected by the Marpori and Chakpori hills on both sides, to which the Shol residents could repair in case of attack and upon which fortresses were later built. This was the typical settlement pattern in Tibet before the establishment of centralized political authority capable of providing protection from raids from rival areas or bandit gangs.

The fortress style of Tibetan settlement is still visible in towns like Gyantse, where the area of settlement is beneath a fortress, and Shekar Dzong. Even as large a settlement as Shigatse had its fortress, but this was also due to the wars that raged between Shigatse and other areas of Tibet, particularly Lhasa, for political dominance in the era between the empire period of the seventh to ninth centuries and the reestablishment of centralized political authority under the Gelugpa Dalai Lamas in the mid-seventeenth century. The Potala still has the character of a fortress, with its wall for the protection of the government buildings and residences of Shol.

Some eastern Tibetan areas in southern Kham are dominated by tall stone towers dating from ancient times when the absence of centralized political authority required that every settlement have a fortress for protection. Even many of the early monasteries were built like fortresses, often with surrounding walls, since the different religious sects also conducted warfare against each other, led by their contingents of *dob dob*, or fighting monks, until the Gelugpa, with the assistance of Mongol chieftains, established their predominance. Until then the different sects cultivated patrons among the various Mongol Khans and used them in their rivalries with other sects.

The Kyichu Valley, beginning at Lhasa and continuing to the northeast into Phenpo, is one of the largest agricultural areas of Tibet, rivaled only by the area between Gyantse and Shigatse. Srongtsan Gampo chose Lhasa as his capital partly because his Yarlung dynasty was the heir to a previous political confederation, centered in Phenpo, that had unified many of the areas of central Tibet into a loose political confederation. One has only to compare the broad agricultural area of Phenpo, and the central location of Lhasa, with the narrow and relatively isolated valley of Yarlung to see why Srongtsan Gampo shifted his capital from Yarlung to Lhasa. From this location, he was able to conquer the rival Zhang Zhung Empire of western Tibet and the nomadic tribes of northern Tibet to create a military empire, based upon the agricultural resources of central Tibet combined with the mobility and "food on the hoof" provided by the nomads—an empire that quickly expanded to control the entire Tibetan Plateau and threaten the Turks to the north and China to the east.

Tibetan political authority was established by means of conquest and confederation. The nomadic tribes to the north needed little coercion to join Central Tibetans in an enterprise of political confederation for the sake of conquests farther afield. Nomadic confederations were most often established for the purpose of conquest of agricultural areas. Tibet had both an agricultural center and the military power and mobility of the northern nomads. The nomads confederated with Lhasa in a system of indirect rule that was to typify the Tibetan style of political organization. The nomads pledged a certain degree of allegiance to Lhasa in return for a share of the spoils. In later Tibetan history, nomadic chieftains had a similar arrangement with Lhasa in which the Tibetan government had some influence over the nomads but did not directly administer them. As the monastic system grew, some monasteries gained political authority over certain areas, mostly in Kham, and they administered those areas independently while acknowledging a certain degree of allegiance to the head of their sect, usually in Lhasa, and to the Tibetan government.

As Tibetan political organization grew, the system of indirect rule was continued and consolidated by the allocation of feudal estates to government officials, who became a social aristocracy. The authority exercised by the estates was similar to that of nomadic chieftains or monastic estates. They had juridical authority, which was subject to abuse, but Tibetan history does not record a pattern of abuse of tenants by feudal authorities, no doubt due to the influence of the moral principles of Buddhism and the presence of monasteries in every area. Tibetan feudalism was more a political than a social system. It was a system of indirect rule typical of rudimentary state organization where the central authority does not yet have the ability to directly administer all of the territory it claims. Political authority has to be delegated to traditional authorities like nomadic chieftains, to religious authorities that controlled certain areas, and to an aristocracy created in order to provide officials for government.

It was this aristocracy that built the manor houses in Lhasa and at the estates they were allocated by the Tibetan government. The manor houses were built in the same style as monasteries, with a courtyard surrounded on three sides by servants' quarters and stables of one or two stories, and a two- or three-story manor house on the northern side of the courtyard facing south. Lhasa grew as Tibetan political authority was centered there and an aristocracy grew up to serve and to benefit from that authority. The aristocracy built their manor houses in the area around the Barkhor, and they financed the nearby temples and monasteries and provided many of their monks. The temples, monasteries, and manor houses were usually separated by privately owned land, parks, streams, and marshes. Only later did the space between these major buildings get filled in with secondary buildings of traders, craftsmen, and others associated with the manors or monasteries.

Until the mid-twentieth century, the old city around the Jokhang was separated from the Potala by an uninhabited area of streams, parks, and marshes. The only building between the Potala and the city was the famous Yutok Samba, or turquoise-roofed bridge, which crossed a stream on the path between the two centers. The stream was channeled at places as it flowed from the northeastern part of the valley, entering the city at the Banakshol area and continuing along what is now the eastern end of Beijing Shar Lam to the junction with Ramoche Lam, then between the Jokhang and Ramoche to the south of the Potala and to the Kyichu. The stream must have provided water for people and animals in the city and also probably served some sanitary functions. It survived to the mid-twentieth century as a pond for watering animals near Banakshol.

The architecture and style of the great Tibetan temples, monasteries, and manor houses were determined by the materials available and environmental conditions. Lhasa was fortunate to have a readily available building material in the durable white granite that was mined from the surrounding mountains. Timbers for support were less readily available but could be brought from farther afield. Environmental considerations included the arid climate, making flat clay roofs feasible; wind, from which protection needed to be sought; and cold, which dictated a southern orientation. Other considerations were the lack of interior heat or light, and thus an emphasis on skylights, and the lack, until the twentieth century, of building materials such as glass or metal, which meant that windows had to be shuttered and the size of interior spaces was dictated by the availability of wooden support pillars and beams.

Existing traditional buildings in Lhasa display the typical method of construction, using granite shaped into rectangular blocks of the size that could be carried from the quarry site by one person. The uniform size of the stones in all Tibetan construction, even those in the lower walls of the Potala, indicates that size was usually limited by the weight that could be carried on the back of one person. At the most, the size was limited to what could be carried by two men in a cradle sling or on a wheeled cart. Some have assumed that large timbers must have been transported by animals, like horses or yaks. However, a yak can carry at most only one short timber on each side. Yaks cannot be hitched together to carry larger timbers. Men, on the other hand, can carry timbers of almost unlimited lengths by means of rope cradles tied to poles held by one man on each side. A very large timber of medium length can be carried by four men in this way. The number of these two-man cradles can be multiplied to carry timbers of almost any length.

The best stone walls still extant in Lhasa are constructed of dressed stone. Less well-built stone walls used stone dressed only on the corners. In both styles, the spaces between stones were filled by thin layers of stone chips, all held together with clay mortar. Even when covered in whitewash, the beautiful and solid granite stonework is often visible. The outer stone wall slopes toward the interior while the interior wall is vertical. In large multistory buildings, this means that the base is often several feet thick. The exterior and interior wall faces are of dressed stone while the space between is filled with smaller rough stones, stone rubble, and clay mortar.

Roofs are supported by pillars of usually squared timbers at regular spaces, usually only six or seven feet apart. Spacing of pillars is not limited by the short length of beams—since long beams as well as pillars can be transported in the same way—but by the need to support a heavy clay roof or, in multistory buildings, the floors above. Pillars support capitals upon which beams rest. The ceiling is built up with several layers of increasingly smaller but more closely spaced wooden poles, decreasing in size until a solid surface is achieved. A layer of small stones comes next, meant to keep the wood separate from the wet clay above, and then multiple layers of clay are added, from coarse lower levels to a fine top layer that is virtually waterproof.

Starting from these basic construction methods, determined by materials available, Tibetan architecture evolved to create innovative methods to transcend the limitations of materials and the constraints of environment, particularly in the use of skylights to get heat and light into the lower interior of temples. Massively thick stone walls kept buildings cool in summer and warm in winter. Decorative elements included the benma friezes on temples and monasteries, elaborately decorated window treatments, golden temple roofs, and interiors decorated with frescoes, hanging thankas, textiles, and carved and colorfully painted wooden surfaces. The Tibetan style of decoration adds perspective by means of sloping outer walls and window edges painted to produce a receding effect. It adds a rich sense of color to Tibetan buildings, both public and private. And it gives a distinctive character to every Tibetan building and settlement of any size.

Tibetan architecture reached its height along with that of the Potala in the late seventeenth century. The Potala is an expression of all of the best elements of the Tibetan architectural style. From its site on an already-prominent outcropping in the middle of the Lhasa Valley, to the way it seems to be an organic part of the hill upon which it is built, to its massive bulk that conceals a surprisingly open and sun-filled interior space, to its magnificent decorations, the Potala is the epitome of Tibetan architectural style. The Potala makes the ultimate use of the materials and construction methods available on the Tibetan Plateau and it is decorated in a style that defines the Tibetan character, both individually and collectively. Other Tibetan buildings, in Lhasa and elsewhere, are also magnificent expressions of architectural style and of the Tibetan character, but all fail in comparison to the Potala. Many other Tibetan constructions were no doubt inspired by the Potala as an example of what could be achieved, given enough energy and effort.

The Tibetan talent for architecture that was appropriate to the environment but also improved upon that environment was on display all over Tibet in the temples and monasteries that decorated every valley. The Tibetan physical environment is magnificent in the extreme; perhaps it was the beauty of this environment that inspired Tibetans to decorate it with tastefully placed and constructed villages, temples, and monasteries. This talent for environmental improvement and decoration is one of the greatest achievements of Tibetan civilization. Tibet was famous not only for its magnificent Potala but for the temples and monasteries that dotted the Tibetan landscape and the chortens and mani walls along every trail. Every village had its temple and every valley its monastery. There were innumerable holy sites and protected areas where nature spirits were thought to reside. Springs were surrounded by small groves and protected from any sort of pollution because they were thought to be the residence of the naga water spirits. Prayer flags flew at mountain passes and at innumerable sacred sites.

The destruction of all these expressions of the Tibetan character and the Tibetan national identity, even to the extent of painting over all the colorful decorations with drab colors in houses, is evidence of China's crime of the destruction of the expressions of the unique Tibetan culture and civilization. The attempted eradication of the achievements of Tibetan civilization, by destroying thousands of temples and monasteries, leaving only those too big or too well-known to destroy, and burning Tibetan texts and the woodblocks used to print them, was a conscious attempt to eradicate Tibetan civilization and all evidence of Tibetan cultural identity that distinguished Tibet from China. The looting of Tibet's thousands of monasteries was a blatant theft of Tibet's cultural heritage. The destruction of most of the accomplishments of Tibetan civilization may have had Tibetan participants but it was inspired by Chinese political imperatives.

When China opened Tibet to foreigners in the early 1980s, the intent may have been to impress them with its new correct policy, a reversal of the disastrous but also correct policies of the past. But the impression one got in Tibet at that time was of a massive destruction of a culture and civilization that could be explained only by China's need to eradicate all evidence of Tibet's separate national identity. Enough of the rubble of that civilization still lay around to provide irrefutable evidence of the destruction that had taken place. And, of course, Tibetans themselves, free at least temporarily to speak the truth without fear of immediate persecution, testified to the magnitude of the destruction of Tibetan culture and the repression of the Tibetan people.

As October turned to November, the weather in Lhasa was getting colder. For the whole month of November, I was the only foreigner in Lhasa. Some days I went to the Jokhang and sat near the Jowo just to get some warmth from the flames of the hundreds of butter lamps. Dolma was preparing to leave. She was going to Nepal and from there to India and Dharamsala. I was, by this time, fully committed to writing the book about Tibet I had promised her. She suggested that I should do my research in Dharamsala, where, if I would go with her, she would introduce me to those who could help me and would also arrange an audience with the Dalai Lama. She was leaving on a bus for Tibetans from exile and for those given permits to visit India or Nepal. I fit into neither of those categories. At that time, it was not permitted for foreigners to travel from Tibet to Nepal (or the other way). Foreign travelers to Tibet that summer had to return to China. A few foreigners had set out on the road to Nepal and had never returned, so presumably they had been allowed to cross the border, but no one knew for sure. I asked the friendly Chinese Public Security Bureau official if I could go to Nepal, since that was where I had lived for the past ten years. He said that the only way I could do so was if I could get a letter from the Nepalese Consul in Lhasa certifying that I was a resident of Nepal.

The Nepalese Consulate was in a small building near the Norbulinka. I went there without much hope for getting the required letter. However, the staff there was very friendly and I was shown into the office of the Consul, G. B. Shah, who immediately declared that he recognized me. His house was in Kupondole, just across the Bagmati on the way from Kathmandu to Patan, very close to where I lived in the house of my friend and patron, Hemanta Mishra. He said that he had often seen me walking on the short driveway that led to both his and Hemanta's houses. He also declared that he had seen me in a wildlife film on tigers, a mistake that was possibly due to the fact that Hemanta was in charge of the Tiger Project, sponsored by the US Smithsonian Institution, dedicated to saving the tigers in the Chitwan National Park in Nepal. Wildlife biologists were often at Hemanta's house and some had even rented the house next to Hemanta's. One of those was a well-known wildlife biologist, Dave Smith, who was with the Smithsonian Tiger Project and who might very well have been in a tiger film. Our same last name might have confused Shah, but he insisted quite confidently that it was me that he had seen in the film. I had never been in any such film and I said so, twice for the sake of the truth. But he was unconvinced, so finally I admitted that yes, he was right, it was me in the film. He was now so pleased with himself that he declared that he would of course certify that I was a resident of Nepal, being an eyewitness to that fact himself!

Armed with the Nepal Consul's letter, I returned to my Chinese friend at the Public Security Bureau, who seemed as surprised as I was that I had been successful. Nevertheless, he promised to put me on the next available bus for Tibetans going to Nepal. That turned out to be at the end of the month, the buses being scheduled only when filled with applicants. Dolma's bus was set to leave about three weeks earlier than that, but she promised to wait for me in Kathmandu, where she had relatives. Given what I had heard from Dolma and those who had conveyed their stories to me through her, I was now deeply committed to the Tibetan political issue. My five months in Tibet had been an extraordinary experience, but what made it a life-changing experience was my association with Dolma.

Many years later, long after I had written and published the book I had promised her, she revealed to me that she had visited Dharamsala before she went to Tibet, where the Dalai Lama had suggested to her that she should recruit some eager foreigner like myself to write the story of Tibet! He said that Tibetans' own accounts of their sufferings under Chinese rule were usually dismissed as too subjective. I had experienced this myself in Nepal. I knew many Tibetans and had heard their stories, but I also knew that there was an unfortunate reluctance on the part of international journalists and others to believe that they were not exaggerated. It was hard to believe that the Chinese were as evil as Tibetans claimed, especially since they declared their intentions in Tibet and their actual results to be exactly the opposite. They produced much propaganda, all of it readily available in Kathmandu, about their benevolent intentions in Tibet and the selfless assistance they had provided to Tibetans. Since Tibet was closed to the outside world, there was no one but a few Tibetan refugees to refute their story. Now, however, Tibet had opened and it was finally possible for a more objective account to emerge. Foreigners were presumed to be more credible, just because they were not as personally involved and interested as were Tibetans, and could therefore be more objective.

Dolma had done exactly as the Dalai Lama suggested and had found an appropriately eager foreigner, one who was fortunately also an amateur scholar and a sucker for political causes. Dolma's assignment also gave my life a needed purpose, so I accepted it with enthusiasm. In undertaking the task Dolma and, through her, the Dalai Lama, had assigned me, I needed to have my own understanding of what was possible and what was not. Nothing of what I had learned so far gave me any illusions that Tibet might recover its independence. The Chinese had loosened their stranglehold at the time and Tibetan culture was already making a rapid recovery, but this was the very reason that they would probably have to clamp down again, as they eventually did.

The revival of Tibetan culture I had witnessed revealed that the Chinese had underestimated the strength and persistence of Tibetan culture and Tibetan national identity. The Chinese Communists originally thought that their Marxist-Leninist nationality policies would allow them to rapidly assimilate Tibet. They thought that Tibet was already a part of China and they disregarded how strongly Tibetans believed otherwise. They regarded Tibetan culture as barbaric, so they could not comprehend why Tibetans might prefer to retain their own culture when offered the obviously superior "Chinese socialist culture." A few of the Chinese Communists, Mao in particular, knew that revolt in Tibet was a possibility, but his strategy was to seduce the Tibetans with promises of autonomy while increasing Chinese military, political, and logistical control over Tibet until the time when any revolt could be repressed. Then, Mao said, either Tibetans would acquiesce or they would revolt, either scenario being advantageous to China. A Tibetan revolt might be embarrassing but it would finally give China a free hand in Tibet.

The Chinese miscalculated after the death of Mao in thinking that Tibetan nationalism was dead and that, therefore, some small degree of cultural autonomy could be allowed. They were surprised to find that Tibetans were not loyal Chinese and that they preferred to revive their own culture and religion and national identity. The Chinese were deceived by their own indoctrination of Tibetans, which had taught them how to repeat enough of the Party line to avoid repression, but had prevented their expression of their true feelings to the Chinese. They were prepared, however, to reverse their policies and crush any resistance if necessary.

It was already obvious to me that Chinese promises of autonomy to Tibetans were a subterfuge from the beginning, with the words of the 1951 Seventeen Point Agreement. Autonomy was never intended to be a permanent policy; assimilation was always the ultimate goal. China, having conquered Tibet, had to absorb it in every way, militarily, politically, economically, and culturally. Tibet could not be allowed to remain an unassimilated nation within the Chinese "multinational state." Tibetan national identity had to be eradicated in order to prevent any reemergence of Tibetan nationalism and separatism. Anyhow, the Tibetans themselves were never China's primary concern in Tibet. As Mao's "bargain" offered to Tibetans revealed, the Chinese were far more concerned about the territory of Tibet, or the Tibetan Plateau, which was some 25 percent of that of the PRC, than with the people, who were an easily ignorable one-half of one percent of the PRC's population. The Chinese were constantly surprised that Tibetans still retained their cultural identity and their hopes for independence and a return of the Dalai Lama, but they were always prepared to crush any such hopes.

I never imagined that the Chinese would allow Tibetans even so much as to breathe freely. So I never imagined that I or anyone else could have any effect on China's ultimate goal to crush any Tibetan aspirations for cultural autonomy, much less political freedom. National identity is based on culture, so China could not, as it discovered in the 1980s, allow cultural autonomy of the type that it had once promised. The only thing that I or any other foreigner could have an effect upon was the outside perception of Tibet, as the Dalai Lama had suggested to Dolma. I could have no effect on the tragedy of Tibet, except to try to counter the Chinese lie that it was no tragedy at all. The false interpretation of Tibetan history promoted by China was like a double tragedy. Tibetans not only suffered the loss of their country but, under Chinese occupation and coercion, they had to deny that their country had even existed, or at least that it had any legitimate reason for existence. Tibetans had to deny their own history and denigrate their own culture as if it had no value, at a time when the value of Tibetan culture was beginning to be recognized in the world outside of China.

China's lies about Tibet were almost as infuriating as the stories of repression of Tibetans that were revealed to me in Lhasa. I could do nothing about the repression, and nobody could, but I, as an individual, might make a contribution to an accurate history of Tibet. The history of Tibet at that time was being written mostly by the Chinese. Their version of Tibet's history was that Tibet had no history as a nation or as a country separate from China. China claimed that it had not repressed Tibetans' aspirations to retain their own culture, to practice their own religion, and to rule themselves free of foreign interference, but instead that it had provided Tibetans the freedom they had been denied through their own misrule. The Chinese falsification of Tibet's history, in order to justify China's rule over Tibet, was so illogical and so improbable that it had to be refuted for the sake of historical truth. I thought that I, as a foreigner, might make some contribution to this historical truth.

My bus finally left at the end of November. First, I had to go have all my baggage inspected at the Lhasa customs office. I had several books in Tibetan that I intended to donate to the library in Dharamsala, so I made sure to buy only books that were not *nei bu*, or for internal distribution only. Sharpa Tulku was on the same bus. The first day, we went via Gyantse to Shigatse and stopped there at the guest house. The next day, we went through Lhatse and Tingri to Nyalam, the last town before the road descended from the edge of the Tibetan Plateau through the narrow valley of the Sun Kosi River, which cuts through the Himalaya to Nepal. The last view in Tibet was of the Himalaya from the height of the plateau. Unlike the view from the lowlands of Nepal, where one is looking up toward the mountains, here one is almost looking down on the Himalaya, or at least down on the lowlands of Nepal beyond. From near Nyalam, one could see all the peaks from Everest to Cho Oyu to Gauri Shankar, all east of the road, to Shisha Pangma to the west, an 8,000-meter peak that is entirely in Tibet and that appears to magnificently rise out of the plateau itself.

From Nyalam the road descends abruptly through a narrow gorge to the border town of Dram. There we again had to stay at a government guest house for the night before being processed through the border the next day. Sharpa Tulku and I shared a room. We were visited by a Chinese PLA officer who spoke very good English and was as sophisticated as any Chinese I had met in Tibet. He asked about our impressions of Tibet and what we thought about the Tibetan political issue. Sharpa Tulku had family in Lhasa so he was more restrained than I. I openly said what I thought about Tibet's right to political independence, which the Chinese officer received with surprising equanimity. We engaged in an objective and unemotional discussion about Tibetan and Chinese politics. He was not angry that I thought the Chinese were colonialists in Tibet. He simply argued that the Tibetans he knew were cooperative and seemed to bear no resentment. He told of using Tibetans as guides to patrol the border area looking for other Tibetans trying to sneak across the border. When he left, both Sharpa Tulku and I realized that we had been debriefed by a very sophisticated Chinese. He was not interested in getting incriminating information about Tibetans we had spoken to in Lhasa or Sharpa Tulku's relatives. He just wanted to know what impressions we had gained from our extended visits to Tibet.

The next day we had to go through Chinese customs. Everything was inspected. I got caught trying to smuggle a very small and not very valuable statue I had bought on the street in Lhasa. A Chinese customs officer accused me, in Chinese, of stealing a Chinese cultural relic. I replied, in my rudimentary Chinese, "*Bu shir Zhong Gou de dongxi. Je shir Xizang de dongxi*," or "It's not a Chinese thing (*dongxi*), it's a Tibetan thing." The Chinese officer, having fully understood the implication of my words, exploded from behind his desk, jumping up so abruptly I thought he would land on top of it. To say that an item from Tibet was not Chinese was to say that Tibet was not a part of China. He angrily threatened to have me arrested on the spot for insulting China's dignity, or denying its territorial sovereignty, or some such crime. He phoned his superior, who fortunately happened to be the officer with whom I had the very interesting conversation the day before. He arrived, and unlike his colleague, was calm and unruffled by my crimes and insults. He just commented to his colleague: "That's what he thinks," and ordered me released. The explosive anger of the customs officer is a typical Chinese cultural characteristic; emotions are usually so contained or repressed that they tend to burst forth with unexpected vehemence when provoked. Tibetans often spoke of the intimidating nature of this sort of Chinese anger.

The border at that time was connected by road but was unconnected by any transportation. One had to hire Nepalese porters to carry one's baggage down a steep hill from the Chinese customs house and across the "Friendship Bridge" to the Nepal side. Our group soon found a driver to take us to Kathmandu. Immediately upon arriving in Nepal, there was a perceptible change in atmosphere. The tension of Tibet dissolved as soon as one crossed the border. I'm sure it was worse for the Tibetans in my group, but even I could feel the release from the tension that anyone could experience due to the political situation in Tibet. Only when you crossed the border did you realize how tense you had been. I had almost been arrested at the border, so maybe that was part of my feeling, but much of it had to do with the nature of the Chinese regime in Tibet. I was reminded of the reply I got to my question on the steps of the Potala: "Rangzen mindu."

Figure 1. Tibetan nomad girl

Figure 2. Tibetan nomad girl with braided hair

Figure 3. Potala from Jokhang

Figure 4. Broken mani stones

Figure 5. Roof of Ramoche Monastery

Figure 6. Ruins of Shide Monastery

Figure 7. Broken mani stones at Reting Monastery

Figure 8. Ruins of Ganden Monastery

Figure 9. Derge Monastery in Kham

Figure 10. Tibetan manor house architectural style in Lhasa

Figure 11. Monastery skylight architectural style

Figure 12. Ramoche Jowo restoration procession

# Chapter 3

# Tibet Studies

## Dharamsala

I returned to Nepal to find myself a minor celebrity among my friends. I was the first to go to Tibet and everyone wanted to hear my story. I didn't have long to enjoy my unusual popularity, however. Dolma had been in Kathmandu for three weeks already and needed to get to Dharamsala. She had even sent a bogus telegram to me in Lhasa, purporting to be from the National Parks Department of the Nepal government, for whom I had previously worked, saying that I had a new contract and needed to be in Nepal immediately. When she left Lhasa, I thought I had little prospect of being allowed to leave Tibet via Nepal, so she had tried to help, but I didn't need to use her telegram with the Nepalese Consulate in Lhasa. After about a week in Kathmandu, Dolma and I and her half-brother Tenzin, who had recently come from Tibet, left by air for Delhi.

In Delhi we stayed at 16 Jor Bagh, a house in a pleasant residential neighborhood that was for many years the location of Tibetan refugee offices like the Dalai Lama's Charitable Trust as well as *Tibetan Review*, the Tibetan refugee monthly newsletter. There I met Tsering Wangyal, who was so identified with his job as editor of *Tibetan Review* that he was known in the Tibetan exile community simply as "Editor."

Dolma was informed that a car belonging to the Tibetan Government in Exile (TGiE) was returning empty to Dharamsala and that we could use it if we wanted. The trip from Delhi to Dharamsala at that time was an ordeal. The best option was to take the overnight train to Pathankot and then a four-hour bus to Dharamsala. There was also an overnight bus that I was to take a few times in the next few years that was an ordeal of suffering, partly due to the Hindi videos that played nonstop even in the middle of the night. The bus was billed as the "Deluxe Video Bus," so they were not about to turn off the video.

As it was, even the trip by private car was not without its hazards. We left Delhi early in the morning. Within the first hour, we saw at least a half-dozen overturned trucks; none had struck other vehicles; all had simply run off the road. It was apparent that nighttime driving was precarious, not that it was much better by daylight. The road was packed with every kind of vehicle, from trucks, buses, and cars to motorized rickshaws and oxcarts. There were also pedestrians and animals, including cattle and camels, all sharing the narrow, undivided roadway. In contrast to China, where most vehicles traveled slowly since no one was in any hurry, cars, trucks, and buses traveled at a breakneck speed. They made a game of dodging each other and the much slower rickshaws and oxcarts. Buses and trucks would pull out to pass slower vehicles, accelerating to their maximum speed and honking furiously as traffic approached, then ducking back into their own lane at the last second. This was probably why there were so many overturned trucks on the road. The whole game was made even more exciting by the need to dodge the much slower animals, oxcarts, and motorized rickshaws, the latter often crowded with dozens of schoolchildren hanging off all sides. Our Tibetan driver was fully into the game and subjected us to several hours of terror as he played chicken with oncoming trucks and buses.

Dharamsala is about twelve hours by road from New Delhi. We arrived in the evening and went directly to the home of the late Trijang Rinpoche, one of the two tutors of the Dalai Lama, with whom Dolma had a family relationship. The house was one of the original buildings in the area known as Gangchen Kyishong, or Gangkyi, where the TGiE had established its governmental offices and a library. Gangkyi was about a thousand feet up a ridge above the village of Dharamsala (4,780 feet, 1,457 meters). Another thousand feet above Gangkyi was McLeod Ganj, a former British hill station and now the main Tibetan refugee settlement. Between Gangkyi and McLeod Ganj was a small knoll on which the residence of the Dalai Lama and the new Tsuklhakhang were located. "Dharamsala" is a Sanskrit word meaning "spiritual sanctuary." In common usage, it referred to rest houses built for religious pilgrims, one of which was located on the site of lower Dharamsala, now the administrative center of Kangra District of the Indian state of Himachal Pradesh. Since the Dalai Lama relocated there in 1960, the whole area became known as Dharamsala, the name being auspiciously appropriate for the nature of the Dalai Lama's "spiritual sanctuary" there.

McLeod Ganj has a spectacular view out over the Kangra Valley some 2,000 feet below and is nestled under the nearby 12,000- to 15,000-foot snow peaks of the Dhauladhar Range. It is surrounded by forests of graceful and lovely Deodar cedars, the name meaning "tree of the gods," which are protected by law in Himachal Pradesh. Although McLeod Ganj still retained the character of a refugee camp, some houses being built out of biscuit tins, the settlement had gradually become more prosperous and permanent. A rueful joke among Tibetans was that they had kept their bags packed, perpetually thinking that they would soon return to Tibet upon the rightful restoration of Tibetan independence, and had been reluctant to permanently settle in Dharamsala or anywhere else in India.

I was set up in one of the small rooms built for visiting foreign scholars near the Library of Tibetan Works and Archives. Dolma was well-known in Dharamsala, having been the first woman to have an official position with the TGiE. She did not so much ask anyone to help me as tell them to do so with a certain authority. My association with her resulted in a great deal of cooperation from many Tibetans. They were already primed to solicit the help of any and every foreigner who showed up in Dharamsala, born out of conviction in the justice of their cause as well as a tradition of reliance on foreign patronage for Tibet's monastic and political systems. Dolma also set into motion a request for me to have a private audience with the Dalai Lama.

Dolma left after a few weeks to return to the United States. She said that she had made a request for me to meet with the Dalai Lama but I didn't really know what to expect. I was unfamiliar about how such audiences were arranged or how likely my chances were until, one day, I was visited in my room by someone from the Private Office and told to get ready for an audience immediately. I put on my best clothes and followed the official up to the Dalai Lama's residence. At that time, there wasn't even any security to speak of. I was ushered into the Dalai Lama's reception room and greeted by him with the open and effusive charm with which he both defuses the nervousness and disarms the pretensions of all with whom he meets. He was alone except for Tenzing Geyche, his longtime assistant. We talked for an hour and a half about conditions inside Tibet and in Inner Mongolia. I gave him a blue khatag of the type favored by Mongols and we talked a lot about comparisons between Inner Mongolia and Tibet, both of which are autonomous regions of the PRC, the former being the model for the latter. He gave me a pen that had been given to a Tibetan by the Panchen Lama in Tibet, who had then given it to the Dalai Lama, and told me to use it to write my book.

Writing the book I had promised to Dolma was why I was in Dharamsala, so I began my research on Tibetan history and politics. The Tibetan library had a very good collection of English books on Tibet, so I spent most of my time there. They even had a copy of my *Mythological History of Nepal Valley*! I also delivered to the library several books that I had bought in Tibet. Since the liberalization had begun in Tibet, the publication of some books, mostly on secular subjects, had been allowed and even sponsored by the government. I had acquired several volumes on the Gesar epic and a history of Amdo. In this way, I met Tashi Tsering, the resident scholar at the library who, like Tsering Wangyal, was so identified with his job that he was often referred to just as "Scholar." Tashi Tsering visited me in my room to thank me for the books, which was the beginning of a long friendship and beneficial association with him. Tashi Tsering knew everything about Tibetan history or, if he didn't know it, he knew where to find it.

The Private Office staffer who had come to fetch me for my audience with the Dalai Lama had told me at the time that, because I was interested in politics, I must meet Jamyang Norbu, then the director of the Tibetan Institute of Performing Arts (TIPA), located in the forest above McLeod Ganj. I went there at the first opportunity and found the person who would be my guide to the ins and outs of Tibetan politics in Dharamsala. I made a pilgrimage to his cozy little cabin behind the institute every Sunday after that, the institute's day off, for stimulating conversation, after which we would repair to the Hotel Tibet in McLeod Ganj for endless quantities of awful Indian beer and dinner. Jamyang was a product of St. Joseph's College, a Jesuit school in Darjeeling, but was mostly self-educated, to which his book-lined cabin was a testimony. As director of TIPA, Jamyang had reenergized that institution and revitalized the performing arts by his research on traditional Tibetan operas and the introduction of new operas and other music and dance dramas. The place was a beehive of activity among the twenty or so performing artists, all of whom were also treated to an education that included exposure to the fertile mind of the director. During the summer opera season, all of Dharamsala would trek up to TIPA for day-long performances of traditional operas during which they would picnic and drink large quantities of Indian beer and Tibetan chang.

Jamyang had been in Dharamsala since the late 1960s and had already made a name for himself as an outspoken intellectual and critic. Jamyang's criticism extended to the fallacies of the Dharamsala government and thus got him into frequent controversies. He was one of the founders of the Tibetan Youth Congress and in 1973 had joined the Chushi Gangdruk guerrillas in Mustang. He and Lhasang Tsering, another of the founders of the Youth Congress, were the only two young Tibetans to join the guerrillas in Mustang in the early 1970s. Jamyang admitted that the old veterans in Mustang, now confined to scratching out a living after the end of US assistance and fighting among themselves, got a good laugh when he arrived as an idealistic and enthusiastic youth accompanied by a library of books on guerrilla warfare. Both Jamyang and Lhasang stayed until the surrender in 1974, Lhasang making the intriguing proposal in the end that the resistance should declare itself an independent government and Mustang as sovereign Tibetan territory as a matter of principle before surrendering to the Nepal Army. Jamyang was a prominent skeptic about the possibility of negotiating with China in the new period of liberalization after 1979. He had warned that Tibetans were deceiving themselves if they thought that the recent

Dharamsala delegations sent to Tibet were likely to achieve anything substantial except to perpetuate Tibetans' typical unrealistic hopefulness.

In the 1970s, Tibetan exiles tended to think that the justice of their cause was self-evident, much like they had previously thought that their independence from China was obvious, as it was, at least to them. They had neglected to explain their situation to the world, both before the Chinese invasion and since the revolt of 1959. Because of Tibetan isolationism and neglect, China's claim that Tibet was under Chinese jurisdiction before 1950 tended to be accepted by foreign governments, with adverse consequences for Tibet when it appealed to other countries and to the United Nations when the Chinese invaded in 1950. Tibetan exiles had similarly neglected the diplomacy and public relations arts, with the result that Chinese propaganda about Tibet was essentially unrefuted before Tibet opened and foreigners could see for themselves.

Dharamsala had realized to some extent that they needed to publicize the facts about the reality inside Tibet and had created an Information Office within the exile government which, in 1976, published a small book of refugee accounts, *Tibet Under Communist Chinese Rule*. The accounts are typically limited by each individual's experience and characterized by a lack of understanding of the intricacies of Chinese politics and policies in Tibet, but are very enlightening about many Tibetans' actual experiences. While this series of personal accounts was a goldmine of information about what had really happened during and after the revolt when Chinese propaganda was the only information available to the world, it lacked the coherence of a more eloquent and comprehensive account.

Jamyang Norbu had also published a small book, *Horseman in the Snow: The Story of Aten, an Old Khampa Warrior*, printed by the Information Office in Dharamsala, about a resistance fighter named Aten from the Nyarong area of Kham. Jamyang's book, later published in the United States and the United Kingdom as *Warriors of Tibet*, was by far the best account of what Tibetans had experienced since the Chinese invasion. Since it was about what happened in eastern Tibet where the Chinese implemented their transformative policies before doing so in the TAR, it provided a very rich picture of the Tibetan experience under Chinese rule.

The book was based upon Aten's account as both an official recruited and trained by the Chinese and as a rebel and refugee, elaborated and enriched by Jamyang's developing narrative style. *Horseman in the Snow* paints a picture of the life of a Tibetan from a prosperous family in Nyarong in the Kham area of eastern Tibet. Nyarong was close to Sichuan and had experienced many Chinese attempts at control, always fiercely resisted or sullenly tolerated. Chinese regimes had usually been brutal and corrupt, but the Communists were different, at least at first. PLA soldiers actually adhered to their principles of good treatment of locals and sought opportunities to demonstrate their benevolence by helping Tibetans with work or chores. Given their promises and their good behavior, the Chinese Communists had been successful in recruiting many collaborators, like Aten, especially since there was little alternative.

As the son of a local chieftain, Aten was recruited by the Chinese for training as an official of what was promised to be an autonomous Tibetan administration of Nyarong. He was sent for training in Chengdu, but this experience was the beginning of his opposition to the Chinese. Aten and several other Tibetans and other minorities were subjected to what the Chinese Communists imagined were enlightened minority policies, but which appeared to the minorities as typical Chinese arrogance toward those they regarded as primitive and inferior. These Tibetans and others, particularly Lolos, objected to Chinese plans to transform their societies according to what they imagined was an obviously superior Chinese socialist model. They found their instructors deaf to their complaints that their own societies were in some ways quite advanced and without need to be transformed according to the Chinese model. All their objections were met with uncompromising and condescending rejection by their Chinese instructors.

While Aten was in Chengdu, the Chinese had begun their deceptively named democratic reforms in eastern Tibet. Aten returned to his village to find that many Tibetans were seething with resentment against the Chinese or had already risen up in open revolt. Thinking Aten a loyal collaborator, the Chinese revealed to him their plan to undermine Tibetan loyalty to their traditional political and religious leaders, who would be replaced with Tibetans recruited and trained by the Chinese. Many of these were formerly of the lowest level of Tibetan society, including beggars and thieves, who the Chinese considered the most virtuous because they had been the most exploited in the old feudal society. With the exception of a few, like Aten, many of these Tibetans were uneducated and incompetent, so it was obvious that they would be little more than puppets manipulated by the Chinese.

Aten remained in his position until the Chinese began their campaigns of persecution of local Tibetan leaders and prominent lamas, when he, like many Tibetans, could take it no longer and decided upon violent opposition. The rest of Aten's story is of the futility of that opposition against Chinese repression and overwhelming force. In the face of Tibetan revolt, the Chinese abandoned all their policies of respectful treatment and resorted to violent and merciless repression of all opposition. The organization of an effective Tibetan resistance was hampered by the fact that those who chose revolt had to take their families along with them so that they would not suffer repression. Aten's resistance and flight is a heartbreaking story of the death of his family and the massacre of most of those who tried to flee to Central Tibet to escape Chinese "reforms."

Dharamsala at that time was still a sleepy hill station/refugee camp. There were quite a few foreigners there, some longtime residents, and the usual tourists and spiritual pilgrims. Dharamsala was full of lots of interesting foreigners and was even better than Nepal for meeting such types, if one's interest was focused on Tibet. Tibetans refer to all foreigners as *Inji*, a derivative of "English." Most Tibetans were gratified when Dharamsala began to attract the interest of foreigners. If nothing else, they stimulated the economy that was mostly based on small hotels and lodges, cafes, handicraft shops, and bookstores. Many of the foreigners were spiritual seekers attracted by Buddhism, the Dalai Lama, and other Tibetan lamas. Tibetans were desperate for any international interest and support and they regarded the foreigners as patrons of the Tibetan religion within the traditional context in which Tibetan Buddhism had survived and propagated itself through cultivation of foreign patronage.

Jamyang Norbu was one of the few who saw a negative effect of the arrival of so many spiritual pilgrims in Dharamsala. He wrote, in an article published in *Tibetan Review* in 1990, that the arrival of this type of foreigners in Dharamsala in the 1970s reversed the trend of secularization and democratization in Tibetan exile society. They had, he said, re-empowered the religious establishment and thus stifled more modern and healthy secular interests among Tibetans and encouraged them to revert to their old and fatal way of dealing with reality by burying their heads in magic, ritual, and superstition.

I began my studies at the Gangkyi library by reading all the back issues of *Tibetan Review*. There was no better way to get current with Tibetan politics and the issues of Tibetan exiles than to read the semi-official publication. *Tibetan Review* had been founded with TGiE support, but Tsering Wangyal had made it a habit to irritate the exile government. He understood that the journal had to be independent in order to have any credibility, but the exile government tended to regard criticism as disloyalty. Tsering Wangyal himself wrote editorials for each issue that were famous in the Tibetan community for their insight and eloquent expression of the issues affecting many Tibetans. He honored the responsibility of a free and independent press to be completely honest and objective. Under his editorship, *Tibetan Review* was so essential to Tibetans and foreigners interested in the issue that the publication was supported on subscriptions alone. In those days it was almost the only publication focused on the Tibet issue and it therefore attracted articles from Tibetans fluent in English as well as foreign scholars and activists.

I wrote my first political article for *Tibetan Review*, at the suggestion of Tsering Wangyal, about my five months in Tibet. My theme was that while Tibet had changed under Chinese rule almost beyond recognition compared to what many exiles remembered, there was a remarkable revival of Tibetan culture happening that was both a surprise to the Chinese and an inspiration to Tibetans. Twenty years of Chinese repression of all aspects of Tibetan identity and culture had not extinguished Tibetans' desire to preserve their own culture. Tibetan culture had experienced a remarkable resurgence that was a testimony to its strength and endurance and a repudiation of all of China's campaigns of destruction and attempts at assimilation.

My conversations with Tashi and Jamyang were usually about Tibetan history or, more often, about alternative historical scenarios that might have seen Tibet emerge into the modern world as an independent country. Most of these scenarios were dependent upon a greater degree of foreign patronage, by the British, Americans, or the United Nations, that might have helped Tibet establish its independence. Such scenarios also required Tibetans, especially the religious establishment, to have been less isolationist and for the country to have been more unified rather than divided by regional interests.

All of these scenarios were of the "alternative history" or "what might have been" kind. One of the most popular was if the British had been willing to make Tibet a colony like India instead of just trying to establish trade privileges there. The problem was that the British Empire was contracting at that point and there was little enthusiasm for another colonial adventure, especially in a place as remote as Tibet, where there was little to be gained except to prevent the Russians from gaining similar advantages. The British also had large economic interests in China and were therefore unwilling to challenge China's claim to sovereignty over Tibet. They tried to have it both ways by support of Tibetan autonomy under Chinese "suzerainty," a term that the last British representative in Tibet, Hugh Richardson, admitted was "incapable of definition."

Another seemingly plausible scenario was if the Americans had been willing to play a role as Tibet's patron after the departure of the British from India in 1947. American interest in Tibet at the time was to counter Soviet Communism and, secondarily, Chinese Communism, in what was an almost seamless transition from the Great Game to the Cold War with the United States now taking the role of Britain. Unfortunately, the Americans, like the British before them, had no real interest in Tibet. The United States did make extraordinary offers of diplomatic, financial, and even small-scale military assistance to Tibetans in 1950 if the Dalai Lama would reject the Seventeen Point Agreement and Chinese sovereignty over Tibet and go into exile, but the religious establishment prevailed and he went back to Lhasa.

My favorite scenario was if the United States and the British in the post-WWII period had demanded that China recognize Tibet's sovereignty, much like the Soviet Union did in regard to Outer Mongolia, which had far less claim to independence than did Tibet. The United States had a large degree of influence over the Chinese Nationalists at the time, having supported them against the Japanese. The boundaries of countries all over the world were being redrawn after the war, but the United States had insufficient interest in or knowledge about Tibet at the time and the British were losing interest altogether.

The recent liberalization introduced by Deng Xiaoping and the opening of Tibet both to foreigners and exiled Tibetans had revived the hopes of Tibetans in Dharamsala. Ever since coming into exile in 1959, Tibetans had been famously unrealistic about their prospects for returning home. Now in Dharamsala, the hope was revived and some Tibetans were thinking about selling their property in India and returning to Tibet. Others were studying Chinese on the assumption that the language would be useful, whatever arrangement was worked out about Tibet's political status. The visits of the Dharamsala delegations to Tibet as well as the meetings in Beijing between Chinese officials and the Dalai Lama's envoys led to speculation that some sort of resolution was imminent. Only skeptics like Jamyang Norbu predicted that the Tibetans were being played by the Chinese and that to expect the Chinese to make any concessions was the height of folly.

Tibetans may have been unrealistic about prospects for a resolution of their issue, but it was undeniable that Tibet was back on the international agenda after an absence of twenty years. China had unintentionally put it there by opening Tibet and by inviting Tibetan exile delegations for inspections and dialogues. They did so because they thought the issue was already resolved and were surprised to find that Tibetan culture and religion and nationalism were not dead, that Tibetans were not reconciled to Chinese rule, and that they had managed to convey that message to the outside world. The sleepy town of Dharamsala had become a bit more exciting with the arrival of Tibetans allowed to leave Tibet and foreigners interested in Tibetan Buddhism or politics.

The "new arrivals," as the recently arrived Tibetans were called, found their experiences of twenty years under the Chinese incomprehensible to those who had been in India since 1959 or those who had been born in exile and had never even seen Tibet. They thought that Tibetans in India had become too Indian, while the old-timers thought the new arrivals too Chinese. Divisions arose over not only recent experiences but superficial things like dress styles and food and music preferences. Many of the new arrivals were conspicuous because of their usually shabby dress and their still typically ruddy faces due to the climate of Tibet.

Despite my resolve to not succumb to unrealistic idealism about the Tibetan political situation, I was also inspired by the political excitement in Dharamsala in those years. If there was still no hope for an ultimately satisfactory solution to the Tibet issue, there was at least interest and some apparent movement both by China and some foreign countries. The Chinese, while not offering what the exiles wanted, were at least edging closer to their own promise about allowing some Tibetan cultural and religious autonomy. Of course, they quickly backtracked as Tibetans revealed their true sentiments and as Tibet once again became an international political issue. Some foreign countries, particularly the United States, began to take an interest in Tibet as their own citizens lobbied on behalf of the issue and the Dalai Lama began making foreign visits.

In Dharamsala, I wrote two more articles for *Tibetan Review*. One, a review of John Avedon's *In Exile from the Land of Snows*, was laudatory and uncritical. My only critical comment was to point out that his caption of a photo showing Chinese troops entering Lhasa in 1951, complete with tubas and large photos of CCP leaders, was incorrect in identifying the leaders shown as Mao and Zhou Enlai. I think he assumed the second leader was Zhou because Zhou eventually was considered second in the CCP hierarchy to Mao, but in 1951 that role was played by Chu Teh, the leader of the PLA. I mentioned that before 1949, the CCP leadership was known collectively as Chu Mao, Chu Teh as the military commander being of equal prominence to Mao. Avedon's book was very influential at the time as one of the first accounts from the Tibetan point of view of what had happened under the Chinese Communists. Many Westerners got their first introduction to the Tibet issue through his book.

I did a much longer review of Israel Epstein's *Tibet Transformed.* Epstein was a Lithuanian Jew whose Socialist parents, members of the Jewish Bund, were purged after the Russian Revolution and fled to China. He grew up in China, became a sympathizer of the Chinese Communists, reported from Yenan, and became the editor of *China Reconstructs*, an English-language pictorial meant to promote the Chinese Revolution to the Western world. He was a lifelong communist and a professional propagandist who never deviated from the Party line but who nevertheless found himself imprisoned as a foreign spy during the Cultural Revolution.

Epstein was privileged with access to Tibet during long visits in 1955, 1965, and 1976, and conducted extensive interviews with Tibetans, mostly "former serfs" supplied to him by local officials, who told horror stories of their suffering before "liberation." Epstein's book, at 550 pages, was full of interesting information about Tibet during those obscure years and was especially valuable in its timeline and description of various Chinese political campaigns among Tibetans. However, he slavishly adhered to the CCP propaganda line that Tibet's "transformation" was "historically determined" according to Marxist doctrine and was a natural, beneficial, and progressive social evolution having everything to do with class conflict and nothing to do with nationalist issues between China and Tibet.

Epstein's book suffered from being published in 1983, when the policies he extols as absolutely correct were being abandoned. He attempted to justify the policies of the past as correct, even as they were being abandoned for "even more correct," if contradictory, doctrines. He claimed that Tibetans were happy under the previous regime but even happier when that regime was abandoned. His book is full of such contradictions, all of which I gleefully pointed out, because of his fidelity to the CCP's "historically determined" ideology and his refusal to admit any political issue of the legitimacy of China's claim to sovereignty over the non-Chinese Tibetans. Epstein was a true believer in the socialist cause whose convictions were unchanged by his imprisonment on false charges during the Cultural Revolution or by any evidence of Chinese abuses in Tibet. To admit any flaw in Communist ideology or the CCP's policies would be to confess that his life had been wasted on a false ideology. His book was useful in providing information, even if biased, about obscure Chinese campaigns in Tibet and in understanding the mentality of those who devote themselves to idealistic and absolutist causes. I took some delight in pointing out that the photo of the Potala on the cover of his book was a reversed image, printed without his or his Chinese editors' notice, despite their claims to intimate knowledge about Tibet, a distortion I suggested was the real meaning of his title.

After some sixteen months in Dharamsala, during three visits from 1982 to 1984, interspersed with periods in Nepal and the United States, I figured I had learned enough about Tibetan history and politics to write the book I had promised Dolma. I had read practically everything in English on the issue available at the excellent library in Gangkyi. I had endless conversations about the politics with my friends, Jamyang Norbu and Tashi Tsering. I thought I knew just about everything there was to know on the subject and I had an inside understanding due to my Tibetan friends, beginning with my tutorial with Dolma in Lhasa. I had learned nothing to convince me that Tibet would ever escape Chinese rule, but I was convinced that it had a right to do so based upon its distinct ethnic, cultural, and national identity as well as a history of political independence and resistance to Chinese claims to control over Tibet.

I developed an analysis of Tibetan nationalism as an ideology that had evolved late among Tibetans due to the absence of any real threats to their independent existence, but that had been stimulated by both the British invasion of 1904 and the Chinese invasion of eastern Tibet. Tibetan nationalism had developed over the first half of the twentieth century, hampered all the while by traditional isolationism and religious otherworldliness, but further progress had been cut short by the Chinese Communists just as Tibet had begun to recognize the Chinese threat to its existence and to seek international recognition.

Traditional Tibet had maintained its independent existence in the pre-nationalist era, when political relationships were only vaguely defined, by acknowledging the imperial pretensions of Mongol and

Manchu empires. However, Chinese nationalism of the twentieth century was not to be satisfied with such vague symbols of sovereignty and demanded actual administrative control in a unified state. Chinese nationalism, which developed simultaneously with that of Tibet, claimed all of the territories of the previous Qing Empire as integral parts of modern China and was intolerant of Tibetan claims for a separate territory or national existence. Tibetan nationalism was an indigenous development in response to foreign threats, both British and Chinese, and not, as the Chinese would later claim, a British and American creation, which came close to achieving its goal of international recognition of Tibetan independence before it was snuffed out by the similar but competing ideology of Chinese nationalism.

Despite its hopelessness, the Tibet issue was still an interesting subject and an attractive cause that inspired many besides me. By confining myself just to refuting Chinese propaganda, I hoped to avoid unrealistic expectations and inevitable disappointment. Tibet had a legitimate case for independence, or national self-determination, and the Chinese denial of Tibet's independent existence was a great injustice. China had successfully incorporated Tibet into the PRC, but it still needed to justify its conquest by refuting the Tibetan claim to an independent national existence. China devoted much propaganda to justifying its sovereignty over Tibet by citing evidence of all that China had done to liberate the Tibetans and to assist them ever since. Part of that propaganda was devoted to a denigration of Tibet's former social and political systems as a "dark, cruel, feudal hell on earth," suitably exaggerated, from which Tibetans were supposedly grateful to have been liberated by the CCP. Chinese distortions of Tibetan history and culture were a subject that an independent scholar might undertake to disprove, in the hope of having some effect on the interpretation of Tibetan history, if not on Tibet's ultimate fate.

I had studied the Tibetan language in Dharamsala both privately and with a tutor, but I had failed to become proficient. It was easy enough to learn the beautiful alphabetic Tibetan script, but the grammar was beyond me. Everyone I knew in Dharamsala spoke perfect English and I was far more interested in deep political discussions than in practicing my Tibetan. Perhaps in Lhasa I could have practiced more easily. Fewer Tibetans there had any English and they were far more forgiving of mistakes and generous in offering help to a foreigner trying to learn their language. It is usually easier to learn a language out in a village where one can begin with simple phrases and no one laughs at your efforts or answers you in English. I had learned more Chinese than Tibetan and had used Chinese in Tibet. Spoken Chinese is relatively easier to learn, at least at a basic level, since it has practically no grammar, but the written language is primitive and archaic. Thus, I could speak some Chinese but couldn't read it and I could read some Tibetan but couldn't speak it.

My lack of language skills determined that I wouldn't be a Tibetologist, as did my interests. I was more interested in the broad history and politics rather than the intricacies of religion or culture. Language scholars tend to spend their lives on textual analysis at the neglect of the overall picture. Of course, their primary research is necessary for anyone who hopes to do a more comprehensive, if derivative, analysis. I had also determined that a failing of most Tibetan scholars was their inability to understand Chinese history and politics and, in regard to modern China, Marxist theory and doctrine. In relation to Tibet, one had to understand Marxist nationality theory as well as Marxist-Leninist and CCP policies on minority nationalism. No one had so far done this most essential task for understanding the modern history of Tibet under Chinese rule. I didn't have the skills to be a traditional Tibetologist, but I did have the interest and ability to understand political theory and politics.

## RETURN TO ACADEMIA

When I returned to the United States in the fall of 1984, I had no real plan for how I would actually write my history of Tibet. As usual, I thought that if I pursued my real interests, circumstances would transpire to facilitate that pursuit. This was, of course, naïve in the extreme, but it had worked for me so far. I tried to begin writing my history, but something was wrong about the way I was going about it. I imagined I could just sit down and do it without any institutional support except that of Westview Press in Boulder, Colorado, which had expressed an interest. I had visited their offices in Boulder and met Fred Praeger, the founder, who was well-known as a publisher of academic studies on obscure or sensitive or controversial political topics that other publishers wouldn't touch. I more or less had a publisher, but the writing wasn't happening. It turns out that one has to learn how to write. I didn't know as much as I thought about the subject either.

A girlfriend, Gay Browning, suggested that I go back to college, where I would find a more congenial atmosphere as well as academic and possibly financial support. I resisted, thinking that I could not afford to return to school, that no school would accept me, that I would find no courses relevant to my subject, and that it would not further my goal of writing a history of Tibet. Eventually, I was proven wrong on all counts. On Gay's advice, I began to explore a return to academia. I would have to finish my BA before going to graduate school. I had almost-but-not-quite graduated from the USAF Academy in 1967. Seniors, or first classmen, were not allowed to quit the academy, but I had expressed some reservations about the Vietnam War and was offered the choice to resign, with the warning that if I graduated, I could end up in Leavenworth Prison if I continued to express such anti-war sentiments. The Air Force was very sensitive at that time about criticism of the war from inside the military. I had more credits from USAFA than most colleges required for graduation, but no degree.

My friend Matthew Kapstein had also returned to academia and was working on a doctorate in Tibetan Buddhist studies at Brown, so I gave him a call for advice. Matthew's first question was "Do you want to be a Tibetologist?" Matthew knew my interests and capabilities as well as anyone in the world and he knew I didn't have the language skills or the interest or even the brains to become a Tibetologist. Matthew was one of a select few who were able to carve out a career in that field. He had begun with Sanskrit and then Tibetan and was an intellectual and a scholar with astounding capabilities. I was not comparable and we both knew it. Matthew asked if what I wanted to do was more in the line of international relations. If so, he recommended the school where his brother, Ethan, had just graduated, the Fletcher School of Law and Diplomacy. Fletcher is a graduate school at Tufts University in Medford,

Massachusetts, near Cambridge and Boston. That sounded right for me, so I began inquiries about Fletcher and Tufts.

Fletcher was very impressive and it seemed to be exactly what I needed. It was founded in the 1930s, jointly by Harvard and Tufts, as America's first graduate school of international relations. Courses were in international law, politics, and political theory, which was exactly what I needed but hadn't known I needed until now. I would have to gain admittance to Tufts as an undergraduate, of course, and then apply to Fletcher, but it was beginning to seem feasible. I contacted Tufts and found that they had an innovative Resuming Education program for older students returning to college and that I might well be admitted on that basis. It turned out that Tufts and other schools with such programs were very happy with older students because they were usually more serious and they almost always graduated. I applied and was accepted into the program. Since I had no financial assets except a Volkswagen van loaded with Tibetan carpets, I qualified for financial aid and loans covering the whole tuition.

With a schedule to go to Tufts in September, 1985, I planned a trip with Gay to Tibet for the summer. The way into Tibet was still through China, the route from Kathmandu having yet to open up, and I was familiar with travel within China, so we planned to fly to Hong Kong and go by boat to Guangzhou and fly from there to Lanzhou. From Lanzhou we took a bus to Labrang Tashikyil, the largest Tibetan monastery in what is now Gansu. Approaching Labrang, the road passes a large Tibetan chorten just as the terrain changes from the yellow loess hills of Gansu to the uplands of the Tibetan Plateau. The chorten appeared as a territorial marker between Tibet and China, as it probably once was.

Labrang was much reduced from the size it was in the past but still occupied the whole side of the large valley for a distance of perhaps a quarter mile. It was entirely Tibetan in character and in population except for some Hui (Chinese Muslim) traders who occupied small stalls along the road in front of the monastery. The local Tibetans appeared very traditional, perhaps because many in the region to the west up the valley were nomadic. Many old travelers had commented on the beauty of the Labrang women, perhaps because they were used to lowering their chubas to the waist as they worked in the fields. We spent three days in Labrang, including a one-day hike up the valley into nomadic areas. I had the feeling that we should have stayed in Labrang, perhaps accepting the offer of some nomads we met to proceed farther up the valley to their encampments, instead of going on to Lhasa. Lhasa proved to have changed much in the three years since I had last been there, whereas Labrang had just opened to foreigners and was essentially unchanged.

Back in Lanzhou, we got on a train to Sining, the capital of Qinghai Province. Walking through the train I unexpectedly encountered a familiar face, a face that I knew well from Dharamsala, a Tibetan official of the TGiE, Atisha, who also recognized me. This was a surprise; it turned out that he and another friend, Thupten Samphel, along with Alak Jigme Rinpoche and Dzasa Kundeling, were on their way to Sining as the fifth official Tibetan delegation from Dharamsala in a process initiated by Deng Xiaoping in 1979. Each of the three preceding delegations had revealed continuing Tibetan reverence for the Dalai Lama and discontent with Chinese rule. A scheduled fourth delegation had been canceled due to shifts in Chinese policy and this, the fifth, would prove to be the last. I witnessed the delegation's greeting by officials as they arrived in Sining and I was able to direct some local Tibetans to the official guest house where they were staying. The local Tibetans were hopeful, as usual, that the delegation would achieve some result; but it didn't, as usual, and was not even allowed to go into the TAR.

This delegation marked the end of the Chinese attempt to put what they thought was the last nail in the coffin of Tibetan separatism by securing the Dalai Lama's return to Tibet. Assuming that the Tibet political issue was already dead, the Chinese had thought that if they allowed the Dalai Lama to return, apologize for his treason in 1959, and assume some meaningless position in the CCP, it would be the end of the Tibetan political issue. However, they had miscalculated, as these delegations' greetings by Tibetans and the unexpected revival of Tibet as an international political issue had revealed. A Tibet Work Group meeting had already reversed much of Hu Yaobang's promise of autonomy and a reduction in the number of Chinese cadres in Tibet by deciding that economic development was the solution for Tibet, for which Chinese experts and entrepreneurs would be necessary. The numbers of Chinese officials were increased and restrictions on the travel of individual traders were removed, leading to a large influx of Chinese officials as well as petty traders, which conflicted with the rise in Tibetan nationalism.

In Sining, we visited the famous Kumbum Monastery just outside the town. It was something of a disappointment to find that it had been turned into a Tibetan Buddhist "Disneyland" for Chinese tourists. I was at first attracted by what appeared to be Tibetan women in their colorful nomadic costumes until I discovered they were Chinese tourists who paid to dress up and be photographed in the Tibetan costumes. From Sining, we went by train to Golmud, at that time the terminus of the railroad. Not wanting to be crammed into a bus for the long trip to Lhasa, I went to the local truck park and soon found a ride on one of a small convoy of five or six trucks carrying large fuel tanks on extended trailers. The Chinese had built an underground pipeline from Golmud to Lhasa in the early 1970s. The pipeline paralleled the road and was said to be two pipes, each about a foot in diameter, one carrying gasoline and the other kerosene. It might seem strange that so much kerosene would be needed, since it is usually only used for cooking and heating, except that kerosene is also jet fuel. The tanks on the trucks in which we were riding revealed that fuel was being stored for emergency use, including the possibility of war with India.

The truck ride was 24-hours nonstop, except for tea breaks, which unfortunately meant that we missed much of the spectacular scenery during the night. Lhasa was amazingly changed in the three years since I had been there. The city had expanded, mostly to the west, with nondescript housing and industrial compounds, occupied mostly by Chinese. There were more Chinese everywhere, and the city, which had already lost much of its character when I visited in 1982, was now much further along in that process. The revitalization of Tibetan culture continued but it had been curtailed by the influx of Chinese, and Tibetans had lost their sense that they might actually control any aspect of their own fate. The optimism generated by the reforms and liberalization initiated by Deng Xiaoping and Hu Yaobang had been overcome by the decision to allow unrestricted Chinese immigration to Tibet in pursuit of economic opportunities fueled by government subsidies. There were also ever more Chinese officials, PLA, and security personnel, now justified as necessary for Tibet's development. Lhasa was still peaceful, but the tension between Tibetan expectations generated by the liberalization and the reality of Chinese control would erupt only two years later in demonstrations and riots. For now, it was just a shock to see how much had changed in the three years since I had last been there.

In 1982, Tibet, and China, were just emerging from the stagnation and repression of the Maoist years. Lhasa was still a mostly Tibetan town and there was optimism among Tibetans due to their finally being allowed some small personal freedoms. Lhasa showed many of the scars of the Cultural Revolution in still unrepaired monasteries and manor houses, but the old city around the Jokhang retained much of its ancient Tibetan quality. Now the old city was being overwhelmed by the vast expansion of new buildings and the Tibetan population was being overwhelmed by the influx of Chinese. The industrious Chinese immigrants were supporting themselves with a variety of small business occupations, always doing it faster and cheaper than Tibetans, and with a new form of garden agriculture in which vegetables were grown in greenhouses made of plastic sheets. This form of intensive gardening, combined with the intensity of sunshine at this altitude, resulted in a profusion of huge vegetables that had transformed the Lhasa marketplace and supported a much larger vegetable-eating population. Rice, which the Chinese preferred over the Tibetan barley, still had to be imported, but could be in the large quantities necessary since the road from Golmud was paved in 1982.

We were in Lhasa for almost two months in the summer of 1985 until forced to leave in mid-August by a purge of foreign tourists in preparation for the twentieth anniversary of the founding of the TAR. Unlike in 1982, when there were fewer than twenty foreign tourists in Lhasa at any time, there were now hundreds and the Chinese had apparently decided that they constituted a security threat and should be removed. The number of tourists was also a great change for me since I no longer had Lhasa mostly to myself nor could I imagine my experience as so unique. Our trip happened to coincide with another visit by Dolma, who stayed with her sister at the old Phala mansion as before.

There was something different about the atmosphere at the Phala house and it had nothing to do with political repercussions from Dolma's last visit. There was a mysterious rectangular object on a shelf covered by a cloth. After the usual pleasantries, the object was uncovered with undisguised pride and revealed to be a television! The only available programming besides Chinese news propaganda was an international soccer game, so that was what we watched. There was no more polite tea drinking and conversation with visitors. TV had changed the cultural atmosphere in an unavoidable way. I didn't want to be one of those who prefers others to be traditional while enjoying the benefits of modernity myself, but I still felt a loss of an important part of Tibetan social tradition.

We were fortunate to be in Lhasa for an important event: the return of the Ramoche Jowo to that temple. The Ramoche Jowo was the Buddha Sakyamuni image brought to Tibet by Bhrikuti, Srongtsan Gampo's Nepalese queen. It was originally placed in the Jokhang, the temple sponsored by Bhrikuti, but later transferred to the Ramoche, the temple sponsored by Wencheng, the Chinese queen, in a process never adequately explained historically. It had disappeared during the chaos of the Cultural Revolution, was rediscovered in two parts in a Chinese metallurgy factory by Rinbur Tulku, and returned to Tibet where it was repaired at the Jokhang until ready to be returned to the Ramoche. It was done so in a grand procession of the image carried on a palanquin accompanied by lamas and monks as well as a dance and drama troupe and seemingly half the Tibetan population of Lhasa.

This was an enormously significant event in that it restored the original Jowo to the Ramoche, thus reconstituting Lhasa's two most famous Buddha images and their temples. Rinbur Tulku had been allowed to search for Tibetan images taken to China before and during the Cultural Revolution and had found several tons of metal statues at several sites in China where they had been taken for melting. Many tons of Tibet's precious artworks as well as common implements such as tea cauldrons had been melted down, but the quantity was so huge that the process was not yet completed even twenty years later. Rinbur Tulku recovered some

13,000 religious statues and artifacts, estimated at less than 5 percent of the total confiscated, among which was the Ramoche Jowo.

I eagerly anticipated seeing another Ganden Serthang with Dolma and her family. I was somewhat surprised that few, if any, of the hundreds of foreign tourists in Lhasa at the time knew anything about it or were planning to attend. I considered myself fortunate to know about it but I was uncertain about whether or not to tell others, thinking that perhaps Tibetans preferred to keep it private. Not so, said Dolma; it was just that other foreigners did not have my advantage of knowing a Tibetan like her! I informed a few selected friends, but at the event there were only a dozen or so tourists. I wondered at the unfortunate ignorance of most tourists while at the same time I was pleased to not have to share the event with them. We went out by truck as before and there was again a festive atmosphere, many more temples now having been restored. The restoration at Ganden had just begun in 1982, with only a few of the most important temples being rebuilt, but now there were many more temples and many more monks there. Ganden was now a functioning monastery, not as huge as before but still impressive given how completely it had been destroyed.

As we prepared to leave Tibet via Nepal, I was once again given the opportunity to travel with Tibetan exiles visiting from India and Nepal. Unlike before when the only such bus was organized by the government and permission was required, this bus was chartered privately by Tibetans from Nepal, one of whom was a friend from Kathmandu. Tsering Dolkar was the former proprietor of a well-known trekking shop in Thamel where one could get any sort of equipment for trekking. She was particularly well-known to Gay, who used to hang out at her shop when she was first in Kathmandu. Tsering was in Lhasa for the first time with her parents, who had fled Tibet in 1959 and were now the owners of one of the carpet factories in Kathmandu. We were able to get seats on the bus they had arranged. Our bus went the usual route for that time, via the Kamba La to the Yamdrok Yumtso Lake to Gyantse and from there to Shigatse.

We were trying to make the border in two days, so passed through Shigatse and continued on to Tingri the first day. Unfortunately, the only place for such a large group to stay in Tingri was at the PLA camp outside the town, which ran a hostel. Gay and I decided to sleep out under the stars, which was wonderful, especially in contrast to the experience of those who stayed at the PLA hostel. They all complained of high prices, poor food, and surly service by the soldiers. One European couple got into a huge argument about a spurious charge for a supposedly missing towel, which led to the soldiers screaming and pointing their weapons at them until they paid up. We drove away shaken at the soldiers' obvious hatred for Tibetans and foreigners as well as their extortionist tactics and coercive methods of fleecing tourists. It was a relief to get away from them and to reach Nepal.

The contrast really hit the next day as we sat in a pleasant café in Kathmandu reading the *International Herald Tribune*. There was a feeling of freedom from the tension in Tibet. Even the ability to get international news was a contrast to the atmosphere of propaganda and censorship in Tibet. The repression was more intense for Tibetans, of course, but even foreigners could feel the tension and lack of freedom, as well as Chinese animosity. Arriving in the vastly more relaxed atmosphere of Kathmandu made one vividly aware of the tensions left behind in Tibet.

Early in September I drove to Massachusetts to begin my resumption of formal studies. The Tufts campus was tiny, mostly all in one quadrangle with the Fletcher School at one end. Tufts was a not-very-impressive second-tier Ivy League school, but Fletcher was the best in its field with an impressive faculty and only 300 students, many of whom were from foreign countries or had interesting backgrounds. Unlike Tufts undergraduates, Fletcher students were older, more experienced, and often had clearer goals and interests.

I immediately fell in love with everything about Fletcher, not only its elitist academic atmosphere and scholarly intensity but even its architecture. The Fletcher library was a reconstructed gymnasium with a high ceiling to which a modern addition had been so seamlessly added that it was hard to tell where the old building ended and the new one began. There were interesting passageways and alcoves that were a delight to explore. I quickly became known as the "Tibet Guy" around both Tufts and Fletcher and this helped me, given the usual Tibet mystique. Administrators and professors were willing to assist me in my study of what was regarded as an exotic and interesting issue. It helped that I was older and had a long experience in my field, and had lived in exotic and mysterious places like Nepal and Tibet.

Besides Chinese history courses at Tufts, my most interesting and relevant courses were on Marxism. I did two or three courses on Marxist theory, in one of which we actually read the Communist Manifesto and large parts of Marx's *Capital.* I believe it is in the Manifesto where Marx and Engels begin with the assertion that man's consciousness is determined by his economic status—no qualifiers allowing for any other factors like tradition or culture, religion or nationalism, or even personality. I objected that this was overly simplistic and was told by the professor, a reputed Trotskyite, that if I could just accept that part then everything that followed would make sense. That was probably true, but I thought that I had uncovered the fundamental fallacy of Marxism in this simplistic premise.

We read not only Marx and several volumes of Lenin but also the theories of Plekhanov, whose ideas were far more reasonable than the other Marxists, and Trotsky. I read one work by Lenin on nationality policy, followed by one by Stalin who, because of his non-Russian nationality, was designated by Lenin as the expert on nationality theory and policy. Stalin was refreshingly candid in admitting that the Communist Party's supposedly principled policy in favor of nationality self-determination was actually a cynical ploy to win the confidence of minority nationalists while pursuing the real goal of proletarian internationalism and assimilation.

Tufts was an interesting learning experience that contradicted my belief that I would be unable to find courses relevant to my Tibet interest. One of the most valuable lessons was learning to write in an academic style. I was somewhat surprised to find that one has to learn to write a language even if a native speaker. Words do not flow as naturally from mind to paper as one might expect. I had to relearn grammar and punctuation and learn written composition.

Being admitted to Fletcher brought my goal closer to reality. This was a critical step and, once officially a Fletcher student, I thought my history of Tibet might really happen and that the decision to go back to school had been the right one. Not only that but my academic experience was expanding the scope of the book and making it potentially more credible academically. I concentrated on political theory and history at Fletcher rather than the international law and economics offerings. Political theory was particularly valuable to me in regard to nationalism and state formation.

The Tibet issue is all about nationalism, as I increasingly understood, and the creation of a state structure that almost, but not quite, achieved international recognition of Tibet's independent status and thus its survival as a national political entity. I learned that nationalism was a natural evolution of political consciousness within a self-defined political group that took place due to factors of social identity and political cohesion, often stimulated by foreign threats, but not necessarily by foreign political theories. Many political scientists thought of nationalism as a European creation that spread worldwide as a political ideology. However, I saw it as due to indigenous factors of social and economic development combined with the evolution of state formation in the immediate area. This was closer to the Marxist theory of "inevitable stages of history" based upon economic development, with the added factors that the Marxists neglected cultural and ethnic identity as well as political history.

An important part of the support I got at Fletcher came in the form of scholarships and grants, the most significant of which was a FLAS (Foreign Language and Area Studies Fellowships Program) grant from the US Department of Education. This grant, and all the others I got, were awarded to the school and then by the school to selected students. A FLAS at that time was worth about $16,000, which was more than the basic Fletcher tuition for one year. One requirement for the FLAS, as the name implied, was language study. I got the grant to study Tibetan even though neither Fletcher, obviously, nor any other school in the area taught the language. I arranged to be taught by a Tibetan lama in the area who had at one time been some sort of research assistant at Tufts. Since his former status was something vaguely equivalent to a professor,

Fletcher agreed that I could take private lessons with him and get Fletcher credit!

The lama, Thupten Kalsang, ran a tiny meditation center in Malden, where I visited him one evening every week for Tibetan lessons. He wasn't much of a teacher and I wasn't much of a language student but we struggled on for a full year during which I acquired a basic conversational ability. When it came time to get a grade, I presented Thupten Kalsang with a Fletcher form to sign. He saw the blank space where a grade was required and asked me what grade I would like. I said I would like an "A," please, which is what I got and Fletcher accordingly recorded two course credits in Tibetan and certified my Tibetan language proficiency! Unfortunately, my Tibetan was forgotten almost as quickly as my Chinese, but due only to neglect rather than distaste.

At Fletcher I wrote ever-lengthier papers leading up to the requirement for a MALD (Master of Arts in Law and Diplomacy) thesis of approximately 100 pages. I had been building up to this with every course paper I wrote and planned to expand the MALD thesis into my history of Tibet. The MALD paper is done as an expanded course paper during the final semester. I did mine in a human rights law course taught by Philip Alston, a popular young professor who later went on to have a distinguished career at the United Nations. My thesis was the culmination of everything I had studied and written so far and it was an outline of my history of Tibet. Alston wasn't known to have any particular interest in Tibet but he was a passionate human rights advocate. He surprised me by giving my MALD thesis an A+, which he told me was not a recordable grade but was meant as praise and encouragement. I knew that the plus would not appear on any record but it was indeed a huge encouragement, especially coming from someone with such an excellent reputation.

I had assumed that after finishing at Fletcher, I would write the book somewhere, somehow. My plans for supporting myself while writing were as vague as before going to Tufts and Fletcher. Now I began to think about the Fletcher PhD program, since the only requirement was a dissertation and I could continue an association with Fletcher and perhaps even get some financial assistance. I would have to pass an oral examination in order to be admitted into the PhD program, conducted by four professors with whom I had taken classes. Theoretically, the oral exam was on the content of the courses I had taken but I got the usual exception for my special interest and the exam was all about the politics of Tibet. Having passed the oral exam, I began thinking about applying for a grant given to the school every year by the Shell Oil Company designated for dissertation research. The single grant was for $9,000 for research in a country outside the United States. Shell no doubt gave the grant for tax purposes and left the award up to a committee composed of Fletcher professors. There was also one student position on the committee filled by someone I didn't know but who lobbied for me for the usual reason of the Tibet mystique. I got the grant and made plans to go to Dharamsala, for the fourth time, in October 1989.

While in the Boston area, I naturally met the few local Tibet activists. I soon discovered that my experience and theirs were vastly different. There were only a few, but none had any experience in Asia, much less Tibet. Their image of Tibet was very idealistic and their expectations for a resolution of the political issue were unrealistic. I began to understand that my experience in Nepal and Tibet might be beneficial for a realistic appraisal of the issue, but it was alien to the idealism of the US activists. Their idealism led to an expectation that justice would ultimately prevail once the world was made aware of the injustice being perpetrated upon Tibet by China. Tibetans in exile tended to be equally as idealistic, so they just supported the unrealism of the activists. I began to realize that realism was not popular among idealists and that this would estrange me from many Tibetans and foreign activists. Academic objectivity was also not very popular, especially if it contradicted the sanitized version of Tibetan history in which Tibet was absolutely independent and its combined religious and political system was perfectly spiritual. Even though a comprehension of the political phenomenon of nationalism was essential for an understanding of Tibetan history, and Marxist-Leninist nationality theories were essential for an understanding of Chinese policies in Tibet, most Tibetans and their supporters had little patience for such academic analysis.

In 1987, a new cadre of Tibet activists was created from among those foreigners caught up in the violence in Lhasa in October of that year. They had at least some experience of Tibet and they had seen the ruthlessness of Chinese repression. A few of these foreigners, in particular John Ackerly and Robbie Barnett, went on to careers in the Tibet activist or academic field. They were among the many tourists in Lhasa at that time, far more than even the summer of 1985 when I was last there. There were enough of them that they began to refer to themselves as the "Class of 1987." They tended to be more realistic than those who had never been there, but some of them seemed to think that they had essentially discovered the previously unknown tragedy of Tibet. Such passion for the Tibet political issue was not often shared by Western Buddhists, who were more concerned with their own spiritual development than in Tibetan human rights. I had reason to wonder that Tibetan Buddhism seemed to make Tibetans less egotistic while with Westerners it often had the opposite effect.

The demonstrations in Tibet were the subject of a conference at MIT in 1988 where I saw Tenzin Tethong, the official TGiE representative in New York, whom I had met in Dharamsala. With him was a young Tibetan named Jigme Ngapo. I asked if he were related to Ngawang Jigme Ngapo, the notorious collaborator who had signed the infamous Seventeen Point Agreement by which Tibet had lost its independence. I was surprised when he said, "My father." Jigme, one of Ngapo's twelve children, had been an English teacher in Lhasa in the mid-1980s and had fled to India from whence he had come to the United States and was a student at the University of Virginia. Tenzin invited me to dinner with him and Jigme and Ed Bednar. Ed had a one-year sponsorship from a local Christian missionary organization, which had a long history in China, to do a project with Tibetans. Ed had met with local Tibetans who had suggested a project to bring Tibetans from India to the United States. Tenzin agreed, and this was the beginning of the first, and only, official US immigration program for Tibetans.

A few days later we met again at the missionary residence, where the Tibetan-US Resettlement Project was born. It eventually became known to Tibetans as the "Thousand Tibetans Project." Actually, the number was essentially arbitrary. This was the first issue that we discussed. Having no idea how many the US government might actually approve, one of us suggested two hundred; another said 300 or maybe even 500. Someone finally suggested that we go for what we thought a really high and probably unrealistic number of 1,000. A State Department liaison later said that we could have asked for any number we wanted.

Tenzin and I had to argue against some of Ed's impractical ideas. My favorite was Ed's suggestion that all the Tibetans could be resettled in one place where they could preserve their culture, religion, and handicrafts. It would be like a Tibetan theme park, which Americans could visit as tourists. When the objection was raised that they might not want to stay in one place, Ed suggested that they would have to be restricted. Tenzin said, "Ed, this is America; you can't do that." We decided that they would be resettled in sites where sufficient numbers of temporary sponsors could be found. Sponsors would only have to commit to lodging each immigrant for three months, after which they would be on their own. In this way, we could promise the US government that the immigrants would be no burden on the American people or government. They would even have to finance their own transportation from India.

Despite Ed Bednar's occasional unrealism, the project might not have happened without him. It took someone with the time to do all the organizing. First, Ed organized the Tibetan-US Resettlement Project Board which included about twenty members. We met at several sites in Boston, New York, and New Jersey and divided ourselves into different committees to address the issues involved. I became the chairman of the selection committee, which made suggestions for selection criteria. We suggested that 10 percent should be selected from the Tibetan community in Nepal, based upon their relative size in the exile community; that recent arrivals from Tibet should also get a preference; and that active TGiE officials should not be eligible. This was to address the fear that the number of officials as well as teachers and other community leaders in India would be depleted. The most essential criteria was that all selections would be made by a lottery of all those eligible. This of course required an impartial selection committee in India, which was perhaps too much to hope for.

Not everyone in the Tibetan community was in favor of the project, mostly traditionalists like Samdhong Rinpoche, who thought Tibetans better off in the India of Gandhi than in the United States. When the project was officially announced in Dharamsala in March 1990, in conjunction with the first international Tibet Support Group Conference, some Tibetans and even some foreigners were unenthusiastic or even opposed, sometimes, it seemed, just because they hadn't been involved in its conception or organization. The opinion of the proponents of Tibetan settlement in the United States was that Tibetans would not only prove very adaptable and successful but that they would also increase Tibetan political influence in the United States, which would benefit the Tibetan cause. Others thought that Tibetans would not only lose their culture but their Tibetan patriotism as well. But I was aware of the example of my friend Dolma and the first Tibetans who came to the United States to work in Maine for the Great Northern Paper Company.

In India the Dharamsala government organized a selection committee to which we submitted our recommendations. To be selected would of course be an almost unbelievably life-changing opportunity. Those selected would be removed from an Indian refugee-camp lifestyle and dropped into an American suburban environment with a much more prosperous lifestyle. The Tibetan refugee community in India and Nepal naturally became awash in rumors about who might be selected. Many probably assumed that former aristocrats would dominate the process, if only because they also dominated most government positions. Our criteria were intended to prevent that from happening, but we could only make suggestions, which Dharamsala could, and did, ignore. A certain amount of lip service was paid to the principle of impartiality and the lottery process was adhered to, but the criteria for selection were so complex and were decided upon so soon before the selections began that those in the know, which usually meant those close to the center in Dharamsala, had a better chance of being selected.

In the end, notwithstanding a certain amount of chaos and confusion in India, the thousand Tibetans arrived and proved as adaptable as we had expected. Within a few years, the new arrivals took advantage of family reunification provisions in US immigration law to bring their families, and the original one thousand turned into four or five thousand. They also, as predicted, began to lobby their congressional representatives;

many senators and representatives were surprised to find that there were Tibetans in their districts whom they now represented. The State Department came to regard the Tibetan resettlement as one of its most successful programs.

The dire predictions of some Tibetans in India about depleting talent and expertise from the community there were not realized. Nevertheless, there was enough lingering opposition to cause Dharamsala to decline a State Department offer to bring an additional thousand Tibetans in the following year. Dharamsala suggested waiting a few years until the community in India recovered from the departure of so many educated Tibetans and their families. This was a reasonable position to take, but they ignored a changing attitude in the United States toward immigration in general, the result of which was that the offer was not repeated.

On October 5, 1989, only a few days before I was to depart for Dharamsala for my dissertation research, the Dalai Lama was awarded the Nobel Peace Prize. This, of course, was a cause for celebration by Tibetans and their supporters worldwide. Finally, it seemed, the Tibet issue was getting some real attention. The Norwegian Nobel Committee stated that the award was also meant to address the human rights violations in China during the June Tiananmen democracy movement and subsequent violent repression by the PLA. Another factor cited by the Nobel Committee was the Dalai Lama's commitment to a negotiated solution to the Tibet issue based upon his acceptance of an autonomous status for Tibet under Chinese sovereignty. He had officially adopted this policy in a speech in June 1988 before the European Parliament in Strasbourg, France. The Dalai Lama's "Strasbourg Proposal" caused consternation in the Tibetan community because it abandoned the claim to independence. Even though acceptance of autonomy had been the unannounced policy upon which Dharamsala had negotiated with China since the early 1980s, this was the first time that it had been openly articulated and the first time, in most Tibetans' minds, that their claim to independence had been formally abandoned.

At Strasbourg, the Dalai Lama had articulated a "Middle Path" policy that gave up independence but demanded a "high degree" of autonomy or even an "associative status" for Tibet within the PRC. The Tibetan territory to which this status should be applied included the TAR as well as all the Tibetan Autonomous Prefectures and Counties in Qinghai, Gansu, Sichuan, and Yunnan. The PRC would be responsible only for Tibet's defense and foreign affairs, while Tibet would have autonomy in regard to economic, environmental and cultural affairs, and political system. Tibet's associative status in relation to China would allow it to retain a semblance of an independent national identity and foreign relations with other countries in economic, cultural, and religious fields. While international supporters acclaimed the seemingly reasonable and conciliatory nature of the proposal, China condemned it as an attempt to "tamper with history, distort reality, and deny Tibet's status as an inalienable part of China's territory under Chinese sovereignty."

The Strasbourg Proposal was rejected by China as a violation of China's sovereignty over Tibet and lamented by many Tibetans as a tragic abandonment of their rightful claim to independence, but it was hailed internationally as an innovative compromise with potential to resolve the Tibet issue and as a pattern for the resolution of other ethnic nationalist issues. It was conceived out of an overestimation of Tibet's political leverage on China due to the recent demonstrations and riots and increased international support due to the Dalai Lama's lobbying efforts. Dharamsala had made the decision to internationalize the Tibet issue and to seek foreign support after the series of dialogues and delegation visits of the early 1980s had come to an end. Since then, Hu Yaobang's promise to limit the numbers of Chinese in Tibet had been abandoned in favor of economic development with assistance from Chinese experts and private entrepreneurs. The influx of Chinese had resulted in the Tibetan protests, which culminated in a riot in March 1989 and the declaration of martial law in Tibet only two months before the Tiananmen massacre in Beijing.

The Nobel Peace Prize award to the Dalai Lama was a response both to Tiananmen and to Strasbourg and it was cited by proponents of the Middle Path policy as evidence of that policy's efficacy. Strasbourg had led directly to the Nobel Peace Prize and to a substantial increase in attention to and support for the Tibetan cause. However, it did not produce any renewed dialogue with China and it created a serious rift in the Tibetan community. For Tibetans, the independence versus autonomy issue was fundamental to their national identity and their hopes for cultural and political survival. Most foreign supporters focused on Strasbourg and the Middle Path policy as negotiating strategies and were less cognizant and less concerned about its long-term consequences. Many quite naïvely thought that China would negotiate on the basis of the Dalai Lama's concessions and the Tibet issue would be resolved, at least to their satisfaction, if not that of Tibetans, who had experienced the reality of "autonomy" under China. Tibetans knew that their culture and identity would never survive under Chinese control, no matter what promises China made in regard to Tibetan autonomy.

Some of the most perspicacious of the Tibetan critics of the Middle Path, including my friend Jamyang Norbu, recognized that the Strasbourg Proposal seemed to be more popular among foreigners than Tibetans and that some non-Tibetans seemed to have influenced or even written it! Many of the Dalai Lama's foreign friends and advisers thought the hope for Tibetan independence futile and tended to think that some sort of "meaningful autonomy' was the only possibility. They also rather naïvely regarded autonomy as a "solution" to the Tibet issue, one that would allow for Tibetan cultural survival. Tibetan independence was obviously more important to Tibetans than to some of their foreign supporters, who advised a compromise on independence in order to get what they thought was the more feasible autonomy. Tibetan critics responded that autonomy under China was no more possible than the admittedly low possibility of independence, but was far less capable of preserving Tibetan cultural or national identity; therefore, why not maintain the claim to Tibet's rightful independence? They thought it naïve to imagine that China would honor any agreement in regard to Tibetan autonomy, given its violation of all such promises in the Seventeen Point Agreement and the National Regional Autonomy system, or that the survival of Tibetan culture or national identity was possible under Chinese domination.

The role of at least one foreign adviser in the Strasbourg Proposal, Michael Van Walt, was openly acknowledged. Van Walt, the Dalai Lama's "legal adviser," formulated the legal concept of "association" to define Tibet's relations with China in his 1987 book, *The Status of Tibet*. He defined association as a consensual arrangement between two sovereign states and claimed that "Tibet would thereby resume the exercise of its sovereignty." Van Walt also claimed that associative status would allow the associated state to alter that status at any time by democratic choice, thus according it the right of national self-determination. He described the status of association as a path to self-government of other formerly dependent or colonial states and he said that it was particularly relevant to Tibet's situation since it "bears significant similarities to the traditional *Cho-Yon* arrangement."

Van Walt's argument that Tibet's archaic political status in relation to China could be transformed into a modern political status was contrary to the conclusions I had reached in my own research on the issue. My opinion was that Tibet had been caught in the transition between the era of empires and the modern state system that came about due to industrialization and the rise of nationalism. An empire, like that of the Mongols and Manchu, was characterized by relationships of dominance and dependency. The dominant empire had superficial authority over surrounding dependent states but allowed considerable local autonomy. Empires did not have the ability or the need to actually control or administer all their dependent territories. This pattern of political relations was essentially feudal in the sense that authority was delegated rather than directly exercised. The internal administration of Tibet was also based upon a system of indirect or delegated authority. Central Tibet was administered by feudal estates awarded to various aristocratic families as a reward for their government service. Farther afield in eastern Tibet, local chieftains or monasteries administered their own territories while acknowledging a certain degree of allegiance to Lhasa.

The premodern feudal system of indirect rule was changed forever with the advent of the industrial revolution and the rise of nationalism. The Manchu Empire was transformed into the modern Chinese state due to the ambitions of Chinese nationalists, combined with their ability to actually control outlying territories due to improved transportation and communications resulting from the industrial revolution. Empires, at least territorial empires, if not overseas colonial empires, were transformed into states and indirect rule was transformed into direct rule. What Van Walt, and Dharamsala, proposed was a return to a premodern system of feudal relationships in the guise of a modern legal status. This would absolve the old Tibetan elite now in Dharamsala for failing to make the transition from a feudal to a modern political status, but it required a reversal of the history of political evolution. Dharamsala essentially wanted to return to a form of its traditional Cho-Yon relationship with China, and thereby reverse the history of its failure to modernize or to achieve political independence. The conclusion of my research was that Tibet was a distinct national entity with the right to national self-determination in international law, if only symbolic, but that history could not be reversed to erase the mistakes of the past or to restore an idealistic interpretation of Tibet's former relationship with China.

The Middle Path policy's acceptance of autonomy was essentially an abandonment of the claim to self-determination, which I thought was Tibet's best case, since it was a fundamental principle of international law. Thus began my estrangement from Dharamsala policy. Middle Path advocates would later claim that a free choice by Tibetans of autonomy under China would be equivalent to self-determination, but self-determination means self-control, an impossible situation for Tibet if China retained overriding political authority. Also, self-determination is not a one-time choice; it implies a continuous right to choose Tibet's political status, ultimately including independence. For this reason, China would never acknowledge Tibet's right to self-determination, nor would it allow any real autonomy.

What China learned in the 1980s was that Tibetan nationalism was not dead, nor was the international political issue of Tibet. China's relatively liberalized policy of allowing some degree of cultural autonomy had resulted in a revival of Tibetan religion, culture, and nationalism, culminating in the demonstrations and riots of 1987–1989. Dharamsala imagined that the rise in international support, plus the demonstrations inside Tibet, gave it sufficient leverage to demand even more autonomy, but China came to the opposite conclusion that no autonomy could be allowed because it inevitably led to Tibetan separatism.

Strasbourg opened divisions among Tibetans, but they were mostly still latent, given the euphoria that had come with the award of the Nobel Peace Prize, to which the Middle Path undeniably contributed. Tibetans were demoralized and confused by the abandonment of independence and Tibetan politics would later be characterized by the division into independence, or Rangzen, and Middle Path camps, but at the time there was an atmosphere of optimism despite the actual lack of any movement in regard to China. Tibet was once again on the international agenda thanks to Dharamsala's international campaign, assisted by Tiananmen and the subsequent Nobel Prize.

## Writing a History of Tibet

When I was last in Dharamsala, I thought myself well-prepared to write my history of Tibet. Since then, I had added five years of academic study to my knowledge, but had a better understanding of how little I really knew. This time in Dharamsala I intended to do interviews in the anthropological style expected of dissertation research. I made arrangements with the Department of Information and International Relations, then led by Lodi Gyari, to provide me with an interpreter and arrange for interviews with Tibetans whose experience they suggested would be relevant. They even arranged for my interviewees to be excused from work duties, if they were government servants, for what were often several days of interviews. I eventually interviewed some thirty Tibetans in what was sometimes an interesting but also often a laborious process. I gained a respect for other scholars who sometimes interviewed hundreds of subjects.

An immediate disappointment was to learn that my friend Jamyang Norbu would be in Dharamsala only for my first month, after which he was moving to Scotland with his new Scottish wife. Jamyang, in my absence, had continued to be at the center of Tibetan exile politics, having been purged from his position as the director of TIPA, the Tibetan Institute of Performing Arts. Jamyang had fallen afoul of Dharamsala's conservatism and orthodoxy by his criticisms of Dharamsala policy, particularly the abandonment of independence.

Jamyang's outspokenness had finally resulted in the Tibetan Women's Association storming his redoubt at TIPA and demanding that he apologize for some insults they imagined he had made against the Dalai Lama. He was accused of some veiled insult contained in an opera he had composed that supposedly referred by alliteration to the person of His Holiness in a derogatory manner, but which in reality did no such thing. Not persuaded by reason, the mob dragged Jamyang out of his office and subjected him to criticisms and harassment uncomfortably similar to the thamzings to which many Tibetans were subjected after the revolt and during the Cultural Revolution in Tibet. Some of the mob had actually learned this style of political theater in Tibet. Jamyang was falsely accused and was supported by all his staff and performers at TIPA, but his opponents in the exile government, some of whom were said to have instigated this event, used it as a reason to remove him from government service.

Jamyang Norbu's purge from TIPA, where he had inspired and revitalized that institution, was a tragic exposure of the pettiness of exile politics of which all Tibetans should be ashamed. Jamyang, however, rather than being depressed by this apparent victory of his opponents, which he may even have expected, turned adversity into advantage by making the best use of his freedom from official responsibility. When I arrived in Dharamsala, Jamyang showed me the results of his endeavor in the two years since his purge, in the form of the manuscript of a novel with the title *The Mandala of Sherlock Holmes*. The genesis of the novel was a two-year gap in Arthur Conan Doyle's Sherlock Holmes mystery series from 1890 to 1892. Doyle had apparently killed off Sherlock Holmes in his last novel in 1890 but by 1892 was again in need of money so had to resurrect his hero. He had Holmes explain that he had traveled to Tibet in the guise of a Norwegian explorer, Sigerson, and had visited Lhasa and met the Dalai Lama.

Jamyang had expanded this brief two-sentence explanation into a full account of Holmes' trip to Tibet. Since all the Sherlock Holmes novels were told in the voice of Holmes' assistant, Watson, who was not said to have accompanied Holmes to Tibet, Jamyang innovatively retained the second person voice, but had the narrator be the Indian Babu, Huree

Chunder Mookerjee, from Rudyard Kipling's *Kim*, the inspiration for whom was the real Indian scholar and spy in Tibet, Sarat Chandra Das. The book was written in the literary styles of both Arthur Conan Doyle's Sherlock Holmes and Rudyard Kipling's *Kim* and was enriched by Jamyang's research on British India of the Victorian era, the atmosphere of the towns along Holmes' route from Bombay to Lhasa, and the vernacular in use at the time.

Jamyang spent the next ten years in a futile pursuit to get his novel published in Britain, which he thought the first choice because of the Sherlock Holmes connection, and the United States. I maintained all along that he should get it published in India first, after which, if it were successful, it might be picked up by a Western publisher, which is exactly what finally happened. He eventually relented and got it published in 1999 by Rupa in India, which at that time was owned by HarperCollins. It won the Indian Crossword Book Award in 2000 for best English fiction and was soon published in US and UK editions. *The Mandala of Sherlock Holmes* is a delightful read that set Jamyang Norbu apart as not only the best Tibetan political writer in English but also the best novelist.

Dharamsala without Jamyang wasn't quite the same. I found the interviews somewhat onerous and of varying usefulness. Some eyewitness accounts were quite informative and filled in the blanks about events in Tibet as actually experienced by Tibetans. Others were less informative, often depending upon the experience and enthusiasm of the interviewee. Tashi Tsering helped fill in the gap left by Jamyang's absence and then there was Tsering Shakya, who was also writing a history of Tibet and was in Dharamsala for research. Fortunately, he shared my belief in the scholarly principle of free sharing of information and he agreed that the more histories of Tibet there were, the better. His history was to begin in 1947, while my plan was to start at the beginnings of time, so our histories would be considerably different. Tsering furthered my career in Tibet studies by inviting me to a conference on Tibet at the London School of Economics in the Spring of 1991.

Sometime in early 1990, Lodi Gyari told me about the international Tibet support group conference to be held in Dharamsala in March and offered to get my return ticket changed by his sister Dolma Gyari, who owned a travel agency in Delhi, so that I could attend. This was to be the first-ever such conference and it signified the saliency the issue had achieved. A few hundred foreigners and Tibetans were supposed to attend and the new office of the Department of Information and International Relations in Dharamsala was hurried to completion so that the conference could be held there. The conference truly was a high-point for Tibet activism; never again would so many activists from all over the world gather with such unity of purpose as well as enthusiasm and optimism. The conference was mostly a rally for the cause and an expression of support for Tibet and for the Dalai Lama's Middle Path policy before the divisions caused by that policy began to emerge. The Tibetans showed their talent for cultivating and rewarding supporters by giving each participant a silk scroll imprinted with an image of the Lhasa treaty pillar of 842 and an English translation in which China and Tibet each promised to respect the territorial integrity of the other.

Before Jamyang left Dharamsala, we planned a speaking tour for him and Lhasang Tsering in the United States. The plan for this tour was that it should be entirely self-financed and independent. Lhasang was brought in at Jamyang's suggestion because he was such a dynamic and eloquent speaker and because he, like Jamyang, had been with the resistance in Mustang during its last few years. The tour became billed as a talk by Tibetan resistance fighters. Unfortunately, I was a poor organizer of the speaking events. The first talk was at a church in Harvard Square. My only attempt at organizing was to put up flyers, since I imagined that the Tibetan resistance was as exciting to others as it was to me. We got only about a dozen people. At other places where others had done the organizing, we got bigger crowds. We went to Brown University in Rhode Island and Hampshire College in western Massachusetts, Cornell in upstate New York and to Burlington, Vermont. We then went to Canada, first to Toronto where Jamyang's sister Rigzin lived and then to Montreal and Lindsay, Ontario, where we were impressed by the Rabgey family and their organization of Tibetan cultural programs and events. We also did events in New York and Washington.

At one point, Lhasang had to return briefly to Dharamsala, so I decided to fill in as an introductory speaker for Jamyang in order to improve my speaking skills, which were poor at best, in front of a few small but receptive audiences. I thought I was successful at this, although Jamyang said that nobody understood my explanations of Marxist nationality theory, which was probably true. Later, while driving through upstate New York through what seemed like an almost endless forest, Lhasang remarked that all Tibetans in exile or even all the six million Tibetans in the world could be resettled in that forest with little impact upon the United States or even the forest itself! That was an example of Lhasang's cosmic thinking. Why, he wondered, were Tibetans destined to be located next to the Chinese rather than in this peaceful and virtually uninhabited forest?

After the relative excitement of Dharamsala, and the tour with Jamyang and Lhasang, I settled down to write my dissertation. I intended to analyze the origins of Tibetan national identity, so I had to start from the very beginning, going back all the way to the geological events that elevated the Tibetan Plateau and created the unique high-altitude homeland of the Tibetans. Then there was the question of the origins of the Tibetan people, a subject, like most associated with Tibet, fraught with controversy and political implications. This was the most difficult part of my research because sources were vague in the extreme about the origins and movements of peoples in prehistoric and early historic periods. The mythological nature of the prehistorical period made it difficult to make any sense of what the sources meant, but since my goal was to discover the origins of Tibetan national identity, the prehistorical period, when proto-Tibetans migrated to the Plateau and became Tibetans, was an essential subject for research.

The most reliable sources were the Chinese accounts of peoples known as Ch'iang, which means shepherds, who were indigenous to the Gansu area and were pushed out of that area to the west to higher altitudes during the former and later Han dynasties (206 BCE–220 CE), as Chinese agriculturalists began to be differentiated from the seminomadic pastoralists on the Chinese cultural frontier. As the Ch'iang migrated further onto the plateau, their cultural ecology was further differentiated to create a subjective sense of ethnicity different from that of the lowland Chinese agriculturalists. The Ch'iang absorbed earlier inhabitants on the plateau known as Mon and they may have also been influenced by a group of Indo-Europeans known as Yueh-chih who migrated onto the plateau from the north during the second century BCE. A much later addition to the Tibetan ethnicity was that of Mongol tribes who migrated to the plateau from the fourth century CE to the thirteenth and fourteenth during the Mongol Empire and later, after the fall of that empire.

A primary component of Tibetan ethnic identity was determined by the cultural ecology of the plateau. Tibetans were differentiated by the altitude and climate of the plateau itself. Given this ecological, cultural, and finally ethnic and national differentiation, I came up with an expression of Tibet as a "nation defined by altitude." Tibetan mythological sources tended to confirm the origins of the proto-Tibetans as scattered tribes of seminomads who became more purely nomadic as they migrated to the high-altitude grasslands of the northern Tibetan Plateau. The northern tribes were disorganized politically and in competition for pasturelands, typical of nomads who usually do not politically unify except for conquest of adjacent settled agricultural areas.

In Central Tibet, a somewhat different cultural ecology of mixed agriculture and animal husbandry evolved, which, in contrast to the nomadic style, did allow for political organization. A variety of clans dominated in each separate valley of Central Tibet; these clans engaged in competition for land and conquest of each other until one clan and one area managed to create a feudal political system, which then led to a more centralized political organization and the creation of a proto-Tibetan state centered around Lhasa. The politically unified or at least allied clans of Central Tibet made confederations with the nomadic tribes of the western and northern plateau and were thus able to quickly project their combined power farther afield. The Tibetan Empire evolved rapidly because it combined the agricultural resources of Central Tibet with the military skills of mounted nomads. The nomads' yaks and sheep and goats provided an additional mobile food source ideal for military campaigning. Within a little over a decade, the original confederation of the Central Tibetan clans expanded to incorporate all the tribes of the plateau and then began campaigns against the Turks to the north and the Chinese to the east.

The Cambridge area was ideal for this sort of dissertation research, given the libraries available, especially those at Harvard like Widener and Yencheng. All the Harvard libraries allow access to the stacks, so one could explore the vast basements of Widener for obscure works on China and Tibet, finding interesting books that could never be found using a card catalogue. Unfortunately, in the summer of 1991, I had to move because my landlord was selling his house. Rather than find another place locally, I decided to take my show on the road. David Peterson, a friend from Nepal, offered to let me stay in his small cabin in Moose, Wyoming, for the winter.

Peterson's cabin was right at the base of the Tetons in a residential development along the Snake River on the southern edge of Grand Teton National Park. At Moose I wrote the section on the Tibetan Empire, for which there were many historical sources, the only problem being the interpretation of the evolution of the Tibetan state and national identity during that period and Tibet's relations with China. This was the time when Tibetans all over the plateau were most unified politically and when they dealt with China on an almost equal basis, the evidence for which was that Tibetan armies were able to defeat Tang dynasty Chinese armies and even briefly capture the Tang capital at Changan, the modern Xian, and make a treaty with China in 842 that acknowledged Tibetan territorial sovereignty.

I got a huge amount of work done during this winter and was sorry to see it end, especially since I would have to give up the cabin in April. Not knowing where to go next, I gave a call to my friend Judith Weitzner in California, whom I had met in Nepal and had corresponded with over the years. Judy immediately invited me to stay on a property she owned with her brother and a few others in Sonoma County. In Sonoma, I wrote about Tibetan relations with the Mongol Empire and the Mongol Yuan dynasty and with the Manchus and the Manchu Qing dynasty, during which the Buddhist church became the predominant political power within Tibet by means of the Cho-Yon relationship between Tibetan lamas and Mongol and Manchu patrons. This unique political relationship allowed the Buddhist religion to flourish, but within it lay the seeds for China's later claim that Tibet became a part of China because of its subordination to the Yuan and Qing dynasties of China. Tibetans maintain that their relationship was with the Mongol and Manchu Empires, not with China, since China was also only a part of those empires.

From California, I intended to return to Cambridge and figure out my next move. My departure was timed to put me in Washington, DC, for a conference intended to bring together Tibetan exiles and Chinese democracy activists exiled since Tiananmen in 1989. The conference was billed as a Sino-Tibetan dialogue and the speakers and most of the participants were Tibetans and Chinese. At that time, the memory of Tiananmen was still fresh and the hopes that China might democratize were still alive. The Chinese democracy advocates who had escaped into exile were still thought to be relevant to China's future, so a dialogue between them and Tibetan exiles was certainly a good idea. My friend Jigme Ngapo, along with Tseten Wangchuk, another Tibetan who had grown up under the communist system in China, were the organizers of the conference. Neither the Tibetan Government in Exile nor the International Campaign for Tibet (ICT) officially sponsored or participated in the conference due to the usual fear of offending Beijing and preempting official contacts or dialogues.

The Sino-Tibetan dialogue idea was hampered from the start by the lack of a common political culture or even language. The Chinese mostly argued among themselves and the Tibetans did the same. There were only a few Tibetans who spoke Chinese and had experience in China and almost no Chinese with any experience in or interest in Tibet. There were a few notable exceptions, particularly Phuntsok Dekyi, the daughter of Bapa Phuntsok Wangyal, and Tang Daxian, a journalist who had been in Lhasa in March of 1988 and had claimed that there had been a massacre of Tibetans in numbers far greater than had been revealed. Tang was very outspoken in challenging the Chinese participants to be more supportive of Tibet's right to self-determination. Phuntsok Dekyi defended the role of Tibetan Communists like her father, whose misplaced idealism and their hopes for social reform and fraternal relations between nationalities as promised by Marxist-Leninist ideology had been sabotaged by the national chauvinism of the Chinese.

The absence of any real dialogue was altered on the first day of the conference by a surprise appearance of Wang Ruowang, a famous Shanghai journalist who had been characterized by Deng Xiaoping as more responsible for the 1989 democracy movement than any other individual. Wang, who had not previously spoken publicly on the issue of Tibet, declared that given the forcible inclusion of Tibet within China, Tibetan independence was both "justifiable and legitimate." Wang's position transcended that of most Chinese democracy advocates, who were willing to accept Tibetan self-determination only in theory and only if Tibet were to remain a part of a democratic China.

The Chinese were further challenged by Jamyang Norbu, who declared Tibetan self-determination, meaning independence, a precondition for democracy in China. This was in contrast to the Chinese who considered that Tibetan self-determination would come about as a result of democracy in China and would not mean independence or, in other words, that democracy in China was a precondition for self-determination in Tibet. Jamyang's position was supported by Tang Daxian, who maintained that the Chinese democracy movement could not call itself democratic unless it recognized the Tibetan right to independence. This exchange forced many of the Chinese to reexamine their positions.

On the second day, some Chinese held to their stance that Chinese democracy must come first while others accepted that the Tibet issue was separate from that of China, or even that Tibetan self-determination was a precondition to democracy in China. Many of the Chinese democracy advocates had their positions on Tibet challenged by others who had more experience in Tibet and knew more about the abuses of Chinese rule there. The conference was thus successful in producing statements by at least a few Chinese in support of Tibet's right to independence.

Unfortunately, those were only a tiny minority even among the Chinese in exile. Nevertheless, in contrast to the few academic conferences or the Tibet supporters' rallies, this dialogue among the actual participants on both sides challenged the convenient and chauvinistic assumptions of many of the Chinese that they could offer some ambiguous degree of self-determination to Tibetans only after they had achieved democracy for themselves. The challenge to that position from Tibetans as well as from some Chinese forced many of the Chinese, perhaps for the first time, to recognize Tibetans' right to decide for themselves.

From DC, I went to Cambridge without an offer of another free place to write and without enough funds to rent a place. Once again, friends came through with offers that kept me going for almost another two years. First, Pam Putney and Todd Stuart let me stay the winter of 1992–1993 at their small house on Martha's Vineyard. Then Mike and Mary Amato let me stay for a full year at their cabin, or camp as such summer places are called, at Norway, Maine. I was able to make monthly trips to Fletcher to meet with my dissertation supervisors.

Hurst Hannum, a Fletcher professor of international human rights law and expert on self-determination, was the obvious choice for dissertation supervisor. I had also asked Alfred Rubin, Distinguished Professor of International Law, to be on my dissertation committee. I happened to know that he had written the first draft of the 1959 International Commission of Jurists report on Tibet and had maintained an interest in the subject. He had been a young graduate student at the time and still harbored some resentment that he had not received any credit for his work in the final report. Hardly anyone at Fletcher knew of Rubin's interest in Tibet, so he was flattered and intrigued when I approached him to be on my committee.

Hurst Hannum proved not very helpful. The problem with Hannum was that he didn't really believe in self-determination. He was of such a liberal mentality that he thought nationalism somewhat reactionary and preferred autonomy as a solution to most self-determination issues. Since he was my dissertation supervisor, he had to read every chapter, most of which he returned with few comments or advice.

Rubin was a different story. My dissertation revived and piqued his interest in Tibet and he read every chapter multiple times, usually returning each draft with numerous comments and suggestions, many of which were quite useful. Rubin taught me not only to accept criticism but to value it and use it to improve my work. I also had to appreciate the very considerable effort he put into my work, which I later learned was rather rare for a dissertation adviser.

At this time, I was working on the history of the early twentieth century. My interest was the post-1950 period, although it was taking me a long time to get there. I thought it arduous enough to deal with US relations with Tibet after 1950, much less the British relationship with Tibet from their invasion of 1904 until they left India in 1947. However, Rubin repeatedly emphasized that the British period was the key to understanding the Tibet issue and essential to a comprehension of the later American role. Rubin kept telling me, "You have to read the Blue Books." The Blue Books were the British Government of India records, some of which dealt with Tibet. Harvard had the Blue Books, stored in a subbasement area known as "Government Docs," that was reached through a long tunnel that ran from Widener to the basement of the adjacent Lamont Library.

I eventually gave in and read some of the Blue Books, not as many as Rubin suggested I should, but enough to get a feel for the period. Then I discovered the books by Alastair Lamb about British relations with Tibet, particularly his two-volume comprehensive history of the 1914 Simla Convention. Lamb had read all the Blue Books, so I didn't have to. I spent a month absorbing Lamb and then revised my chapter on that period, which I had titled "The Thirteenth Dalai Lama and the Quest for Independence." This was a very long chapter, 80 pages in its final published version and longer in the draft, and Rubin had already read at least two versions and had left each page littered with his usual red marks and comments, but he was so pleased that I had finally accepted his advice and focused more closely on this period that he seemed absolutely delighted to read yet another draft.

Rubin was famous at Fletcher for his international law classes, taught in the rigorous and challenging law school style, but my personal experience with him was more revealing of his dedication to his students and to their scholarship, the qualities that made him a great professor. In graduate school one learns that there are two kinds of professors. One type publishes and becomes famous, but necessarily neglects his students. The other kind of professor publishes less (although Rubin published quite a lot in international law journals) but is devoted to his students. The second type of professor is often less well-known, except to his students, but sometimes achieves a level of respect among his students that approaches reverence. Rubin achieved that, at least with me.

Rubin was right that the post-1950 period of Tibetan history could not be understood without studying the British role in the first half of the century. The British invaded Tibet in 1904 because of their fear that Russia was gaining influence there. They did not want to make a colony of Tibet because Britain had little commercial interest there relative to their interests in China. Britain tried to keep Russia out of Tibet by recognizing Chinese "suzerainty" there and to keep China out by supporting Tibetan autonomy. Britain helped Tibet to keep the Chinese out, at least temporarily, but did not go so far as to support or recognize Tibetan independence. Britain then quit India and left Tibet without a political patron and without an internationally recognized political status. Tibetan autonomy had no definition and the British recognition of Chinese suzerainty over Tibet was a terminology of a prior era of indefinite political relationships.

After almost four years of dissertation research and writing, I had barely reached the modern period after the Chinese invasion, which was supposed to be my focus and would ultimately comprise half of my dissertation and book. I was beginning to be envious of Tsering Shakya whose history would begin only with 1947. Fortunately, the modern period of Tibetan history was relatively well-documented, at least by the Chinese, and there were a multitude of written sources available compared to the earlier time. My research and writing of the modern period would take only another year.

These years of research were a highlight of my life; being a graduate student is an ideal life, if one can afford it for any time. To be engaged in an intellectual endeavor to which one is passionately committed and with the support of benevolent professors is a fortunate fate. Those who are able to cite professors who have had an important impact upon their lives are usually graduate students. It is usually only when one reaches this level that they are afforded such a personal relationship with professors. I also sought out other professors in the area, all of whom were very generous with their time, particularly Lucian Pye of MIT who never refused a request for a meeting, even though I was not one of his students and he had no obligation toward me except the usual desire of the scholar to share knowledge.

## Washington, DC

By the summer of 1994, I had run out of free places to stay and was nearing the completion of my dissertation. I had never contemplated any other move at this point other than to go to Washington, DC, to look for a job. The logic of this move was that Washington was where the politics were, so DC was the only place where I might find useful employment related to my interest. It was often suggested that I should work for ICT. I considered myself both academic and activist, but I was to find those roles a difficult combination. Lodi Gyari, the then-president of ICT, was well-aware of my friendship and association with Jamyang Norbu, Lhasang Tsering, and other critics of Dharamsala policy. Lodi himself had been, along with Jamyang and Lhasang, one of the founders of the Tibetan Youth Congress, which remained the primary critic of Dharamsala policy, but Lodi had assumed the role of defender of that policy because of his position with Dharamsala and ICT and later as the Dalai Lama's Special Envoy in negotiations with China. Although ICT was theoretically an independent NGO (nongovernmental organization), it was in fact closely associated with Dharamsala, as Lodi's simultaneous positions in both organizations made apparent.

My prospects improved when I met Maura Moynihan, daughter of Daniel Patrick Moynihan, the senator from New York. Maura was a fervent advocate for Tibet. Maura also appreciated, as did few others, that I had returned to school and educated myself about Tibet just in order to best explicate Tibet's cause. She was therefore determined to help me get a job in Washington and offered to use her father's influence to do so.

My close friendship with Maura led to a meeting with her father and a subsequent association with him that was a highlight of my life. If I had the opportunity to know one prominent politician in Washington, Daniel Patrick Moynihan would be my first choice. He was almost universally admired for his intelligence and integrity and he was the author at that time of more than a dozen books on public policy. Maura arranged for us to meet with her father one day at his favorite French restaurant on Capitol Hill.

Senator Moynihan had also done a Fletcher School PhD in the 1950s after finishing at Tufts on the GI Bill after the war. So we had a connection. Still, I could tell that I needed to convince him that I was not one of Maura's often unrealistic Tibet-advocate friends. This was immediately made obvious by his attempt to taunt me with an assertion that Tibet was a hopeless cause, to which he seemed to expect me to object. I later came to recognize this as a Moynihan ploy to challenge others when they had adopted an irrational position, just to see if they were foolish enough to try to defend that position or smart enough to withdraw.

Moynihan was distinguished by his respectful attention to others' opinions, but if you said something stupid, it was best to escape as gracefully as possible to avoid being skewered by his impeccable logic. I soon came to recognize his tactic and determined never to be drawn onto indefensible ground in his presence. In response to his assertion that Tibet was a hopeless cause, I replied "Yes, but it's the best of the hopeless causes." Still trying to draw me in, he objected that it surely wasn't the best of all causes. I immediately agreed, with the caveat that it was at least among the best. If I had learned anything in graduate school it was that qualifiers render your assertions unchallengeable. His face lit up and I could tell that this was the moment when I established a rapport with him. I was relieved and not a little proud of myself that I could just hold up my side of the conversation with such a deservedly famous intellectual. I had convinced him that I had actually learned something at Fletcher and could be somewhat objective about the Tibet issue, which he knew was rare.

Moynihan, like many people who impress with their intelligence, did so partly by listening respectfully to others and thus making you think yourself intelligent as well. Moynihan had a tremendous thirst for knowledge and was willing to listen to anyone who knew what they were talking about. Over the next few years, Maura invited me many times for conversations with her father, many at their apartment on Pennsylvania Avenue. She was quite aware of how much I valued my contact with him and he also seemed to genuinely enjoy our conversations. I called him

"Senator" at first until the memorable day when he said to me, "Warren, call me Pat."

Maura was working for ICT at the time and was talking me up with Lodi Gyari. This resulted in a contract to write an analysis of the system of autonomy promised to Tibet, if not actually practiced there, and that being proposed for Hong Kong and, eventually, Taiwan. Hong Kong was due to return to full Chinese sovereignty in 1997 under a political regime that the CCP termed "One Country, Two Systems." Hong Kong would be guaranteed extensive autonomy for at least fifty years. Taiwan was offered the same deal, and the CCP even promoted a "Tibet model" to Taiwan, which was an acknowledgement that the original Seventeen Point Agreement was the model for One Country, Two Systems. The Taiwanese scornfully rejected the CCP's offers and pointed out that Tibet enjoyed none of the autonomy that the CCP had promised. Despite the lack of any real autonomy in Tibet, the Dalai Lama's Strasbourg Proposal and his Middle Way policy were based upon the autonomy promised in the Seventeen Point Agreement, not the autonomy that had actually resulted.

ICT wanted a comparison of Tibet, Hong Kong, and Taiwan that would substantiate the potential for meaningful autonomy, based upon the One Country, Two Systems formula, the original promises to Tibet, and the Middle Way proposal. I wrote an extensive analysis that, unfortunately, reflected my own conclusions rather than the hopes of Dharamsala and ICT. My previous research had led me to the conclusion that the Chinese Communists never intended for the autonomy they had promised to be a permanent status for Tibet. The assimilation of Tibet, culturally and politically, had always been the ultimate goal for Tibet. I assumed that the same was true for Hong Kong, despite the CCP's promises, and ultimately, for Taiwan as well.

This was not what ICT wanted to hear, and they never published my paper. They wanted to believe that the autonomy promised to Tibet could be revived and that the system about to go into effect in Hong Kong could be the model for Tibet just as the Seventeen Point Agreement had been the theoretical model for One Country, Two Systems. They wanted to see autonomy as not only possible within the PRC but as a constantly expanding system of rights rather than the opposite. Eventually, I had the bittersweet satisfaction of being proven right, as China constantly circumscribed Hong Kong's autonomy and refused to seriously contemplate the Dalai Lama's Middle Way proposals or any expansion of the autonomy allowed in Tibet.

While my so-far unsuccessful job search was going on, I was editing my dissertation for publication. I had lost contact with Westview Press since I had made a tentative contact there in 1985, but I happened to see Fred Praeger at an Association of Asian Studies meeting in DC. He said that Westview would still be interested and he seemed impressed that I had not dropped the idea but had been diligently working on it for ten years and had turned it into a PhD. I made a proposal to Westview and it was accepted by the Asian studies editor, Susan McEachern. So, my strategy of writing the book and then getting a publisher rather than the other way around worked out. This was typical of my whole philosophy, or leap of faith, actually—that if I pursued the goal of writing a good history of Tibet, then the book would get published and the book plus the PhD would somehow get me a job.

When I sent the manuscript to Westview, it had the same title as the dissertation: *A History of Tibetan Nationalism and Sino-Tibetan Relations.* I had thought for a long time about a more concise title that would define Tibet as a nation. I was fond of my description of Tibet as a nation "defined by altitude" and searched for some title to express both that Tibet was in fact a nation and that its defining characteristic was altitude. Tibetans distinguished themselves from the Chinese and other ethnicities by their cultural and ecological adaptation to the high-altitude environment of the plateau. It was the altitude of the plateau that had kept them separate and protected their independence. Tibetans referred to their country as the "Land of Snow" and as a highland ringed by mountains that is translated in English as "Roof of the World." I thought of such things as "Highland Nation," or "Mountain Nation," but finally I realized that what I wanted to express was that Tibet was in fact a distinctive nation. It suddenly dawned on me that the appropriate title was *Tibetan Nation.*

My quest to write a history of Tibet had taken fourteen years, including ten years in a formal academic atmosphere. I had no hope that my book would change anything, only that it would help to counter Chinese propaganda, which distorted Tibetan history and obscured the reality of Tibet under Chinese rule. Whatever the reception the book received, it was for me the foremost achievement of my life—finally honoring a promise I had made to Dolma in 1982, granting me a PhD and, perhaps almost coincidentally, a career. I still had no job, but at least I would soon be a published author and an acknowledged expert, if only on an admittedly obscure and arcane subject, a subject with a certain universal appeal but with little relevance to the interests of the modern world.

## International Commission of Jurists Report

I owe my first real job to my friend, Maura Moynihan. Maura became aware of a proposal to produce an International Commission of Jurists (ICJ) report on Tibet, which would be the third such report, the first being in 1959 and the second in 1960. The first ICJ report, *The Question of Tibet and the Rule of Law*, published only four months after the revolt, was a preliminary analysis of Tibet's status. It was authored by the Indian international lawyer, Purshottam Trikamdas, but, as I knew, was drafted by my professor, Alfred Rubin. The report concluded that Tibet's legal status was "not easy to appraise," but that Tibet was to all intents and purposes an independent country over which China could not claim domestic jurisdiction. The report accused China of "a *prima facie* case of imperialism and colonialism, coming precisely from the very people who claim to fight against it." On the basis of this preliminary report, the ICJ had constituted a Legal Inquiry Committee, composed of eleven international lawyers, who were tasked to examine the evidence that the crime of genocide had been committed in Tibet.

In its second report, *Tibet and the Chinese People's Republic*, the ICJ determined that there was sufficient evidence to accuse China of an attempt to destroy Tibetans as a religious group, but insufficient evidence to conclude that China intended to destroy Tibetans as a national or ethnic group. This conclusion was based upon interviews with Tibetans who had fled into exile, many of whom were monks. Monks seemed to have been particularly targeted by the Chinese, thus the ICJ's conclusion. However, this introduced much confusion into the issue about whether or not the ICJ had accused China of genocide.

The closest that the Chinese came to a genocidal act against religion was their subjection of some lamas in eastern Tibet to thamzing, which was meant to demonstrate their lack of any spiritual power to save themselves from this torment. These lamas were subjected to punishment in the absence of any demonstrated guilt. However, for the most part, monks and lamas as well as most Tibetans could avoid repression by cooperation. Therefore, what the Chinese were guilty of in Tibet was an imperialist conquest in which they repressed all who resisted, but not genocide against all Tibetans or even Tibetans as a religious group. Both ICJ reports did determine that the issue of Tibet was one for the legitimate concern of the United Nations, which led several countries to support the eventual UN resolutions on Tibet, which accused China of violating Tibetans' human rights if not Tibet's sovereignty.

Maura's information about a new ICJ report came from Reed Brody, who was formerly the ICJ executive secretary and who was encouraging the organization to do another report on Tibet. Maura, who was in New York at the time, insisted to Reed that he should have me write the historical part of the report. She later told me that she had told him that he wouldn't be invited to any more of her parties if he didn't. I was an unknown to Reed, and to many others involved with the Tibet issue at the time, but Maura was persuasive and her parties were not to be missed, so Reed contacted me about being involved. The proposal then got delayed due to some unknown ICJ reluctance. Reed then suggested that if I wanted it to happen, I should call the ICJ executive secretary in Geneva, Sigrid Higgins, and encourage her to go ahead with the report. I did call her and managed to inspire her with my enthusiasm, so she agreed to proceed. Reed had to admit that it was my call that got the project back on track, since he had almost given up on it.

I was given a three-month contract to write the first draft of the report. I was determined that the focus of the report should be on self-determination, since that was the conclusion of my own studies. This was contrary to the current policy of the Dalai Lama and the Tibetan

Government in Exile, to accept Tibetan autonomy under Chinese sovereignty. Although it had given up the claim to independence, the TGiE maintained that it had not given up the right to self-determination, since self-determination could be achieved by a free Tibetan choice of autonomy under China. However, this was just semantics since it was a safe assumption that Tibetans, or any other people, would choose independence if given a truly free choice. Also, self-determination implies a continuous right, not a one-time choice. Even if Tibetans were to choose autonomy under China, they would have the right to revisit that choice at any time. China could claim that Tibetans already enjoyed autonomy, but they could never answer the question why they denied Tibetans the right to self-determination.

The first two ICJ reports had been very significant, having led to and been cited in the United Nations debates and resolutions on Tibet in 1959, 1960, and, after a follow-up ICJ report, in 1965. The ICJ itself was far more influential in the 1950s and 1960s before it was revealed that the CIA was a major funder. The CIA had also been involved in the creation of Radio Free Europe and other Cold War propaganda efforts when the agency itself was less controversial and the ideological competition with international Communism was more intense and secret funding more acceptable. Now, however, the ICJ's reputation had forever been harmed by its previous association and the organization itself was less influential. Nevertheless, given the ICJ's previous role in regard to Tibet, a new report would certainly have some significance.

I wrote a historical background and an outline of the human rights and self-determination issues. Christa Meindersma, a Dutch woman who had been shot in the abdomen during the demonstrations in Lhasa in 1987, added sections on current issues of human rights and autonomy and edited some of my draft. Manfred Nowak, a distinguished international human rights lawyer and a member of the ICJ, added a legal analysis of self-determination in international law. Several others made contributions and the final product was published in December 1997. The report focused on self-determination throughout and recommended that an internationally supervised referendum be held in Tibet to determine Tibetans' true wishes in regard to their political status. None of us imagined that China would actually allow any such referendum, but we knew that the principle of self-determination was what China most feared and that the refusal to allow Tibetans to express their own political preference would be most difficult for China to rationalize and explain. I and others involved in the new ICJ report, *Tibet: Human Rights and the Rule of Law*, were rightly proud of our result, which was by our estimate and that of independent observers one of the best reports on the Tibet issue ever.

The report, like most books and reports by anyone on any subject, did not achieve the impact the authors had hoped. It did not even receive wide distribution or promotion by any Tibet-related organization. The problem, we later learned, was that it was not promoted by Dharamsala—mainly, I was told, because the report had taken its stand on the principle of self-determination rather than the Dalai Lama's Middle Path policy. The result was that Dharamsala did not promote the ICJ report and it failed to achieve the influence it deserved.

Michael Van Walt, TGiE's legal counsel, expressed some complaints about the new ICJ report in an article in the December 1998 issue of *Tibetan Review*, still at that time the primary venue for discussion and debate on Tibet. While purporting to approve the emphasis of the report on self-determination, Van Walt criticized the historical background, the part for which I was almost solely responsible, for a variety of errors, all of which happened to deviate from his version of Tibetan history, and that of the TGiE, as explicated in his book *The Status of Tibet*. In *Tibetan Nation*, I criticized his role as adviser to the TGiE in proposed negotiations in 1988 just after the Dalai Lama's Strasbourg Proposal. I was also critical of Van Walt's interpretation of Tibet's political status, which was that Tibet's traditional relationship with China, the Cho-Yon relationship between political patron and religious adviser, was sui generis, or original. In fact, the cultivation of religious authorities was typical of Mongol rule. Patronage of religious authorities could be manipulated to defuse discontent among subject populations while preventing the rise of any secular authority around which resistance might coalesce.

Van Walt and Dharamsala's position would absolve the Tibetan political system, which combined religion and politics, of having compromised Tibet's independence in the past. According to this position, Tibet's former independence was uncompromised; Tibet was deprived of its independence in 1951, and therefore had the right to regain that independence according to the principles of international law. This theory conveniently ignored the fact that the Dalai Lama's government had ratified the Seventeen Point Agreement in 1951. Van Walt had proposed that Tibet could regain most of its former sovereignty, except for defense and foreign relations, by means of an associative relationship with China, which was essentially a high degree of autonomy functionally equivalent to sovereignty in many aspects and potentially leading even to full sovereignty according to the principles of self-determination.

In the *Tibetan Review* article, Van Walt complained that the new ICJ report had declared that it did not intend to repeat the analysis of the earlier ICJ reports on Tibet's legal status, which concluded that Tibet was a de facto independent state before 1950, but that the new report had in fact repeated that analysis in a way that was inconsistent with the earlier reports and their conclusions. However, the conclusion of the earlier ICJ reports was that Tibet was independent before the Chinese invasion or, more specifically, between 1912 and 1951. As to Tibet's status before 1912, they reached no definitive conclusion. I thought that Van Walt's real complaint was that I had deviated from his and Dharamsala's position and had analyzed Tibet's traditional relationship with China as ambiguous, with the implication of Tibet's political dependency in relation to certain Chinese dynasties, mainly the non-Han Mongol and Manchu dynasties, rather than sui generis with no implications of a subordinate relationship of Tibet to China.

Van Walt's analysis of Tibet's political status in *The Status of Tibet* was like a lawyer's brief for a client, starting from a conclusion and searching for evidence to prove that point. This is contrary to the academic method of starting from the evidence and searching for a conclusion. My critique of his book was that, rather than being an objective analysis, it faithfully followed Dharmsala's version of Tibetan history and attempted to reincarnate the archaic Cho-Yon as a status of association, that was furthermore purported to be a pattern for the future for the transition to self-government of former dependent or colonial states. Contrary to the Dharamsala position, the self-determination argument that the ICJ reports adopted did not require Tibet to demonstrate uncompromised independence in the past. Because the authors of the new ICJ report defined the issue as self-determination, we did not have to adhere to an unrealistically idealistic interpretation of Tibetan history.

In contrast to the mystification of Tibetan history required for Dharamsala's position, the principle of self-determination is not dependent upon Tibet's historical or legal status. Tibet does not have to demonstrate an unbroken history of political independence in order to demand self-determination in the present. Tibet does not have to deny the reality that the Cho-Yon relationship involved Tibet's political subordination to the Mongol and Manchu Empires. Sakya Pandita, after all, initiated that relationship by inviting the Tibetans to submit to Godan Khan. Self-determination is an issue of Tibet's current situation, not its past history. Tibet can demand the right to self-determination while admitting to having been dominated to some extent by China, or at least by Mongol and Manchu conquest dynasties of China. Most UN member states could not claim independent statehood if they had to demonstrate a history of continuous and uncompromised independence, as was pointed out in the UN debates on Tibet. The position of the new ICJ report was that Tibet's best case is the whole truth, unobscured by fairy-tale interpretations of the past or denials of the realities of the present.

# Chapter 4
# Radio Free Asia

## Working for RFA

The idea for a Radio Free Asia, an American surrogate radio on the model of Radio Free Europe of the Cold War era, came out of the 1989 Tiananmen democracy movement and the subsequent massacre of students and workers by the PLA. The first proponents were Chinese democracy activists who had escaped China and reached the United States. However, the Chinese democracy activists never created a unified organization in the United States and, as they began fighting among themselves, their influence waned, particularly their ability to lobby the US Congress. Lobbying for Radio Free Asia was then taken up by Tibetans through the International Campaign for Tibet, which had become a very effective lobbying organization after being established in Washington in 1988.

The Voice of America already broadcast to China and, after 1990, to Tibet, but Radio Free Asia was to be a surrogate radio, meaning that it was intended to be a substitute for a free media in China and to broadcast as if it were actually located in China. As such, Radio Free Asia was to be far more political and potentially offensive to China; therefore, like Radio Free Europe, it was to be created and funded by the US Congress but given a status outside the government in order to provide it with an independent credibility. The US government had created several organizations with a similar status outside the government, for the same purpose of objectivity, including the Public Broadcasting System and the National Endowments for the Arts, Humanities, and Democracy. The

National Endowment for Democracy was most like the proposed Radio Free Asia in that it was intended to promote democracy in nondemocratic countries.

I had been following the status of the efforts to create a Radio Free Asia since around 1992 when Lodi Gyari suggested that it might be the place where I could find employment. After moving to Washington in late 1994, I followed it more closely, often going to ICT to inquire about its status. Whenever I went to ICT, I would also talk with Jigme Ngapo, then at ICT, and I interviewed him there on his reflections about his father. I often mentioned to Jigme that Radio Free Asia was my main hope for employment. Jigme never gave any indication that he might also be interested, but that may have just been his typical discretion. By 1995 there were indications that it might actually happen and in 1996 it was finally funded. The Radio Free Asia that appeared in 1996 was due to the lobbying of many people and organizations, but I believe that of ICT was probably most effective.

At its creation, RFA was intended to broadcast to China, Tibet, Vietnam, Cambodia, Laos, Burma (now Myanmar), and North Korea. All of these countries were RFA's targets because they all lacked a free media. A separate Tibetan Service was created despite the undeniable fact that Tibet was a part of China. This reflected the lobbying of ICT and its efforts to create a separate status for Tibet whenever possible in US government resolutions and organizations. RFA was created just as I was finishing the final draft of my book and getting it ready for publication; therefore, my attention was somewhat diverted at the time. It was also difficult to determine to whom to apply for positions there.

One day in June 1996, while having a beer with John Ackerly of ICT and Jigme Ngapo, Jigme announced that he had just been hired as the director of the Tibetan Service of RFA. I was more than surprised. Jigme knew that I had an interest in RFA, and he was sympathetic, but neither he nor I could imagine what my role might be. In the end Jigme's hiring proved to be extremely fortuitous for me.

I know that Lodi Gyari had assumed that he would be consulted about RFA Tibetan Service staffing and perhaps even asked to name the director. But Jigme had secured the job without even a recommendation from Lodi and without revealing to anyone that he was even interested in the job. Lodi undoubtedly assumed that the new RFA president would ask ICT for recommendations. What he did not anticipate was that the president of RFA would be unaware even of the existence of ICT and would not know whom to ask. Dick Richter, the newly named RFA president, had a background in media but knew little about the political issues of the countries that RFA was to cover.

Jigme was apparently recommended by a Chinese friend who was interviewed for the position of Mandarin Service director but who did not take the job. Jigme was the first Tibetan that Dick Richter had ever met and he hired him on the spot. He was lucky in that Jigme was just about the best possible choice. Jigme had excellent Chinese and Tibetan language and adequate English skills. He was as knowledgeable about China and Chinese policy in Tibet as any Tibetan could possibly be. Jigme's choice proved fortuitous not only to me but to the Tibetan Service as well. Jigme knew many Tibetans in China, so he was able to recruit several who were extremely knowledgeable about Chinese policies in Tibet. About half the eventual Tibetan Service staffers were from exile and half from China, but those from China were the best resources for all subsequent programming. Jigme himself was a model of fairness and objectivity, perhaps partly because of his sensitivity about his father's legacy.

In January 1997, my friend Maura Moynihan called me up one day to say that RFA was having a party to celebrate its first broadcasts and that she had called Jigme and asked if we could come. This was typical Maura. Jigme didn't really know if the party was meant to be open to outsiders or not, but Maura was hard to refuse. Anyhow, we went, as did a few other outsiders, all Tibetans. Jigme introduced me to Dan Southerland, the editorial director, saying, "This is the guy I've told you about," and Dan immediately invited me into his office. He suggested that I might be able to do some programming on contract, in English, to be translated and broadcast by one of the Tibetan staff, if I could think of a subject. I don't know if this was Jigme's idea or Dan's, but it had not occurred to me, and I don't know if it would have ever come up had Maura not intervened to get us invited to the event.

However, it did dawn upon on me on the spot that an ideal subject would be the recently released Panchen Lama's famous 1964 petition to Chinese leaders. The Panchen Lama's petition had never before been revealed until the Tibet Information Network in London (TIN) obtained a copy from a mysterious source. They were still in the process of translating it, but I thought if I could get a prepublication copy from them, it would make an ideal subject for a series of programs. Dan agreed on the spot and I found myself with, if not a job at RFA, at least a contract. I sent an appeal to Robbie Barnett and Kate Saunders at TIN telling them that my life depended upon their agreeing to send me an advance copy of their translation, which fortunately they did.

The Panchen Lama's appeal, known as his "70,000-Character Petition," based upon its length in Chinese, was a full-length book, so I had sufficient material for a very long series of programs. The Panchen Lama had described the devastation in Tibet due to misguided Chinese policies after the 1959 revolt. His appeal was couched in the most respectful terms and addressed to Zhou Enlai and Mao with the expectation that they would take steps to correct the mistakes that had led to Tibetan suffering. Instead, Mao denounced the Panchen's petition as "an arrow aimed at the Party," and purged the Panchen from all his positions in Tibet.

The Panchen Lama was summoned to Beijing, where he was subjected to thamzing in a football stadium by Tibetan students of the National Minorities Institute and then imprisoned in the notorious Qincheng Prison for three years and kept under house arrest for the next ten years. The Panchen Lama's petition was a gold mine of information about one of the most important but most obscure periods of Tibetan history. After the revolt, Tibet was transformed almost beyond recognition to those like the Panchen Lama, who until then had believed the Chinese leaders' promises that they would respect and protect Tibetan religion and culture and allow cultural and even political autonomy in Tibet.

In this unexpected way I found myself working on contract for RFA only two months after its first broadcast. I had to deliver one program of about ten minutes once a week, so I came into the new RFA office at 2025 M Street only on Fridays and used the computer of one of the Tibetan staff who was off that day. After this series of programs was finished, I did another very long series using my own book and, with that and other projects, managed to extend my contract for a year and a half. In September 1998, at the end of the US government fiscal year, I was offered a permanent position, not because I had become indispensable, but because there was an allocated position that had not been filled.

After a talk with Jigme, I accepted. I wanted to be sure that he approved my taking a permanent position, which he did. He said that there was no issue of my taking a position that might go to a Tibetan, since one of the Tibetan staff would still be needed to translate and broadcast my programs. Unstated was the fact that my programs would, therefore, cost twice that of any other programming. Also unstated was any justification for the presence of one non-Tibetan in the Tibetan Service. I became, and remained, the only non-native in any of RFA's language services.

Although my job did not pay very much, it was still a job and one designed by and for me. I was privileged to be paid to pursue my own interests and I was very proud to be considered capable of broadcasting to a Tibetan audience. RFA was a surrogate radio, so we were supposed to be as credible as if we were located in Lhasa. Of course, I was supposed to do more on Chinese and international politics, but I still thought of myself as on the tip of the spear in the ideological battle with China about the interpretation of the reality of Tibet. Over the years my role became more refined as I sought to refute the lies, misrepresentations, and obfuscations of Chinese propaganda about Tibet. My previous research and my long-held determination to refute China's rewriting of Tibetan history prepared me well for this role. I never lost the feeling of privilege to be paid to pursue my most passionate interest and to be in a unique position as the only "Inji" in the Tibetan Service.

In the beginning there were only eight Tibetans in RFA's Tibetan Service, but the number gradually increased as RFA was required to increase its broadcast hours to Tibet. As additional hours of broadcast time were added, more positions were created, until there were more than forty Tibetan staff, including clerical and administrative positions, and me. We then broadcast four hours of original programming each day along with an additional four hours of repeats. We quickly became popular in Tibet as well as with Tibetans in India because we were far more political and reported more on Tibetan events than did the Tibetan Service of VOA. Our listener surveys, conducted among recent arrivals from Tibet in Kathmandu, showed that we were popular, although Tibetans tended to refer to both RFA and VOA as "American Radio" without distinction.

VOA was usually easier to hear inside Tibet because it used more powerful transmitters and was less subject to jamming. VOA used transmitters in Thailand and Sri Lanka that RFA was not permitted to use because we, as a surrogate radio, were considered more offensive to China. We were relegated to transmitters on the American-owned Pacific island of Tinian, from where B-29s took off to bomb Japan in the Second World War, and a former Soviet jammer in Tajikistan on which we rented time.

RFA broadcasts were hard to hear inside Tibet because of our distant or weak transmitters, but also because of relentless Chinese jamming. Jamming consisted of broadcasts, usually of Chinese music or opera, on exactly the same frequency as ours, which was contrary to international law but that the Chinese claimed was accidental. I was able to monitor our broadcasts on two short trips to Tibet, one in 1997 and another in 2000. RFA's signal was almost impossible to hear in Lhasa even at night on the roof of a hotel after stringing up a wire antenna. Later, the Chinese installed jammers in Lhasa and other towns that made it almost impossible to hear our signals. We began to hear from listener surveys that RFA could be heard only in rural areas. That still left many monasteries—traditionally located in the most remote areas—nomads, and those sent out from villages in the summer months to take care of animals. These listeners were said to tell others about the contents of our broadcasts, and we began to claim a multiplier effect, given that our news was transmitted by word of mouth from actual listeners to others.

My signature program was called *Expert on Tibet*, not a name I chose, which proved to be popular, at least among Tibetans in India. Jigme characterized my role as something like an editorial writer for a newspaper, whose opinions were not necessarily those of the publisher. We decided to include a disclaimer at the beginning of my programs, stating that any opinions expressed were my own and not those of RFA. However, while in Dharamsala in an audience with the Dalai Lama, the first translator of my program, Tseten Namgyal, was asked why RFA disclaimed my opinions. The Dalai Lama reportedly said, "His opinions are the same as ours," after which we no longer used the disclaimer. Since he considered me an editorial writer, Jigme never censored or altered a single word I wrote. Neither did the RFA administration. Despite the imaginings of some, including many Chinese, that we were a US government propaganda organ, RFA operated independently, as Congress intended it to do by placing it outside the government structure.

In refuting Chinese propaganda, I had abundant opportunity to heap scorn and ridicule upon the Chinese for their lies, which were believed only by the Chinese people themselves. The Chinese people tended to dismiss almost all their government's propaganda as false except that about Tibet, which they were generally content to accept. There was a psychological component to their willingness to believe whatever their government told them about Tibet, since they preferred to see themselves as the benevolent benefactors of the poor Tibetans rather than as their oppressors. Foreign criticism of China in regard to Tibet was typically dismissed as "groundless," "baseless," or "without foundation." Ultimately, foreigners were warned to avoid "hurting the feelings of the Chinese people" with their criticisms, the unstated threat lying in the very large numbers of such feelings that might be hurt.

China's propaganda provided me with a perpetual supply of material for my programs, in particular the Chinese White Papers about Tibet, each of which I refuted in detail. China also published a full-length book, *The Historical Status of China's Tibet*, for which I was particularly grateful since it kept me occupied for quite a long time. The book attempts to substantiate China's claim that Tibet is an inalienable part of China. It was originally published in Chinese and distributed widely within China. It was claimed to have attracted great attention in China and was awarded the Excellent Book Award in 1996. It was published in English in 1997 in order to publicize China's version of Tibetan history to an international audience. The introduction says that it describes the close relations between Tibet and China, showing that Tibet has been a part of Chinese territory since the Yuan dynasty. It claims to forcefully deny the entire ideological system of "Tibetan Independence," which the Chinese always put in quotes, and to systematically refute the theories put forward by the "Dalai Clique."

China's Patriotic Education Campaigns in Tibet and the instruction booklets used to educate Tibetans provided me with additional material. The Patriotic Education Campaign was intended to transform Tibetan national identity into Chinese identity, to eradicate Tibetans' loyalty to the Dalai Lama, and to cultivate Tibetan loyalty to China.

My program, *Expert on Tibet*, allowed me the pleasure of responding to China's propaganda and interpreting Chinese policies as they applied to Tibet. I also followed any world events that applied to or that I thought would be interesting to Tibetans, including the Dalai Lama's travels and expressions of international support for Tibet or criticisms of China's policies there. It was hard to know how effective we were. We literally broadcast into the ether and got very little feedback, so it was important to remember that there were actually listeners on the other end.

Since the relatively liberal period of Chinese policies in Tibet of the 1980s, Chinese policy hardened considerably after the demonstrations and riots in Lhasa from 1987 to 1989, the declaration of martial law in the TAR in March 1989, and the Tiananmen democracy movement and subsequent massacre of June 1989. China reverted to a policy of central control, denial of all aspects of autonomy, repression of opposition, and renewed attempts to assimilate Tibet and Tibetans. China began a campaign to denigrate the Dalai Lama and to indoctrinate Tibetans in a new identity as Chinese. China also increased its propaganda internationally through visits by Chinese and Tibetan officials and various cultural activities. Numerous Tibetology institutes were established employing Chinese and Tibetan researchers whose purpose was to prove the essentials about the Chinese version of Tibetan history. Several State Council White Papers were produced with the same historical themes, accompanied by evidence about how China had liberated Tibetans and improved their lives.

Several Tibet Work Forums were held in which the new policy for Tibet was formulated. Emphasis was placed on economic development as the solution in Tibet, which could only be accomplished by sending more Chinese officials and "experts" and allowing individual Chinese to come there for business opportunities. Infrastructure development and resource exploitation was increased, which also led to an influx of more Chinese. The economic development policy was accompanied by the abrogation of Chinese promises in regard to Tibetan autonomy and renewed repression of all opposition. China's new policy made it apparent that it had identified the sort of Tibetan autonomy that had been allowed in the 1980s as the breeding grounds for separatism and had determined not to allow it again.

Above all else, it was the affair of the Panchen Lama's reincarnation that demonstrated China's decision to rely on control and repression in Tibet and to deny any role to the exiled Dalai Lama. The Tenth Panchen Lama died in Shigatse in January 1989 at age 51 under mysterious circumstances, shortly after delivering a speech describing the damaging effects of "democratic reforms" on Tibetan culture. His untimely passing removed the most important proponent for Tibetan autonomy. The sensitivity of his role delayed the discovery of his reincarnation until 1995. A possible precedent had been set in 1992 in the choice of the reincarnation of the Karmapa that might have allowed some cooperation with the Dalai Lama in the choice of the Panchen. Exiled officials of the Karmapa sect had cooperated with those in Tibet to choose a new Karmapa, who was thus accepted as legitimate by both sides.

In the search for the Panchen Lama's reincarnation, there was also some initial communication allowed between Tibet and Dharamsala. However, the Tashilhunpo search committee's choice was secretly conveyed to the Dalai Lama for his approval, which he provided without coordination with China, thus preempting Chinese approval. China still could have rejected the Dalai Lama's recognition as inconclusive while proclaiming their choice of the same child as authoritative and official, thus having a Panchen Lama accepted by the Tibetan people.

However, they chose to reject the Dalai Lama's choice in favor of a boy whose acceptance would have to be imposed upon the Tibetan people. The "Chinese Panchen Lama" was eventually installed at the Jokhang in secret, in the middle of the night.

The Panchen Lama affair demonstrated China's lack of concern about the wishes of the Tibetan people when it felt that its authority was threatened. It also represented the end of any attempt to cooperate with the Dalai Lama. It was also the end of the Chinese government's cooperation with prominent Tibetans within China, like Ngapo Ngawang Jigme and Bapa Phuntsok Wangyal, who had tried to play a role in cooperating with the Dalai Lama in the selection of the Panchen Lama. After this time, China's policy in Tibet hardened even further.

China's disdain for the opinions of the Tibetan people was demonstrated in another autocratic policy that it imposed upon Tibetans, one that had drastic implications for the survival of Tibetan culture. China's policies in Tibetan areas outside the TAR were sometimes more arbitrary than those inside, which at least at the beginning were restrained by the promises of the Seventeen Point Agreement. In nomadic areas of Amdo, the Chinese initiated ambitious programs to "improve" the grasslands. In the 1950s, China promoted the draining of many wetlands in the grassland areas in order to increase the area of grassland, which resulted in an overall drying of the area. Nomads were then made to increase their herds in order to improve meat and butter production, but this resulted in overgrazing. China then tried to settle the nomads and make them fence their pastures, which resulted in degradation of grasslands because the nomads could not rotate their herds to different areas.

Beginning in 2003, China decided to restore the grasslands and marshes by removing the nomads and their animals altogether. The rationale was that the headwaters of the Yellow, Yangtze, and Mekong Rivers were China's water storehouse which must be preserved for the sake of those living downstream as well as for the viability of the numerous hydroelectric projects being built on all these rivers. Hydroelectricity was in turn needed if China were ever to mine Tibet on an industrial scale. Restoring the water retention capacity of the headwaters of China's rivers required that the nomads, the supposed beneficiaries of previous projects, should now give up their animals and their nomadic lifestyle. Although the stated purposes of the resettlement project were to restore the environment, Chinese officials also revealed that they hoped that the settlement of nomads in towns would improve their access to social services and facilitate their economic and cultural development. This reflects the Chinese belief that nomadism is equivalent to barbarism and that civilization is furthered by settlement. The settlement of the Tibetan nomads would also facilitate Chinese social and political control and programs for their assimilation to Chinese socialist culture.

China claimed that resettling nomads was beneficial both to the nomads and to the grasslands and was popular with the nomads being resettled, who were well taken care of by the government during their transition to a more modern lifestyle and economy. However, contrary to these claims, the nomads were not always voluntarily resettled nor were they adequately assisted in adapting to a new, more commercial lifestyle. Tibetans who complained were told that all land belonged to the Chinese government. In Tibet, any opposition to government plans is interpreted as harming national unity or even as separatist. China's projects are always described as scientific and all opposition as backward and reactionary. Chinese claims that resettlement was necessary because of degradation of grasslands due to overgrazing have also been questioned by international experts who point out that the nomadic lifestyle was adapted to the grasslands and had maintained an ecological balance there for thousands of years. China's motives in resettling the nomads seemed to outside observers to be mostly political rather than ecological.

The settlement of Tibetan nomads meant the demise of an important component of Tibetan culture. The Chinese state's autocratic interference in Tibetan nomadic culture was breathtaking in its disregard for the wishes or traditions of Tibetans, but difficult to oppose because the nomads had absolutely no political power. China went about its massive alterations without regard to the opinions of Tibetans or outside experts. The result was a massive alteration of Tibetan cultural traditions and the displacement and often impoverishment of the former nomads who often had great difficulty adapting to a new lifestyle. The state assistance promised to the displaced nomads was limited and often failed to reach the nomads due to the corruption of Chinese officials.

During the 2002 to 2010 period, a series of dialogues took place at the rate of about one inconclusive meeting per year between Chinese officials and representatives of the Dalai Lama. There was much speculation about why China engaged in the dialogue at all, given that it denied that there was any "issue of Tibet" about which it should negotiate. China continued its policy of confining the discussions to the personal status of the Dalai Lama, while his representatives tried to broaden the discussion to include Tibetan autonomy and the territorial extent to which it should apply. In the opinion of skeptics, myself included, Beijing was simply playing on Tibetan hopefulness and wishful thinking in order to get concessions from Dharamsala and to convince the world that they were serious about dialogue and a "resolution" of the Tibet issue.

The revival of Sino-Tibetan contacts was begun, as in 1979, by a visit of the Dalai Lama's brother, Gyalo Thondup, to China in 2002. In September of that year, a four-man delegation representing the Dalai Lama, led again by Lodi Gyari, made a visit to Lhasa, the first official contact between Dharamsala and Beijing since 1993, the first visit of a delegation to Tibet since 1985, and the first to Lhasa since 1980. In order to preclude anything like the frenzied welcome the last delegation received in Lhasa, the visit was kept secret and the delegation was surrounded by Chinese security personnel at all times. This event predictably aroused hopes in the Tibetan community, but the Chinese characterized the visits as private and denied that there was any dialogue going on or, indeed, anything to dialogue about except an unconditional return of the Dalai Lama. Nevertheless, the Kalon Tripa, Samdhong Rinpoche, suggested to Tibetans that it would help "create an atmosphere conducive to talks" if Tibetans in exile refrained from demonstrations against Chinese officials during their international travels. Since the substance of the talks was kept secret, there was speculation that it was the Chinese who had suggested that the Tibetans needed to prove their sincerity in this or some other way.

The same group of Tibetan exile representatives made a second visit in June 2003, but were not allowed to visit Tibet. They were taken to the Tibetan county in Yunnan that China had turned into a tourist site under the name "Shangri-La." They also went to Buddhist sites in Chinese provinces. The delegation reported that they had hopefully increased China's confidence in dealing with the Dalai Lama's representatives. In the only statement that revealed anything about the substance of talks, Lodi Gyari said that the Chinese had acknowledged the efforts made by Dharamsala to create a "conducive atmosphere" for the continuation of visits, which tended to confirm that it was they who had suggested such steps to the delegation during their first visit. After the second visit, Samdhong Rinpoche expressed his determination to continue creating a conducive atmosphere for the dialogue process. The Chinese responded by stating that there was no issue of Tibet about which it should engage in dialogue with the Dalai Lama, that he did not represent the interests of the Tibetan people, and that Tibetan resistance to Chinese rule was exclusively the product of American imperialist interference there.

Within Tibet, China did nothing to show any willingness to allow Tibetan autonomy. In the Tibetan area of Kham, now in Sichuan Province, authorities shut down a popular Tibetan monastery school, Larung Gar, where thousands of Tibetans and as many as a thousand Chinese had been studying Buddhism. A popular Tibetan lama, Tenzin Delek Rinpoche, was sentenced to death for conspiracy in regard to a bombing attempt by one of his disciples in Chengdu, which appeared to be an attempt to associate Tibetan nationalism with terrorism. Chinese tolerance for Tibetan cultural activities outside the TAR had previously been thought to demonstrate the possibility of Tibetan autonomy so long as it had no political implications. Chinese intransigence led critics to complain that China's purpose in engaging in contacts was to discourage the anti-China activities of Tibetans in exile, to silence the TGiE by playing upon its hopes for dialogue, and to defuse international criticism by pretending to be willing to dialogue.

The Tibetan envoys returned for a third visit in September 2004. They had discussions with United Front Work Department officials in Beijing and then traveled to the Kham Tibetan area of Sichuan. Lodi Gyari reported an extensive and serious exchange of views on matters related to Tibet. They next met with Chinese officials in Switzerland, in what Dharamsala characterized as the fourth round of talks but that China dismissed as a routine meeting between Chinese officials and Tibetan exiles about private matters. In contrast to the Chinese, the Tibetans typically tried to give as much substance to the dialogue as possible in order to demonstrate some success for the Dalai Lama's Middle Path policy.

The envoys returned to China in February 2006 for what they described as the fifth round of talks. They again met with United Front officials and went to other nationality autonomous regions but not to Tibet. While Dharamsala described the delegation as official envoys of the Dalai Lama, Beijing said they were visiting in a private capacity. Upon his return to Dharamsala, Lodi Gyari made a statement that indicated that the talks were essentially deadlocked, saying that there was a fundamental difference even in the approach in addressing the issue, meaning that there was no mutual understanding even about the definition of the issue that they should be discussing.

Despite the stalemate, both sides vowed to continue the process. Beijing apparently wanted to appear conciliatory, while Dharamsala was desperate to show some results for the Middle Path policy. While the Middle Path had produced no results with China, it was very popular with foreign governments, who were required only to support dialogue, which was the one thing that they could easily do. Beijing also benefitted from Dharamsala's efforts to create a "conducive atmosphere" for dialogue. Before the visit of Hu Jintao to the United States in early 2006, Dharamsala went so far as to send a public appeal to Tibetans and their supporters to avoid embarrassing him. There were rumors that the Chinese had told Dharamsala that if there were no demonstrations against Hu during his US visit, then China might invite the delegates for another visit or even invite the Dalai Lama to visit a Buddhist pilgrimage site in China. China continued to oppose all the Dalai Lama's international activities, particularly meetings with foreign leaders, with warnings that this would jeopardize the "conducive atmosphere" for dialogue.

There was not another meeting until July 2007, when the Tibetan delegation was invited to China for what the Tibetans said was the sixth round of dialogue but that the Chinese typically dismissed as a private visit. They again met with officials of the United Front but reported no concessions from the Chinese, including about a proposed visit by the Dalai Lama. An incident at the horse fair in Lithang that summer in which a nomad jumped on stage and shouted out for Tibetan independence had produced a Chinese crackdown in Kham. Tibetan officials were replaced with Chinese and the Patriotic Education Campaign was required for all, monks as well as civilians. Regulations were introduced requiring Chinese government approval for the recognition of all reincarnations, because it was thought that the Dalai Lama was using his approval of reincarnations to continue his influence in Tibet. Eastern Tibet, where there were formerly fewer restrictions on Tibetan cultural practices than in the TAR, because it was thought to be less political and more assimilated, was now subjected to more restrictions and repressions, more Patriotic Education Campaigns, and a greater presence of Chinese officials and security personnel.

## Uprising of 2008

Tibetan protests within Tibet as well as in exile traditionally occur around March 10, the anniversary of the 1959 revolt in Lhasa. March 2008 was particularly tense because Tibetans in exile as well as those in Tibet hoped to use the forthcoming Beijing Olympics in August to put pressure on China. Beijing had campaigned for the honor of hosting the Olympics for many years and had been denied the right in 2000 because of opposition due to its poor human rights record. Having won the award for 2008, Beijing was determined to make the Olympics a testimonial to China's greatness and that of the CCP. There was much Chinese idealism about how the Olympics would allow China to invite the world and to demonstrate China's readiness to be a respected member of the world community. The CCP as well as the Chinese people were therefore very sensitive to any embarrassment that might detract from its glorious Olympics. Tibetans were well aware of this opportunity to put pressure on China to address the issue of Tibet, which was already an embarrassment that China might perhaps want to ameliorate in some way.

Tibetans in India mounted a campaign to march to the border with Tibet, which they gave the rather provocative title of Tibetan Peoples' Uprising Movement. This title was meant to commemorate the 1959 uprising in Lhasa, but it later provided the Chinese with propaganda to accuse the exiles of instigation of unrest within Tibet. Tibetans within Tibet were not unaware of the opportunity presented by the Olympics, since they were already being subjected to propaganda about the event and what it meant for China.

The uprising in Tibet began on March 10, a Monday, when some 500 monks of Drepung Monastery attempted to march on the city center and were stopped by security forces. At the same time, a few monks from Sera were arrested in front of the Jokhang for carrying the banned Tibetan flag and shouting slogans for Tibetan independence. On Tuesday, some 600 monks from Sera marched on the city to demand the release of their fellows. They were also stopped and some were beaten and arrested. On the next day, monks of Ganden, located 20 miles east of Lhasa, were prevented from marching. By this time all three of Lhasa's great monasteries were surrounded by security forces.

Monks of the smaller Ramoche Monastery in the center of Lhasa attempted to march on Friday and were stopped, setting off large-scale rioting by Tibetans living in the area. The riot grew and resulted in the destruction of some 1,200 Chinese shops and the deaths of twenty-two, mostly Han Chinese shopkeepers. After withdrawing from the Tibetan section of Lhasa for several hours, the Chinese security forces returned and killed an estimated 50 to 100 Tibetans, none of whose deaths were admitted by the Chinese. On the same day, some 400 monks demonstrated at the large Labrang Tashikyil Monastery in Gansu and were repressed by force, leading the next day to rioting by 5,000 to 10,000 Tibetans and the burning of many Chinese shops, as well as the deaths of several Tibetans when security forces responded.

The Chinese government designated the Lhasa riot as the "3.14 incident" and concentrated its propaganda on the rioting in Lhasa and the deaths of Chinese. However, far more significant was the fact that another ninety places in mostly eastern Tibet outside the TAR erupted in demonstrations and riots over the next month. All of these demonstrations were accompanied by Tibetan flags and slogans for independence and resulted in the deaths of an estimated additional 100 Tibetans. Most of the demonstrations after the first week were in eastern Tibet near the traditional border between Tibet and China. The unrest in Tibet received a considerable amount of international attention and was a serious embarrassment for China. China responded by blaming all the disturbances on outside instigation and further accused the Western media of intentional distortion of the nature of the riots in Lhasa.

Several world leaders threatened to boycott the opening ceremonies of the Olympics if China did not take some measures to alleviate the crisis, such as meeting with the Dalai Lama's representatives. China quickly agreed to such a meeting in May, the seventh round of dialogue, according to the Tibetan side, which produced nothing but an agreement for another meeting in July, shortly before the Olympics. This resulted in the withdrawal of the world leaders' threats, accompanied by their taking credit for having moved the Chinese to dialogue.

In July, during what the Tibetan side counted as the eighth round of dialogue, the Chinese agreed only to another meeting after the Olympics, accompanied by vague hints of compromise, thus defusing the threat of protests before or during the Olympics. The hint of compromise came in the form of an invitation to the Tibetans to explicate exactly what they meant by "genuine autonomy." Doubts about the significance of the invitation arose because the Chinese had, before this meeting, scrupulously refused to allow that the nature of autonomy in Tibet was a subject about which they were willing to dialogue. The invitation may have been no more than an inexperienced Chinese official's remark that he didn't even know what the Tibetans meant by their demand for autonomy when Tibet already had autonomy.

In anticipation of the next round of dialogue, after the Olympics, at which the Chinese had ostensibly agreed to talk about autonomy, the TGiE worked up a "Memorandum on Tibetan Autonomy," an impressive and well-researched document that laid out Dharamsala's position on autonomy, including evidence that their proposals were in total conformity to China's own National Regional Autonomy Law, now translated by the Chinese as Regional Ethnic Autonomy Law. The new designation put the regional before the national (now changed to "ethnic") character of Tibet and other minority regions—signifying that territory was more important than people and that those people did not rise to the level of a nation, or even a nationality, but only to an ethnicity.

The Tibetan Memorandum was scornfully rejected by the Chinese at the next meeting in November, accompanied by a return to a refusal to talk about anything but the Dalai Lama's personal status. China expressed no willingness to dialogue further with the Dalai Lama's representatives. Chinese duplicity in pretending to dialogue only in order to prevent protests against its Olympics was exposed, but the Olympics had been a success and China believed it had won the world's admiration, while the Tibetan issue had been forgotten.

The 2008 Tibetan Uprising produced no positive results for Tibetans; it aroused Chinese anti-Tibetan and anti-Western nationalism, furthered by Chinese government propaganda. Popular Chinese resentment was stimulated by the perception that Tibetans were ungrateful for all that China had done for them, while foreigners were ignorant of the real history of Tibet or were intentionally trying to harm China's reputation. Tibetan protests against the Olympic Torch Relay, which China had unwisely expanded to an international venue, further aroused popular Chinese resentment and nationalism. The Chinese government tolerated this phenomenon of popular outrage on the internet because the nationalist fervor was in support of the CCP, the government's repression of protests in Tibet, and China's glorification by means of the Olympics.

In May, at the height of interest in events in Tibet and how they might affect the Beijing Olympics, my second book, *China's Tibet?: Autonomy or Assimilation*, came out. The title's question mark was awkward, but I added it after being asked by Tibetan friends about whether or not my title was intended to express approval of China's claim to Tibet. In press for the past six months, of course the book didn't deal with the uprising, but its release was fortuitously timed, nonetheless. It had, in fact, taken four years to write and publish, but it appeared to have been perfectly timed to coincide with the uprising. The subject of the book was Chinese propaganda about Tibet and the fellow travelers who had promoted that propaganda. It was inspired by Paul Hollander's *Political Pilgrims*, an exposé of the naïve idealism of Western socialists who had traveled to the Soviet Union during the 1930s and who had seen nothing but economic prosperity and political freedom, when Stalin was engaged in his murderous purges and subjecting Ukraine to starvation in the pursuit of collectivization.

A characteristic of the political pilgrims as revealed by Hollander was that they saw what they wanted to see. Because they firmly believed in the socialist future, they tended to alter reality to fit their preconceptions. Even when they recognized that the reality was not as proclaimed, they were often willing to pretend otherwise in the belief that, even if the socialist paradise was not reality now, it would be so in the near future. The end, the socialist and communist ideal, was thought to justify the means used to promote that ideal, including misleading and overly optimistic reporting and even intentionally deceptive propaganda.

Tibet also had a series of political pilgrims, whose numbers were fewer but whose observations, even if biased, were useful just because no other information was available during the periods when they were allowed access. One notorious journalist, actually propagandist, Israel Epstein, had taken Chinese citizenship and was editor of China's main propaganda publication in English, *China Reconstructs*. He was favored with exclusive access to Tibet during three lengthy trips in 1955, 1965, and 1976. He wrote a book, *Tibet Transformed*, in which, among the faithful repetitions of Chinese propaganda, one could find much information about the actual goals and processes of that transformation. Anna Louise Strong, an elderly American communist, was allowed a trip to Lhasa in late 1959, only months after the revolt. In her subsequent book, *When Serfs Stood Up in Tibet*, she saw a self-liberation of the Tibetan serfs, magnanimously assisted by the CCP, and a bright future for Tibetans under their own self-rule and pursuit of the socialist paradise.

An English couple, Stuart and Roma Gelder were allowed a visit to Lhasa in 1962—when Tibetans were suffering the effects of Chinese repression of the 1959 revolt, when many of their relatives were in prisons and labor camps, and when Tibet was, like all of China, suffering from the famine due to Mao's disastrous Great Leap Forward. None of this was seen by the Gelders, who reported in their book, *The Timely Rain*, only on the happiness of the liberated serfs and their actual exercise of democracy and autonomy. Han Suyin was a Chinese national and well-known author who wrote biographies of Mao and Zhou Enlai. She was a communist sympathizer, but preferred to live in the West where she wrote and published her books. She went to Lhasa in 1976 and wrote that Lhasa was free and open, contrary to Westerners who thought it closed off by the Chinese. Her book, *Lhasa, the Open City*, was infused with Chinese chauvinism.

In order to contrast the reports of the fellow travelers with the reality of Tibet at the time, and also to make use of their reports and some other newly obtained information to try to understand what Tibet and Tibetans went through from the revolt to the Cultural Revolution, I included parts of the Panchen Lama's account as well as the memoir by Rinbur Tulku. The Panchen Lama's petition was an antidote to the accounts of Anna Louise Strong and the Gelders, who were blissfully unaware of the trauma, repression, starvation, and suffering that the Panchen Lama so vividly described. Rinbur's account revealed the massive theft of Tibetan art and the looting of monasteries at precisely the time when Strong and the Gelders were in Tibet and reporting that religion was flourishing as usual with no restrictions by the Chinese.

I included two other pieces of recently obtained Chinese propaganda, both of which revealed much about what the Chinese thought about Tibet, or at least what the CCP wanted them to think. The first was a film, *Serf*, of near legendary status since it was one of the few sources of popular Chinese opinion about Tibet in the early years of Chinese control. It was made in 1962 by a PLA film company and portrayed the life of a supposedly typical Tibetan serf in the darkest light. The serf lived a life of abuse and drudgery until the arrival of the PLA, who were supposedly called the "Army of Bodhisattvas" by the serfs. I had heard of this film for years. It was said to have been extremely popular in China and influential in forming Chinese opinions about Tibet since it was the sum total of what they knew about the supposedly typical life of a poor Tibetan serf. The film had recently been obtained by Robbie Barnett, now at Columbia, who supplied me with a DVD version complete with English translation of the script.

The second piece of Chinese propaganda was equally famous in forming the opinions of not only Chinese but of young Tibetans as well. It was a display at the "Museum of the Tibetan Revolution," located in the Shol area below the Potala, of 106 life-sized clay sculptures depicting the suffering endured by the Tibetan serfs. The sculptures had been created in 1975 by a group of Chinese art students who had interviewed former serfs about their lives before liberation. The exhibition, titled *Wrath of the Serfs*, was the highlight of the museum that had been inaugurated in 1965 and was devoted to displays of torture instruments and other evidence of the miserable lives of the serfs. There was an accompanying book of photos of the sculptures issued at the same time. The sculptures were magnificent in their portrayal of the Tibetan serfs' suffering and their eventual revolt against the serf-owners in 1959, which never happened, of course. I was told by an RFA colleague who had been a young student in Lhasa in the 1970s that he and his class were taken to see the exhibit and were very impressed by the lifelike nature of the sculptures. They were swayed to believe this Chinese depiction of old Tibet in the absence of any counternarrative from their parents, who were no doubt terrified to bring up any such subject.

Given the interest in Tibet at this time due to the uprising, I proposed another book to my publisher that would actually be about the uprising. I promised to finish it in a few months, by October, so that it could be issued in March on the first anniversary of the uprising. I titled it *Tibet's Last Stand?: The Tibetan Uprising of 2008 and China's Response*. I chose the title as an analogy to the uprising of the American Indians that culminated in the Battle of Little Bighorn, popularly known as "Custer's Last Stand," but which, while a gratifying victory for the Indians was actually their last stand against American efforts to curtail their freedoms and confine them to reservations. I feared that the Tibetan Uprising was similar; it had been gratifying to many Tibetans to be able to express their rejection of Chinese rule and to fly the Tibetan flag, even if only briefly, but all knew that Chinese repression would follow. Such was the case, with Tibetan freedoms curtailed as never before in eastern Tibet, while the Chinese admitted to no faults in their policies and no reasons to change. Again, the question mark in the title was awkward, but I felt the need to allow that this was not inevitably Tibet's last stand.

The book was easy to write, since the events were very recent. The themes I pursued were the duplicitous way that China used promises of meetings with the Dalai Lama's representatives to defuse international protests and to safeguard China's Olympics, the incredible distortion of the nature of events inside Tibet and the acceptance of those distortions by the Chinese public, and the rise of Chinese nationalism in defense of China against Tibetan protests, particularly those around the International Olympic Torch Relay. Popular Chinese nationalism became a major factor after this time, while Sino-Tibetan dialogue ceased. China celebrated the success of its Olympics and most Chinese believed that they had won the propaganda war about Tibet.

The book began with a short chronology of the events of the uprising, emphasizing the fact that most of the demonstrations after the first week of the Lhasa riot took place in eastern Tibet along the traditional Sino-Tibetan cultural frontier. In fact, a map of the occurrences redefined that border, almost duplicating the frontier posts that were established during the Tibetan Empire. China's response to the uprising was to blame it on foreign instigation, primarily that of the "Dalai Clique" but also "hostile Western forces." Western media were accused of intentionally distorting reality in their coverage of the uprising.

One photo of police beating Tibetan monks was incorrectly labeled as happening in Lhasa when it was actually from Kathmandu. This honest mistake was regarded by many Chinese as intentional distortion with hostile motive. Another photo taken during the riot in Lhasa left out a group of stone-throwing Tibetans in the far margin of the photo. This was also denounced as intentional distortion of the reality of the events. Chinese propaganda as well as popular opinion focused on the deaths of the innocent Chinese shopkeepers and ignored reports of brutal repression by Chinese security forces and the deaths of Tibetans. Many Chinese seemed unaware of why Tibetans should oppose Chinese rule; having been taught that China had liberated Tibetans from their own feudal misrule, they imagined that Tibetans were ungrateful and that Western supporters of Tibet were just ignorant of this history.

China also put out a flurry of propaganda in all of its state-controlled media with the usual themes that Tibet has always been a part of China, that it was "peacefully liberated" in 1950, and that old Tibet was a "dark, barbaric, cruel, feudal Hell on Earth" from which Tibetans were grateful to have been liberated by the CCP. The Dalai Lama was accused of having never given up Tibetan independence, despite his Middle Path policy, which was interpreted as a demand that China's regional autonomy law should not apply in Tibet and that Tibetan regions should be reunited into a territory where he intended to practice Tibetan separatism and eventually achieve independence. His refusal to give up the claim that Tibet was once independent was regarded as equivalent to accusing China of imperialism, and setting the conditions for Tibet to demand national self-determination in international law.

China's seventh White Paper on Tibet issued at this time attempted to refute the Dalai Lama's charge that it was guilty of "cultural genocide." The paper cited all of China's economic assistance to Tibet, much of which was declared to have been devoted to the protection and development of Tibetan culture. A secondary theme was to expose the Dalai Lama's demand for cultural autonomy as really meant to achieve independence. China compared the 1959 Tibet rebellion to the secession of the slave states in the American Civil War, and its liberation of the Tibetan serfs to the emancipation of the slaves during that war. It challenged the United States to explain why it did not see the comparison between its preservation of the Union and elimination of slavery with China's similar acts in Tibet. The TGiE was equated with the Ku Klux Klan, both of which were said to have hoped to preserve slavery.

The uprising in Tibet and the international response, including threats against the Beijing Olympics, were a serious challenge to the CCP, which had hoped to use the Olympics as evidence of China as a modern and responsible member of the international community. China's first response was to deny the validity of the uprising. The second tactic was to defuse international protests and sympathy for Tibetans by pretending to dialogue with the Dalai Lama's representatives. I emphasized

China's duplicity in pretending to dialogue, and the ambiguity of the invitation to the Tibetans to explicate exactly what they meant by "genuine autonomy." The validity of this interpretation was demonstrated by the scornful Chinese rejection of Dharamsala's "Memorandum on Tibetan Autonomy" after the Olympics and their termination of the dialogue.

I also tried to emphasize the rather amazing effect that the uprising had on the explosive growth of a virulent anti-Tibetan and anti-Western Chinese nationalism. Young Chinese "netizens" rallied around their government and the CCP in defense of China's role in Tibet and the Beijing Olympics. Popular Chinese sentiments, usually censored on the internet, were allowed to proliferate as long as they supported the government and condemned protests by Tibetans and their supporters against the International Olympic Torch Relay. Popular Chinese nationalism became an important factor for the first time, due to the challenge posed by the uprising to China's reputation and the popular reaction in support of the Party and government.

China's uncompromising response to the uprising as well as the rise of anti-Tibetan Chinese nationalism were why I had chosen *Tibet's Last Stand?* as the title for my book. China's final analysis was that it had defeated the supporters of Tibet in the international propaganda war and had conducted a highly successful Olympics, and thus that it had "won" the competition about the interpretation of Tibetan reality. So confident was China of its victory in the propaganda war that it demanded that other countries should alter their thinking about Tibet to accord with China's interpretation of Tibetan reality as a precondition for good relations with a rising China.

To consolidate its sense of victory, the CCP revived much of its most simplistic and offensive propaganda about the liberation of Tibet's "serfs and slaves" from the feudal serf system. An exhibition was opened in Beijing of images of serfs in old Tibet and a film was released of scenes in Tibet in the 1950s before "democratic reforms." The most notorious examples of Chinese propaganda about the suffering of the serfs were revived, including the *Serf* film and the book of photos of the *Wrath of the Serfs* exhibition. For the first time, a "Serf Emancipation Day" was inaugurated as an annual celebration on March 28 to commemorate the day in 1959 that the traditional Tibetan government was dissolved and Tibetan serfs supposedly gained their freedom. As was usual in this type of propaganda exercise, particularly that of 1965 when the TAR was inaugurated and the Museum of the Tibetan Revolution opened, former liberated serfs were invited to relate their experiences in order to remind all Tibetans of how much better off they were now than in old Tibet before liberation. Residents of Lhasa were required to gather in the square in front of the Potala for the celebration of the first Serf Emancipation Day.

China's reversion to its "liberation of the serfs" propaganda was, as usual, meant to obscure the political issue of the legitimacy of Chinese rule over Tibet. According to China, there is no political or national issue of Tibet, only a class issue of the liberation of the serfs. China's response to the Tibetan uprising demonstrated that it had no intention of changing its policy in Tibet, no matter how much Tibetans revealed their discontent or how much international criticism of China the Tibet issue evoked. Its refusal to dialogue with the Dalai Lama, even during threats to its Olympics performance, was further evidence. The CCP was gratified by the popular Chinese support it received in regard to Tibet and its promotion of China's reputation through a successful holding of the Olympics. Ultimately, China had to rely upon repression and propaganda in Tibet, since it could not change its policy. The lesson of a more relaxed policy in Tibet in the 1980s was that a revival of Tibetan nationalism was the result. In order to forever eliminate the separatist threat in Tibet, China had to rely upon repression to keep Tibetan opposition under control, until economic development accompanied by colonization achieved the ultimate goal of cultural and political assimilation.

In August 2010 I became aware of a ceremony that was to take place at Camp Hale, Colorado, to commemorate the site where the CIA had trained Tibetan Resistance fighters. A Colorado senator, Mark Udall, had convinced the US Forest Service to erect a plaque at the site, which was the first official acknowledgment by any US government agency that the United States had trained and assisted the Tibetan Resistance. Camp

Hale was a former US Army base high in the mountains of Colorado that was used to train troops of the US Army's 10th Mountain Division during World War Two. The base was abandoned after the war and was selected as the site for the training of Tibetans because of its similarity to the terrain and environment of Tibet. Tibetans who were at the site gave it the Tibetan name *Dumra*, or "garden."

I asked Jigme if I could cover the ceremony for RFA. I convinced my friend Jamyang Norbu to be there as well. We were both eventually very proud to have been there since it turned out to be a memorable gathering of old CIA trainers and some of the Tibetans who were trained there. We both also achieved a long-time goal of seeing the famous site where the Tibetans were trained.

The camp is at a 10,000-foot elevation about ten miles northwest of the old Colorado mining town of Leadville. The site was a mile-long valley, about a quarter mile wide, and there were a series of plaques commemorating the 10th Mountain Division. There were traces of the army base roads still visible and one rusty steel framework of a barracks to be seen. There was no trace of the CIA camp and the three or four old CIA types at the ceremony very disappointingly couldn't remember exactly where the camp was. A few current Chushi Gangdruk Tibetans showed up and decorated the site with their flags, that of Tibet and a string of prayer flags, giving the ceremony a bit more color.

The ceremony was attended by perhaps forty people, mostly very interesting characters, giving one the feeling of being at a memorable event. In a statement at the ceremony, Senator Udall said that the plaque will be a lasting memorial to the brave Tibetan freedom fighters who were trained there and to their dedicated CIA instructors. He described the training of Tibetans there as a shared worthy endeavor of the American and the Tibetan people. The plaque was unveiled and read:

> *From 1958 to 1964 Camp Hale played an important role as a training site for Tibetan Freedom Fighters. Trained by the CIA, many of these brave men lost their lives in the struggle for freedom. "They were the best and bravest of their generation and we wept together when they were killed fighting alongside their countrymen." Orphans of the*

*Cold War, by John Kenneth Knaus. This plaque is dedicated to their memory.*

The significance of this event was that finally Americans could openly acknowledge and be proud of their support for Tibetan resistance to Chinese control of their country. Americans could rightly be proud of their support for Tibetans' rights and freedoms. The designation of the Tibetans as "Freedom Fighters" was a refutation of all of China's propaganda about its "liberation" of Tibet.

After the ceremony, some of us went around the very large site in search of any traces of the CIA camp. Even though it was fifty years ago, I found it incomprehensible that none of the old CIA agents could remember where the camp was. We didn't find any traces, but I later located the site through old photos. It was a very small camp on the eastern edge of the valley, as could be discovered from the photos once it was determined that one confusing photo had been reversed when it was published. A group of some twenty Tibetans and a few non-Tibetans went into Leadville that evening for dinner at an old-fashioned restaurant. The next day Jamyang and I drove over Independence Pass to Aspen, where I had lived in the late 1960s. It was a beautiful drive, memorialized for me by Jamyang "Tibetanizing" Independence Pass as "Rangzen La."

## Chapter 5

# Tibet's Fate

It is often said that history will tell, as if history is some autonomous decision maker that always, eventually, discerns what is true from what is false. This expression is similar to others, such as the "verdict of history" or "time will tell," again giving to some impersonal phenomenon the power to sort out the historically true from the false. However, the reality is that what passes as "history" is told by historians, who are entirely mortal beings with typical human biases and prejudices. Historians are not even always free to write history as they see it but often work under constraints imposed by others. The victors in human conflicts, most often governments, typically decide what version of history will be promoted and what other versions, those of the losers, will be suppressed. The Chinese tradition of each new dynasty rewriting the history of the last, the one that it has conquered or superseded, is well known. This process is going on right now, with the Chinese Communist Party promoting its version of Tibetan history and denying that of Tibetans and their sympathizers.

Even in regard to the Tibetan version of its own history, the victor in the historical process, the Buddhist church, has promoted its version of historical truth. According to this version of history, the prevalence of Buddhism in Tibet and the establishment of a political system combining religion and politics, or church and state, is Tibet's greatest accomplishment. The Buddhist version of Tibetan history credits the Tibetan Empire of the seventh to ninth centuries with having established Buddhism as the state religion. It blames an apostate king, Lang Darma, for having persecuted Buddhism, thus leading to his justifiable assassination by a Buddhist monk and the consequent collapse of the kingdom and empire.

The Tibetan state was eventually reestablished, by the church, but only four centuries later and only with the patronage of a foreign military power, the Mongol Empire. Despite this reliance upon foreign patrons, inherent to the rule of an organization that professes nonviolence, the Tibetan Buddhist church maintains that Tibetan independence was not sacrificed, due to the unique Cho-Yon, or Priest-Patron, relationship which, it claims, did not imply subordination of the priest to the patron.

Recently, some Tibetan historians have challenged the Buddhist version of Tibetan history, particularly during the formative empire period. Samten Karmay, one of the foremost historians of the pre-Buddhist Bon religion of Tibet, has offered a different version of the role of Buddhism in the establishment of the empire, particularly as opposed to that of Bon, and the circumstances of the collapse of the empire due to the assassination of Lang Darma. Karmay has revealed that Lang Darma, characterized in Tibetan Buddhist history as a persecutor of Buddhism, was actually only trying to curtail the excess privileges granted to the clergy by his predecessor, and brother, Ralpacan.[1]

According to Karmay's interpretation, the Tibetan Empire may well have been brought down not by an apostate but by a reaction from Buddhist monks denied the privileges to which they had become accustomed. With the collapse of the empire came the collapse of organized Buddhism as well, at least temporarily, given that the clergy had also benefitted from the patronage of a centralized state. Karmay writes that the monk, Palkyi Dorje, who assassinated Lang Darma was not just a simple monk, as is implied in the usual histories, but the abbot of Samye, the first (founded in 779) and most important monastery in Tibet at that time. The assassination therefore presents a situation of conflict between the head of the church and the head of state. As Karmay writes:

> *In my opinion, based upon this piece of the Dunhuang document, the murderer of the king was the ninth abbot of bSam-yas. It would not be very surprising if the abbot of the monastery had taken*

*such action against the king since the latter was hostile to the clergy. The elimination of the king had definitely put an end to the conflict between church and state, but then it threw the whole country into turmoil. The Buddhist clergy, however, continued its struggle, though no longer under any single authority. It finally won supremacy in Tibet, so to speak, but Buddhism in Tibet never managed to reestablish an institution that would have authority over all subsequent development of the various Buddhist schools. Till very recent times when Tibetan Buddhists gathered together, there was not even a common prayer readily known to all.*

*None of the sources that I have been able to consult has ever stated that the king was a follower of the Bon religion and yet this idea has crept into some western works on Tibetan religion. . . . As we have seen, the conflict was about political power between the clergy and the secular authority and not the struggle between two religious establishments. The Bon religion as a belief certainly existed in the ninth century, but it did not have an institutional form that put it in a position to compete at the time with Buddhism which was the state religion with monastic institutions and enjoying imperial favor even though one cannot exclude the likelihood that some of the ministers involved in the conflict had leanings toward the Bon faith.*

*The btsan-po lHa-sras Dar-ma [Lang Darma] appears to have been sympathetic to a faction consisting mainly of lay ministers of the imperial government. This movement, which was led by the minister rGya-to-re, viewed the government as weakened by the influence of Buddhism in its policies and particularly objected to the involvement of Buddhist monks in the government. However, there is a strong suggestion that the king himself personally remained Buddhist and during his reign Buddhism certainly continued to flourish. In the early sources there appears no suggestion that he persecuted Buddhist monks, but as he was against the involvement of Buddhist clergy in politics it is likely that he was not in favor of maintaining the special privileges of the Buddhist monastic establishment as had been the case especially during the reign of King Ral-pa-can.*[2]

The Tibetan Empire, the only era of a unified and indisputably independent Tibet, was the creation of a secular aristocracy, united for the first time by the kings of Yarlung. The king of Yarlung, Namri, created what can best be described as a feudal confederacy, which united the clans of Central Tibet in a relationship that was mutually beneficial. The clans retained much of their autonomy over local affairs, but at the same time they gained the unified political and military power necessary for conquests further afield. A feudal aristocracy and state administration were created by the practice of having each of the clans provide one or more nobles who swore oaths of loyalty to the king and who literally shared the same fate, having to enter the king's burial chamber with him. This feudal aristocracy was based upon the clan but also transcended the clan and created a higher political structure based upon personal loyalty to the king. The political system under Yarlung gradually developed from a relationship between clans, in which the clans held the actual power and retained autonomy, to a system of feudal privilege based upon personal and class relationships between the aristocracy and the ruling sovereign.[3]

The feudal system enabled the Yarlung sovereign to establish military and administrative authority over territory far beyond the ability of Yarlung to directly administer, creating the political basis for the Tibetan state and, later, the empire. The union of the clans under Yarlung exhibited some of the characteristics of a confederation of the nomadic type in which tribes unite only for conquests further afield. Nomads typically create state structures only due to a relationship with a neighboring agricultural society, either tribute relations which provide the nomadic leader with gifts sufficient to ensure the loyalty of his subordinates or actual conquest of a sedentary society.

In other aspects, the creation of the Tibetan state differed from the nomadic type. Central Tibet was an area of mixed agricultural and animal husbandry economy. Tibet was not dependent upon the raiding or conquest of neighboring sedentary societies in order to create centralized political authority. What actually happened was that the central Tibetan state quickly expanded to incorporate surrounding nomadic societies, thus combining the strengths of both sedentary and nomadic societies. Within a period of little more than a decade, the Yarlung confederation expanded to include all the peoples of the Tibetan Plateau, creating in the process a centralized Tibetan state.

Some of the nomadic tribes had to be militarily conquered, but most seem to have joined the Tibetan confederation after little resistance, combined with promises of an alliance of convenience with their distant cousins from Central Tibet. In addition to the political and agricultural resources of the Central Tibetan valleys, nomadic economy, especially the wealth of mounted manpower, played a large role in Tibetan state formation. The nomadic tribes of the plateau were weak in political organization but strong in resources of men and animal power. All of these resources shared the characteristics of nomadic mobility and were therefore ideal for military campaigning. The nomadic tribes provided mounted warriors, porterage by means of man and animal power, and food on the hoof.

Owen Lattimore never visited Tibet, but based upon his study of the Inner Asian societies on the frontiers of China, he deduced much about the political formation and state structure of Tibet. Writing during the period before 1950, when Tibet was relatively open to foreigners, he was distinguished by his analysis of state formation based upon the nomadic model. Lattimore was able to deduce the course of Tibetan state formation based upon the facts of a mixed economy in Central Tibet surrounded by nomadic tribes. He was also able to deduce the role of the Buddhist church in Tibetan state formation during the empire period, based upon universal principles of church-state relationships. Lattimore was also aware, of course, of the history of the post-empire dominance of the Buddhist church in Tibet and its dependence upon foreign patrons.

> *Tibetan Lama-Buddhism . . . was at first the instrument of the secular kings, who used it to circumvent the feudal power of local nobles. The church was corporate; its institutions could be established in every locality and could penetrate both the settled and the nomadic societies, yet in doing so it did not succumb to particularism [localism] but retained its corporate, centralized interest and character. It successfully eliminated the danger and difficulty of imposing the rule of one great family or one locality over other families and localities, for the*

*hierarchical succession to power is relatively impersonal. . . . Because its corporate interest was always continuous and at the same time resistant to both local and family bias, the Lama church eventually superseded the secular kings of whom it had originally been the instrument.*[4]

*[I]n alliance with the kings of Lhasa it [the church] assisted in creating a Tibetan state, incorporating widely scattered communities that until then had almost certainly been ruled by powerful families but could hardly be called states. Thereafter it superseded the kings themselves by subordinating the state and incorporating it within the church. No new form of state arose, however, to displace, in turn, the church. This was partly for internal reasons—the extreme dispersion of the Tibetan communities, the small scale of local organization, and the difficulty of community and concerted action—and partly for an external reason. In Tibet as in Mongolia the processes of history ceased to develop and became stagnant, though at a different stage of development; and as in Mongolia this was because of consideration of imperial and frontier policies in China. The church maintained at a dead, unchanging level the supremacy that it had acquired within Tibet because it allied itself, externally, with the dynastic interests of the Manchu Empire in China and its corona of stabilized frontier societies.*[5]

*For the social and political history of Tibet this period [Tibetan Empire] was clearly of great importance. . . . the growth of church property and power increased until it threatened the secular authority. In the tenth [ninth] century, there was an anti-ecclesiastical reaction under the king Langdharma—known ever since in Lama tradition as the incarnation of wickedness. The persecution failed and the church was not destroyed. On the contrary, it was the kingdom that fell, giving way to a constellation of principalities . . . From this time on the church was ascendant in Tibet over the divided state; but though its interests were more generally spread throughout the Tibetan population than the influence of any principality or noble family, the church itself was not yet centralized under a "papal" hierarchy.*[6]

The Tibetan Buddhist church recovered after about two hundred years, due to the "second diffusion" of Buddhism from India in the eleventh century, but the secular state never recovered. As Lattimore writes:

In the eleventh century, there was a great reforming activity in Tibetan Buddhism, or Lamaism. The formal tradition of the church refers this to saints coming from India and Kashmir, like Atisa, who founded the Kadampa reformed sect. The tendency to split up into rival sects led to the formation of rival hierarchies associated with rival secular principalities. These particular tendencies were offset by the effort to create a supreme ecclesiastical authority.

*In this way there was prepared the next stage in the history of Tibet, under Mongol influence. . . . Then, in 1270, Kubilai Khan, the grandson of Chingghis, who had become Emperor of all China and overlord in title of the several Mongol empires, settled the tributary or feudatory status of Tibet by recognizing the head of the Sakya sect as primate of the Lama church and concurrently the supreme secular authority in Tibet.*[7]

Tibet was unified again, four hundred years after the end of the empire, when Sakya Pandita submitted to the Mongols. Submission may have been the only alternative to an all-out Mongol invasion, but Sakya Pandita and his nephew Phagspa willingly sacrificed Tibetan independence for the sake of Buddhism. They were primarily interested in promoting Buddhism to the Mongols and Chinese and they were amazingly successful in doing so, but they forever compromised Tibetan independence.

The Cho-Yon relationship was established by Sakya Pandita and his nephew Phagspa as a means to forestall a Mongol invasion of Tibet in the mid-thirteenth century. Sakya Pandita's goal was also to promote the authority of his own sect within Tibet by means of Mongol patronage and to promote Buddhism further abroad among the Mongols and their subjects. Tibetan Buddhism thereby gained Mongol patronage, while the Mongol Khans gained Tibetan spiritual legitimization as *chakravartins*, or universal Buddhist kings. Sakya Pandita's nephew Phagspa, who formalized the Cho-Yon system under Kubilai, declared Kubilai an incarnation of Manjushri.

Contrary to modern Tibetan claims that this system was unique, or sui generis, this sort of relationship was not unique to Tibet within the Mongol Empire. The Mongols favored religious practitioners of all types in all the countries they conquered. This was due not only to their interest in all manifestations of religion and, no doubt, to their fear of the supernatural, but also to a policy of using local religious authorities to impose and legitimate Mongol rule. Patronage of religious authorities could be manipulated to defuse discontent among subject populations while at the same time preventing the rise of any secular authority around which resistance might coalesce.

As Turrell Wylie wrote,

> *The exploitation of religious leaders at the expense of secular lords in order to subjugate foreign populations was a sociological pattern not unknown to the Mongols. Therefore, given the fragmented and dichotomous nature of Tibetan society at the time, it was logical that Prince Kotan would select a lama [rather] than a layman to surrender Tibet.*[8]

Max Weber also writes of Tibet as an example of a type of government, a hierocracy, that is particularly vulnerable to foreign domination:

> *Wherever hierocracy in this sense occurred . . . it had far-reaching effects on the administrative structure. Hierocracy must forestall the rise of secular powers capable of emancipating themselves. . . . Hierocracy seeks to prevent the king from securing sufficient resources; it impedes the accumulation of the thesaurus which was indispensable to all kings of early history. . . . Hierocracy checks as much as possible the rise of an autonomous and secular military nobility. . . . This opposition to [secular] political charisma has everywhere recommended*

*hierocracy to conquerors as a means of domesticating a subject population. Thus, the Tibetan, the Jewish and the late Egyptian hierocracy were in part supported, and in part directly created, by foreign rulers.*[9]

Lattimore recognized that the rise of the church in Tibet overcame regionalism but that it was flawed by its dependence upon foreign patronage:

*Politically, the supreme pontiffs in Tibet have from the beginning acted as the agents of one or another alien overlord. This converted regional politics into sect politics. The rise of a new sect normally reflected an increase in the relative importance of a region; if the increase went far enough the sect could assert control over the whole church. Thereupon, however, the pontiff in whom this control was vested had to attempt to arrest the native Tibetan processes that tended to make different regions and the sects representative of them vary in importance and influence. This could be most simply managed by leaning on a power external to Tibet. The supreme pontiff, in other words, is to be understood as the symbol of stagnation within Tibet and of alien political power over Tibet.*

As the Mongol Yuan dynasty declined and with it its influence in Tibet, the fortunes of the Sakyapa also declined along with a rise of regionalism, now led by rival Buddhist sects, but also a revival of secular interests in the glories of the Tibetan Empire. Lattimore saw that the collapse of the Mongol Yuan dynasty and its patronage for the Sakyapa would lead to a revival of regionalism:

*Although this system [Cho-Yon] was already foreshadowed in the time of Kublai Khan, it could not yet become rigid because from the fourteenth to the seventeenth century no one empire succeeded in controlling both China within the Great Wall and the steppes beyond the Great Wall. Consequently, the fall of the Mongol (Yuan) dynasty in 1368 was followed by schism in the Tibetan church. Different sects claimed either independence or primacy, each of them being headed by*

> *one of the notable monasteries and each monastery being, in fact, the political "capital" of a region. Certain of these church parties, moreover, negotiated for the patronage of the Ming dynasty in China, while others gravitated toward the successive Mongol coalitions that attempted to win supremacy over the steppe.*[10]

The Chinese Ming dynasty (1368–1644 CE) made some halfhearted efforts to continue relations with Tibetan Buddhist sects and lavished expensive gifts upon any lamas willing to travel to the Ming capital at Nanking. The lamas rather shamelessly fell over each other to accept such gifts as well as the pledges of allegiance to Ming overlords that went along with them. However, the Mongol threat to China had diminished; therefore, the Ming had less need of Tibetan religious influence over the Mongols in order to control them. Political authority in Tibet at the time reverted to regionalism but under the now well-established control of the various monasteries and sects.

The most prominent of the Tibetan lamas who visited the Ming capital was the Karmapa, in 1403. He was honored with lavish gifts and ceremonies and offers to escort him back to Tibet with titles and a military escort sufficient to establish the Karmapa sect as predominant over others. The Karmapa refused the offer, along with a political relationship of the Cho-Yon type with the Ming emperor. Presumably the Karmapa calculated that the Ming lacked the interest or the ability to create the same sort of relationship as had existed during the Yuan. The Ming patronized lamas of most of the sects of Tibetan Buddhism, including the Sakya and Gelugpa. Tibetan Lamas, with only a few exceptions, including Tsongkhapa, displayed little reluctance to accept Ming titles and gifts. The Ming finally had to limit the numbers of Tibetan visits, their duration, and frequency.

Tsongkhapa established the new Gelugpa, or "reformed" sect, in the Lhasa area at the beginning of the fifteenth century with the founding of Ganden Monastery to the east of Lhasa in 1409, Drepung in 1416, and Sera in 1419. Because the Gelugpa were a new sect, they lacked a network of clan patronage like the older sects enjoyed. They were therefore even more dependent upon foreign patronage. The Gelugpa also adopted succession by reincarnation, unlike the older sects that were ruled by hierarchical succession (uncle to nephew), which combined spiritual and secular lineages. Succession by reincarnation was relatively autonomous of clan influence; clans thus had less incentive to patronize the Gelugpa because they could not thereby gain any hereditary influence.

In 1578, Sonam Gyatso, the abbot of Drepung and the most important Gelugpa lama at the time, traveled to the camp of Altan Khan, the most powerful of the Mongol chieftains, to reestablish a relationship of the Cho-Yon type. Sonam Gyatso identified himself as an incarnation of Phagspa, and Altan as an incarnation of Kubilai Khan, thus providing Altan with a spiritual claim to the Chingghisid lineage and securing Altan's patronage for himself and the Gelugpa sect. Altan gave Sonam Gyatso the name Dalai, which, like Gyatso, means "oceanic," and Sonam Gyatso thus became the First Dalai Lama, or the Third after two abbots of Drepung were recognized as previous incarnations. The relationship was firmly solidified when Sonam Gyatso died in 1588 and his reincarnation was found in the great-grandson of Altan Khan.

Mongol patronage strengthened the Gelugpa position in Tibet, but it aroused opposition from their rivals, mainly the Karmapa sect whose stronghold was at Shigatse. The death of the Fourth Dalai Lama in 1617 led to open conflict. The Gelugpa under the new Fifth Dalai Lama found a new patron in Gushri Khan of the Khoshot, one of the Mongol tribes that had recently migrated to the Kokonor (Qinghai) area. Gushri Khan defeated the Karmapas' patron, the Khalkha, thus eliminating them as a threat to the Gelugpa. Gushri Khan then came to Central Tibet and attacked the Karmapa strongholds, including Shigatse. In 1642 Gushri Khan conferred upon the Fifth Dalai Lama political authority over all of Tibet, the first time that a Dalai Lama, and the Buddhist church, had attained both temporal and spiritual rule. Gushri Khan was declared "King of Tibet," but he retired to the Kokonor with his armies. The effect of Gushri Khan's intervention on behalf of the Gelugpa was that regional and sectarian conflicts were finally eliminated and Tibet was politically unified, but once again this was accomplished only by means of Mongol patronage and reliance upon Mongol military force. The Fifth Dalai

Lama also acquiesced in the conversion of many monasteries of the older sects to the Gelugpa.

The Gelugpa and the Fifth Dalai Lama were quick to establish and monopolize relations with the new Manchu Qing dynasty (1644–1912). The Gelugpa hoped to establish a Cho-Yon type relationship with the Manchu, who needed Tibetan influence in their relations with the remaining Mongol tribes. The Dalai Lama accepted an invitation to visit the Manchu court at Peking in 1652. The Tibetans requested an initial meeting outside the Great Wall, because the symbolism of the emperor traveling some distance to meet the Dalai Lama would signify a relationship of equality consistent with the Tibetan conception of the Cho-Yon. The emperor agreed, but the meeting was sabotaged by the objections of Chinese advisors citing inauspicious astrological signs as calculated by a German Jesuit resident at the court, who may have considered the Dalai Lama a rival for religious influence. Ultimately, the emperor descended from his throne and advanced thirty paces to greet the Dalai Lama, who was not required to perform the kowtow.

The Dalai Lama was awarded titles and given seals that implied recognition of his rule over Tibet but only due to having been appointed by the Manchu court. The Dalai Lama was accorded extraordinary respect, but this was not equivalent to his having been recognized as the head of an independent state, as later Buddhist historians would claim. Independent heads of state did not travel to meet each other at this period in Inner Asian history; instead, they sent envoys. The significance of the emperor being able to summon another political potentate to his court was an unmistakable one of nominal submission of the latter.

From 1652 until the Fifth Dalai Lama's death in 1682, the Qing did not directly interfere in Tibetan affairs. The Qing hoped to use the Dalai Lama's influence to control the still-independent Mongol tribes but were somewhat suspicious that the Dalai Lama was operating too independently with the Mongols and that a union of the Mongols with the Dalai Lama could still pose a threat to the Qing. The Dalai Lama's death in 1682 was concealed by the Desi Sangye Gyatso (reputed to have been the son of the Dalai Lama) who hoped to rule on his own. At this time, the Qing adopted a more active policy of military campaigning against the remaining Mongols and thus their need for the Dalai Lama's mediation decreased. The Qing emperor began to hear rumors from some of the defeated Mongols that the Dalai Lama was actually dead and that the Desi was ruling in his stead. This they considered an act of deceit and sent envoys to Lhasa in 1696 to determine if the Dalai Lama was dead or alive. The Desi Sangye Gyatso attempted to placate the Qing envoys by proclaiming that the Dalai Lama was indeed alive but now in his sixth reincarnation!

In 1703, Lhazang Khan, grandson of Gushri Khan, heir to the title of Chogyal, or Dharmaraja of Tibet, with the support of the Qing, took a more activist role in Tibetan politics. In 1705 he invaded Lhasa, executed the Desi, and deposed the Sixth Dalai Lama, who had proved an unfortunate choice. In 1709 a Qing envoy was sent to Lhasa to support Lhazang Khan and to supervise the Tibetan administration, the first time that the Qing had intervened so directly in Tibet. Along with him were specialized personnel who were charged to draw up maps of Tibet, an act that confirmed that the Qing considered Tibet a part of their empire.

Lhazang was unpopular among the Tibetans, particularly the lamas, who had been supporters of the Desi. They conspired with the Dzungar Mongols, from the area beyond the Tian Shan Mountains, the last independent Mongol tribe, in an invasion of Tibet in 1717. The Dzungar surrounded Lhazang Khan at Lhasa, who appealed to the Qing for assistance. The Qing sent armies that arrived too late to save Lhazang Khan, but who now established direct Qing rule over Tibet. The Qing established a provisional government composed of two Khalkha Mongols, two Khoshot Mongols, and two Tibetans.

Thus was established the first direct foreign rule in Tibet, but also the first secular government. The reasons that the Qing established a secular government were because they were dissatisfied with ecclesiastical rule under the Desi, and the Seventh Dalai Lama was still a minor. A more permanent government under a Kashag of three Tibetans, under the supervision of a Mongol *Amban*, was created the next year. The Tibetans were a few of the aristocrats, all from areas outside Lhasa, who had remained loyal to the Qing against the Dzungars. The Dalai Lama, when he reached maturity, would still have great influence, mostly due to continued Mongol loyalty to him. The Qing appointed only Mongols as ambans in Tibet, rather than Han Chinese, which was to continue until the end of the dynasty.

The system of secular rule in Tibet, under the supervision of a Qing amban, did not last for very long. The Lhasa aristocracy considered the Tibetans who were in charge of the administration as too subservient to the Qing. Lhasa Tibetans revolted against them but were put down by Qing loyalists assisted by the dispatch of Qing armies. Even the young Seventh Dalai Lama, whose father was considered less than loyal, was exiled to eastern Tibet near Dartsendo.

This administration remained stable until the middle of the century when another revolt occurred and the Qing again reorganized the administration, this time under a Kashag of four members, one of whom was to be a lama, all under the authority of the now mature Seventh Dalai Lama, who had finally demonstrated loyalty to the Qing. The Dalai Lama was invested with spiritual and temporal rule and this was announced as a restoration of the system that had existed under the Fifth Dalai Lama. The Dalai Lama's temporal authority, however, was in name only; the Qing emperor through the amban was now more than ever in actual control of Tibetan affairs. After their experience that the Tibetan aristocracy was too nationalistic to accept foreign authority, the Qing reverted to a modified Cho-Yon system based upon their recognition of the anti-nationalist nature of ecclesiastical rule and its dependence upon foreign political patronage.

The Qing made another, final, restructuring of their protectorate over Tibet after invasions of Tibet by the Gurkhas of Nepal in 1788 and 1791. The Qing sent an army to drive them out and took advantage of the occasion to make further reforms, including increasing the power of the ambans and instituting the "golden urn" method of selection of incarnations of the Dalai, Panchen, and other high lamas. The amban was to supervise the selection, which meant that the Qing had final authority over political succession in the Tibetan system of combined spiritual and temporal rule. This was meant to separate the aristocracy from the church by limiting the ability of important families to have their sons named as incarnations of high lamas and thus preventing any of the aristocracy from gaining both secular and religious power. The same system was instituted among the Mongol tribes at the same time.

After a succession of Dalai Lamas who failed to gain maturity, some due to intrigues, the Twelfth Dalai Lama was selected in 1858 by the traditional Tibetan method, but was confirmed by means of the golden urn lottery. The regent during the minority of the Twelfth Dalai Lama, Reting Rinpoche, precipitated an evolution of the Tibetan political system by his abuse of authority. Reting was accused of having employed the lottery system only in order to win favor for himself with the Qing. Reting was attacked by Ganden and Drepung monks (Reting was associated with Sera) and forced to flee to China. The alliance of monks and secular officials that had ousted Reting formed a *Tsongdu*, or national assembly, and assumed control of the Tibetan administration. By the late nineteenth century, the Tibetans were beginning to evolve a political system that was a combination of ecclesiastical and secular interests and thus had the potential to resolve the faults of the exclusively ecclesiastical method of rule.

The Qing dynasty, like the previous conquest dynasty, the Yuan, distinguished its Inner Asian domains from China in both political status and administrative divisions. China, the inner empire for the Qing, was regarded as a subjugated state. Inner Asian tribes and states, or the outer empire, were treated as dependent states or even allies, at least during the early Qing. The system of ecclesiastical rule in Tibet, while creating internal cultural and political unity and preserving Tibetan autonomy by an astute use of Tibetan influence in Inner Asian affairs, also perpetuated its fatal dependence upon foreign political patrons. Tibet enjoyed autonomy only when its political patron was disinterested in Tibetan domestic affairs, as were Gushri Khan and his descendants to Lhazang Khan. In the case of a politically involved patron, whether Lhazang Khan, the Dzungar Mongols, or the Manchu Qing, Tibetan sovereignty was effectively in foreign hands.

Tibet fell under British influence, after their invasion of 1904 and after the fall of the Manchu Qing dynasty in 1912, and saw an increase in Tibetan secular nationalism and efforts to establish Tibetan independence of China. These efforts were opposed at every turn by the religious establishment, which saw the government's expenses in creating an army as taking away resources and influence from the monks. They also opposed a British school established in Gyantse and managed to shut it down. The lamas opposed the British for bringing changes to Tibet that decreased their influence, while believing that China would remain a disinterested and generous patron without any interest in being directly involved in Tibet. The Thirteenth Dalai Lama himself, of course, was head of the religious establishment, while at the same time being the foremost proponent of modernizing changes and the creation and funding of an army. But he was forced by the religious establishment before his death in 1933 to curtail many of the modernizing changes. The role of the Buddhist church in preventing any social or political modernization in Tibet is an excellent example of what Lattimore and Weber called the "stagnating effect" of ecclesiastical rule.

A later example of the deleterious effect of religious rule can be found in the efforts of Reting Rinpoche to elicit Chinese support to restore his regency in 1947 during the minority of the Fourteenth Dalai Lama. Reting had been the regent appointed at the time of the Thirteenth Dalai Lama's death, with the responsibility to find the new reincarnation and to administer the government during his minority. Like a previous Reting Rinpoche, he was known to be pro-Chinese. He had to, temporarily he thought, abandon the regency because he was known to have had several sexual affairs and was therefore not qualified to administer the vows of celibacy to the young Fourteenth Dalai Lama. Reting was unsuccessful in his attempt to revive his regency, with Chinese assistance, but his intrigues with the Chinese weakened Tibet just when unity was needed against Chinese efforts to reestablish their control over Tibet.

After the Chinese Communists invaded Tibet in 1950 and imposed their "Seventeen Point Agreement for the Peaceful Liberation of Tibet," the Dalai Lama fled to the border with India. There ensued a debate about whether to accept the Chinese terms or to go into exile in India in order to preserve Tibet's claim to independence. The religious establishment was predominantly in favor of the Dalai Lama's return to Lhasa and acceptance of the Chinese terms. The lamas focused their attention on one of the seventeen points that promised that the religious establishment would continue to function as before and that none of the monasteries' estates would be confiscated. Few clerical officials, ignorant of communist ideology, could imagine why, if unprovoked, the Chinese would want to destroy the Tibetan Buddhist church, the example of the Russian communists' destruction of the Mongolian Buddhist church notwithstanding. The lamas' ignorance of the true nature of the Chinese Communists was "rewarded" with the church being designated as one of the "three pillars of feudalism" in Tibet (the other two were the government and the aristocracy) that had to be eradicated in order to achieve "democratic reforms" and "socialist transformation." After 1959, the church and all its monasteries with the exception of a few of the largest and most famous, were indeed eradicated.

The Tibetan Buddhist church made a comeback, if only in exile, in the mid-1970s when Western spiritual seekers began showing up in Dharamsala, looking to meet lamas and the Dalai Lama himself. The Dalai Lama became far more accessible to such Westerners due to an official policy to transfer the Dharma to the West. It was hoped that this would also promote the Tibetan political cause, but most of the Westerners were more interested in their own "enlightenment" than in political issues, which they tended to consider beneath their lofty spiritual pursuits. Some of the Tibetan lamas who were active in teaching Western students, and who set up Buddhist centers in Western countries, also advised their students against political involvement. The situation became so bad that the Dalai Lama had to tell the lamas to stop advising their students against involvement in politics because of their conspicuous absence in political activism in support of Tibet.

Some Tibetans in Dharamsala complained that every Western hippie who came along could get an audience with the Dalai Lama, whereas Tibetans living there had greater difficulty. Jamyang Norbu writes that Tibetan society in exile was aware that the old political system had failed to sustain Tibet in the modern world and that a more democratic system had to be created in exile. An assembly of delegates was created that was democratically elected and a democratic constitution was written and adopted.

*The feeling was pervasive that our old institutions had failed us, and that it was vital to learn from the outside world. Though people's faith in Buddhism had not diminished, it was felt that the ultra-conservatism of the church and the apathy of the aristocracy had been largely responsible for the disaster that had befallen Tibet. The Dalai Lama himself acknowledged how much Buddhism in Tibet had become mired in arid rituals and ceremonies, and set about trying to put his house in order.*[11]

Norbu writes that an important development was the organization of the Tibetan Youth Congress in 1970, which he says was "consistently democratic, and sometimes progressive." However, the Government in Exile began immediately to undermine the TYC, which posed an alternative to itself and was unrestrained in its criticisms of the government:

*The arrival of Western travelers in Dharamsala did not help matters. . . . The influence of such people on Tibetan society was essentially obscurantist. They patronized everything traditional; the more magical, superstitious and primitive, the better. The forces of reaction in Tibetan society in exile were given a new lease of life. . . . Religious fundamentalism began to supersede any idea of learning from the West. . . . Through their constant disdain of Western rationalism, democracy and science, Western travelers effectively discouraged Tibetan curiosity about the West, and encouraged Tibetans to revert to their old and fatal way of dealing with reality by burying their heads in the sands of magic, ritual and superstition.*[12]

Western Buddhists were not the only supporters of the Dalai Lama's Middle Path policy, announced at Strasbourg, France, in 1988. However, those who advised him to give up independence and settle for autonomy were certainly idealists for whom the issue of Tibetan independence was not as important as it was to Tibetans and, at least one, Jimmy Carter, was a religious idealist of the Christian faith. The result of giving up the political issue was, of course, more official international support, and the Nobel Peace Prize, but the subsequent emphasis on cultural preservation redirected the Tibet issue to the promotion of Buddhism. Buddhism is certainly the most salient aspect of Tibetan culture, and one of the only aspects that it was thought could be preserved, both by its promotion within China as well as its transferal to the West. Efforts were made to promote Buddhism among the Chinese, with the hope that they would consequently become more sympathetic to the situation in Tibet. Dharamsala made great efforts to cite evidence of the spread of Buddhism in China, but could find very little evidence of how that had led to political support. Chinese Buddhists, like those in the West, were much more concerned with their own spiritual fate.

The role of Buddhism in Tibetan history and politics may be regarded as the key to whether or not Tibetan independence was ever anything more than a hopeless cause. Tibet's traditional system of government was distinguished by the union of politics and religion, or church and state. This system is extolled as appropriate for Tibet, without question or even without thought, by many Western supporters, who no doubt would adhere to the principle of separation of church and state in their own societies. For many, the unity of religion and politics was the very characteristic that made Tibet unique and worthy of their support. Perhaps they thought Tibetan Buddhism so different, or so pure, that its association with the state was harmless, or they assumed that the normal rules of politics did not apply to otherworldly Tibet.

Many were attracted to the issue because of Tibet's exotic reputation, as a sort of spiritual sanctuary in the world, or as the Dalai Lama himself proposed, a "Zone of Peace." Many were able to project their fantasies upon Tibet as a place immune to, or that ought to be immune to, the cares and troubles of the world. Tibet, after all, came into the consciousness of most Westerners as "Shangri-La," where the inhabitants did not age and were devoted to exclusively spiritual pursuits. The exotic nature of Tibetan Buddhism had much to do with this reputation, as did Tibet's traditional isolation and exclusion of all but Buddhist pilgrims. Tibet's otherworldly reputation was attractive to idealists but a potential hindrance for those, especially Tibetans, who wanted for Tibet only that it should be a normal country in a normal world. However much the role of religion in Tibet may have done to create an exotic and spiritual reputation, it can be shown to have done little to promote and much to have hindered Tibet's quest for an independent political existence.

Tibetan history is replete with examples of the anti-nationalist, universalist interests of the Buddhist establishment, in contrast to the more nationalist interests of the secular aristocracy. The question thus arises whether Tibet under a different form of government, or a different religion, might have maintained its independence against the ambitions of Inner Asian empires and, later, China, to control it. The essentially secular government of the Tibetan Empire has to be taken as an example of the possibility of a predominantly secular government throughout its history right up to the present.

Despite the claims of Buddhist historians of Tibet that Buddhism was firmly established during the empire period, that claim is rather tenuous given that Bon rites were celebrated as late as the 822 treaty with China, during the reign of Ralpacan, one of the most devoutly Buddhist of the Tibetan kings. Buddhism did not finally prevail over Bon so much by subjugation as by incorporation of its rites and ceremonies and by having a more institutional structure, including a literature acquired from India, and monasticism. In addition, while the nobility used Buddhism to consolidate and support its power, they, not the religious establishment, remained in control of government. In fact, it was the attempt by Ralpacan to give the monks a greater role in government that precipitated a backlash under Lang Darma. The Tibetan government during the empire may be said to have been predominantly secular. That empire, of course, unified Tibet and established Tibetan military power and political independence for the first and only time in Tibetan history. Buddhism, although it played a role in the creation of the Empire, also had a role in its demise.

Buddhist scholasticism, acquired from India, and monasticism, helped the Buddhist church reestablish itself in Tibet after the fall of the empire before any central state was able to do so. Eventually, the church acquired the role of the state with the help of foreign patrons. But what if the state had not completely collapsed, or if it had reestablished itself, perhaps only in Lhasa and Central Tibet? Would the history have then been different? Would a secular Tibetan regime have been able to resist the incursions of the Mongols or to have made an arrangement with them that preserved Tibetan independence?

The Mongols were attracted to the rituals and mysticism of Buddhism and they were familiar, like all subsequent overlords, with the advantage of using a religious establishment to prevent the rise of a more nationalistic secular nobility. However, if such a nobility was all they had to work with, would they have been content to have made some arrangement, perhaps a dependency relationship, that would have satisfied the Mongols' need for conquest and control? As Sakya Pandita said, the Mongols were immensely powerful and could easily have conquered Tibet. However, the Mongol need to control Tibet was primarily in order to control the Buddhist church, or various sects of that church, because of its influence over other Mongols. Absent that, Tibet offered little in terms of population to exploit and it posed little military threat to the Mongols. Might they have been content with a dependency relationship with a culturally similar secular Tibetan state?

The Tibetans themselves created an empire by strategic alliances with nomadic tribes of the Plateau, a pattern that was familiar to the Mongols. The Mongol Yuan dynasty lasted only a relatively brief time (1270–1368), in terms of Asian history, and the subsequent Ming was a domestic dynasty without the same ambitions in Inner Asia. If Tibet could have maintained a unified secular government during the Mongol Empire, perhaps even benefiting from a political alliance with the Mongols, then the tradition of a centralized Tibetan political administration would have been established on a firm basis.

Tibet could surely have maintained its independence during the Ming dynasty (1368–1644) against the Ming emperors whose only interests in Inner Asia were to prevent attacks upon their borders by the remaining Mongol tribes. All of this is speculative, of course, but there were no outside threats to Tibet that would have compromised Tibetan independence. Some attempts were made, in fact, particularly by the Pagmodrupa, to revive the secular traditions of the Tibetan Empire. A more difficult question arises with the advent of the Manchu Qing dynasty (1644–1912), another Inner Asian conquest dynasty that had ambitions similar to those of the Mongols and an increasing ability to carry them out.

The Manchu patronized Buddhism for political purposes but, unlike the Mongols, did not become Buddhist. It is clear that the Manchu Qing emperor considered the Fifth Dalai Lama to have made a submission in 1652 and that Tibet thereby became part of the Manchu Empire. However, the Manchu at that time seem to have had little interest in actually intervening or administering Tibet. They did so only after the Desi deceived them about the Dalai Lama's death, and Tibetans conspired with the Dzungar Mongols, the last Inner Asian tribe independent of Qing control. They showed no preference for ecclesiastical over secular rule in Tibet until the secular aristocracy began to show nationalistic opposition to Qing control. However, it is important to note that some of the secular nobles, usually those from far outside Lhasa, were loyal to the Qing. The Qing intervened again only to drive out the Gurkhas of Nepal, and finally adopted the tradition of ecclesiastical rule under the Dalai Lamas, but constrained by supervision by the ambans and limited by dividing the aristocracy from the church by prohibiting reincarnations being found in noble families.

So, had there been a well-established secular government in Tibet that made the same nominal submission to the Qing as did the Fifth Dalai Lama, might Tibetan history under the long rule of the Qing (268 years) been any different? Had Tibetans not conspired with the Mongols, had they not rebelled against the Qing, and had the Gurkhas not invaded or had the Tibetans been able to repulse the Gurkhas, then the answer is yes, perhaps. However, this answer depends on many factors not due to the flaws of ecclesiastical rule, which survived under the Qing only in a substantially symbolic role. It is hard to blame the Qing imposition of almost direct rule over Tibet on the flaws of the Cho-Yon system or the church's dependence upon foreign patrons. Secular rule might have left modern China with little justification to imagine that Tibet became a part of China during the Qing. Given the early ambitions of the Manchu Qing to control Inner Asia, it is hard to imagine that any Tibetan government could have avoided at least a nominal submission. The final analysis has to be that any Tibetan government, secular or ecclesiastical, sufficiently competent to avoid giving the Qing overlords any reason to send armies and to impose supervisory officials and make reforms to the Tibetan political system would have required less actual Qing control over Tibet and provided less of an argument for the Chinese to make that Tibet became a part of China during the Qing.

The British invaded Tibet in 1904 due to Tibet's refusal to allow any trade relations. Had there been a secular government in Tibet, that particular turn of history might never have happened. Tibet's isolation was not only due to the Buddhist church but to Qing China's attempt to keep foreign influences out of Tibet. Although it is generally thought that Tibet denied entry to all but Buddhists from neighboring countries, there were no such restrictions. Citizens of China, India, and Nepal could travel freely to Tibet whether they were Buddhist or not. It was only Europeans who were excluded, due to Tibetan and Chinese fears of European imperialism. Tibet under an independent secular government might have had reason to fear British imperialism but, in reality, the British were in no position to impose their authority over Tibet, even after Tibetans wished they would do so. Once Tibetans became familiar with the British, they realized that they could use British help in creating an army and establishing secular schools. However, the British were at the end of the expansionist phase of their empire and were unable to administer Tibet even if they had wanted to. In addition, the British had economic interests in China that would be jeopardized if they were too supportive of Tibet against Chinese ambitions.

The modernizing role of the British in Tibet was opposed at every step by the religious establishment. Had the church been less powerful, then British India might have played a more extensive role in Tibet and, at the withdrawal of the British from India in 1947, Tibet might have had better relations with independent India with which to counter China. It was the secular aristocracy that supported the British modernizations in Tibet in actuality so it can be assumed that they would have favored a greater role if they were dominant over the religious establishment. This would have placed Tibet in a much more advantageous position after the Second World War when some of the Tibetan aristocracy did indeed try to establish diplomatic relations with other countries. Had Tibet allowed the transit of military supplies to China requested by the Americans, then Tibet would predictably have had well-established international relations at the end of the war when borders were being redrawn and political statuses were being redefined.

Mongolia, which had less justification for an independent status than did Tibet, achieved independence after the war solely due to Soviet support. Nationalist China was under such American and international influence after the war that Chiang Kai-shek actually made a statement that Tibet might have the right to self-determination, although what he meant by that is unclear. Chiang, following Sun Yat-sen, had defined Tibetans as one of China's "Five Races," so he may have meant only that Tibet might "voluntarily" join with Republican China. Tibet's appeal to the United Nations, the United States, Britain, and India, when the Chinese Communists announced their intention to "liberate" Tibet, was rejected primarily because those states and organizations professed ignorance of Tibet's true political status. They would not have been in such ignorance and could not have used this as an excuse if they had previously established diplomatic relations with Tibet.

When the Chinese Communists invaded Tibet and the Dalai Lama fled to the border with India, he (or possibly a secular government leader) would not have been so much influenced by the religious establishment to return and acknowledge Chinese rule over Tibet. And he would not have made that decision based upon an archaic ritual of divination that Tibetans then, and to this day, resort to when making difficult political decisions. This exercise in alternative history is of course speculative, but it is not too unreasonable to suggest that Tibet under a secular government established as far back as the empire period, or actually at any time in Tibet's history, might have had a better chance to survive China's ambitions—which are the only imperialistic ambitions that ever really threatened Tibetan independence—and emerge in the modern world as an independent country. Tibet might still have its Dalai Lama and its monasteries that are so important to its exoticism, but the Buddhist church would not have been the government.

One has only to look to the history of Afghanistan to imagine how Tibetan history might have been different, were it an Islamic country.

This is not so far-fetched a possibility, given how Islam conquered the countries to the north and west of Tibet and wiped out Buddhism in India. Islam is a far more militant religion than Buddhism and has fueled the resistance of the Afghan people to any and all foreign invaders. My own experience of Afghanistan during two months there in 1971 was that the Afghan people loved nothing more than their guns. I saw Afghans lovingly polishing their Lee-Enfield and other types of rifles, the stocks of which were inlaid with silver filigree. Tibetans themselves were not as nonviolent as some of their Western Buddhist admirers imagine. Especially among the nomads and the Khampas, a rifle was an essential accoutrement and many Tibetans were very knowledgeable about the various types of weapons that made their way to Tibet. Monasteries had stockpiles of weapons that they had persuaded Tibetans to abandon for the sake of nonviolence, but with little effect on the total number of weapons in Tibet. The Chinese effort to confiscate weapons in Kham in 1956 was an important factor in the Khampas' decision to revolt.

As to the possibility of a small country (at least in population) remaining independent in an area of ambitious and expansionist larger neighbors, one has only to look at Switzerland. Similar to Tibet as a mountainous refuge, Switzerland has remained independent by means of diplomacy, nonalignment with any of its neighbors (except financially), and a strong military defense of its territory. And Switzerland has always had a secular government. Swiss territory is small and thus not that attractive to any of its neighbors, while Tibet's territory is vast in comparison, even though it is in large part uninhabitable. Tibetan territory was always attractive to the Chinese due to its sparse population and its reputed mineral resources. Tibetan territory would be harder to defend than that of Switzerland, especially against the overwhelming masses of Chinese. Nevertheless, Tibet would have had a better chance of defending itself had it recognized the threat from China earlier, and had it had a secular government without any reason for dependency on China and a strong military capable of defending the country.

I spent many hours sitting in the bars of Dharamsala with my Tibetan friends, speculating on the "what ifs" of Tibetan history. However, even the most secular of my friends were reluctant to criticize the role of the Buddhist church. This little essay has been an attempt to do so by a non-Tibetan who is (hopefully) somewhat immune to the vitriol that would certainly be heaped upon any Tibetan who might suggest such a thing. The failure of the Dalai Lama's Middle Path policy to produce any results with China has led Dharamsala and many Tibetans to become more intolerant of those who criticize that policy.

There was also a sentiment, encouraged by the Chinese, to believe that if only every Tibetan would support the Middle Path policy, then China would have no reason to doubt its sincerity. Chinese officials have openly said that they cannot trust the Dalai Lama's vow that he has given up independence when other Tibetans still call for independence or self-determination. However, Chinese duplicity is obvious in that they do not allow any of the autonomy promised by their own Regional Ethnic Autonomy law, upon which the Tibetan exiles' proposals are based. In addition, the current trend among Chinese nationality experts is toward restricting the signs and symbols of nationality identity as a means to create greater cultural conformity with Chinese society. One has only to look at China's coercive assimilationist policies in Xinjiang to see what its real policies and interests are. The conformist impulses in Tibetan exile society do not bode well for any who should have the temerity to suggest that the Tibetan political system itself was and is part of the problem.

There is a darker side to the confluence of religious idealism with political intolerance. The Dalai Lama is considered to be above criticism by Tibetans and most foreign supporters as well. Therefore, his Middle Path policy is also considered to be not really debatable. This is a hindrance to the development of real democracy in Tibetan society. Critics of the Dalai Lama's policy are condemned as not just wrong but as disloyal to the Dalai Lama and thus to the Tibetan cause itself.

Some of my Tibetan friends have experienced this conformity and intolerance to a far greater degree than I. My friends Jamyang Norbu, Tashi Tsering, Lhasang Tsering, and Pema Bhum founded the Amnye Machen Institute in Dharamsala (named for the holy mountain of Amdo), which published many important documents on Tibetan history. Jamyang tells the story that George Soros met with Amnye Machen in Dharamsala to discuss funding their efforts. This never happened, however, and many years later Jamyang found out why. As related by someone who worked at the Latse Institute, founded by Soros' daughter, Andrea, George Soros was dissuaded from separately funding Amnye Machin by Lodi Gyari, who argued that the young Tibetans involved there were indeed some of the most impressive intellectuals in Tibetan society, but that they had "narrow nationalist" interests, whereas the Dalai Lama's policy for the peaceful resolution of the Tibetan issue was more universalist, involving the integration of China within the democratic world and a vision for world peace. Lodi Gyari was notorious for insisting that all foreign support for Tibet should be controlled by Dharamsala, and himself, but "narrow nationalism" is the exact term also used by the Chinese Communists to condemn Tibetan independence in favor of the supposed benefits to be enjoyed by Tibetans by joining with China and the world in the socialist revolution.

This story illustrates the reality that the Dalai Lama and his government are still more universalist than nationalist, more concerned with the promotion of Buddhism and its ideals than Tibetan nationalism or Tibetan national identity. This is the traditional problem of the system of *Chosi Shungdrel*, or the system of unity of church and state, the founding principle of the Dalai Lama's government. The church was always more universalist than nationalist, more concerned with the promotion of Buddhism than in resisting foreign influence in Tibet. Rather than promote the archaic system of unity of church and state, which hinders the development of any legitimate form of democracy, Tibetans in exile should pursue the separation of church and state, the principle behind every working democracy in the world today.

The Dalai Lama could sometimes be less intolerant than his followers. In May 2018 at a conference of rangzen (independence) advocates, the Dalai Lama made an appearance in what appeared to be an act of reconciliation, his attendance alone absolving the rangzen activists of the accusation from other Tibetans of disloyalty to the Dalai Lama, to his policy, and thus to Tibet. Afterward, he reportedly asked his staff about the absence of Jamyang Norbu, who was actually there but whom the Dalai Lama had not seen. Being informed that Jamyang actually was there, the Dalai Lama requested that Jamyang meet with him the next day. Usually, it is Tibetans and anyone else who request audiences with the Dalai Lama, not the other way around. Jamyang had done so, but had been refused by the Dalai Lama's staff. At the audience, the Dalai Lama attempted to convince Jamyang of the potential of the Middle Path policy, based mostly upon its acceptance by world leaders but without acknowledging that they did so mostly for convenience to themselves, since it required them to do nothing but call for dialogue and preservation of Tibetan culture and did not involve offending the Chinese by demanding anything more, like self-determination for Tibet. He also said that his policy was based upon the fact of Tibet's independence before the Chinese invasion. Jamyang pointed out that he and other rangzen activists had done much to authenticate Tibet's former independence. The Dalai Lama's conciliatory action in meeting with the rangzen activists and with Jamyang personally did much to alleviate the animosity that had previously prevailed between the two camps in Tibetan politics.

The popular Tibetan saying that "Tibetans are betrayed by their hopefulness, the Chinese by their suspiciousness" really means that Tibetans are betrayed by their faith. Faith is the antithesis of reason; therefore, faith-based decision-making does not lead to reasonable outcomes. Some of the Tibetan aristocracy attempted to introduce rational decision-making into Tibetan politics, but were opposed by the religious establishment. When the British invaded Tibet in 1904, the Tibetans who resisted them had perfect faith in their amulets, until they were cut down by British bullets. When the Chinese invasion was imminent, the Tibetan government resorted to prayers and rituals to protect Tibet. Such unrealistic faith in the efficacy of Buddhist rituals and protections is what is meant by the saying that Tibetan hopefulness, meaning naïveté, is what has betrayed its people and the country itself.

Similar hopefulness that the Chinese will see the advantages of allowing real autonomy in Tibet is the source for support for the Middle Path policy. Many Tibetans and their international supporters wonder why the Chinese can't see that genuine autonomy in Tibet would be better for China than continual Tibetan discontent. They say that the Dalai Lama is the solution to the Tibet issue, since his presence in Tibet would result in the happiness and contentment of the Tibetan people. However, the Chinese have shown that they do not care about the happiness of the Tibetan people. They care only about the territory of Tibet and that it should remain firmly a part of China. They know very well that autonomy preserves culture and culture leads to nationalism and nationalism leads to separatism, which they are bound to prevent. Tibetans are betrayed by their faith to believe that China actually cares about the happiness of the Tibetan people and will therefore someday see the advantages to allowing the sort of autonomy proposed by the Dalai Lama's Middle Path policy.

All the foregoing having been said, it has to be acknowledged that Tibet would not be such an attractive issue and Tibetans themselves such an attractive people without Buddhism. Many Westerners are attracted to the rich religious philosophy of Buddhism and, certainly, Tibetan exoticism, also an attraction, would hardly exist without Buddhism. Few Americans were inspired by Afghan resistance to the Soviet invasion, while at the same time, the already almost-hopeless issue of Tibet aroused a great deal of support. Anyone who knows Tibetans, myself very much included, knows of their innocence, honesty, compassion, openness, and the surprising sophistication and cosmopolitanism among many. It is sometimes said that the Dalai Lama institution is the best thing and the worst thing about Tibet—the best due to the unifying effect of a common religion, rule by the church, and the Dalai Lama's reputation which evokes so much support in the outside world; and the worst because of the stagnating effect on social and political development in Tibet and on the society in exile. The same may be said for the role of Buddhism itself in Tibetan history.

# AFTERWORD

It is my hope in publishing this collection of writings that they might contribute to the history of Tibet and the international Tibetan political issue. Although many scholars and activists (I consider myself a bit of both) have been inspired by the story of Tibet, few have had the opportunity to pursue a career in the subject. Tibetan history and politics are almost entirely absent in academia. I have known many who would have loved to have made a career of Tibetan academics or activism, but who have had to drop the issue due to lack of paying positions. I consider myself exceedingly fortunate that the pursuit of my passion actually resulted in a career.

China has pursued its goals in Tibet with almost total impunity, having sought to make Tibet an integral and inalienable part of China with little regard to the wishes of Tibetans. True, in the early 1950s, when China was pursuing a United Front policy of alliance with the still-existent Tibetan upper class and traditional leadership, Tibetan opinions were at least ostensibly respected. However, given that the Chinese Communists' announced policy was for "democratic reforms" and "socialist transformation," the Tibetan elite had to realize that it was cooperating in its own demise. The Chinese Communists' nationality policies aimed to convince all but the elite that their class interests should prevail over those of nationality. The elite would be gradually dispossessed of their leadership positions as well as their wealth with the support of those who were promised that they would get their positions and possessions. To imagine that this scenario was feasible, the Chinese had to dismiss the issue of Tibetan nationalism, which their Marxist doctrine told them they could convince the Tibetan lower classes was not as important as their class interests.

The Chinese Communists' dismissal of the nationality issue was based not only upon Marxist doctrine but also the belief that Tibet was and had "always" been a part of China. They thus had absolutely no doubt about the legitimacy of their plans for the incorporation of Tibet and the transformation of Tibetan society. However, the Chinese belief that Tibet had always been a part of China was actually only a never-realized ambition, while Tibetans imagined themselves independent of Chinese rule, whether they acknowledged the authority of Lhasa or only their own traditional leadership. The Chinese Communists thought that Tibetans, or at least the lower classes who would benefit from their "democratic reforms," could be convinced to abandon their allegiance to their traditional authorities in favor of the benefits they were promised under Chinese socialism.

To say that the Chinese underestimated the strength of Tibetan nationalism is an understatement. Because the Chinese denied the legitimacy of Tibetan nationalism, they had to ascribe any Tibetan resistance to change to the intrigues of the former upper classes or to foreign imperialism. The history of China's role in Tibet is defined by this denial of Tibetan nationalism, or indeed, any legitimate reason for Tibetan nationalism, since the Chinese firmly believed in the legitimacy of Chinese sovereignty over Tibet. China has thus been dependent upon the class argument to justify all its policies in Tibet.

A major campaign in the Chinese transformation of Tibet was to make class divisions among Tibetans and then convince them to pursue their class interests, with the help of their Chinese big brothers, against their own traditional leadership. However, Chinese activists' impatience to achieve "democratic reforms" in the parts of Kham outside the TAR in 1956 resulted in revolt there of individuals of all classes who still identified with their nationality over class. Mao's impatience in 1958 to achieve socialist transformation led to the abandonment of the United Front, the condemnation of upper-class leaders as "local nationalists," and the precipitous and violent imposition of simultaneous democratic reforms and communization in Amdo, thus also resulting in revolt there.

The spread of the revolt to Central Tibet, where Mao had only recently promised no reforms for the next six years or even longer, was predictable. However, Mao was apparently not too concerned by the possibility of revolt, given his belief that the revolt of the Tibetan upper classes could be easily repressed, since they represented only their own class interests, thus giving China the freedom to pursue the socialist transformation of all of Tibet without any further resistance.

Mao even declared that he would not be too upset if the Dalai Lama were to escape into exile, thus allowing China to operate in Tibet with impunity. Thus, when the Dalai Lama did escape, he was (after several years of pretense that he had been abducted) declared a traitor to his country, meaning China. That both the Dalai Lama and many Tibetans disagreed about what was the country to which they should be loyal is the essence of the political issue of Tibet. Chinese repression of Tibetan resistance was characterized by an absolute lack of any sympathy for Tibetans' beliefs that they were not part of China. Tibetans' resistance was denounced as "treason" against the Chinese Motherland. Tibetans who tried to flee from Kham and Amdo to the TAR were often massacred, as if flight to what the Chinese claimed was just another part of China was also equivalent to treason against the Chinese state.

Tibetans who were captured and imprisoned after the 1959 revolt were treated as criminals, sometimes just for having been Tibetan government officials with whom the policy until that time had been to cooperate. Tibetans in prison died in great numbers, due to the treatment they received, or from starvation due to the famine that resulted from Mao's misguided and disastrous "Great Leap Forward." Tibetans in prisons and labor camps were not allowed to suffer in peace but were subjected to relentless thought reform meant to coerce them into the belief that they were indeed traitors to China rather than patriots to their own country.

It has been said that prison literature, or the accounts of those who have survived imprisonment by a state, is the most revealing about the character of that state. By all accounts, the worst psychological aspect of Chinese prisons was the pressure to "reform one's thoughts." Prisoners could not just quietly try to survive their imprisonment, they had to admit that they were guilty and that the state was fully justified in imprisoning them. For Tibetans, this meant that they had to confess that they were guilty of treason against China because what they had thought was patriotism to Tibet was actually a crime. As Tibetan prison literature reveals, resistance against thought reform was virtually impossible.

Tibetan prison and resistance literature is the most evocative about the post-revolt politics of Tibet. I begin this book with a sample of such accounts for that reason. What these accounts reveal is that Tibetans defended their country against what they considered a foreign invasion and were condemned as traitors to a country with which they did not identify for doing so. Those imprisoned for their resistance to the imposition of Chinese rule were coerced to confess that they were mistaken in their belief that their country was independent and made to declare their gratitude to the Chinese Communist Party for correcting them. It is obvious from many of the accounts that only a few survived their imprisonment; therefore, we are fortunate to have as many such accounts as we do.

Tibetan resistance and prison accounts alone tell the story of recent history better than any outside observer can possibly hope to do. However, there is also a story to be told of the rather remarkable international interest in and support for Tibet evidenced especially after Tibet opened to foreigners in the early 1980s. Having been one of the first to travel to Tibet and to spend an extended amount of time there, I believe my own experience also tells something about the appeal of the Tibetan story. That experience was significant to me because it led to a forty-year career in Tibetan studies. I was deeply involved in the international Tibet issue in those years when there was actually an optimism that international pressure could convince the Chinese to improve their treatment of Tibetans and respect some of their rights to cultural autonomy that had been promised. Unfortunately, the exact opposite was the result, as both Tibetan resistance and international interest convinced the Chinese that Tibetan autonomy and the consequent survival of Tibetan culture inevitably led to a perpetuation of the separatist issue.

Sino-Tibetan negotiations in the early 1980s were aimed at a return of the Dalai Lama, thus, in the Chinese mind, resolving the final issue of Tibet. Chinese policy in Tibet hardened after the demonstrations of

1987–1989 and Tiananmen in June 1989. The affair of the selection of the reincarnation of the Panchen Lama in 1995 revealed that China was no longer interested in cooperation with the Dalai Lama and intended to choose its own Fifteenth Dalai Lama when the time came.

Tibetan hopes were revived by the series of Sino-Tibetan talks between 2002 and 2010, but the history of those meetings reveals that the motive of the Chinese side was solely to counter international criticism with a pretense of willingness to dialogue and compromise. China made absolutely no compromises and maintained throughout that there was no issue of Tibet about which it should negotiate. Even the pretense of a willingness to actually negotiate ended after the Tibetan Uprising of 2008 and the Chinese rejection of the Memorandum on Tibetan Autonomy presented by Dharamsala after the Olympics.

Since 2008, China's policy has only hardened further as its economic power has grown along with its ability to ignore international criticism. There seems to be little or no criticism of Tibet policy within the upper levels of the Chinese government. Chinese tourism to Tibet, especially since Tibetan protests have been thoroughly quelled, is increasingly a part of the policy to assimilate Tibetan culture. The numbers of foreign tourists have dwindled while Tibet is turned into something like an ethnic theme park for Chinese. Even the more than 150 self-immolations have not impressed the Chinese people nor have they aroused much of an international response. The Chinese state seems at last free to act in Tibet with total impunity.

Just as there was nothing to be done about China's abrogation of Hong Kong's autonomy, except for sympathetic countries to offer asylum to those who fear persecution, there is apparently nothing anyone can do about Tibet. Tibetans will never give up, of course, but Tibet's fate as an integral part of China seems determined. Current opinion among Han Chinese nationality experts is that national separatist issues can only be solved with less autonomy, not more, even to the extent of eliminating nationality distinctions and autonomous status altogether.

Even a change in the character of the Chinese regime offers little hope, since any future Chinese leader who thinks it might be a good idea to offer more autonomy to Tibetans, or to Uighurs or to the people of

Hong Kong, has only to be reminded that more autonomy has always led to more nationalistic feelings and thus a perpetuation, not a resolution, of separatist issues. I am often irritated by the naïveté of many Tibetan supporters who express wonder why China cannot see that the Dalai Lama is the solution to the Tibet issue, not the problem. They wonder why, if China cares about the happiness of the Tibetan people, it does not talk to the Dalai Lama. The answer is that China does not care about the happiness of the Tibetan people; it only cares that they should be obedient and subservient. Ultimately, what China cares about is not the Tibetan people at all but their territory, which it coveted for centuries before being able to gain actual control and which it is not about to give up control over in any way or by any measure.

Some well-meaning foreigners have suggested to Chinese leaders that they should talk to the Dalai Lama, as if the Tibet issue is just a little misunderstanding about the Dalai Lama's intentions that could be cleared up with a friendly chat. However, China has defined Tibet as one of its "core" or existential issues, not a misunderstanding with the exiled Dalai Lama. The Tibet issue is a fundamental conflict between nations about the nature of sovereignty that can only be resolved by the elimination or absorption or assimilation of one of those nations.

I do not doubt the sincerity of any of the international Tibet supporters, but it seems that some have read all the books about Tibetan Buddhism and none about the history or politics of China or Tibet. Idealism is a wonderful thing, but realism operates in politics. A certain amount of idealism is surely a prerequisite for becoming a Tibet activist, but one has to accept historical and political realities. Most foreigners cannot imagine the ruthlessness with which China is prepared to deal with any opposition in Tibet.

The Chinese Communists' "peaceful liberation" of Tibet finally achieved China's ambition to actually control Tibet. Despite the fact that the Chinese invasion and annexation of Tibet wasn't actually peaceful or a liberation, this was one of the Chinese Communists' proudest success stories. Their pride and optimism are reflected in the often-attempted effort to revive the "Old Tibet Spirit" that once prevailed among Chinese cadres who imagined that they would be greeted as liberators in Tibet, or at least that resistance would come only from the upper classes, who could be bought off with the United Front policy. They imagined that after suitable education, the lower classes would have the same ambitions as the Chinese to achieve democratic reforms and socialist transformation. Their Marxist doctrine told them that Tibetan nationalism, like all nationalisms, was a phenomenon exclusively of the "bourgeois-democratic" period of economic history and political development, which Tibet had not yet experienced, but which Leninist doctrine had determined could be skipped over altogether, with the assistance of outside "proletarian activists," meaning the Chinese, in order to achieve socialism. Nationalism, whether Chinese or Tibetan, would disappear in favor of "proletarian internationalism."

The Chinese Communists' dismissal of nationalism was epitomized by Mao's saying that the national issue is, in essence, a class issue. What this means, as derived from Marx, is that class identity always ultimately prevails over national identity. Some members of the Tibetan lower classes did indeed support the Chinese, mostly since they were promised that they would inherit the wealth and power of the formerly rich. Those whom the Chinese promised would become the "masters of their own fate" were the lower classes, not the formerly upper classes who would be co-opted, dispossessed, or repressed. Thus, the Chinese expected no resistance from the lower classes who were to become the ultimate benefactors of China's "liberation" of Tibet.

That the Chinese Communists underestimated the power of Tibetan nationalism was demonstrated by the fact that much of the lower class participated along with the upper classes in revolt against Chinese reforms and imposition of their control. The Chinese came into Tibet expecting to be welcomed as liberators of the Tibetans from exploitation by their own upper classes as well as by foreign imperialism but found that they themselves were regarded as conquerors and imperialists. They were taught that Tibet was already a part of China but were surprised to find that Tibetans did not agree.

As Tibetan resistance was aroused by Chinese "reforms" of Tibetan society, Chinese sentiments hardened toward the Tibetans until, after only nine years of the Chinese occupation of Tibet, Mao was welcoming a revolt in order to finally gain total control and achieve a final resolution of the issue. Even after the revolt and the deaths, imprisonment, and flight into exile of hundreds of thousands of Tibetans, Mao and the CCP thought that the remainder of Tibetans could be convinced or coerced to support the Chinese in their efforts to control and transform Tibet. The Chinese still dismissed nationalism as a factor, even after the revolt had demonstrated that it was a huge factor for Tibetans.

Chinese policy in Tibet has consistently denied the reality of Tibetan nationalism. The Tibet issue for the Chinese has to be solely about class since the alternative would invalidate all their justifications for the imposition of Chinese rule over Tibet. China has thus never been able to deal realistically with the political issue of Tibet. Contemporary Chinese nationality experts' attempts to eliminate all nationality distinctions altogether is the ultimate manifestation of that refusal to acknowledge the reality. This is why China has found that it cannot allow any meaningful semblance of even cultural autonomy in Tibet, because culture is associated with nationality, and nationality with political separatism.

China's problems in Tibet are entirely of its own making and can only be resolved by the final elimination of Tibetan nationalism, which means the elimination of all aspects of Tibetan identity and culture with nationalist implications, which means almost all aspects. Chinese confidence in the ultimate success of their policy is undiminished, however, because since the time of Mao, it has had the resources in terms of power, population, and ruthless determination to overwhelm Tibetan resistance.

The historical, political, legal, and moral arguments such as I have made will therefore have no significance to the Chinese, who now think they have no option but to eliminate Tibetan identity altogether, or at least to turn it into a subservient, abject form consisting only of song and dance and other innocuous forms that are comfortable and unthreatening to Chinese tourists. Having repressed almost all resistance in Tibet and having coerced almost all countries to deny meetings of their government leaders with the Dalai Lama, the Chinese apparently think that they are almost at their final goal. They betray no lack of confidence in their policies and they show no willingness to acknowledge any faults that would lead them to discuss the issue with anyone, whether the Dalai

Lama or foreign governments. The fate of Tibet, as far as the Chinese are concerned, is determined, and that fate is to be an integral part of China with no separate ethnic or national identity that would make Tibet, or the sentiments of the Tibetan people, an issue with which China should have to deal, not least with the Tibetans themselves.

None of the scenarios by means of which Tibet might regain its independence of the sort that I used to sit around Dharamsala with my friends and spin out has transpired, of course. And the chances have not improved, as China's economic and political power has constantly increased, along with its ability to ignore foreign criticism. Perhaps only the scenario of the total collapse of China's government holds any possibility for Tibet. And even that is increasingly implausible.

Events in Tibet have resulted in a consistent hardening of Chinese policies there. Chinese confidence in the ultimate solution to the Tibet issue, by means of repression, colonization, and assimilation, has only grown over the years, despite certain setbacks. Whenever a lessening of restrictions on Tibetan autonomy has been attempted, the result has been a revival of Tibetan culture and nationalism, after which the Chinese have had to abandon all their promises to allow any significant degree of Tibetan autonomy.

Chinese repression in Tibet is merciless, as some Chinese officials have openly declared in righteous indignation at Tibetans' lack of gratitude to the CCP and loyalty to the PRC. But perhaps more insidious than the disincentives for resistance are the incentives for loyalty. How much would it cost, after all, to buy off the loyalty of six million Tibetans? China now has the means and certainly the willingness to do so.

Tibetans and the world are constantly reminded not to "hurt the feelings of the Chinese people." The threat implied in this is obvious. It is a reminder to the world of the danger of offending 1.3 billion people. To Tibetans it is a reminder that there are 200 Chinese for every Tibetan. The obvious solution to the issue for China is to swamp Tibet with Chinese, which is increasingly possible. Ultimately, a little problem of only six million Tibetans in a sea of Chinese is manageable. The territory of Tibet, not the people, has always been the object of China's ambition anyhow.

As the hopes for any resolution to the Tibet issue that would allow for the survival of Tibetan culture have dwindled, the Dalai Lama has aged, and Tibetan desperation has increased, Dharamsala has nevertheless clung to its Middle Path policy with religious intensity. It has encouraged and even dictated conformity to that policy out of a misguided and deluded hope that if Tibetans could convince China that all Tibetans, without exception, had given up the campaign for independence, China would then allow the autonomy promised in its own laws. There is evidence that China itself has suggested to Dharamsala, by complaining that it was impossible to accept the Dalai Lama's position while other Tibetans in exile were not in agreement, that it should curtail the independence advocates. However, the duplicity of the Chinese was revealed by their contention that the existence of the Tibetan Government in Exile was itself an example of Tibetan nonacceptance of Chinese sovereignty over Tibet and the legitimacy of the already supposedly autonomous government in the TAR.

Despite China's obvious motive to eliminate Tibetan exile criticism and even the political organization of the Dharamsala government, some Tibetan leaders have indeed discouraged demonstrations against Chinese officials during their travels abroad and have tried to ostracize and curtail the activities of independence advocates. Conformity to the Middle Path has become a test of loyalty to the Dalai Lama himself and there have been some unfortunate instances of Tibetans in positions at important advocacy organizations abroad, even those founded and funded by foreign governments, being purged for lack of sufficient fealty to the Middle Path policy. Even foreign supporters who cast doubt on the Middle Path policy have found themselves ostracized. This enforced conformity to a policy that is very convenient to foreign governments but that has shown no evidence of success or potential for success has demoralized both Tibetans and their foreign supporters.

The statements from the Chinese government, particularly those in its White Papers, leave no doubt that China will not negotiate on the basis of the Middle Path policy. China has declared repeatedly that it will not negotiate with anyone about the nonexistent "issue" of Tibet. Chinese policies under Xi Jinping to assimilate the Uighurs and other minorities in Xinjiang to "Chinese socialist culture" leave little doubt about Chinese attitudes toward minority nationality autonomy. The employment of coercive assimilation tactics, including what are equivalent to concentration camps where minorities are confined and indoctrinated with Chinese propaganda, has led foreign critics to label Chinese policy there as "cultural genocide." Such is the severity of Chinese repression in Xinjiang that Tibet is almost forgotten, even though assimilation policies in Tibet are comparable with the exception of the use of concentration camps. Tibetan monasteries, rightly identified by the Chinese as incubators of Tibetan nationalism, serve as convenient sites where a concentrated population may be indoctrinated.

China's most recent abrogation of its promises to allow autonomy in Hong Kong is indicative of the fate of all such autonomous systems in current CCP policy. The One Country, Two Systems policy in Hong Kong was actually based upon the Seventeen Point Agreement and the system of National Regional Autonomy intended to be implemented in Tibet. Those Tibetans and others who predicted that all such promises were duplicitous or, at best, incompatible with the Chinese Communists' "democratic centralism" have been vindicated by the fate of autonomy in Hong Kong. The temporary nature of such promises and the ultimate goal of centralized control has been repeatedly revealed by Chinese explanations that Tibet did not need any sort of One Country, Two Systems formula—as supposedly implemented in Hong Kong and promised to Taiwan—because Tibet had already "returned to the Motherland" while Taiwan had not yet. Those Middle Path proponents who always cited Hong Kong as an example of the possibility of any sort of autonomy in China have now been disappointed.

China's expansionist policy in the South China Sea has made the preposterous claim that an ocean is part of the "territory" of China, the equivalent of an inland lake. The PRC has adamantly maintained its rather outrageous posture there, rejecting international court rulings that its position is in violation of the international law of the sea, thus creating one of the world's most volatile scenes of possible conflict with other states surrounding the South China Sea as well as all those that support the freedom of navigation in international waters. China's demands that

Taiwan must, like Tibet and Hong Kong, "return to the Motherland," are another source of international tension and potential conflict.

China has been in a confrontational mood in regard to all such irredentist issues, thus rendering the potential for conciliation on the issue of Tibet, an issue regarded as already resolved, almost nonexistent. This confrontational mood is popular and not just a manifestation of the politics of the CCP or its current leader Xi Jinping. Chinese nationalism has been fostered by the CCP, of course, particularly in its "hundred years of imperialist domination" propaganda, which has made the Chinese people believe that they have been held back from their rightful place in the world and that their past glory as the world's foremost civilization must be restored. The Chinese government and people may once have cared what the outside world thought about such issues as Tibet, but they clearly no longer do so. Thus, whatever slight potential there may have been for any "resolution" of the Tibet issue favorable to Tibetans has faded from sight and China seems on a course of confrontation with the world rather than having any concern or sympathies for such a minor issue as Tibet. Tibet's tragic fate thus seems decided, at least by China and its people.

The Tibet issue has faded from international news even as the situation there gets worse. China's assimilation strategy, particularly in regard to language, has become more blatant with the prohibitions on private Tibetan language classes and the adoption of Chinese language as the medium in almost all schooling. Tibetan Buddhist statues have been destroyed in acts of state-supported intolerance that can be compared to the Taliban's destruction of the Buddhist statues at Bamiyan in Afghanistan. International criticism of Chinese human rights abuses on the occasion of the 2022 Winter Olympics in Beijing failed to mention the role of the March 2008 Tibetan Uprising as the origin of similar protests surrounding the 2008 Summer Olympics. The 2008 Tibetan protests were an important stimulant to what has now become a virulent Chinese popular nationalism that is both anti-American, partly because of US criticisms in regard to Tibet, as well as anti-Tibetan. Tibet has played a large role in the development of Chinese policies toward other "separatist" issues such as Hong Kong and Taiwan and in regard to the issues about centralism versus autonomy in general.

Tibet has been and remains a far more important issue to China than most outsiders realize. China will do whatever is necessary to retain control over the vast territory of the Tibetan Plateau. To Westerners, on the other hand, Tibet retains some of its mystical or spiritual character due to what can be called the Shangri-La Syndrome. Tibet is not taken as seriously as other international issues because of an otherworldly image of Tibet as an imaginary spiritual paradise, even given recent political history, and of Tibetans as all lamas and holy beings for whom worldly problems are not important. The issue of Tibet can be said to be simply that Tibet and Tibetans should be thought of as part of this world and their fate under Chinese rule should be regarded as worthy of international outrage.

Tibetans received no sympathy from the Chinese government or people when they expressed their discontent during the 2008 Uprising, quite the opposite. There was some international interest, but it was quickly defused by Chinese promises to dialogue with the exile Tibetans. Dharamsala contributed to the downplaying of the issue by buying into Chinese promises that they would dialogue after the Olympics if Tibetans would allow them to go forward without protests. Many Chinese were incensed that Tibetans dared to embarrass China before the Olympics, which were a major propaganda exercise about the greatness of China and its emergence on the world stage. Popular Chinese nationalism against the Tibetans was particularly aroused by international protests against the International Torch Relay, another blatant propaganda exercise. In desperation to find some means for protest, Tibetans, mostly monks and nuns, began self-immolating. More than 150 Tibetan self-immolations have aroused precious little international concern and absolutely no sympathy among the Chinese.

Tibetans in exile have reverted to coercing conformity to the Middle Path policy and prohibiting criticism of the Dalai Lama or his "legacy," presumably including his Middle Path policy. Tibetans in exile have thus damaged their own claim to have created democracy in Tibetan society, one of their strongest points of contrast with the pseudo-democracy inside Tibet. Many Tibetans, the Dalai Lama included, continue to naïvely believe that if the Chinese people could just see the justice of the Tibetan cause, they would do something to improve conditions in Tibet and to allow Tibetan culture to survive. The Dalai Lama continues to maintain that more Chinese are becoming interested in Buddhism and that this will eventually alter their perceptions of the Tibet issue. However, most of the Chinese with whom the Dalai Lama comes into contact and who donate money to Tibetan lamas are from Taiwan. Those few Chinese Buddhists from the mainland, like most Western Buddhists, appear mostly interested in their own spiritual welfare and scrupulously avoid the political issue.

Tibetans within Tibet have seemingly exhausted their options to alter the conditions of Chinese rule over Tibet or even to express their discontent. China now seems confident that neither Tibetan protests nor international criticisms can affect its policies in Tibet. And Chinese policy is increasingly evidently aimed at cultural assimilation of Tibet and Tibetans. There is apparently little that Tibetans or the outside world can do to preserve Tibetan culture against the relentless Chinese determination to eliminate what it regards as the separatist threat posed by an autonomous Tibetan culture and national identity.

This seemingly disparate collection of memoirs and musings is offered in the hope that it may shed some light on Tibet's history and the internationalization of the Tibetan political issue. The magnitude of the injustice imposed upon Tibetans by the Chinese can be judged by the accounts and experiences of Tibetans as well as by the international support that their cause has been capable of arousing. By combining excerpts from the memoirs of Tibetans and my own memoir on my involvement with the issue, I have attempted to tell the story of Tibet from the points of view of Tibetans themselves as well as from the viewpoint of one inspired by their political cause. My speculations on Tibet's political fate are offered with respect to all Tibetans and their international supporters who have fought for the cause of Tibet and with the hope that I will not offend too much those who have devoted their lives to the struggle for Tibet's cultural and political survival.

I do not like to be in the position of predicting Tibet's fate. However, I am confident in making the prediction that any hopes for the survival of Tibetan culture that depend upon the benevolence toward Tibet of any Chinese government, the current one or any in the foreseeable future, as the Dalai Lama's Middle Path policy does, are doomed to failure. Tibetans cannot hope for any sympathy from the Chinese people either, who demonstrated after the Tibetan Uprising of 2008 that anti-Tibetan sentiments are now a part of modern Chinese nationalism. China has exploited Tibetans' unrealistic hopes in the past to defuse Tibetan exile and international criticism, while policies aimed at the elimination of all of those rights that Tibetans might hope for are steadily implemented. This is despite the fact that Tibetans themselves acknowledge that unrealistic hopefulness is their worst national characteristic.

Most Tibetans, of course, will never reconcile with the idea that China must be allowed the last word on the fate of their country. I agree, but the only field of endeavor in which I can see opportunity is in the interpretation of Tibetan history. This is the field to which I have devoted my own career and I recommend it to anyone, Tibetan or non-Tibetan, who wishes to play a role, however small, in the opposition to Chinese lies and propaganda in regard to the history and reality of Tibet. China may indeed accomplish its ambition to turn Tibet into a part of China distinguished only by its altitude, but China should not be allowed to control the interpretation of Tibetan history and deny the reality of Tibetan national identity.

# Notes

## Chapter 1

1. *Tibet Under Chinese Communist Rule: A Compilation of Refugee Statements, 1958–1975* (Dharamsala: Information and Publicity Office of His Holiness the Dalai Lama, 1976), 13.

2. Personal interview, Dharamsala, 1989.

3. Naktsang Nulo, *My Tibetan Childhood: When Ice Shattered Stone* (Durham: Duke University Press, 2014).

4. Personal interview, Dharamsala, 1989.

5. Markham was a part of what the Chinese KMT had claimed as the province of Sikang, following on the Chinese invasion from Sichuan in response to the British invasion of Tibet in 1904. Markham and Chamdo became part of what the Chinese Communists called the Chamdo Liberation Committee, which was separate from what became the TAR until 1955. The Chinese entered Central Tibet only after the conclusion of the Seventeen Point Agreement in May 1951.

6. The CCP set up Political Consultative Committees in minority areas to ostensibly provide for joint administration by the CCP and the national minorities themselves. The national Chinese People's Political Consultative Committee ostensibly provided for United Front rule that included political parties other than the CCP as well as the national minorities under the overall leadership of the CCP.

7. Markham and Jomda are the eastern-most districts of what eventually became the TAR.

8. The Chinese always made the deprivation of political rights a part of sentencing of prisoners and labeling of reactionaries and counterrevolutionaries, in accordance with their ideology of "people's democracy," but it is difficult to see what political rights any Tibetans actually had. Certainly few, if any, Tibetans complained about being deprived of any such theoretical rights.

9. *Tibet Under Chinese Communist Rule*, 29.

10. The valuable articles looted from Tibetan monasteries at the same time were also taken from Tibet to Loyang.

11. *Tibet Under Chinese Communist Rule*, 29.

12. Personal interviews, Lhasa, 1982, 1985; Dharamsala, 1989.

13. This letter, or at least this sentiment, may have influenced the Dalai Lama to accept the Seventeen Point Agreement and return to Lhasa rather than seek refuge in India since one of the reasons he cited for returning was to protect the Tibetan people from the Chinese.

14. Personal interview, Dharamsala, 1989.

15. Children of poor families from all parts of Tibet seem to have been mostly sent to the provincial minority nationality institutes in Sichuan and Qinghai and particularly to the large school at Xiangang near Xian in Shanxi Province.

16. Tsering Dorje Gashi, *New Tibet: Memoirs of a Graduate of the Peking Institute of National Minorities* (Dharamsala: Information Office of His Holiness the Dalai Lama, 1980).

17. Personal interview, Dharamsala, 1990.

18. Drapchi was originally built as a Chinese Army post when the Chinese occupied Lhasa in 1910–1912. It later became the headquarters of the Tibetan Army. It was turned into a prison after the 1959 revolt and remains one of the largest prisons in the Lhasa valley.

19. Tsongkhapa was the founder of Ganden Monastery in 1409 and the Gelugpa, or "reformed" sect that later (1642) under the Dalai Lamas became the ruling authority in Tibet. His body was interred in a chorten, or Buddhist stupa, at Ganden, east of Lhasa.

20. Ling Gesar is the subject of an epic poem recited from memory about Gesar, the ruler of the kingdom of Ling in northern Kham, about 1050. Hor, which originally meant Mongol, is now used to refer to all of the nomads of eastern and northern Tibet.

21. Namtsho, "Sky Lake," northwest of Lhasa is the largest lake in central Tibet. Markham is in western Kham, now on the border between TAR and Sichuan. What this means is that virtually all the populated areas of the TAR were involved in the revolt.

22. In December 1978 Gyalo Thondup, the Dalai Lama's elder brother, met with Deng Xiaoping in Beijing and was promised that the exile government could send a series of delegations to Tibet to see conditions for themselves. This promise was based upon his belief that conditions were far better than the reality and would impress the exiles and convince them to return along with the Dalai Lama, thus finally resolving the issue of Tibet. The result was a disaster as the delegations were mobbed by Tibetans with pleas to deliver them from the oppression of the Chinese.

23. I was in Lhasa in the summer and fall of 1982 where I heard the 85 percent number constantly repeated and saw buses of Chinese leaving from the #2 Guest House on their way back to China.

24. "Doing a round" of the Jokhang, or circumambulation (*kora*), was a Tibetan Buddhist practice for gaining religious merit.

25. Hu Yaobang's death in April 1989 led to the Tiananmen protest demonstrations of June and the subsequent massacre.

26. Dhondub Choedon, *Life in the Red Flag People's Commune* (Dharamsala: Information Office of His Holiness the Dalai Lama, 1978).

27. Rinbur Tulku's biography was published in Tibetan in Dharamsala in 1989. It has been translated and not yet published in its entirety by Matthew Akseter. Several excerpts,

including his experiences in the Cultural Revolution, were published in André Alexander, *The Temples of Lhasa* (Chicago: Serindia, 2005).

28. See Warren W. Smith Jr., *China's Tibet?: Autonomy or Assimilation* (Lanham, MD: Rowman & Littlefield, 2008), 129.

29. Rinbur Tulku, *The Search for Jowo Mikyoe Dorje* (Dharamsala: Office of Information and International Relations, 1988).

30. Gatar Tulku (Tenzing Norbu), personal communication, Washington, DC.

## CHAPTER 2

1. Some of my "observations," particularly about Tibetan architecture, were not made at the time but are the results of later research. Primary sources were Knud Larsen and Amund Sinding-Larsen, *The Lhasa Atlas: Traditional Tibetan Architecture and Townscape* (London: Serindia, 2001); and André Alexander, *The Temples of Lhasa: Tibetan Buddhist Architecture from the 7th to the 21st Centuries* (Chicago: Serindia, 2005).

2. See Mana Bajra Bajracharya and Warren W. Smith, *Mythological History of the Nepal Valley from Svayambhu Purana* (Kathmandu: Avalok, 1978).

## CHAPTER 5

1. Samten G. Karmay, "King Glang Dar-ma and his Rule," in *The Arrow and the Spindle: Studies in History, Myths, Rituals and Beliefs in Tibet*, vol. II (Kathmandu, Nepal: Mandala, 2005), 15.

2. Karmay, 28.

3. *Tibetan Nation*, 55.

4. Owen Lattimore, *Inner Asian Frontiers of China* (Oxford: Oxford University Press, 1988), 218.

5. Lattimore, 220.

6. Lattimore, 224.

7. Lattimore, 225.

8. Turrell V. Wylie, "The First Mongol Conquest of Tibet Reinterpreted," *Harvard Journal of Asiatic Studies* 37, no. 1 (June 1977): 112.

9. Weber defines a hierocratic organization as an "organization which enforces its order through psychic coercion by distributing or denying religious benefits." As examples of hierocracy Weber lists: 1) a ruler who is legitimated by priests, either as an incarnation or in the name of God; and 2) a high priest who is also king. The second example Weber classes as the only true theocracy. Max Weber, *Economy and Society* (Berkeley: University of California Press, 1968), 54, 1160.

10. Lattimore, 225.

11. Jamyang Norbu, "Opening of the Political Eye: Tibet's Long Search for Democracy," in *Shadow Tibet: Selected Writings 1989–2004* (New York: High Asia, 2004), 14.

12. Norbu, 16.

# Index

**Abu Chonga, 48–54**
Ackerly, John, 261, 292
Afghanistan, 342–43, 347, 360
Akseter, Matthew, 189
Alak clan, 22
Alak Jigme Rinpoche, 251
Alak Kuncho Senge, 14
Alston, Philip, 259
Altan Khan, 329
Amato, Mary, 278
Amato, Mike, 278
*Ambans*, 331
Amchok, 9, 10, 11
Amdo, 4, 6, 9, 12, 15, 17, 19, 42, 101, 111, 114, 147, 148, 179, 206, 210, 213, 236, 300, 350, 351
Amdo Gyatok, 67, 68
Amdowas, 186
American Indians, 196
Amnye Machen Institute, 344–45
Ansi, 10, 11
Anti-Rightist and Anti-Local Nationalist Campaign, 10, 58, 59, 60, 63, 68, 70, 71
Anti-Tibetan nationalism, 1
Aspen, 317
assimilation, 1, 257, 283, 315, 344, 353, 354, 357, 359, 360, 362
Aten, 238–40
Atisha, 251, 325
Aufschnaiter, Peter, 122
autonomy, 1, 228, 229, 242, 251, 257, 265, 266, 267, 278, 280, 283–84, 287, 289, 299, 302, 303, 307, 313, 314, 333, 336, 344, 346, 347, 352, 353, 356, 357, 359
Avedon, John, 244

**Baby Austin, 149**
Bagmati, 226
Bamiyan, 360
Banakshol, 221
Barkhor, 48, 134–35, 140, 141, 150, 151, 158, 216, 221
Barnett, Robert, 261, 294, 310
Bathang, 26, 39, 174, 179, 182, 183
Bednar, Ed, 261–62
Beijing Olympics, 305–8, 312, 313, 315, 353, 360, 361
Beijing Shar Lam, 221
Bentzang Monastery, 95

Bhatt, Ami, 173–75
Bhrikuti, 129–30, 136, 137, 139, 254
Bhutan, 39, 46, 56, 77, 78, 83
Blue Books, 279
Bomi, 53, 179, 182
Bonism, 60, 62, 320, 321, 338
Brahmaputra, 182
Britain, 132, 180, 182, 202, 219, 242, 247, 279, 280, 333–34, 346
Brody, Reed, 286
Browning, Gay, 249, 250, 255, 256
Buddhist church, 203, 275, 319, 320, 321, 323, 324, 325, 327, 329, 334, 335, 338, 339, 340, 341, 342, 343, 345, 346, 347
Buryatia, 148

**Camp Hale, Colorado, 315–17**
Carter, Jimmy, 336
Central Intelligence Agency (CIA), 27, 29, 41, 49, 169, 287, 315–16
Central Tibet, 267, 274, 322, 323, 329, 338, 351
Chakpori, 158, 219
Chakra Pembar, 41, 50
*Cham* dances, 129
Chamdo, 24, 26, 28, 29, 48, 49, 50, 51, 66, 122, 157, 179, 180, 193–95, 209
Chamdo Liberation Committee, 25, 194
Chamdo Monastery, 29, 194
Chamdo Prison, 53
*chang*, 94, 237
Changan, 132, 275
Changchung Gyalpo, 194
Changtang, 38, 42, 74, 75, 168, 169, 179, 209
Chengdu, 15, 57, 73, 74, 113, 114, 239, 303
*Chetral*, 95
Ch'iang, 273
Chiang Kai-shek, 342
*China Reconstructs*, 245, 309
China's "Five Races," 342
*China's Tibet?*, 3, 308–11
Chinese Army, 6
Chinese Nationalists, 243
Chinese Navy, 194
Chinese-Tibetan Friendship Language, 109
Chingghis Khan, 325
Chingghisid lineage, 329
Chitwan National Park, Nepal, 226
Cho La, 188, 190, 192
Cho Oyu, 230
Cho-Yon, 267, 268, 275, 288, 290, 320, 325–26, 327, 328, 329, 330, 332, 340
Choni, 10
chorten, 90, 109, 126, 141, 164, 215, 224, 250
*Chosi Shungdrel*, 3, 345
chromium, 38
*chuba*, 150, 151
Chu Teh, 244
Chugama Monastery, 16

Chumarleb, 16, 22, 23
Chumbi valley, 56, 57
Chundo, 29, 53
Chushi Gangdruk, 31, 33, 34, 46, 49, 50, 83, 111, 183, 237, 316
CIA airdrops, 27, 29, 41, 49
Cold War, 242, 287, 291
collectivization, 5, 10, 43, 90, 209, 217
Communist Youth League, 62, 97
communization, 5, 15, 23, 91, 96, 153, 217
Crafts Union, 44, 45
Cultural Relics Bureau, 112
Cultural Revolution, 5, 13, 14, 29, 47, 54, 81, 84, 86–89, 108–9, 112, 125, 136, 140, 142, 143, 152, 157, 163, 214–16, 245, 246, 253, 254, 270, 310

**Dahm, Jurgen, 171, 177**
"Dalai Clique," 312
Dalai Lama audience, 235–36
Damchu, 29, 53
Damshung, 40, 41
*Danwei*, 180
Darjeeling, 205, 237
Dartsendo, 179, 181, 186, 209, 332
Das, Sarat Chandra, 270
Dawu Gompa, 187
*dayan*, 26, 43, 44, 48, 110
Dekyi Shar Lam, 132, 141, 143, 145
Delhi, 233, 234
democratic reforms, 2, 10, 24, 49, 51, 52, 76, 78, 86, 95, 152, 185, 186, 204, 210, 212, 213–14, 215, 239–40, 335, 349, 350
Democratic Reforms Campaign, 5, 9, 16, 17, 18, 20, 37, 55, 66, 111, 112, 349
Deng Xiaoping, 119, 125, 154, 243, 251, 252, 277
Deodar cedars, 235
Department of Information and International Relations, 269, 272
Derge, 49, 179, 182, 188–89, 190, 192, 193
Derge Monastery, 188
Desi Sangye Gyatso, 330–31
Deyang, 148
Dharamsala, 3, 6, 48, 117, 160, 176, 210, 225, 226, 229, 233, 234, 235, 237, 240–41, 243, 244, 246, 247, 251, 260, 261, 264, 265, 268, 269, 271, 272, 281, 288, 289–90, 297, 299, 302–5, 307, 335, 337, 344, 345, 353, 357, 358, 361
Dharamsala delegation, 47, 91, 126–27, 135–36, 159–60, 218, 238, 243, 251
Dhargyal Ling Monastery, 93, 94
Dhauladhar Range, 235
Dhondub Choedon, 93–110
Dorje Phagmo, 162
Dorje Tsering, 6–9
Doyle, Arthur Conan, 270–71

Dragyab, 31
Dram, 230
Drapchi Prison, 30, 44, 45, 84, 90, 91, 171, 209
*dratsang*, 143, 148, 167
Drepung Monastery, 48, 83, 115, 142, 143, 145, 147–48, 154, 306, 328, 329, 333
Dri Chu, 26
Drigung Monastery, 83
*Drokpa*, 9
*Dumra*, 316
Dunhuang, 38, 74, 114, 120, 121, 213, 320
Dza Chu, 193
Dzachuka, 21
Dzasa Kundeling, 251
Dzi Chu, 193
Dzongba, 168
Dzongna, 29, 53
Dzungar Mongols, 331, 333, 340

**Ear Society, 63**
Epstein, Israel, 245–46, 309
Estonia, 177
Everest, 2, 230

**Fifth Dalai Lama, 44, 128, 130, 148, 329, 330, 340**
Fifteenth Dalai Lama, 353
First Dalai Lama, 167
Fletcher School of Law and Diplomacy, 3, 249–50, 256–57, 258–60, 278, 282
Food and Agriculture Organization of the United Nations (FAO), 2
Ford, Robert, 122
"four olds," 54, 86, 215
"four pests," 98, 153
Fourth Dalai Lama, 329

**Gande Gompa, 26**
Ganden Monastery, 44, 85, 90, 142, 143, 145, 147, 149–50, 159–61, 180, 205, 255, 306, 328, 333
Ganden Podrang, 148
Ganden Serthang, 159–61, 255
Ganden Tripa, 149
Gang of Four, 125
Gangchen Kyishong, 234
Ganges River, 169
Gangkyi, 234, 235, 241, 246
Gansu Province, 9, 16, 114, 250, 265, 306
Gartok, 168, 169
Gashi, Tsering Dorje, 55–83
Gatar, 186
Gatar Gompa, 186
Gatar Tulku, 114
Gatok, 25
Gauri Shankar, 230
Gelder, Roma, 309
Gelder, Stuart, 309
Gelukpa, 147, 149, 159, 163, 219, 328, 329, 330
genocide, 285–86, 313
*geshe*, 83, 205

Giamda, 180
Godan Khan, 290, 326
Goldstein, Melvyn, 157, 174
Golingtang, 29
Golmud, 38, 40, 74, 120, 121, 170, 182, 213, 252, 253
Golok, 16
Gomang, 148
Gompo Tashi, 50
*Gong An Ju*, 155, 173, 191, 197
Goshang, 53
Grand Teton National Park, 275
Great Game, 242
Great Leap Forward, 5, 15, 16, 23, 51, 73, 76, 80, 84, 85, 87, 153, 209–10, 215, 217, 309, 351
Great Northern Paper Company, 151, 176, 263
Griffon vulture, 173
Guangzhou, 250
Guest House (#2), 123, 124, 126, 147, 156, 160, 170, 171, 180
Gurkhas of Nepal, 332, 340
Gurtsa Prison, 30
Gushri Khan, 329, 331, 333
Gyalo Thondup, 127, 302
Gyantse, 63, 154, 161–65, 170, 219, 230, 255
Gyantse Kumbum, 163–64
Gyari, Dolma, 271
Gyari, Lodi, 269, 271, 281, 283, 292, 293, 302–5, 345
Gyatak, 136
Gyenlok, 87–89
Gyume Monastery, 33, 37, 143, 145–47, 218
Gyutok Monastery, 142

**Han dynasty, 273**
Han Suyin, 310
Hannum, Hurst, 278
HarperCollins, 271
Harrer, Heinrich, 122
Harvard University, 250, 272, 274, 275
Higgins, Sigrid, 286
Himachal Pradesh, 235
Himalaya, 167, 230
Hollander, Paul, 309
Hong Kong, 1, 82, 121, 250, 283–84, 353, 354, 359–60, 361
Hor, 90
Hor Yetar, 39
Hormuka, 6, 7, 10
Hotel Everest View, 2
Hotel Tibet, 237
Huhohaote, Inner Mongolia, 119
Hu Jintao, 304
Hu Yaobang, 90–92, 125, 132, 160, 218, 251, 252, 265
Huang Yuan, 114
Hui, 44, 250
Hundred Flowers Campaign, 10, 58, 205

**Independence Pass, 317**
Indus River, 169
*Inji*, 240, 295
Inner Mongolia, 197, 199, 236

Inner Mongolian cavalry, 20, 21
Inner Mongolia University, 119–20
International Campaign for Tibet (ICT), 276, 281, 283, 291, 292–93
International Commission of Jurists (ICJ), 278, 285–90
*International Herald Tribune*, 256
Islam, 343

**Jamyang Norbu, 236–41, 242, 243, 246, 266, 269–71, 272–73, 277, 281, 316–17, 335–36, 344, 345–46**
Je Tsongkapa, 141
Jebumgang Lhakhang, 141–42
Jincheng, 138
Jinsha Jiang (Yangtze), 188
Jokhang Jowo, 138
Jokhang Temple, 44, 47, 48, 85, 89, 112, 115, 124, 126, 132–35, 137, 139–40, 143, 150, 151, 154, 171, 215, 219, 221, 225, 253, 254, 300, 306
Jomda, 25, 26, 193
Jowo, 44, 136, 138, 225
Jowo Mikyoe Dorje, 369
Jumla, 2
Junbesi, 3
Jyekundo, 190, 191, 192, 193

**Kadampa, 325**
Kalimpong, 205
Kalmykia, 148
Kalon Tripa, 302
*Kamalok*, 9
Kamba La, 162, 255
Kang Rinpoche (Kailash), 54, 164, 168, 169
Kangding, 179
Kangra District, 235
Kangsar Monastery, 19
*kangtsens*, 147, 148
*Kangyur*, 167, 168, 188
Kannan, 23
Kansu, 186, 213
Kanze, 187, 190
Kapstein, Ethan, 249
Kapstein, Matthew, 249
Karmapa, 299, 328, 329
Karnali, 2, 169
Karo La, 162
Karpo, Lama Shabdung, 8
Kashag, 46, 331, 332
Kashgar, 120
Kashmir, 46
Kathmandu, 137, 191, 226, 227, 231, 233, 250, 255, 256, 296, 312
Katsara, 86, 135
Kazakhs, 57
Kesang Dekyi, 68
*Khabzes*, 94
Khalkha Mongols, 329, 331
Kham, 4, 15, 24, 31, 42, 48, 49, 57, 83, 101, 110, 111, 114, 147, 148, 174, 179–96, 206, 213, 219, 220, 238, 239, 303, 304, 343, 350, 351

Khampas, 24, 30, 46, 49, 135, 186, 195–96, 343
*Khatags*, 18, 108
*khel*, 6
Khoshot Mongols, 329, 331
Khumbu, 2
King Birendra, 2, 30, 48
Kipling, Rudyard, 270, 271
Knaus, John Kenneth, 317
Kokonor, 66, 329
Kongpo, 29, 38, 49, 75, 83, 181–82, 209
*kora*, 134, 136
Korea, 28, 53
Kubilai Khan, 168, 325, 326, 327, 329
Kumbum Monastery, 252
Kundeling Monastery, 34
Kuomintang (KMT), 7, 8, 25, 26, 44, 342
Kupondole, 226
Kyi Chu, 33, 46, 47, 160, 162, 180, 207, 212, 219, 221

**Labrang Tashi Kyil Monastery, 9, 10, 12, 16, 17, 250–51, 306**
Ladakh, 42
Ladakhi Tibetan Muslims, 141
Lamb, Alastair, 279
Lammergeier vulture, 173
Lamont Library, 279
Lang Darma, 319–21, 324, 338
Langtang National Park, 2
Lanzhou, 10, 12, 250, 251
Larung Gar, 303
Latse Institute, 344
Lattimore, Owen, 323–25, 327
Latvia, 177
Leadville, Colorado, 316, 317
Lee-Enfield rifles, 343
Lenin, Vladimir, 174, 257, 355
*lhakhangs*, 147, 148, 161
Lhasa Middle School, 90
Lhasa Radio, 88
Lhasa Religious Affairs Department, 146
Lhasang Tsering, 237, 272–73, 281, 344
Lhatse, 168, 169, 230
Lhazang Khan, 331, 333
Lho Dzong, 48, 49, 50, 51
Lhoka, 33, 83, 93, 103
Lhora Gompa, 26
Library of Tibetan Works and Archives, 235, 236, 241, 246
Lin Biao, 166
Ling, 190
Ling Gesar, 90, 190, 236
*Lingkor*, 134
Lithang, 179, 182, 184–86, 304
Lithuania, 177
Liu Shao-chi, 76, 80, 87
Liuyuan, 74, 114, 120, 213
Lobsang Rampa, 177
Lobsang Samten, 135
Lolo, 239
London School of Economics, 271
Long March, 73
Losar, 189

Loseling, 148
loudspeakers, 88, 164, 216
Lower Tantric College, 145
Loyang, 38
Luhou, 187
Lukhang, 132

**Ma Chu, 14, 16, 17, 19**
Ma Pufang, 44, 50
Madame Blavatsky, 177
Magshikhang, 131
Mahatmas, 177
Maitreya, 131, 154, 167
Man Shan, 114
Manchu Empire, 182, 247, 267, 275, 289, 290, 324, 329, 330, 340
Manchu Qing dynasty, 275, 329, 330–33, 339–41
*Mandala of Sherlock Holmes*, 270–71
mani stones, 41, 82, 109, 215, 224
Maniganggo, 190, 192
Manjushri, 326
Mansarovar, 169
Mao Zedong, 8, 12, 13, 14, 24, 53, 58, 59, 87, 109, 124, 142, 166, 200, 204, 205, 209, 214, 216, 244, 294, 310, 350, 351, 356
Markham, 24, 25, 26, 28, 30, 90, 110, 111, 183
Markham Gatok, 27
Marpori hill, 128, 219
Marx, Karl, 13, 63, 257, 355
Marxism, 1, 63, 69, 106, 160, 174, 175, 198, 199–200, 245, 248, 257, 258, 349
Marxist-Leninist nationality policies, 174, 199–203, 227, 248, 260, 273, 276
Mazong Xian, 11
McEachern, Susan, 284
McLeod Ganj, 234, 235, 236, 237
Megasthom, 138
Meindersma, Christa, 287
Mekong, 49, 183, 193, 195, 300
Memorandum on Tibetan Autonomy, 307–8, 314, 353
Meru Monastery, 140, 143, 145, 146–47, 218
Meru Nyingpa Temple, 140, 158
Meru Sarpa, 145
Middle Path (Middle Way Approach), 264, 266, 268, 269, 272, 283–84, 288, 304, 313, 336, 344, 346, 347, 358, 359, 361, 363
MiG jet, 176
Mi La, 180
*Mimang*, 46
Ming dynasty, 328, 339
Mishra, Hemanta, 226
*momos*, 126
Mon, 273
Mongol Empire, 168, 246, 267, 274, 275, 288, 320, 325, 326, 339
Mongolia, 148, 324, 335, 342
Mongol Khans, 168, 219

Mongol Yuan dynasty, 167, 168, 275, 289, 290, 327, 339
Mongols, 58, 120, 167, 168, 182, 274, 288, 325, 326, 327, 330, 331, 332, 338, 339
Mookerjee, Huree Chunder, 270
Moose, Wyoming, 275
Moynihan, Daniel Patrick, 281–83
Moynihan, Maura, 281–83, 285, 286, 293
Museum of the Tibetan Revolution, 132, 311, 315
Mustang, 169, 237, 272

**Nachen Trang, 33, 34, 35, 36, 38, 39, 45, 75, 152, 154, 207–8, 216**
Naga Lake of Nepal, 137
*Nagas*, 132, 136, 224
Nagchu, 38
Nagchuka, 40, 74
Nagtsang Lake, 38
Naktsang Nulo, 16–24
Nam Tso, 90, 121, 209
Namche Barwa, 182
Namdrel, 86–89
Namgyal Monastery, 128
Namri, 322
Nangdap, 53
Nangkartse Monastery, 162
*nangkor*, 134
Nangra, 6, 7, 8, 9, 10
Nangtsesha, 141
Narendradeva, 137
Narthang Monastery, 167
National Endowment for Democracy, 291, 292
National Endowment for the Arts, 291
National Endowment for the Humanities, 291
National Minorities Institute, 55, 57, 59, 64, 67, 71, 81, 215, 294
National Planning Commission (NPC) of Nepal, 2
National Regional Autonomy, 1, 70, 266, 307, 313, 349, 359
Nechung, 140, 148
Nehru, Jahawarlal, 205
Nei Mongu Daxue, 119, 173, 180
Nepal, 2, 31, 54, 119, 121, 123, 129, 135, 136, 137, 138, 152, 167, 168, 169, 170, 225, 230, 231, 233, 246, 255, 256, 260, 262, 263
Nepal Army, 237
Nepal Department of Agriculture, 2
Nepal National Parks Department, 2, 233
Nepalese Consul, 226
Nepalese Consulate, 46, 225–26
Nepalese Embassy, 141
Nepalese Jowo, 138, 254
Newari, 135, 137, 164, 165
Ngadep, 29
Ngapa, 147, 148
Ngapo, Jigme, 261, 276, 292–93, 295, 296, 297, 316

Ngapo Ngawang Jigme, 24, 87–88, 261, 300
Ngari, 169
Ngom Chu, 193
Ngu Barkhang, 131
Nishi, 15
Nobel Peace Prize, 264–65, 269, 336
Nomads, 300–1
Norbulinka, 31, 32, 34, 44, 46, 47, 126, 137, 148–49, 154, 176, 226
Norwegian Nobel Committee, 264
Nose Society, 64
Nowak, Manfred, 287
Nyalam, 230
Nyang River, 165
Nyarong, 238–39
Nyatri Tsanpo, 104
Nyemo Ani, 91, 172
Nyemo Gompa, 26
Nyemo rebellion, 54, 90–91, 216
Nyenchenthangla, 121, 170
Nyethang, 93, 94, 103
Nyetho Jigme, 63
Nyima Assam, 24–31
Nyima Pon, 27
Nyingtri, 181, 209

**Olympic Torch Relay, 307, 312, 314, 361**
*Om Mani Padme Hum*, 215
One Country, Two Systems, 283, 359
Oring Nor, 42
Outer Mongolia, 243

**Pabongka, 158**
Pagmodrupa, 339
Paksho Gompa, 49
Palkyi Dorje, 320
Panchen Lama, 25, 45, 63, 76, 77, 85, 117, 123–25, 166, 167, 170, 206, 210, 236, 294, 299–300, 310, 332, 353
Panchshila, 204
*pangden*, 150
Parkhang Chenmo, 131
Patan, 226
Pathankot, 234
Patriotic Education Campaign, 304
Patron-Priest relationship, 168, 202–3
Patsang Monastery, 41
Pelkor Chode Monastery, 163–64
Pema Bhum, 344
Pemako, 182
People's Liberation Army (PLA), 7, 8, 9, 25, 27, 39, 42, 43, 45, 48, 49, 71, 74, 88, 89–90, 95, 101, 139, 157, 158–59, 165, 186, 204, 207, 212, 230, 253, 256, 264, 291, 310
People's Militia, 98
People's Republic of China (PRC), 247
Peterson, David, 275
Phagspa, 168, 325, 326, 329

Phala house, 47, 151–52, 158, 198, 254
Phari, 55, 56, 77–80, 83
Phenpo, 219–20
Phuntsok Dekyi, 175, 276
Phuntsok Wangyal, 174–75, 203, 276, 300
Plekhanov, 257
Po Tramo, 29, 49, 51, 54
Political Consultative Committee, 15, 24
Pon Choeje, 7
Pon Wangchen, 7, 8
Pongog Lake, 38
Poor Farmers League, 98
Potala, 32, 34, 44, 46, 75, 112, 121, 122, 126, 128–31, 132, 137, 154, 166, 176, 219, 221, 223–24, 231, 246, 311, 315
Praeger, Fred, 248, 284
Precious Metal Smelting Foundry, 113
Preparatory Committee for the Tibet Autonomous Region, 25, 45, 111
Private Office (of the Dalai Lama), 236
Public Broadcasting System (PBS), 291
Public Security Police, 88, 119, 155, 158, 225, 226
Putney, Pam, 278
Pye, Lucian, 280

**Qincheng Prison, 294**
Qinghai, 16, 40, 42, 44, 57, 74, 120, 121, 182, 186, 190, 191, 265
Qinghe Prison, 125

**Rabgey, 272**
Radio Free Asia (RFA), 3, 291–97, 311, 316
Radio Free Europe, 287, 291
Radio Nepal, 42
Rakshas Tal, 169
Ralpacan, 144, 146, 320, 321, 338
Ramoche Jowo, 47, 113, 115, 138, 139, 142, 254
Ramoche Lam, 141, 143, 221
Ramoche Monastery, 31, 32, 47, 113, 115, 126, 136, 138, 141, 145, 221, 254, 306
Ramoche Tsuklakhang, 136, 142
Rangzen, 131, 179, 231, 269, 345, 346
Rangzen La, 317
Rara National Park, 2
Rato Rinpoche, 39
Rebkong, 7
Reception Committee, 178, 198
Red Flag Commune, 97–110
Red Guards, 47, 85, 86–89, 108–9, 140, 143, 146, 215, 216
Red Palace, 128
Reform Through Labor, 2, 12, 29, 154, 208
Regional Ethnic Autonomy Law, 307, 344
Republican China, 342

Reting Monastery, 144
Reting Rinpoche, 144, 333, 334
Richardson, Hugh, 122, 242
Richter, Dick, 293
Rinbur Tulku, 110–17, 254, 310
Rinzing Paljor, 42–48, 154, 165, 167, 212
*Rogyapas*, 172
*rongpa*, 9
Rubin, Alfred, 278–80, 285
Russia, 15, 38, 199, 242, 280, 335
Rutok, 168

***Saga Dawa*, 94**
Sakya Lama, 157
Sakya Lhakhang Chenmo, 167
Sakya Monastery, 115, 164, 167–68
Sakya Pandita, 168, 290, 325–26, 339
Sakyamuni Buddha, 94, 113, 254
Sakyapa, 163, 327, 328
Salween, 183
Samba Droka, 26
Samdhong Rinpoche, 262, 302, 303
Samten Karmay, 320–21
Samye Monastery, 320
Sangchu, 26
Sangey Gyatso, 128
Sangyip Prison, 30, 83, 171
Saunders, Kate, 294
Second Dalai Lama, 148
Self-determination, 4, 99, 200, 247, 267, 268, 276, 277, 278, 287, 288, 289, 290, 342, 344, 346
Self-immolation, 361
Sera Je, 147
Sera Me, 147
Sera Monastery, 44, 90, 110, 111, 115, 125, 142, 143, 146, 147, 171, 172, 306, 328, 333
Serdrag, 31
*Serf*, 310, 314
Serf Emancipation Day, 314–15
Serthang, 159–61, 163
Serti Rinpoche, 8
Serxu, 191–92
Seventeen Point Agreement, 24, 25, 43, 45, 70, 87, 88, 111, 156, 185, 203, 228, 242, 261, 266, 283, 289, 300, 334, 359
Seventh Dalai Lama, 149, 186, 331, 332
Shabdung Karpo, 8
Shah, G. B., 226
Shalu Monastery, 154, 165
Shalupa, 163
Shanghai, 82, 114
Shangri-La, 303, 337, 361
Shanxi, 57
Sharpa Tulku, 176–77, 230
Shekar Dzong, 219
Sherpas, 2, 119, 124, 152
Shide Dratsang, 143
Shide Monastery, 143–44, 146, 218
Shigatse, 63, 125, 154, 162, 165–67, 170, 205, 219, 230, 255, 329

Shisha Pangma, 230
Shol, 75, 131, 141, 176, 219, 311
Shol Dekyiling, 131
Shol Lekhung, 131
Shol Parkhang, 131
Shopa Do, 48, 50
Shota Lhosum, 48, 49
Si Gompa, 26
Sichuan, 42, 49, 57, 73, 113, 179, 186, 193, 265, 303
Sikang, 24, 180, 194
Sikkim, 56, 78
Siling Tamak, 50
Silingbu, 47, 111
Simla Convention, 279
Sining, 44, 57, 114, 120, 251–52
Sino-Tibetan dialogue, 302–5, 307–8, 312, 313, 352, 353
Sirhor, 42
Sitru Prison, 171
Sixth Dalai Lama, 132, 331
Smithsonian Institution, 226
Snake River, 275
socialist transformation, 16, 17, 20, 55, 56, 335, 349, 350, 351
Sokchu Dan Monastery, 41
Sokchu River, 41
Sonam Cheodron, 47, 48, 152–54
Sonam Gyatso, 329
Sonam Rinchen, 44, 207
Soros, George, 344–45
South China Sea, 359
Southerland, Dan, 293
Soviet Union, 25, 85, 166, 177, 199, 209, 243, 347
Srongtsan Gampo, 128, 129, 136, 137, 140, 158, 219–20, 254
St. Joseph's College, 237
Stalin, 209, 257
State Council White Papers, 298
Strasbourg Proposal, 264–65, 266, 269, 283, 288, 336
Strong, Anna Louise, 309
Stuart, Todd, 278
Suge La, 170
Sun Kosi River, 230
Sun Yat-sen, 342
Sutlej River, 169
suzerainty, 242, 280
*svayambhu*, 137
Switzerland, 343

**Ta Dzong, 48, 50**
Taiwan, 283, 359, 360, 361, 362
Taiyuan, 114
Tajikistan, 296
Taliban, 360
Talung, 29, 53
Tan Kuan-san, 72
*Tang*, 35
Tang Daxian, 276, 277
Tang dynasty, 132, 133, 138, 275
Tang Taizong, 136
Tara Tsamkhang, 31
Tarim Basin, 133
Taring, 45
Tashi Dorje, 39–42
Tashilhunpo Monastery, 48, 63, 115, 125, 154, 164, 166–67, 299
Tashi Palden, 31–35

Tashi Tsering (Dharamsala), 236, 242, 246, 271, 344
Tashi Tsering (Lhasa), 156–57, 174
*Tengyur*, 167, 168, 188
Tenpa, Dolma Yudon, 47, 150–56, 158, 161, 176–77, 198–99, 202, 205–6, 214, 218, 225, 226–27, 229, 233–35, 236, 246, 254–55, 263, 285
Tenth Dalai Lama, 186
Tenzin Delek Rinpoche, 303
Tethong, Tenzin Geyche, 236
Tethong, Tenzin Namgyal, 261–62
Tetons, 275
Teykhang house, 75
Thamel, 255
thamzing, 9, 11, 13, 14, 22, 28, 29, 37, 39, 41, 45, 51, 52, 53, 61, 64, 67, 69, 106, 110, 112, 185, 210–12, 270, 286, 294
*thankas*, 41, 42, 82, 109, 129, 212
Theosophical Society, 177
Third Dalai Lama, 329
Thirteenth Dalai Lama, 130, 131, 149, 279, 334
Thongo La, 74
Thonmi Sambhota, 140, 158
Thupten Kalsang, 259
Thupten Samphel, 251
*thukpa*, 126
Tian Shan Mountains, 331
Tiananmen, 264, 265, 269, 276, 291, 298, 353
Tianjin, 114
Tibet Autonomous Region (TAR), 5, 17, 45, 87, 90, 112, 116, 132, 134, 179, 185, 193, 194, 205, 210, 215, 251, 253, 265, 298, 303, 306, 315, 350, 351, 358
Tibet Buddhist Association, 111, 112, 113, 117
*Tibet Daily*, 55, 75, 84, 88
Tibet Information Network (TIN), 294
*Tibet's Last Stand?*, 3, 311–15
Tibet Support Group Conference, 263, 271–72
*Tibet Under Chinese Communist Rule*, 6, 238
Tibet Work Forum, 251, 299
Tibetan Academy of Social Science, 188
Tibetan Army, 24, 34, 43, 93, 96, 100, 194
Tibetan Empire, 3, 70, 133, 274, 275, 312, 320, 322, 324, 327, 338
Tibetan Government in Exile (TGiE), 1, 5, 127, 210, 233, 234, 235, 241, 251, 261, 262, 264, 265, 268, 276, 281, 287, 288, 289–90, 299, 302–5, 307, 313, 314, 336, 344, 353, 358, 361
Tibetan Institute of Performing Arts (TIPA), 236–37, 269–70
*Tibetan Nation*, 3, 191, 284, 288

Tibetan Peoples' Uprising Movement, 1, 306
Tibetan Plateau, 133, 179, 182, 220, 224, 228, 230, 273, 274, 323, 361
Tibetan Resistance, 169, 315
*Tibetan Review*, 233, 241, 244, 288, 289
Tibetan Service of Radio Free Asia, 3, 292–93, 295
Tibetan Uprising of 2008, 205–8, 311–12, 353, 360, 361, 363
Tibetan-US Resettlement Project, 261–64
Tibetan Women's Association, 83, 269
Tibetan Youth Congress (TYC), 237, 281, 336
Tibetology institutes, 298
Tiger Project, 226
*ti momo*, 11, 126
Tinian, 296
Tingri, 230, 255–56
Tokyo, 82
Tramdub Dolma Lhakhang Monastery, 103
Trijang Rinpoche, 111, 234
Trikamdas, Purshottam, 285
Trisong Detsen, 9
Trotsky, 257
Trulnang Tsuklakhang, 137
Tsa Pomda, 28, 29
Tsaidam, 74
*Tsaidam* Basin, 120
Tsala Karpo, 38, 39, 74, 75, 209
Tsam Lung, 41
Tsampa, 33
Tsangpo River, 121, 162, 165, 168, 169, 182
Tsaring Nor, 42
Tsayul Tulku, 9–15
Tsemoling Monastery, 143, 144–45, 146, 218
Tsering Dolkar, 255
Tsering Shakya, 271, 280
Tsering Wangchuk, 83–93
Tsering Wangyal, 233, 236, 241
Tsetang, 30
Tseten Namgyal, 297
Tseten Wangchuk, 131–32, 276
Tsomchen, 148
Tsomoling Monastery, 32
*Tsongdu*, 333
Tsongkhapa, 90, 147, 148, 159, 160, 167, 328
Tsuklakhang, 133, 235
Tubten Khétsun, 188–89, 207–8, 209, 216–17
Tufts University, 249–50, 256–57, 258, 282
*tulkus*, 53
Turks, 182, 220, 274
Tuva, 148
Twelfth Dalai Lama, 333

**Udall, Mark, 315, 316**
Uighurs, 57, 58, 59, 60, 61, 71, 353, 358
UNDP-FAO, 2

United Front, 79, 84, 199, 203, 303, 304, 305, 349, 350, 355
United Nations, 242, 259, 286, 287, 290, 342
United States, 27, 28, 85, 157, 242, 243, 247, 263, 279, 313, 315, 341
Upper Tantric College, 31, 142, 145
Urumchi, 120
USAF Academy, 249
US-China Education Foundation, 119
US Forest Service, 315
US Tibet Committee, 177
U-Tsang, 15

**Van Walt, Michael, 266–67, 268, 288–90**
Vietnam, 249
Vihara, 137–38, 139
Vise Gompa, 27
Voice of America, 291, 295, 296

**Wang Chimei, 87**
Wang Ruowang, 277
Wangdu, 66
Weber, Max, 326
Wei Jingsheng, 175
Weitzner, Judith, 275
Wengcheng, 129–30, 134, 136, 137, 138, 254
Westview Press, 248, 284
White Palace, 128
White Papers, 297, 298, 313, 358
Widener Library, 274
Women's Federation, 98
World War II, 243
*Wrath of the Serfs*, 132, 218, 311, 314
Wujud, 21
*Wulag*, 93
Wutitu Prison, 30
Wylie, Turrell, 326

**Xi Jinping, 358, 360**
Xian, 57, 87, 132, 157, 215, 275
Xianyang, 57, 157, 215
*Xinhua*, 126, 166
Xinjiang, 1, 10, 12, 38, 57, 74, 85, 112, 114, 120, 133, 168, 199, 207, 344, 359

**yak, 184–85, 189–90, 222**
Yamdrok Yumtso, 162, 255
Yangbachen, 162, 170
Yangtze River, 26, 183, 193, 300
Yarlung dynasty, 163, 165, 219, 220, 322
Yarphel, 66, 67
Yatung, 43
Yellow River, 300
Yenan, 245
Yenching Library, 275
Yitritu Prison, 30, 171
Yuan dynasty, 167, 168, 298, 333
Yuan Shikai, 44
Yueh-Chih, 273
Yumbu Lhakhang, 103
Yumen Xian, 11

Yunnan, 26, 186, 265, 303
*Yutok Samba*, 126, 205, 221

**Zangmu, 31**
Zhaggo, 187
Zhang Zhung Empire, 169, 220
Zhou Enlai, (Chou En-lai), 46, 80, 124, 154, 164, 205, 244, 294, 310
Zimbook house, 31, 32
Zu Xian, 11

# About the Author

**Warren W. Smith Jr.** was a broadcaster at the Tibetan Service of Radio Free Asia for twenty-two years, where he wrote more than 1,000 articles on all aspects of Tibetan history and politics, Chinese policy on Tibet, and Sino-Tibetan relations. He was a long-term resident of Nepal and has traveled extensively in Tibet. He is the author of *Tibetan Nation: A History of Tibetan Nationalism and Sino-Tibetan Relations*; *China's Tibet?: Autonomy or Assimilation*; and *Tibet's Last Stand?: The Tibetan Uprising of 2008 and China's Response*. He is currently a resident of Alexandria, Virginia.

Author with the Dalai Lama—Dharamsala, 1983

www.ingramcontent.com/pod-product-compliance
Lightning Source LLC
Chambersburg PA
CBHW020406100426
42812CB00001B/226
* 9 7 8 1 5 3 8 1 7 3 9 8 5 *